# Lecture Notes in Artificial Intelligence 10633

Subseries of Lecture Notes in Computer Science

More information about this series at http://www.springer.com/series/1244

Félix Castro · Sabino Miranda-Jiménez
Miguel González-Mendoza (Eds.)

# Advances in Computational Intelligence

16th Mexican International Conference
on Artificial Intelligence, MICAI 2017
Enseneda, Mexico, October 23–28, 2017
Proceedings, Part II

 Springer

*Editors*
Félix Castro
Universidad Autónoma del Estado de
Hidalgo
Pachuca, Mexico

Miguel González-Mendoza
Tecnológico de Monterrey
Atizapán de Zaragoza, Mexico

Sabino Miranda-Jiménez
INFOTEC Aguascalientes
Aguascalientes, Mexico

ISSN 0302-9743 ISSN 1611-3349 (electronic)
Lecture Notes in Artificial Intelligence
ISBN 978-3-030-02839-8 ISBN 978-3-030-02840-4 (eBook)
https://doi.org/10.1007/978-3-030-02840-4

Library of Congress Control Number: 2018958467

LNCS Sublibrary: SL7 – Artificial Intelligence

This Springer imprint is published by the registered company Springer Nature Switzerland AG
The registered company address is: Gewerbestrasse 11, 6330 Cham, Switzerland

*In memoriam*
Dr. José Negrete Martínez

# Preface

The Mexican International Conference on Artificial Intelligence (MICAI) is a yearly international conference series that has been organized by the Mexican Society of Artificial Intelligence (SMIA) since 2000. MICAI is a major international artificial intelligence forum and the main event in the academic life of the country's growing artificial intelligence community.

We dedicate this set of two volumes to the bright memory of Dr. José Negrete Martínez, the founder of the SMIA back in 1986, its first president, whose contribution to the promotion of artificial intelligence in our country is difficult to overestimate.

MICAI conferences publish high-quality papers in all areas of artificial intelligence and its applications. The proceedings of the previous MICAI events have been published by Springer in its *Lecture Notes in Artificial Intelligence* series, as volumes 1793, 2313, 2972, 3789, 4293, 4827, 5317, 5845, 6437, 6438, 7094, 7095, 7629, 7630, 8265, 8266, 8856, 8857, 9413, 9414, 10061, and 10062. Since its foundation in 2000, the conference has been growing in popularity and improving in quality.

With MICAI 2017, we celebrated the 30th anniversary of the SMIA, which was officially registered in 1987. Accordingly, MICAI 2017 featured a round table with the participation of a number of former presidents of the SMIA, including its founder Dr. José Negrete Martínez; this happened to be one of his last public appearances.

The proceedings of MICAI 2017 are published in two volumes. The first volume, *Advances in Soft Computing*, contains 30 papers structured into four sections:

- Neural Networks
- Evolutionary Algorithms and Optimization
- Hybrid Intelligent Systems and Fuzzy Logic
- Machine Learning and Data Mining

The second volume, *Advances in Computational Intelligence*, contains 30 papers structured into three sections:

- Natural Language Processing and Social Networks
- Intelligent Tutoring Systems and Educational Applications
- Image Processing and Pattern Recognition

This two-volume set will be of interest for researchers in all areas of artificial intelligence, students specializing in related topics, and for the general public interested in recent developments in artificial intelligence.

The conference received 203 submissions for evaluation from 23 countries: Argentina, Belgium, Brazil, Chile, Colombia, Cuba, Ecuador, France, India, Iran, Ireland, Malaysia, Mexico, Morocco, Pakistan, Paraguay, Peru, Portugal, Russia, South Africa, Spain, Ukraine, and USA. Of these submissions, 61 papers were selected for publication in these two volumes after the peer-reviewing process carried out by the international Program Committee. Thus, the acceptance rate was 30%.

The international Program Committee consisted of 192 experts from 19 countries: Argentina, Benin, Brazil, Canada, Colombia, Cuba, Finland, France, Greece, Israel, Italy, Japan, Mexico, Portugal, Singapore, Spain, UK, USA, and Uruguay.

MICAI 2017 was honored by the presence of renowned experts, who gave excellent keynote lectures:

- Pierre Baldi, University of California, Irvine, USA
- Hamido Fujita, Iwate Prefectural University, Japan
- Thamar Solorio, University of Houston, USA
- Eduardo Morales Manzanares, INAOE, Mexico
- Jeff Dean, Google, USA

The technical program of the conference also featured eight tutorials:

- "Artificial Hydrocarbon Networks and Their Applications," by Hiram Eredín Ponce Espinosa
- "Building a Digital Ecosystem Using FIWARE," by Nestor Velasco-Bermeo, Miguel González Mendoza, and Jesus Favela
- "Computational Biology," by Gabriel Del Rio and Carlos Brizuela
- "Data Science: A Quick Introduction," by Mauricio Alonso Sánchez Herrera
- "Introduction to Data Mining with Python," by Mario Garcia Valdez
- "Sentiment Analysis," by Alexander Gelbukh
- "Similarity, Correlation and Association Measures in Data Analysis: New Looks and New Measures," by Ildar Batyrshin
- "The Wavelet Transform in Soft Computing," by Oscar Herrera Alcántara

Three workshops were held jointly with the conference:

- HIS 2017: 10th Workshop on Hybrid Intelligent Systems
- WIDSSI 2017: Third International Workshop on Intelligent Decision Support Systems for Industry
- WILE 2017: 10th Workshop on Intelligent Learning Environments

The authors of the following papers received the Best Paper Awards based on the paper's overall quality, significance, and originality of the reported results:

- Best paper: "On the Many-Objective Pickup and Delivery Problem: Analysis of the Performance of Three Evolutionary Algorithms," by Abel García-Nájera, Antonio López-Jaimes, and Saúl Zapotecas-Martínez (Mexico)
- Best student paper: "Human Activity Recognition on Mobile Devices Using Artificial Hydrocarbon Networks," by Hiram Ponce, Guillermo González, Luis Miralles-Pechuán, and Lourdes Martínez-Villaseñor (Mexico)

The latter paper was selected among all papers of which the first author was a full-time student, excluding the paper that received the best paper award.

In addition, at MICAI 2017 the winners of the national contest of theses on artificial intelligence, organized by the Mexican Society of Artificial Intelligence (SMIA), were announced:

- Best PhD thesis, first place: "Image Classification Through Text Mining Techniques," by Adrián Pastor López Monroy with his advisors Manuel Montes-y-Gómez, Hugo Jair Escalante, and Fabio A. González
- Best PhD thesis, second place: "Hardware Acceleration of Frequent Itemsets Mining on Data Streams," by Lázaro Bustio Martínez with his advisors René Cumplido and Raudel Hernandez-León
- Best PhD thesis, third place: "Evolución Diferencial par Resolver Problemas de Optimización Dinámica con Restricciones," by María Yaneli Ameca Alducin with her advisors Nicandro Cruz Ramírez and Efrén Mezura Montes
- Best MSc thesis, first place: "Redes Neuronales de Tercera Generación Aplicadas al Reconocimiento de Imaginación de Movimientos en Registros de Electroencefalografía," by Ruben Isaac Cariño Escobar with his advisors Roberto Antonio Vázquez Espinoza de los Monteros and Josefina Gutiérrez Martínez
- Best MSc thesis, second place: "Distinción de Estados de Actividad e Inactividad Lingüística para Interfaces Eerebro Computadora," by Luis Alfredo Moctezuma Pascual with his advisors Maya Carrillo Ruiz and Alejandro A. Torres Garcia
- Best MSc thesis, third place (shared): "Clasificación de Patrones de Bandeo Obtenidos Mediante Western Blot para el Diagnóstico de Cáncer de Mama," by Diana María Sánchez Silva with her advisors Héctor Gabriel Acosta Mesa and Tania Romo González de la Parra
- Best MSc thesis, third place (shared): "Multimodal Sentiment Analysis in Social Media using Deep Learning with Convolutional Neural Networks," by Navonil Majumder with his advisor Alexander Gelbukh

The cultural program of the conference included tours to the La Bufadora natural attraction and the tour of wine production route.

We want to thank all people involved in the organization of this conference. In the first place, these are the authors of the papers published in this book: It is their research effort that gives value to the book and to the work of the organizers. We thank the track chairs for their hard work, the Program Committee members, and additional reviewers for their great effort spent on reviewing the submissions.

We would like to thank Dr. Juan Manuel Ocegueda Hernández, Rector of the Universidad Autónoma de Baja California, and Dr. Silvio Guido Lorenzo Marinone Moschetto, Director General of the Centro de Investigación Científica y de Educación Superior de Ensenada, along with all the members of their teams, for their invaluable help in the organization of the conference. We express our great gratitude to Dr. Blanca Rosa García Rivera, Dr. Juan Iván Nieto Hipólito, and Dr. Juan Crisóstomo Tapia Mercado for all the support provided to this event. We are deeply grateful to the student assistants from UABC and CICESE, who were very helpful at all stages of the organization. We are deeply grateful to the conference staff and to all members of the Local Committee headed by Dora Luz Flores Gutiérrez, Everardo Gutiérrez López, and Carlos Alberto Brizuela Rodríguez. The entire submission, reviewing, and selection process, as well as preparation of the proceedings, was supported free of charge by the

EasyChair system (www.easychair.org). Finally, yet importantly, we are very grateful
to the staff at Springer for their patience and help in the preparation of this volume.

February 2018                                                      Félix Castro
Sabino Miranda-Jiménez
Miguel González-Mendoza

# Organization

MICAI 2017 was organized by the Mexican Society of Artificial Intelligence (SMIA, Sociedad Mexicana de Inteligencia Artificial) in collaboration with the Universidad Autónoma de Baja California (UABC), the Centro de Investigación Científica y de Educación Superior de Ensenada (CICESE), the Universidad Autónoma del Estado de Hidalgo (UAEH), the Centro de Investigación e Innovación en Tecnologías de la Información y Comunicación (INFOTEC), the Tecnológico de Monterrey CEM, the Centro de Investigación en Computación del Instituto Politécnico Nacional (CIC-IPN), and the Universidad Autónoma Metropolitana Azcapotzalco (UAM).

The MICAI series website is www.MICAI.org. The website of the Mexican Society of Artificial Intelligence, SMIA, is www.SMIA.org.mx. Contact options and additional information can be found on these websites.

## Conference Committee

### General Chair

Miguel González Mendoza      Tecnológico de Monterrey CEM, Mexico

### Program Chairs

Félix Castro                 Universidad Autónoma del Estado de Hidalgo, Mexico
Sabino Miranda Jiménez       INFOTEC, Mexico
Miguel González Mendoza      Tecnológico de Monterrey CEM, Mexico

### Workshop Chairs

Obdulia Pichardo Lagunas     Instituto Politécnico Nacional, Mexico
Noé Alejandro Castro         Centro Nacional de Investigación y Desarrollo
  Sánchez                      Tecnológico, Mexico

### Tutorials Chair

Félix Castro Espinoza        Universidad Autónoma del Estado de Hidalgo, Mexico

### Doctoral Consortium Chairs

Miguel Gonzalez Mendoza      Tecnológico de Monterrey CEM, Mexico
Antonio Marín Hernandez      Universidad Veracruzana, Mexico

### Keynote Talks Chair

Sabino Miranda Jiménez       INFOTEC, Mexico

**Publication Chair**

Miguel Gonzalez Mendoza    Tecnológico de Monterrey CEM, Mexico

**Financial Chair**

Ildar Batyrshin    Instituto Politécnico Nacional, Mexico

**Grant Chairs**

Grigori Sidorov    Instituto Politécnico Nacional, Mexico
Miguel Gonzalez Mendoza    Tecnológico de Monterrey CEM, Mexico

**Organizing Committee Chairs**

Dora Luz Flores Gutiérrez    Universidad Autónoma de Baja California, Mexico
Everardo Gutiérrez López    Universidad Autónoma de Baja California, Mexico
Carlos Alberto Brizuela    Centro de Investigación Científica y de Educación
    Rodríguez        Superior de Ensenada, Mexico

# Area Chairs

**Machine Learning**

Eduardo Morales    Instituto Nacional de Astrofísica, Óptica y Electrónica,
    Manzanares        Mexico
Raul Monroy Borja    Tecnológico de Monterrey CEM, Mexico

**Natural Language Processing**

Sabino Miranda Jiménez    INFOTEC, Mexico
Esaú Villatoro    Universidad Autónoma Metropolitana Cuajimalpa,
    Mexico

**Evolutionary and Evolutive Algorithms**

Hugo Jair Escalante    Instituto Nacional de Astrofísica, Óptica y Electrónica,
    Balderas        Mexico
Hugo Terashima Marín    Tecnológico de Monterrey CM, Mexico

**Neural Networks**

Angel Kuri Morales    Instituto Tecnológico Autónomo de México, Mexico
Pilar Gómez Gil    Instituto Nacional de Astrofísica, Óptica y Electrónica,
    Mexico

**Computer Vision and Robotics**

José Martínez Carranza    Instituto Nacional de Astrofísica, Óptica y Electrónica,
    Mexico
Daniela Moctezuma    Centro de Investigación en Ciencias de Información
    Geoespacial, Mexico

## Hybrid Intelligent Systems

Carlos Alberto Reyes Garcia    Instituto Nacional de Astrofísica, Óptica y Electrónica, Mexico

Juan Jose Flores    Universidad Michoacana, Mexico

## Intelligent Applications

Gustavo Arroyo    Instituto Nacional de Electricidad y Energias Limpias, Mexico

Humberto Sossa    Instituto Politécnico Nacional, Mexico

# Program Committee

Rocío Abascal-Mena    Universidad Autónoma Metropolitana Cuajimalpa, Mexico

Giner Alor-Hernández    Tecnológico de Orizaba, Mexico

Matias Alvarado    CINVESTAV, Mexico

Nohemi Alvarez Jarquin    Centro de Investigación en Geografía y Geomática Ing. Jorge L. Tamayo, A.C., Mexico

Gustavo Arechavaleta    CINVESTAV-Saltillo, Mexico

García Gamboa Ariel Lucien    Tecnológico de Monterrey CEM, Mexico

Gustavo Arroyo    Instituto Nacional de Electricidad y Energías Limpias, Mexico

Maria Lucia Barrón-Estrada    Instituto Tecnológico de Culiacán, Mexico

Rafael Batres    Tecnológico de Monterrey, Mexico

Ildar Batyrshin    Instituto Politécnico Nacional, Mexico

Edmundo Bonilla    Instituto Tecnológico de Apizaco, Mexico

Maricela Claudia Bravo Contreras    Universidad Autónoma Metropolitana, Mexico

Davide Buscaldi    LIPN, Université Paris 13, Sorbonne Paris Cité, France

Felix Calderon    Universidad Michoacana de San Nicolas de Hidalgo, Mexico

Hiram Calvo    Instituto Politécnico Nacional, Mexico

Nicoletta Calzolari    Istituto di Linguistica Computazionale – CNR, Italy

Erik Cambria    Nanyang Technological University, Singapore

Sergio Daniel Cano Ortiz    Universidad de Oriente, Cuba

Jesus Ariel Carrasco-Ochoa    Instituto Nacional de Astrofísica, Óptica y Electrónica, Mexico

Victor Carrera    Instituto Nacional de Astrofísica, Óptica y Electrónica, Mexico

Mario Castelan    CINVESTAV-Saltillo, Mexico

Oscar Castillo    Instituto Tecnológico de Tijuana, Mexico

Felix Castro Espinoza    Universidad Autónoma del Estado de Hidalgo, Mexico

| | |
|---|---|
| Efrén Mezura-Montes | Universidad Veracruzana, Mexico |
| Sabino Miranda-Jiménez | INFOTEC, Mexico |
| Daniela Moctezuma | CONACYT, CentroGeo, Mexico |
| Raul Monroy | Tecnologico de Monterrey CEM, Mexico |
| Manuel Montes-y-Gómez | Instituto Nacional de Astrofísica, Óptica y Electrónica, Mexico |
| Marco Morales | Instituto Tecnológico Autónomo de México, Mexico |
| Eduardo Morales Manzanares | Instituto Nacional de Astrofísica, Óptica y Electrónica, Mexico |
| Annette Morales-González | CENATAV, Cuba |
| Alicia Morales-Reyes | Instituto Nacional de Astrofísica, Óptica y Electrónica, Mexico |
| Masaki Murata | Tottori University, Japan |
| Antonio Neme | Universidad Autónoma de la Ciudad de México, Mexico |
| C. Alberto Ochoa-Zezatti | Universidad Autónoma de Ciudad Juárez, Mexico |
| Diego Oliva | Universidad de Guadalajara, Spain |
| José Luis Oliveira | University of Aveiro, Portugal |
| Fernando Ornelas | Universidad Michoacana de San Nicolás de Hidalgo, Mexico |
| Jose Ortiz Bejar | Universidad Michoacana de San Nicolás de Hidalgo, Mexico |
| José Carlos Ortiz-Bayliss | Tecnológico de Monterrey, Mexico |
| Ivandre Paraboni | University of Sao Paulo, Brazil |
| Alvaro Pardo | Universidad Católica del Uruguay, Uruguay |
| Miguel Perez | Instituto Nacional de Electricidad y Energías Limpias, Mexico |
| Airel Pérez Suárez | CENATAV, Cuba |
| Humberto Pérez-Espinosa | CICESE-UT3, Mexico |
| Obdulia Pichardo-Lagunas | Instituto Politécnico Nacional, Mexico |
| Garibaldi Pineda | The University of Manchester, UK |
| Raul Pinto Elias | Centro Nacional de Investigación y Desarrollo Tecnológico, Mexico |
| Hiram Ponce Espinosa | Universidad Panamericana, Mexico |
| Soujanya Poria | Nanyang Technological University, Singapore |
| Belem Priego-Sanchez | Benemérita Universidad Autónoma de Puebla, Mexico; Université Paris 13, France; Universidad Autónoma Metropolitana Azcapotzalco, Mexico |
| Luis Puig | Universidad de Zaragoza, Spain |
| Vicenc Puig | Universitat Politècnica de Catalunya, Spain |
| J. R. G. Pulido | The University of Colima, Mexico |
| Juan M. Ramírez-Cortés | Instituto Nacional de Astrofísica, Óptica y Electrónica, Mexico |
| Gabriela Ramírez-De-La-Rosa | Universidad Autónoma Metropolitana Cuajimalpa, Mexico |
| Juan Ramirez-Quintana | Instituto Tecnológico de Chihuahua, Mexico |

| | |
|---|---|
| Juan Manuel Rendon-Mancha | Universidad Autónoma del Estado de Morelos, Mexico |
| Orion Reyes | University of Alberta Edmonton, Canada |
| Carlos Alberto Reyes García | Instituto Nacional de Astrofísica, Óptica y Electrónica, Mexico |
| José A. Reyes-Ortiz | Universidad Autónoma Metropolitana, Mexico |
| Roger Rios-Mercado | Universidad Autónoma de Nuevo León, Mexico |
| Noel Enrique Rodriguez Maya | Instituto Tecnológico de Zitácuaro, Mexico |
| Hector Rodriguez Rangel | University of Oregon, USA |
| Katya Rodriguez-Vazquez | Universidad Nacional Autónoma de México, Mexico |
| Alejandro Rosales | Tecnológico de Monterrey, Mexico |
| Jose Sanchez Del Rio | IMDEA Materiales, Spain |
| Cuauhtemoc Sanchez-Ramirez | Tecnológico de Orizaba, Mexico |
| Christian Sánchez-Sánchez | Universidad Autónoma Metropolitana, Mexico |
| Guillermo Santamaria | CONACYT, Instituto Nacional de Electricidad y Energías Limpias, Mexico |
| Oliver Schuetze | CINVESTAV-IPN, Mexico |
| Carlos Segura | Centro de Investigación en Matemáticas, Mexico |
| Ángel Serrano | Universidad Rey Juan Carlos, Spain |
| Grigori Sidorov | Instituto Politécnico Nacional, Mexico |
| Jesus Antonio Sosa Herrera | CentroGEO, Mexico |
| Juan Humberto Sossa Azuela | Instituto Politécnico Nacional, Mexico |
| Efstathios Stamatatos | University of the Aegean, Greece |
| Eric S. Tellez | CONACYT, INFOTEC, Mexico |
| Hugo Terashima | Tecnológico de Monterrey, Mexico |
| Esteban Tlelo-Cuautle | Instituto Nacional de Astrofísica, Óptica y Electrónica, Mexico |
| Luis Torres | General Electric, Mexico |
| Alejandro Antonio Torres García | Tecnológico de Monterrey, Mexico |
| Nestor Velasco-Bermeo | Tecnológico de Monterrey CEM, Mexico |
| Esau Villatoro-Tello | Universidad Autónoma Metropolitana, Mexico |
| Aline Villavicencio | Universidade Federal do Rio Grande do Sul, Brazil |
| Francisco Viveros Jiménez | Instituto Politécnico Nacional, Mexico |
| Carlos Mario Zapata Jaramillo | Universidad Nacional de Colombia, Colombia |
| Saúl Zapotecas Martínez | Universidad Autónoma Metropolitana Cuajimalpa, Mexico |
| Ramón Zatarain | Instituto Tecnológico de Culiacán, Mexico |
| Alisa Zhila | Target, USA |
| Carlos Zozaya | Grupo BAL, Mexico |

## Additional Reviewers

Maria-Yaneli Ameca-Alducin
Ildar Batyrshin
Jan Burchard
Jingcao Cai
Katy Castillo-Rosado
Barbara Cervantes
Sankha Deb
David Estévez
Alexander Gelbukh
Lázaro Janier González-Soler
Betania Hernandez Ocaña
Pablo H. Ibarguengoytia
Azah Mohamed
Gianluca Morganti
Rosa María Ortega-Mendoza

Daile Osorio Roig
Ferdinando Pezzella
Eduarda Portela
Marcela Quiroz-Castellanos
Alberto Reyes
Jorge Rodríguez-Ruiz
Alfonso Rojas
Manuel Schmitt
Ricardo Sousa
Yasushi Tsubota
Francisco Viveros Jiménez
Lunche Wang
Lei Wang
Rolf Wanka
Rodrigo Wilkens

## Organizing Committee

### Chairs

| | |
|---|---|
| Dora Luz Flores Gutiérrez | Universidad Autónoma de Baja California, Mexico |
| Everardo Gutiérrez López | Universidad Autónoma de Baja California, Mexico |
| Carlos Alberto Brizuela Rodríguez | Centro de Investigación Científica y de Educación Superior de Ensenada, Mexico |

### Members

David Cervantes Vasquez
Manuel Castañón Puga
Omar Álvarez Xochihua
Evelio Martínez Martínez
José Ángel González Fraga
Adrian Enciso Almanza
José Manuel Valencia Moreno
Christian Xavier Navarro Cota
Sergio Omar Infante Prieto
Yolanda Angélica Baez López
Eunice Vargas Viveros
Luz Evelia López Chico
Ariel Arturo Quezada Pina, Universidad Autónoma de Baja California, Mexico

# Contents – Part II

## Intelligent Tutoring Systems and Educational Applications

## Image Processing and Pattern Recognition

# Contents – Part I

## Hybrid Intelligent Systems and Fuzzy Logic

## Machine Learning and Data Mining

# Natural Language Processing and Social Networks

# Binary and Multi-class Classification of Lexical Functions in Spanish Verb-Noun Collocations

Olga Kolesnikova[1(⊠)] and Alexander Gelbukh[2]

[1] Escuela Superior de Cómputo, Instituto Politécnico Nacional,
07738 Mexico City, Mexico
kolesolga@gmail.com
[2] Centro de Investigación en Computación, Instituto Politécnico Nacional,
07738 Mexico City, Mexico
https://www.gelbukh.com

**Abstract.** Collocations as semi-fixed lexical combinations present a challenge in natural language processing. While collocation identification on the shallow level is a task in which a significant advance has been reached, a deeper semantic representation and analysis of collocations remains an open issue. One of the possible solutions is detection of lexical functions of the Meaning-Text Theory in collocations thus resolving their semantic interpretation. We experimented with four lexical functions (Oper1, Real1, CausFunc0, and CausFunc1) for the special case of Spanish verb-noun collocations. In our experiments we also identified free verb-noun combinations as opposed to lexical functions. We used WordNet hypernyms as features and various algorithms of supervised machine learning; the best result with an F-measure of 0.873 was achieved for detecting Oper1 in binary classification.

**Keywords:** Lexical functions · Spanish verb-noun collocations
Hypernyms · Supervised learning

## 1 Introduction

Natural language processing (NLP) is an area of Artificial Intelligence that has been developing rapidly in the last years showing substantial advance. However, most robust language techniques are shallow and do not allow for deeper semantic analysis. This work contributes to the development of semantic representation of recurrent phrases or collocations. Collocations are frequent combinations, commonly consisting of two words, in which the lexical choice for one word called the collocate is bound by the other word called the base. This fact is the lexical criterion to distinguish collocations from free word combinations: semantics of the latter can be interpreted by the compositional analysis which is not applicable to the former.

Statistically, two words are a collocation if they occur together more frequently than independently. Semantically, the meaning of the collocate in a collocation deviates (to different degrees) from its typical or most common meaning when used in free word combinations, i.e., independently of the base. Examples of collocations are *make the*

© Springer Nature Switzerland AG 2018
F. Castro et al. (Eds.): MICAI 2017, LNAI 10633, pp. 3–14, 2018.
https://doi.org/10.1007/978-3-030-02840-4_1

*bed, do the homework, take a risk, give someone advice, open an account, forgive a debt, land a deal, receive a discount*[1].

Collocations present a challenge in NLP because they cannot be analyzed compositionally as we mentioned above, that is, their meaning cannot be generated by adding the meaning of one word to the meaning of the other word. Other methods have been proposed in the literature, however, they still leave room for improving. Most recent methods for collocation detection are reviewed in Sect. 2. These techniques were developed for verb-noun collocations as they are in the focus of our research.

In this work we analyzed Spanish verb-noun collocations as a special case using lexical functions of the Meaning-Text theory (Mel'čuk [4]) briefly explained in Sect. 3. We used the lexical resource compiled by us in previous work [3] and supervised machine learning for detecting four lexical functions and free word combinations. The data and methodology are discussed in Sect. 4, and the results of our experiments are presented and discussed in Sect. 5. Section 6 includes conclusions and future work.

## 2 Related Work on Verb-Noun Collocations

Much work has been done on identification of verb-noun constructions in general and collocations in particular. It seems that the so-called light verb constructions are a type of verb-noun collocations most frequently met in corpora, so many methods have been proposed to automatically detect them in texts.

The term *light verb* represents the idea that the meaning the verb acquires in a collocation is not lexically full as it only verbalizes the noun, aiding it in conveying the verbal categories of tense, aspect, person, and number, and actually does not add any semantics since nouns in light verb constructions often include the action component. Light verb constructions are collocations because they fulfill the lexical, statistical and semantic criteria which distinguish collocations from free word combinations. These criteria were defined in the Introduction.

Due to a high interest of researchers to collocations and a variety of approaches designed, diverse terminology has been proposed to denote light verb and its constructions: support verbs, operator verbs, linking verbs, complex predicates, support verb construction, function verb construction.

Among state of the art methods of extracting light verb constructions from corpora, we can mention the work of Nagy and Vincze [6] who developed a rule-based technique for English. The rules were crafted manually according to observations of light verb behavior in texts. In the experiments, 368 light verb constructions were found in the corpus.

Vincze et al. [10] applied a dependency parser to detect light verb constructions in Hungarian texts. The authors noticed that the role of the noun in a light verb construction is different from the role of the noun in the common predicate-argument relation and assumed the view of the noun as a quasi-argument in light verb constructions. They suggested to add the relation of a quasi-argument to the parser used in

---

[1] https://www.thoughtco.com/collocation-examples-1210325.

experiments expecting that in the process of extracting events the parser would recognize this relation in such sentences as *The plan received support of the company* and produce the following output: 'event: receiving-support, argument 1: plan, argument 2: company' instead of 'event: received, argument 1: plan, argument 2: support, argument 3: company'. The experimental results demonstrated that this approach was feasible: the authors achieved an F-score of 0.7563 for the light verb construction specific relations, which exceeded the baseline of the dictionary matching method with an F-score of 0.5438.

Another set of rules for detecting support verb constructions was developed by Rassi et al. [8] in Brazilian Portuguese. The authors integrated support verb constructions in a parser and evaluated its performance in the experiments. The method achieved a precision of 85%, a recall of 79%, and an accuracy of 76%.

Chen et al. [1] reported a supervised learning method for light verb constructions identification. The method includes two stages. At the first stage, the OntoNotes corpus [7] was used to identify candidate verb-noun pairs. The second stage consisted in application of the LibLinear machine learning technique. The features used for classification were lemma, part of speech, voice, subcategorization frame, dependent words, the distance between the verb and the noun, OntoNotes word senses, WordNet senses, WordNet noun types, WordNet hyponyms, among other features. The method achieved an F-measure of 88.90% on the British National Corpus and of 64.20% on the OntoNotes data set.

Tutin [9] designed a lexicon/grammar method to annotate and extract French verbal collocations using a shallow analysis based on finite state transducers. In the experiments on a corpus of about 233,000 words, a precision of 90% and a recall of 86.2% were achieved.

Foufi, Nerima, and Wehrli [2] designed a system for identification of collocations and other multiword expressions. The principal part of the system was a multilingual constituent parser based on dependency grammar. To enhance the procedure of collocation detection, lexical information derived from a collocation database was fed into the parser resulting in a precision of 0.4815, a recall of 0.4680, and an F-measure of 0.4746.

In our work, we represent the meaning of verb-noun collocations with lexical functions, a concept of the Meaning-Text Theory (Mel'čuk [4]) and experiment on Spanish collocations using supervised machine learning. In the next section, the concept of lexical function is explained briefly.

## 3   Representing Verbal Collocations with Lexical Functions

Lexical function (LF) is a formal concept proposed within the Meaning-Text Theory (Mel'čuk [4]) to generalize and represent both semantic and syntactic structure of a collocation. It has the form $LF(w_0) = \{w_1, w_2, ..., w_n\}$, where $w_0$ is the LF argument which is the base of a collocation (noun), and the LF value is the set $W = \{w_1, w_2, ..., w_n\}$ of collocates (verbs). The set $W$ may include one or more verbs, all of which can be used with the base to convey one particular meaning.

Now we explain and illustrate the concept with most common lexical functions we selected for our experiments. First, the lexical function termed Oper1, from Latin *operari* meaning 'do, carry out', formalizes the action of carrying out of what is denoted by the noun (LF argument). Examples of verb-noun collocations which belong to Oper1 are *pursue a goal, make an error, apply a measure, give a smile, take a walk, have lunch, deliver a lecture, make an announcement, lend support, put up resistance, give an order.*

Integers in the LF notation are used to specify the predicate-argument and syntactic structure. In Oper1, 1 means that the word used to lexicalize the semantic role of agent of the action denoted by the verb (agent is considered to be the first argument of a verb) functions as the grammatical subject in a sentence, so Oper1 represents the pattern 'Agent performs $w_0$' in which $w_0$ is the argument of the lexical function. Notice, that the LF argument $w_0$ is not the agent of the action, it is another word. For example, the value of Oper1 for the argument *smile* is *give*, so the verb-noun phrase is *give a smile* as in the sentence *The boy gave her a smile*, here *the boy* is the agent and its syntactic function is subject.

Real1 means that the first argument (the verb's agent) realizes, fulfills the requirement of the second argument (the verb's object): *drive a car, follow a recommendation, hoist/put up/spread a sail, prove an accusation, succumb to illness, turn back an obstacle.*

Oper1 and Real1 discussed above represent one simple meaning or a single semantic unit, so such functions are called simple. There are lexical functions that formalize combinations of unitary meanings, they are called complex lexical functions. Now we consider two complex LFs: CausFunc0 and CausFunc1.

Caus, from Latin *causare* (to cause), represents the meaning 'cause, do something so that $w_0$ begins occurring', and Func0, from Latin *functionare* (to function), represents the meaning 'happen, take place'. The noun argument $w_0$ of Func0 is the name of an action, activity, state, property, relation, i.e., it is such a noun whose meaning is or includes a predicate in the logical sense of the term thus presupposing arguments. Zero in Func0 means that the argument of Func0 is the agent of the verb and functions as the grammatical subject in a sentence. Therefore, Func0 formalizes the patterns '$w_0$ occurs'. Examples of Func0 are *snow falls, silence reigns, smell lingers, time flies.*

Combining Caus and Func0, we get CausFunc0 which means 'to cause the existence of $w_0$' and represents the pattern 'Agent does something such that $w_0$ begins to occur'. The examples of collocations which can be used in this pattern are *bring about the crisis, create a difficulty, present a difficulty, call elections, establish a system, produce an effect.* CausFunc1 represents the pattern 'Non-agent argument does something such that $w_0$ begins to occur', the corresponding examples of collocations are *open a perspective, raise hope, open a way, cause a damage, instill a habit into someone.*

In this work, we used Oper1, Real1, CausFunc0, CausFunc1 as well as free verb-noun combinations (FWC) in the experiments on LF and FWC automatic detection. These experiments are discussed in the section which follows.

## 4 Experimental Setup

For automatic detection of Oper1, Real1, CausFunc0, CausFunc1 discussed in the previous section as well as free verb-noun combinations (FWC) as opposed to collocations of the four LFs just mentioned, we used as a dataset a portion of the corpus of Spanish verb-noun collocations [3] annotated manually with lexical functions and the Spanish WordNet version 2000611[2] senses [5].

The dataset was submitted to various supervised machine learning techniques implemented in Weka 3-8-1x32[3] [11], first, to classify each sample in the dataset as belonging or not to a particular LF (binary yes-no classification), and second, to assign one of the five classes (Oper1, Real1, CausFunc0, CausFunc1, FWC) to each sample using multiclass classification; in both approaches 10-fold cross-validation was used to evaluate the performance of classifiers.

As vector features, we used hypernyms extracted from the Spanish WordNet referred to previously in this section. Each verb-noun combination was represented as a vector of all hypernyms of the noun concatenated with all hypernyms of the verb, the noun and the verb were also included as zero-level hypernyms.

Concerning our dataset, we took all 60 samples of Real1 from the corpus of Spanish verb-noun collocations [3], and arbitrarily selected 60 samples of each of the other four classes (Oper1, CausFunc0, CausFun1, and FWC) to make the dataset fully balanced. Examples of the data used in our experiments are presented in Table 1.

**Table 1.** Examples of data used in our experiments

| LF | # samples in experiments | Examples of collocations | |
|---|---|---|---|
| | | Spanish | English translation |
| Oper1 | 60 | *realizar un estudio* | do a study |
| | | *cometer un error* | make an error |
| | | *dar un beso* | give a kiss |
| Real1 | 60 | *alcanzar el nivel* | reach a level |
| | | *utilizar recurso* | use a resource |
| | | *cumplir la función* | fulfill the function |
| CausFunc0 | 60 | *crear una cuenta* | create an account |
| | | *formar un grupo* | form a group |
| | | *hacer ruido* | make noise |
| CausFunc1 | 60 | *ofrecer una posibilidad* | offer a possibility |
| | | *causar un problema* | cause a problem |
| | | *crear una condición* | create a condition |
| FWC | 60 | *tener dinero* | have money |
| | | *defender el interés* | defend the interest |
| | | *vender un producto* | sell a product |

---

[2] http://www.lsi.upc.edu/~nlp/web/index.php?Itemid=57&id=31&option=com_content&task=view.

[3] http://www.cs.waikato.ac.nz/ml/weka/downloading.html.

## 5   Results and Discussion

Tables 2, 3, 4, 5, and 6 present the results for LFs classification: first, in the binary classification mode, then, as multi-class classification. For classification, the available algorithms applicable for our type of data in Weka 3-8-1x32[4] [11] were used. The performance of algorithms was evaluated in terms of precision, recall and F-measure using 10-fold cross-validation. The highest values of precision, recall and F-measure in the Tables 2, 3, 4, 5, and 6 are in bold.

**Table 2.** Experimental results for Oper1

| Classifier | Binary classification | | | Multiclass classification | | |
|---|---|---|---|---|---|---|
| | Precision | Recall | F | Precision | Recall | F |
| BayesNet | 0.741 | 0.786 | 0.763 | 0.605 | 0.767 | 0.676 |
| NaiveBayes | 0.762 | 0.711 | 0.735 | 0.558 | 0.800 | 0.658 |
| NaiveBayesUpdateable | 0.762 | 0.711 | 0.735 | 0.558 | 0.800 | 0.658 |
| NaiveBayesMultinomialText | 0.000 | 0.000 | 0.000 | 0.200 | 1.000 | 0.333 |
| Logistic | 0.777 | **0.906** | 0.837 | 0.573 | 0.717 | 0.637 |
| SimpleLogistic | 0.867 | 0.861 | 0.864 | 0.754 | 0.867 | 0.806 |
| SMO | 0.856 | 0.872 | 0.864 | 0.716 | 0.800 | 0.756 |
| IBk | 0.549 | 0.793 | 0.649 | 0.459 | 0.650 | 0.650 |
| KStar | 0.594 | 0.714 | 0.648 | 0.474 | 0.600 | 0.529 |
| LWL | 0.786 | 0.470 | 0.588 | 0.344 | 0.900 | 0.498 |
| AdaBoostM1 | 0.970 | 0.365 | 0.530 | 0.278 | 0.083 | 0.128 |
| AttributeSelectedClassifier | 0.874 | 0.861 | 0.867 | **0.785** | 0.850 | **0.816** |
| Bagging | 0.879 | 0.850 | 0.864 | 0.739 | 0.850 | 0.791 |
| CVParameterSelection | 0.000 | 0.000 | 0.000 | 0.200 | **1.000** | 0.333 |
| FilteredClassifier | 0.876 | 0.853 | 0.865 | 0.610 | 0.783 | 0.686 |
| LogitBoost | 0.833 | 0.861 | 0.847 | 0.773 | 0.850 | 0.810 |
| MultiClassClassifier | 0.777 | **0.906** | 0.837 | 0.643 | 0.750 | 0.692 |
| MultiScheme | 0.000 | 0.000 | 0.000 | 0.200 | **1.000** | 0.333 |
| RandomCommittee | 0.782 | 0.850 | 0.814 | 0.605 | 0.767 | 0.676 |
| RandomSubSpace | 0.892 | 0.714 | 0.793 | 0.732 | 0.867 | 0.794 |
| Stacking | 0.000 | 0.000 | 0.000 | 0.200 | **1.000** | 0.333 |
| Vote | 0.000 | 0.000 | 0.000 | 0.200 | **1.000** | 0.333 |
| JRip | 0.860 | 0.853 | 0.857 | 0.662 | 0.750 | 0.703 |
| OneR | **0.983** | 0.218 | 0.357 | 0.278 | 0.083 | 0.128 |
| PART | 0.881 | 0.865 | **0.873** | 0.698 | 0.733 | 0.715 |
| ZeroR | 0.000 | 0.000 | 0.000 | 0.200 | **1.000** | 0.333 |
| J48 | 0.876 | 0.853 | 0.865 | 0.610 | 0.783 | 0.686 |
| RandomForest | 0.840 | 0.827 | 0.833 | 0.658 | 0.800 | 0.722 |
| RandomTree | 0.718 | 0.786 | 0.750 | 0.600 | 0.550 | 0.574 |
| REPTree | 0.859 | 0.850 | 0.854 | 0.696 | 0.800 | 0.744 |
| DecisionStump | **0.983** | 0.218 | 0.357 | 0.278 | 0.083 | 0.128 |

---

[4] http://www.cs.waikato.ac.nz/ml/weka/downloading.html/.

**Table 3.** Experimental results for Real1

| Classifier | Binary classification | | | Multiclass classification | | |
|---|---|---|---|---|---|---|
| | Precision | Recall | F | Precision | Recall | F |
| BayesNet | 0.396 | 0.317 | 0.352 | 0.761 | 0.583 | 0.660 |
| NaiveBayes | 0.143 | 0.017 | 0.030 | 0.729 | 0.583 | 0.648 |
| NaiveBayesUpdateable | 0.143 | 0.017 | 0.030 | 0.729 | 0.583 | 0.648 |
| NaiveBayesMultinomialText | 0.000 | 0.000 | 0.000 | 0.000 | 0.000 | 0.000 |
| Logistic | 0.379 | **0.650** | 0.479 | 0.686 | 0.583 | 0.631 |
| SimpleLogistic | 0.844 | 0.450 | 0.587 | 0.754 | 0.717 | 0.735 |
| SMO | 0.706 | 0.600 | 0.649 | 0.733 | 0.733 | 0.733 |
| IBk | 0.407 | 0.400 | 0.403 | 0.477 | 0.517 | 0.496 |
| KStar | 0.523 | 0.383 | 0.442 | 0.492 | 0.533 | 0.512 |
| LWL | 0.625 | 0.333 | 0.435 | 0.500 | 0.300 | 0.375 |
| AdaBoostM1 | 0.625 | 0.333 | 0.435 | 0.269 | **0.900** | 0.414 |
| AttributeSelectedClassifier | 0.628 | 0.450 | 0.524 | 0.642 | 0.717 | 0.677 |
| Bagging | 0.875 | 0.467 | 0.609 | 0.613 | 0.767 | 0.681 |
| CVParameterSelection | 0.000 | 0.000 | 0.000 | 0.000 | 0.000 | 0.000 |
| FilteredClassifier | 0.769 | 0.500 | 0.606 | **0.800** | 0.667 | 0.727 |
| LogitBoost | **0.889** | 0.533 | **0.667** | 0.730 | 0.767 | **0.748** |
| MultiClassClassifier | 0.379 | **0.650** | 0.479 | 0.755 | 0.617 | 0.613 |
| MultiScheme | 0.000 | 0.000 | 0.000 | 0.000 | 0.000 | 0.000 |
| RandomCommittee | 0.479 | 0.517 | 0.569 | 0.656 | 0.667 | 0.661 |
| RandomSubSpace | 0.800 | 0.133 | 0.229 | 0.563 | 0.667 | 0.611 |
| Stacking | 0.000 | 0.000 | 0.000 | 0.000 | 0.000 | 0.000 |
| Vote | 0.000 | 0.000 | 0.000 | 0.000 | 0.000 | 0.000 |
| JRip | 0.786 | 0.550 | 0.647 | 0.686 | 0.583 | 0.631 |
| OneR | 0.462 | 0.100 | 0.164 | 0.269 | **0.900** | 0.414 |
| PART | 0.721 | 0.517 | 0.602 | 0.672 | 0.683 | 0.678 |
| ZeroR | 0.000 | 0.000 | 0.000 | 0.000 | 0.000 | 0.000 |
| J48 | 0.769 | 0.500 | 0.606 | **0.800** | 0.667 | 0.727 |
| RandomForest | 0.800 | 0.333 | 0.471 | 0.691 | 0.633 | 0.661 |
| RandomTree | 0.435 | 0.450 | 0.443 | 0.588 | 0.667 | 0.625 |
| REPTree | 0.829 | 0.483 | 0.611 | 0.535 | 0.633 | 0.580 |
| DecisionStump | 0.625 | 0.333 | 0.435 | 0.269 | **0.900** | 0.414 |

For Oper1 (Table 2), the best result in terms of F-measure is demonstrated by the PART algorithm with a value of 0.873 for binary classification, and a slightly lower F-measure for multi-class classification of 0.816 was produced by AttributeS-electedClassifier. The following classifiers were not able to determine Oper1 at all in the binary mode: NaiveBayesMultinomialText, CVParameterSelection, MultiScheme, Stacking, Vote, and ZeroR.

For Real1 (Table 3), LogitBoost generated the highest value of F-measure of 0.667 for binary classification and the same algorithm reached the highest value in the multi-

**Table 4.** Experimental results for CausFunc0

| Classifier | Binary classification | | | Multiclass classification | | |
|---|---|---|---|---|---|---|
| | Precision | Recall | F | Precision | Recall | F |
| BayesNet | 0.558 | 0.578 | 0.568 | 0.569 | 0.550 | 0.559 |
| NaiveBayes | 0.535 | 0.211 | 0.303 | 0.564 | 0.517 | 0.539 |
| NaiveBayesUpdateable | 0.535 | 0.211 | 0.303 | 0.564 | 0.517 | 0.539 |
| NaiveBayesMultinomialText | 0.000 | 0.000 | 0.000 | 0.000 | 0.000 | 0.000 |
| Logistic | 0.383 | 0.706 | 0.497 | 0.655 | 0.600 | 0.626 |
| SimpleLogistic | 0.707 | 0.532 | 0.607 | 0.617 | 0.617 | 0.617 |
| SMO | 0.692 | 0.661 | 0.676 | 0.625 | 0.583 | 0.603 |
| IBk | 0.519 | 0.385 | 0.442 | 0.442 | 0.317 | 0.369 |
| KStar | 0.532 | 0.385 | 0.447 | 0.457 | 0.350 | 0.396 |
| LWL | 0.000 | 0.000 | 0.000 | 0.667 | 0.100 | 0.174 |
| AdaBoostM1 | 0.750 | 0.028 | 0.053 | 0.250 | 0.033 | 0.059 |
| AttributeSelectedClassifier | 0.756 | 0.569 | 0.649 | **0.736** | 0.650 | 0.690 |
| Bagging | 0.704 | 0.633 | 0.667 | 0.725 | 0.617 | 0.667 |
| CVParameterSelection | 0.000 | 0.000 | 0.000 | 0.000 | 0.000 | 0.000 |
| FilteredClassifier | 0.747 | 0.541 | 0.628 | 0.667 | 0.633 | 0.650 |
| LogitBoost | 0.794 | 0.459 | 0.581 | 0.627 | 0.700 | 0.661 |
| MultiClassClassifier | 0.383 | 0.706 | 0.497 | 0.729 | **0.717** | **0.723** |
| MultiScheme | 0.000 | 0.000 | 0.000 | 0.000 | 0.000 | 0.000 |
| RandomCommittee | 0.624 | 0.486 | 0.546 | 0.508 | 0.500 | 0.504 |
| RandomSubSpace | **0.860** | 0.339 | 0.487 | 0.673 | 0.583 | 0.625 |
| Stacking | 0.000 | 0.000 | 0.000 | 0.000 | 0.000 | 0.000 |
| Vote | 0.000 | 0.000 | 0.000 | 0.000 | 0.000 | 0.000 |
| JRip | 0.729 | **0.716** | **0.722** | 0.635 | 0.667 | 0.650 |
| OneR | 0.690 | 0.266 | 0.384 | 0.250 | 0.033 | 0.059 |
| PART | 0.638 | 0.615 | 0.626 | 0.667 | 0.667 | 0.667 |
| ZeroR | 0.000 | 0.000 | 0.000 | 0.000 | 0.000 | 0.000 |
| J48 | 0.747 | 0.541 | 0.628 | 0.667 | 0.633 | 0.650 |
| RandomForest | 0.754 | 0.394 | 0.518 | 0.625 | 0.583 | 0.603 |
| RandomTree | 0.621 | 0.495 | 0.551 | 0.561 | 0.533 | 0.547 |
| REPTree | 0.721 | 0.688 | 0.704 | 0.712 | 0.617 | 0.661 |
| DecisionStump | 0.000 | 0.000 | 0.000 | 0.250 | 0.033 | 0.059 |

class option: an F-measure of 0.748. Comparing with the identification of Oper1, we can notice that Real1 is less distinguishable. However, the classifiers which were not able to determine Real1 at all in both binary and multi-class modes were the same as for Oper1: NaiveBayesMultinomialText, CVParameterSelection, MultiScheme, Stacking, Vote, and ZeroR.

For CausFunc0 (Table 4), JRip produced the highest value of F-measure of 0.722 for binary classification and for the multi-class classification, the best result was shown by MultiClassClassifier with an F-measure of 0.723. The classifiers which were not

**Table 5.** Experimental results for CausFunc1

| Classifier | Binary classification | | | Multiclass classification | | |
|---|---|---|---|---|---|---|
| | Precision | Recall | F | Precision | Recall | F |
| BayesNet | 0.487 | 0.427 | 0.455 | 0.634 | 0.750 | 0.687 |
| NaiveBayes | 0.294 | 0.056 | 0.094 | 0.657 | 0.733 | 0.693 |
| NaiveBayesUpdateable | 0.294 | 0.056 | 0.094 | 0.657 | 0.733 | 0.693 |
| NaiveBayesMultinomialText | 0.000 | 0.000 | 0.000 | 0.000 | 0.000 | 0.000 |
| Logistic | 0.370 | **0.719** | 0.489 | 0.618 | 0.700 | 0.656 |
| SimpleLogistic | 0.735 | 0.685 | 0.709 | 0.793 | 0.767 | 0.780 |
| SMO | 0.731 | 0.640 | 0.683 | 0.780 | 0.767 | 0.773 |
| IBk | 0.495 | 0.551 | 0.521 | 0.565 | 0.583 | 0.574 |
| KStar | 0.470 | 0.438 | 0.453 | 0.563 | 0.600 | 0.581 |
| LWL | 0.762 | 0.539 | 0.632 | 0.528 | 0.633 | 0.576 |
| AdaBoostM1 | 0.762 | 0.539 | 0.632 | 0.479 | 0.583 | 0.526 |
| AttributeSelectedClassifier | 0.726 | 0.685 | 0.705 | 0.891 | 0.683 | 0.774 |
| Bagging | 0.767 | 0.629 | 0.691 | **0.894** | 0.700 | 0.785 |
| CVParameterSelection | 0.000 | 0.000 | 0.000 | 0.000 | 0.000 | 0.000 |
| FilteredClassifier | **0.800** | 0.674 | **0.732** | 0.825 | **0.783** | 0.803 |
| LogitBoost | 0.753 | 0.685 | 0.718 | 0.849 | 0.750 | 0.796 |
| MultiClassClassifier | 0.370 | **0.719** | 0.489 | 0.754 | 0.767 | 0.760 |
| MultiScheme | 0.000 | 0.000 | 0.000 | 0.000 | 0.000 | 0.000 |
| RandomCommittee | 0.671 | 0.596 | 0.631 | 0.722 | 0.650 | 0.684 |
| RandomSubSpace | 0.756 | 0.382 | 0.507 | 0.788 | 0.683 | 0.732 |
| Stacking | 0.000 | 0.000 | 0.000 | 0.000 | 0.000 | 0.000 |
| Vote | 0.000 | 0.000 | 0.000 | 0.000 | 0.000 | 0.000 |
| JRip | 0.765 | 0.697 | 0.729 | 0.721 | 0.733 | 0.727 |
| OneR | 0.762 | 0.539 | 0.632 | 0.479 | 0.583 | 0.526 |
| PART | 0.626 | 0.640 | 0.633 | 0.855 | **0.783** | **0.817** |
| ZeroR | 0.000 | 0.000 | 0.000 | 0.000 | 0.000 | 0.000 |
| J48 | **0.800** | 0.674 | **0.732** | 0.825 | **0.783** | 0.803 |
| RandomForest | 0.745 | 0.461 | 0.569 | 0.730 | 0.767 | 0.748 |
| RandomTree | 0.526 | 0.562 | 0.543 | 0.633 | 0.633 | 0.633 |
| REPTree | 0.743 | 0.618 | 0.675 | 0.878 | 0.717 | 0.789 |
| DecisionStump | 0.762 | 0.539 | 0.632 | 0.479 | 0.583 | 0.526 |

able to determine CausFunc0 at all in both binary and multi-class modes were NaiveBayesMultinomialText, CVParameterSelection, MultiScheme, Stacking, Vote, and ZeroR. LWL did not distinguish CausFunc0 in the binary classification, and in the multi-class option its F-measure was as low as 0.174. The same was true for DecisionStump: zero F-measure for binary classification and an F-measure of 0.059 for multi-class classification.

For CausFunc1 (Table 5), FilteredClassifier and J48 produced the highest value of F-measure of 0.732 for binary classification, and PART reached the best value of F-

**Table 6.** Experimental results for FWC

| Classifier | Binary classification | | | Multiclass classification | | |
|---|---|---|---|---|---|---|
| | Precision | Recall | F | Precision | Recall | F |
| BayesNet | 0.600 | **0.643** | 0.621 | 0.694 | 0.567 | 0.624 |
| NaiveBayes | 0.664 | 0.495 | 0.567 | 0.705 | 0.517 | 0.596 |
| NaiveBayesUpdateable | 0.664 | 0.495 | 0.567 | 0.705 | 0.517 | 0.596 |
| NaiveBayesMultinomialText | 0.000 | 0.000 | 0.000 | 0.000 | 0.000 | 0.000 |
| Logistic | 0.580 | 0.592 | 0.586 | 0.647 | 0.550 | 0.595 |
| SimpleLogistic | 0.692 | 0.469 | 0.559 | 0.661 | 0.617 | 0.638 |
| SMO | 0.669 | 0.587 | 0.625 | 0.690 | 0.667 | 0.678 |
| IBk | 0.556 | 0.607 | 0.580 | **0.778** | 0.583 | 0.667 |
| KStar | 0.590 | 0.551 | 0.570 | 0.735 | 0.600 | 0.661 |
| LWL | 0.552 | 0.352 | 0.430 | 0.615 | 0.267 | 0.372 |
| AdaBoostM1 | 0.571 | 0.327 | 0.416 | 0.000 | 0.000 | 0.000 |
| AttributeSelectedClassifier | 0.711 | 0.413 | 0.523 | 0.478 | 0.550 | 0.512 |
| Bagging | 0.672 | 0.449 | 0.538 | 0.569 | 0.550 | 0.559 |
| CVParameterSelection | 0.000 | 0.000 | 0.000 | 0.000 | 0.000 | 0.000 |
| FilteredClassifier | **0.720** | 0.393 | 0.508 | 0.525 | 0.517 | 0.521 |
| LogitBoost | 0.582 | 0.199 | 0.297 | 0.686 | 0.583 | 0.631 |
| MultiClassClassifier | 0.580 | 0.592 | 0.586 | 0.672 | **0.683** | 0.678 |
| MultiScheme | 0.000 | 0.000 | 0.000 | 0.000 | 0.000 | 0.000 |
| RandomCommittee | 0.649 | 0.622 | **0.635** | 0.660 | 0.550 | 0.600 |
| RandomSubSpace | 0.718 | 0.403 | 0.516 | 0.611 | 0.550 | 0.579 |
| Stacking | 0.000 | 0.000 | 0.000 | 0.000 | 0.000 | 0.000 |
| Vote | 0.000 | 0.000 | 0.000 | 0.000 | 0.000 | 0.0000 |
| JRip | 0.590 | 0.403 | 0.479 | 0.544 | 0.517 | 0.530 |
| OneR | 0.455 | 0.153 | 0.229 | 0.000 | 0.000 | 0.000 |
| PART | 0.647 | 0.551 | 0.595 | 0.541 | 0.550 | 0.545 |
| ZeroR | 0.000 | 0.000 | 0.000 | 0.000 | 0.000 | 0.000 |
| J48 | **0.720** | 0.393 | 0.508 | 0.525 | 0.517 | 0.521 |
| RandomForest | 0.699 | 0.520 | 0.596 | 0.736 | 0.650 | **0.690** |
| RandomTree | 0.542 | 0.490 | 0.515 | 0.600 | 0.600 | 0.600 |
| REPTree | 0.639 | 0.434 | 0.517 | 0.424 | 0.417 | 0.420 |
| DecisionStump | 0.551 | 0.332 | 0.414 | 0.000 | 0.000 | 0.000 |

measure of 0.817 in the multi-class option. The classifiers which were not able to determine CausFunc0 at all in both binary and multi-class modes were NaiveBayesMultinomialText, CVParameterSelection, MultiScheme, Stacking, Vote, and ZeroR.

For FWC (Table 6), RandomCommittee produced the highest value of F-measure of 0.635 for binary classification, and RandomForest gave the best F-measure with a value of 0.690 for the multi-class option. The classifiers which were not able to determine CausFunc0 at all in both binary and multi-class modes were

NaiveBayesMultinomialText, CVParameterSelection, MultiScheme, Stacking, Vote, and ZeroR. DecisionStump did not distinguish FWC in the multi-class classification, and in the binary option its F-measure was 0.414.

## 6 Conclusions and Future Work

In this work explored the performance of supervised algorithms on the task of identification of four lexical functions of the Meaning-Text Theory (Mel'čuk [4]) and free word combinations as opposed to them. Lexical functions are used to formalize the semantics and syntax of collocations. We performed experiments for the special case of Spanish verb-noun collocations having selected four lexical functions: Oper1, Real1, CausFunc0, and CausFunc1. Free verb-noun combinations as opposed to collocations were represented as a class and included in the dataset alongside with the collocations of the four chosen lexical functions.

The experimental results showed that application of supervised learning algorithms of collocations represented as vectors of hypernyms of the verb and the noun is feasible. The best result achieved was an F-measure of 0.873 demonstrated by PART algorithm on the binary class detection of Oper1. Identification of free word combinations was less successful. The best result on this class task was an F-measure of 0.690 achieved by RandomForest in the multi-class mode.

In future we plan to perform experiments with other lexical functions not considered in the present work.

**Acknowledgements.** The work was done under partial support of Mexican Government: SNI, BEIFI-IPN, and SIP-IPN grants 20172044 and 20172008.

## References

1. Chen, W.T., Bonial, C., Palmer, M.: English light verb construction identification using lexical knowledge. In: AAAI, pp. 2368–2374 (2015)
2. Foufi, V., Nerima, L., Wehrli, E.: Parsing and MWE detection: fips at the PARSEME shared task. In: Proceedings of MWE (2017)
3. Gelbukh, A., Kolesnikova, O.: Supervised learning for semantic classification of Spanish collocations. In: Martínez-Trinidad, J.F., Carrasco-Ochoa, J.A., Kittler, J. (eds.) MCPR 2010. LNCS, vol. 6256, pp. 362–371. Springer, Heidelberg (2010). https://doi.org/10.1007/978-3-642-15992-3_38. The lexical resource (lexical functions data) can be downloaded at http://148.204.58.221/okolesnikova/index.php?id=lex/ or http://www.gelbukh.com/lexical-functions/
4. Mel'čuk, I.A.: Lexical functions: a tool for the description of lexical relations in a Lexicon. In: Wanner, L. (ed.) Lexical Functions in Lexicography and Natural Language Processing, pp. 37–102. Benjamins Academic Publishers, Amsterdam (1996)
5. Miller, G.A., Leacock, C., Tengi, R., Bunker, R.T.: A semantic concordance. In: Proceedings of the Workshop on Human Language Technology Association for Computational Linguistics, pp. 303–308 (1993)

6. Nagy, I., Vincze, V.: Identifying verbal collocations in Wikipedia articles. In: Habernal, I., Matoušek, V. (eds.) TSD 2011. LNCS (LNAI), vol. 6836, pp. 179–186. Springer, Heidelberg (2011). https://doi.org/10.1007/978-3-642-23538-2_23

7. Pradhan, S.S., Hovy, E., Marcus, M., Palmer, M., Ramshaw, L., Weischedel, R.: Ontonotes: a unified relational semantic representation. Int. J. Semant. Comput. 1(04), 405–419 (2007)

8. Rassi, A., Baptista, J., Mamede, N., Vale, O.: Integrating support verb constructions into a parser. In: Proceedings of Symposium in Information and Human Language Technology, Natal, RN, Brazil, 4–7 September, pp. 57–61 (2015)

9. Tutin, A.: Annotating lexical functions in corpora: showing collocations in context. In: Proceedings of the Second International Conference on the Meaning-Text Model (in Russian). Litres (2017)

10. Vincze, V., Zsibrita, J., Nagy, I.: Dependency parsing for identifying Hungarian light verb constructions. In: Proceedings of IJCNLP, pp. 207–215 (2013)

11. Witten, I.H., Frank, E., Hall, M.A.: Data Mining: Practical Machine Learning Tools and Techniques. Morgan Kaufmann Publishers, MA, USA (2011)

# Surface Realisation Using Factored Language Models and Input Seed Features

Cristina Barros[⊠] and Elena Lloret

Department of Software and Computing Systems, University of Alicante,
Apdo. de Correos 99, 03080 Alicante, Spain
{cbarros,elloret}@dlsi.ua.es

**Abstract.** Natural Language Generation research field needs to move forward to the design and development of flexible and adaptive techniques and approaches capable of producing language automatically, for any domain, language and purpose. In light of this, the aim of this paper is to study the appropriateness of factored language models for the stage of surface realisation, thus presenting an almost-fully language independent statistical approach. Its main novelty is that it can be adapted to generate texts for different purposes or domains thanks to the use of an input seed feature that guides all the generation process. In the context of this research, the seed input is a phoneme and our goal is to generate a full meaningful sentence that maximises the amount of words containing that phoneme. We experimented with different factors, including lemmas or part-of-speech tags, based on a trigram language model. The analysis carried out with several configurations of our proposed approach showed an improvement of 47% and 40% as far as the total meaningful generated sentences is concerned, with respect to traditional language models, for English and Spanish, respectively.

**Keywords:** Natural Language Generation · Surface realisation
Statistical approach · Seed feature · Factored language models

## 1 Introduction

Natural Language Generation (NLG) aims to automatically produce human utterances, either in speech or text format. The task of NLG comprises a wide range of subtasks which are commonly viewed as a pipeline of three stages: document planning, microplanning and surface realisation [22].

However, surface realisation is the one responsible of producing a grammatically well-formed, natural and cohesive output [7]. Indeed, there have been many previous research works focusing in this stage on its own [4,7,11,28], or addressing the entire NLG process integrating a surface realiser with the remaining macroplanning and microplanning components [13,14].

© Springer Nature Switzerland AG 2018
F. Castro et al. (Eds.): MICAI 2017, LNAI 10633, pp. 15–26, 2018.
https://doi.org/10.1007/978-3-030-02840-4_2

Furthermore, NLG has been applied to several fields, ranging from specific tasks concerning the construction of a single sentence, by just addressing surface realisation as it was previously shown, to more complex tasks, including text simplification [23], text summarisation [10] or generation of suggestions/recommendations [15].

Nevertheless, generation is a difficult task and the systems are currently designed for very specific domains [21] and languages [2], as well as for particular predefined purposes [9].

Given this context, research into more flexible, open-domain, multilingual (or language-independent) techniques and approaches able to generate language, that could be adapted to the target audience, or purpose would considerably advance the state of the art in NLG. Towards this ambitious long-term goal, the objective of this paper is to present an almost-fully language independent statistical approach focused on the surface realisation stage using factored language models. The main novelty of our approach is that it can be adapted to generate text for different purposes or domains thanks to the use of an input seed feature that guides all the generation process. Within our scope, the seed feature can be seen as an abstract object (a phoneme, in this paper - please see Sect. 4 for further information) that will determine how the sentence will be in terms of content, and, therefore, it will guide all the generation process in relation to its vocabulary or the word types that the new sentence must contain.

## 2      Background: Factored Language Models and NLG

Factored language models (FLM) are an extension of language models proposed in [5]. In this model, a word is viewed as a vector of $k$ factors such that $w_t \equiv \{f_t^1, f_t^2, \ldots, f_t^K\}$. These factors can be anything, including the Part-Of-Speech (POS) tag, lemma, stem or any other lexical, syntactic or semantic feature. Once a set of factors is selected, the main objective of a FLM is to create a statistical model $P(f|f_1, \ldots, f_N)$ where the prediction of a feature $f$ is based on $N$ parents $\{f_1, \ldots, f_N\}$. For example, if $w$ represents a word token and $t$ represents a POS tag, the expression $P(w_i|w_{i-2}, w_{i-1}, t_{i-1})$ provides a model to determine the current word token, based on a traditional n-gram model together with the POS tag of the previous word. Therefore, in the development of such models there are two main issues to consider: (1) choose an appropriate set of factors, and (2) find the best statistical model over these factors.

In recent years, FLM have been used in several areas of Computational Linguistics, mostly in machine translation [1,6] and speech recognition [26,27]. To a lesser extent, they have been also employed for generating language, mainly in English. This is the case of the BAGEL system [16], where FLM (with semantic concepts as factors) are used to predict the semantic structure of the sentence that is going to be generated; or OpenCCG [29], a surface realisation tool, where FLM (with POS tag and supertags as factors) are used to score partial and complete realisations to be later selected. More recently, FLM (with POS tag, word and lemma as factors) were used to rank generated sentences in Portuguese [19].

To the best of our knowledge, there is no any research focused on generating sentences for Spanish employing FLM, and, moreover, with the restriction of containing words with a specific seed feature, thus leading to a more flexible NLG approach that could be easily adapted to different purposes, domains and languages.

## 3    Seed-Feature-Guided Surface Realisation Using FLM

We propose an almost-fully language independent statistical approach focused on the surface realisation stage that is based on over-generation and ranking techniques, which can be adapted to generate texts for different purposes and domains. This is achieved through the use of input seed features, which are abstract objects (e.g., a phoneme, a semantic class, a domain, or a topic) that will guide the generation process in relation to the most suitable vocabulary for a given purpose or domain.

The overall performance of the approach is explained below.

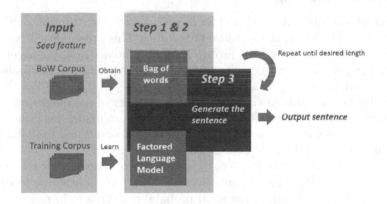

**Fig. 1.** Our proposed approach

### 3.1    Sentence Generation

In a first instance, the approach generates multiple sentences for a specific seed feature, taking as input: (i) a training corpus, (ii) a corpus to build the bag of words (BoW corpus), and (iii) a seed feature. The generation approach consists of three major steps as can be seen in Fig. 1:

1. **Generate the language model.** A FLM is firstly trained over a corpus (i.e., the training corpus).
2. **Generate the bag of words.** A bag of words containing words related with the input seed feature is obtained from the BoW corpus.

3. **Generate the sentence.** The sentence is generated based on both, the FLM and the bag of words. The algorithm follows an iterative process, that is repeated until either the desired length of the sentence or a full stop are reached, such that:
   - We first search if there is a word in the bag of words that follows the word predicted from the previous iteration (in the first iteration is set as the token start of sentence <s>) based on the FLM's factors. If so, the one which has the highest probability based on the FLM is selected.
   - Otherwise, the word, related with the seed feature, which has the highest probability of appearance with the word from the previous iteration based on the FLM's factors is looked for in the FLM. If there is no such word, then, the word with highest probability of appearance with word from the previous iteration is chosen.

In this manner, this process prioritise the selection of words from the bag of words to guarantee that the generated sentence will contain the maximum number of words related with the input seed feature.

## 3.2   Sentence Ranking

Once several sentences are generated for a specific seed feature input, only one of them is selected based on the sentence probability. This probability is computed by the chain rule where the joint probability of a sentence or sequence of words $P(W) = P(w_1, w_2, w_3 \ldots w_n)$ can be calculated as the product of the probability of all the words: $P(w_1, w_2 \ldots w_n) = \prod_{i=1}^{n} P(w_i | w_1, w_2 \ldots w_{i-1})$.

Applying the Markov Assumptiom, the probability of a sequence of n items only depends on the previous item $n - 1$, so in a trigram model, for example, the probability of a sequence is just the product of the conditional probabilities of its trigrams: $P(w_1^n) \approx \prod_{i=1}^{n} P(w_i | w_{i-2}, w_{i-1})$.

This kind of model has the length effect, where longer sentences usually receive lower scores than shorter ones because word probabilities are less than 1 and, with each multiplication, the total probability decrease. In order to avoid this effect, the probability of a sentence is calculated as a geometric mean of the probability of each word in the sentence, as it is suggested in [12]: $P(w_1^n) \approx \prod_{i=1}^{n} P(w_i | w_{i-2}, w_{i-1})^{1/n}$.

Based on these techniques, the probability of a word was calculated as the linear combination of FLMs, where a weight $\lambda_i$ was assigned for each of them: $P(f_i | f_{i-2}, f_{i-1}) = \lambda_1 P_1(f_i | f_{i-2}, f_{i-1}) + \cdots + \lambda_n P_n(f_i | f_{i-2}, f_{i-1})$, where $f$ are the selected factors from the different FLMs employed, the total sum of the weights being 1. The final selected sentence would therefore be the one which is above the average probability, and has the maximum number of words containing the seed feature.

## 4   Experimental Setup

Our experiments were developed in the context of NLG for assistive technologies. Specifically, they were focused on story generation to help children with dyslalia in therapies. Dyslalia is a disorder in phoneme articulation that implies the inability to correctly pronounce a phoneme or group of phonemes.

Based on this scenario, a phoneme is selected as the seed feature, being the main objective of our approach the generation of meaningful sentences having as many words with this phoneme as possible. This kind of sentences would help children with dyslalia to reinforce their phoneme pronunciation through reading and repeating words [24].

In Fig. 2, different illustrative examples of an input phoneme and generated sentence meeting the requirements previously mentioned can be seen.

Spanish
/e/ → Érase que se era, un hombre llamado Esteban.

English
/e/ → My friend Fred said that many people eat bread.

**Fig. 2.** Illustrative example sentences.

Given this scenario, a collection of 158 Hans Christian Andersen tales in two languages (English and Spanish) was chosen as corpora, due to the fact that the vocabulary contained would be suitable for a young audience. In Table 1 are shown the statistics of the corpus employed. Therefore, our approach was tested in these languages for each of their phonemes, according to the correspondence between phonemes and letters provided in [17] for Spanish, and the spelling of the phonemes in English[1].

**Table 1.** Statistics of the corpora employed.

| Corpus | Files | Sentences | Avg. sents. per file | Words | Avg. words per file |
|---|---|---|---|---|---|
| Spanish H.C. Andersen | 158 | 21,310 | 134 | 339,443 | 2,148 |
| English H.C. Andersen | 158 | 17,718 | 112 | 425,846 | 2,695 |

Concerning the tools for carrying out the experiments, SRILM [25] and Freeling [20] were used. On the one hand, SRILM is a software which allows building and applying statistical language models, which also includes an implementation of factored language models. On the other hand, Freeling is a language analyser at a lexical, syntactic and semantic level that works for multiple languages, including English and Spanish.

---

[1] http://www.dyslexia-reading-well.com/support-files/the-44-phonemes-of-english.pdf.

Regarding the factors to be used within FLM, the word itself, its POS tag and its lemma were selected to automatically generate the sentences in the context of the scenario previously described.

To obtain all these factors, except the words, Freeling was employed to automatically annotate the training and the BoW corpus with POS-tags and lemmas. These annotations were subsequently used to obtain the language models.

The experiments were performed to analyse and test if FLM could generate better sentences, thus improving the results obtained over traditional n-gram Language Models (LM), that were considered as baseline. This baseline was obtained, as explained in [3], training trigrams and bigrams LMs only with words, were trigrams proved to perform better than bigrams, so we decided to use this type of LMs in our experiments.

In this case, taking into account the different factors, Spanish and English sentences were automatically generated using trigram FLM with several configurations, WORD+POSTAG (using the words and the POS tags as the features to train the FLM) and LEMMA+POSTAG (using the lemmas and the POS tags as the features to train the FLM), and subsequently these sentences were ranked with a linear combination of three FLM, as explained in Sect. 3.2: $P(w_i) = \lambda_1 P(f_i|f_{i-2}, f_{i-1}) + \lambda_2 P(f_i|p_{i-2}, p_{i-1}) + \lambda_3 P(p_i|f_{i-2}, f_{i-1})$, where $f$ can be can be either a lemma and a word, $p$ refers to a POS tag, and $\lambda_i$ are set $\lambda_1 = 0.25$, $\lambda_2 = 0.25$ and $\lambda_3 = 0.5$ (these values were empirically determined).

## 5   Results and Discussion

Initially we did not apply the ranking stage and the generated sentences by the new approach were analysed in order to compare them with the ones obtained by the baseline.

From all these generated sentences, those ones ending with full stop were selected for evaluation and their meaningfulness was manually analysed, since they are comparable to complete sentences. This manual evaluation was performed in order to ensure the selection of meaningful sentences.

A total of 114 and 101 sentences with the WORD+POSTAG configuration, and a total of 98 and 109 sentences with the LEMMA+POSTAG configuration were generated in Spanish and English, respectively. Considering the full stop ended sentences mentioned before, a total of 67 and 21 sentences with the WORD+POSTAG configuration, and a total of 64 and 33 sentences with the LEMMA+POSTAG configuration were finally obtained for Spanish and English, respectively. From these sentences ending with full stop, meaningful sentences were obtained after a manual analysis, choosing only those ones that provide a complete meaning by themselves.

The results obtained can be seen in Table 2, where the statistics were calculated based on the total number of generated sentences with the corresponding configurations. As it can be seen, the percentages concerning the meaningful generated sentences were subdivided in two, those newly meaningful generated

**Table 2.** Results and comparison of the factored language models employed with respect to the baseline.

| Surface realisation technique | | Total generated sentences | Meaningful generated sentences | Newly meaningful sent. (not in corpus) | Meaningful sent. in corpus |
|---|---|---|---|---|---|
| EN | N grams (baseline) | 140 | 51.43% | 34.29% | 17.14% |
| | FLM-WORD+POSTAG | 21 | 33.33% | 28.57% | 4.76% |
| | FLM-LEMMA+POSTAG | 33 | 75.75% | 72.72% | 3.03% |
| ES | N-grams (baseline) | 95 | 56.84% | 31.58% | 25.26% |
| | FLM-WORD+POSTAG | 67 | 77.61% | 53.73% | 23.88% |
| | FLM-LEMMA+POSTAG | 64 | 79.69% | 54.69% | 25% |

sentences that are not included in the original corpus and those meaningful generated sentences included in the corpus (the sum of their percentages leads to the total percentage of the meaningful sentences).

Although the results obtained for the Spanish generated sentences have significantly improved with regard to the baseline results, the English ones seem not to present so much improvement.

This is because most of the English generated sentences are very long and may lack of meaning caused by some common errors. Moreover, the number of generated sentences has notably decreased in English, whereas not so much for Spanish. This decrease is due to the way the approach selects the first word when generating the sentence.

In particular, the approach firstly selects the most probable POS tag in the FLM that appears with the token start of sentence (<s>), and then, the first word of the sentence to be generated is determined based on both, the token start of sentence and the POS tag. Since the most probable POS tag at the beginning of the sentence is a verb for Spanish, and a pronoun for English, this is the reason why very few sentences beginning with a pronoun and ending with a full stop were generated in English.

When the full approach with our two stages (overgeneration and ranking) is executed, the ranking is performed based on the linear combination seen before in order to verify if the approach is able to select correct sentences.

In Table 3, the results from the ranking performed can be seen, where the statistics were calculated based on the total number of generated sentences (being the maximum of sentences to generate the total number of phonemes for each language). As it is shown in the table, good results were obtained in the meaningful generated sentences chosen in the ranking with the LEMMA+POSTAG configuration, though only some of them are not included in the corpus.

With the experimentation conducted, the best results were obtained with the LEMMA+POSTAG configuration in both languages obtaining an improve-

**Table 3.** Sentence ranking results and comparison of the factored language models employed.

| Surface realisation technique | | Total generated sentences | Meaningful generated sentences | Newly meaningful sent. (not in corpus) | Meaningful sent. in corpus |
|---|---|---|---|---|---|
| EN | FLM-WORD+POSTAG | 22 | 50% | 45.45% | 4.55% |
| | FLM-LEMMA+POSTAG | 40 | 80% | 55% | 25% |
| ES | FLM-WORD+POSTAG | 24 | 100% | 29.17% | 70.83% |
| | FLM-LEMMA+POSTAG | 27 | 77.78% | 29.63% | 48.15% |

ment of 47% and 40% concerning the total meaningful generated sentences in comparison with the baseline. In addition, we also obtain good results with this configuration in the ranking.

In Fig. 3 can be seen several examples generated from the LEMMA+ POSTAG configurations whereas in Fig. 4 can be seen the respective sentences selected in the ranking stage from the examples shown in Fig. 3, which are meaningful sentences not included in the original corpus.

As can be seen in these Figures, with the baseline, more sentences are generated than when applying the ranking, making the evaluation of these sentences more expensive, while employing the ranking, the approach is capable of choosing correct sentences, despite of the coverage loss. So, with the use of the ranking we gain accuracy, making the evaluation of these sentences lighter.

Manual inspection was performed, within the meaningless sentences, in order to identify possible common errors. Several common errors were found affecting its coherence and cohesion. Mostly, these errors are concerned with an incorrect syntactic order of the words, leading to non-sense sequences of words. Also, some errors regarding semantic relation between words were also found, where the words are unrelated to each other.

# 6    Potentials and Limitations of the Approach

This approach has a great potential since it can generate meaningful sentences for different languages due to its statistical nature, leading to a independent language generation. Moreover, the use of the seed feature gives a greater flexibility to this approach being able to be adapted to diverse domains or scenarios, resulting this adaptation cost not really high. Furthermore, with the inclusion of the sentence's ranking, although we lose coverage during the sentence's generation, we gain accuracy in the selection of correct sentences as mentioned in the previous section.

However, since the best results were obtained with the LEMMA+POSTAG configuration as mentioned before, the words in the generated sentences with this configuration are not inflected and, therefore, we should study different ways

**Spanish**
**Phoneme:** /o/
**Sentences:**
*Conocer el bosque de abeto.*
*Contar lo a todo velocidad.*
*Contestar el viejo árbol.*
*Dormir dulcemente.*
*Observar el padre tocar uno redoble en todo dirección.*
*Poder contar le el mano sobre el blanco de el sol brillar en su corazón.*
*Poner el sol brillar sobre el blanco de el mundo.*
*Resonar por todo el mundo.*
*Tomar lo y comprender el cosa ser.*
*Volver a encontrar se en todo dirección.*

**English**
**Phoneme:** /m/
**Sentences:**
*Many thank for the moon become calm and still high mountain seem to come home.*
*My mother be asleep.*

**Fig. 3.** Example generated sentences from the LEMMA+POSTAG configuration.

Spanish
/o/ ⟶ Resonar por todo el mundo.

English
/m/ ⟶ My mother be asleep.

**Fig. 4.** Example ranked sentences from the LEMMA+POSTAG configuration. (*Translation of the Spanish sentence: resonate all over the world.*)

**Spanish**
**Original Sent:** *Resonar por todo el mundo.*
**Original Sent:** *Resonó por todo el mundo.*

**English**
**Original Sent:** *My mother be asleep.*
**Inflected Sent:** *My mother was asleep.*

**Fig. 5.** Example inflections of the generated sentences.

to post-process the sentences. The inflection task of these sentences could be addressed taking several inflection/deslemmatization research works as reference, as the one in [8], that predicts the set of all inflected forms of a lexical items using a discriminative sequence model; or the one in [18], where they approach the task of morphological inflection as a discriminative string transduction. These works mentioned above could be combined with some kind of grammar or structure in order to finally obtain a infected sentence. An example of the resulting sentences after applying the inflection changes mentioned can be seen in Fig. 5.

## 7    Conclusions and Future Work

In this paper, an almost-fully language independent statistical NLG approach that relies on an input seed feature to generate a sentence was presented. This approach allows us to generate sentences containing a large number of words related to a specific seed feature. The approach was tested in a possible application scenario were these type of generated sentences may be useful in different speech therapies.

Regarding the results obtained, the newly meaningful generated sentences showed a significant improvement compared to the baseline approach. In this novel approach, FLM with different factor configurations are employed in contrast to the baseline approach were only n-grams LMs are used, together with an input seed feature to generate the sentences. In addition, automatic ranking techniques have been included obtaining good results on selecting meaningful sentences with the LEMMA+POSTAG configuration, being this configuration the one obtaining the best results which can make our generated sentences grammatically correct.

In addition, one advantage of this approach is that it is easily adaptable to other contexts without requiring a high cost.

However, although the obtained results are promising, in some cases the approach generates meaningless sentences, so in order to avoid their generation, we need to add more syntactic and semantic information. Consequently, in the future we will analyse to what extent such a generation model can be learned using deep learning algorithms. Furthermore, we will analyse beam search techniques for NLG.

In the short term, we also want to test the approach in other types of scenarios in order to evaluate its performance in diverse areas.

**Acknowledgment.** This research work has been partially funded by the Generalitat Valenciana through the projects "DIIM2.0: Desarrollo de técnicas Inteligentes e Interactivas de Minería y generación de información sobre la web 2.0" (PROMETEOII/2014/001); and partially funded by the Spanish Government through projects TIN2015-65100-R, TIN2015-65136-C2-2-R, as well as by the project "Análisis de Sentimientos Aplicado a la Prevención del Suicidio en las Redes Sociales (ASAP)" funded by Ayudas Fundación BBVA a equipos de investigación científica.

## References

1. Axelrod, A.: Factored language models for statistical machine translation (2006)
2. Ballesteros, M., Bohnet, B., Mille, S., Wanner, L.: Data-driven sentence generation with non-isomorphic trees. In: Proceedings of the 2015 Conference of the North American Chapter of the Association for Computational Linguistics: Human Language Technologies, pp. 387–397. Association for Computational Linguistics, Denver, May–June 2015. http://www.aclweb.org/anthology/N15-1042

3. Barros, C., Lloret, E.: Input seed features for guiding the generation process: a statistical approach for spanish. In: Proceedings of the 15th European Workshop on Natural Language Generation (ENLG). Association for Computational Linguistics (ACL) (2015)
4. Belz, A., Bohnet, B., Mille, S., Wanner, L., White, M.: The surface realisation task: recent developments and future plans. In: Proceedings of the Seventh International Natural Language Generation Conference, pp. 136–140. INLG 2012. Association for Computational Linguistics, Stroudsburg (2012). http://dl.acm.org/citation.cfm?id=2392712.2392743
5. Bilmes, J.A., Kirchhoff, K.: Factored language models and generalized parallel backoff. In: Proceedings of the 2003 Conference of the North American Chapter of the Association for Computational Linguistics on Human Language Technology: Companion Volume of the Proceedings of HLT-NAACL 2003-Short Papers, vol. 2, pp. 4–6. Association for Computational Linguistics (2003)
6. Crego, J.M., Yvon, F.: Factored bilingual n-gram language models for statistical machine translation. Mach. Transl. **24**(2), 159–175 (2010)
7. Dethlefs, N., Hastie, H., Cuayáhuitl, H., Lemon, O.: Conditional random fields for responsive surface realisation using global features. In: Proceedings of the 51st Annual Meeting of the Association for Computational Linguistics: Long Papers, vol. 1, pp. 1254–1263. Association for Computational Linguistics, Sofia, August 2013. http://www.aclweb.org/anthology/P13-1123
8. Durrett, G., DeNero, J.: Supervised learning of complete morphological paradigms. In: Proceedings of the North American Chapter of the Association for Computational Linguistics (2013)
9. Ge, T., Pei, W., Ji, H., Li, S., Chang, B., Sui, Z.: Bring you to the past: automatic generation of topically relevant event chronicles. In: Proceedings of the 53rd Annual Meeting of the Association for Computational Linguistics and the 7th International Joint Conference on Natural Language Processing: Long Papers, vol. 1, pp. 575–585. Association for Computational Linguistics, Beijing, July 2015. http://www.aclweb.org/anthology/P15-1056
10. Gerani, S., Mehdad, Y., Carenini, G., Ng, R.T., Nejat, B.: Abstractive summarization of product reviews using discourse structure. In: Proceedings of the 2014 Conference on Empirical Methods in Natural Language Processing (EMNLP), pp. 1602–1613. Association for Computational Linguistics, Doha, October 2014. http://www.aclweb.org/anthology/D14-1168
11. Gyawali, B., Gardent, C.: Surface realisation from knowledge-bases. In: Proceedings of the 52nd Annual Meeting of the Association for Computational Linguistics: Long Papers, vol. 1, pp. 424–434. Association for Computational Linguistics, Baltimore, June 2014. http://www.aclweb.org/anthology/P14-1040
12. Isard, A., Brockmann, C., Oberlander, J.: Individuality and alignment in generated dialogues. In: Proceedings of the Fourth International Natural Language Generation Conference, pp. 25–32. Association for Computational Linguistics (2006)
13. Kondadadi, R., Howald, B., Schilder, F.: A statistical NLG framework for aggregated planning and realization. In: Proceedings of the 51st Annual Meeting of the Association for Computational Linguistics: Long Papers, vol. 1, pp. 1406–1415. Association for Computational Linguistics, Sofia, August 2013. http://www.aclweb.org/anthology/P13-1138
14. Konstas, I., Lapata, M.: A global model for concept-to-text generation. J. Artif. Int. Res. **48**(1), 305–346 (2013). http://dl.acm.org/citation.cfm?id=2591248.2591256
15. Lim-Cheng, N.R., Fabia, G.I.G., Quebral, M.E.G., Yu, M.T.: Shed: an online diet counselling system. In: DLSU Research Congress 2014 (2014)

16. Mairesse, F., Young, S.: Stochastic language generation in dialogue using factored language models. Comput. Linguist. **40**(4), 763–799 (2014)
17. Morales, J.L.O.: Nuevo método de ortografía. Colección Cervantes, Verbum (1992)
18. Nicolai, G., Cherry, C., Kondrak, G.: Inflection generation as discriminative string transduction. In: Proceedings of NAACL (2015)
19. Novais, E.M., Paraboni, I.: Portuguese text generation using factored language models. J. Braz. Comput. Soc. **19**(2), 135–146 (2012)
20. Padró, L., Stanilovsky, E.: Freeling 3.0: towards wider multilinguality. In: Proceedings of the Eight International Conference on Language Resources and Evaluation (LREC 2012). European Language Resources Association (ELRA) (2012)
21. Ramos-Soto, A., Bugarín, A.J., Barro, S., Taboada, J.: Linguistic descriptions for automatic generation of textual short-term weather forecasts on real prediction data. IEEE Trans. Fuzzy Syst. **23**(1), 44–57 (2015)
22. Reiter, E., Dale, R.: Building Natural Language Generation Systems. Cambridge University Press, Cambridge (2000)
23. Reiter, E., Turner, R., Alm, N., Black, R., Dempster, M., Waller, A.: Using NLG to help language-impaired users tell stories and participate in social dialogues. In: Proceedings of the 12th European Workshop on Natural Language Generation, pp. 1–8. Association for Computational Linguistics (2009)
24. Rvachew, S., Rafaat, S., Martin, M.: Stimulability, speech perception skills, and the treatment of phonological disorders. Am. J. Speech-Lang. Pathol. **8**(1), 33–43 (1999)
25. Stolcke, A.: SRILM - an extensible language modeling toolkit. In: Proceedings International Conference on Spoken Language Processing, vol. 2, pp. 901–904 (2002)
26. Tachbelie, M.Y., Abate, S.T., Menzel, W.: Morpheme-based and factored language modeling for Amharic speech recognition. In: Vetulani, Z. (ed.) LTC 2009. LNCS (LNAI), vol. 6562, pp. 82–93. Springer, Heidelberg (2011). https://doi.org/10.1007/978-3-642-20095-3_8
27. Vergyri, D., Kirchhoff, K., Duh, K., Stolcke, A.: Morphology-based language modeling for Arabic speech recognition. In: INTERSPEECH, vol. 4, pp. 2245–2248 (2004)
28. Wan, S., Dras, M., Dale, R., Paris, C.: Spanning tree approaches for statistical sentence generation. In: Empirical Methods in Natural Language Generation: Data-Oriented Methods and Empirical Evaluation, pp. 13–44 (2010). https://doi.org/10.1007/978-3-642-15573-4_2
29. White, M., Rajkumar, R.: Perceptron reranking for CCG realization. In: Proceedings of the 2009 Conference on Empirical Methods in Natural Language Processing, vol. 1, pp. 410–419. Association for Computational Linguistics (2009)

# Comparison of Two-Pass Algorithms for Dynamic Topic Modeling Based on Matrix Decompositions

Gabriella Skitalinskaya[1,2,4(✉)], Mikhail Alexandrov[3,4], and John Cardiff[1]

[1] Institute of Technology, Tallaght, Dublin, Ireland
gabriellasky@icloud.com, john.cardiff@ittdublin.ie
[2] Moscow Institute of Physics and Technology (State University),
Dolgoprudny, Russia
[3] Autonomous University of Barcelona, Barcelona, Spain
[4] Russian Presidential Academy of National Economy and Public Administration,
Moscow, Russia
malexandrov@mail.ru

**Abstract.** In this paper we present a two-pass algorithm based on different matrix decompositions, such as LSI, PCA, ICA and NMF, which allows tracking of the evolution of topics over time. The proposed dynamic topic models as output give an easily interpreted overview of topics found in a sequentially organized set of documents that does not require further processing. Each topic is presented by a user-specified number of top-terms. Such an approach to topic modeling if applied to, for example, a news article data set, can be convenient and useful for economists, sociologists, political scientists. The proposed approach allows to achieve results comparable to those obtained using complex probabilistic models, such as LDA.

**Keywords:** Dynamic topic modeling · Matrix decomposition
Latent Dirichlet Allocation

## 1 Introduction

### 1.1 Problem Setting

In recent years, there has been a sharp increase in the popularity and development of methods for extracting hidden topics in texts. Topic modeling is an approach that allows users to explore collections of text documents, search and analyse information based on topics covered in the documents. Algorithms of topic modeling allow the determination of topics that are covered in the collection of articles, and present the result in a way that enables simple navigation in the corpus of documents using the found topics. Dynamic topic models can track how a particular topic has changed over a certain period of time, for example in months or years, and how it is related to other topics. Thus, dynamic topic

© Springer Nature Switzerland AG 2018
F. Castro et al. (Eds.): MICAI 2017, LNAI 10633, pp. 27–43, 2018.
https://doi.org/10.1007/978-3-030-02840-4_3

modeling can serve as an addition to static modeling, which is associated only with the identification of a set of topics outside the context of time.

In this paper, we propose a dynamic topic model with different matrix decompositions such as latent semantic indexing (LSI), principal component analysis (PCA), independent component analysis (ICA) and non-negative matrix factorization (NMF), which captures the evolution of topics in a sequentially organized corpus of documents. The proposed algorithm allows to achieve results comparable to those obtained using complex probabilistic models, such as latent Dirichlet allocation (LDA), but with less resources and faster. We demonstrate the algorithms applicability by analyzing news articles in the Russian language obtained from [1], that have been published during the year 2016. Under this model, articles are grouped by month, and from each months articles we retrieve a set of topics that evolve throughout the year.

The paper is organized as follows. Section 2 describes the proposed two-pass algorithm and model quality evaluation measures. Section 3 provides information on the dataset used for topic modeling. Sections 4 and 5 provide a comparison of results obtained by different methods during the first pass and second pass of the proposed approach. It is demonstrated how the proposed dynamic topic models allow the exploration of a large document collection distributed in time. Finally, Sect. 6 presents our conclusions.

## 1.2  State-of-the-Art

Topic models are aimed at finding hidden semantic structures or themes in textual data that can be obtained from word coincidences in documents. These models date back to an early work on LSI [2], which proposes the decomposition of Term-Document matrices using singular value decomposition. Here each singular vector is considered as a topic and the most interesting topics are associated with the first singular values.

A lot of studies on topic modeling have focused on the use of probabilistic methods, where the topic is defined as a discrete distribution on a set of terms, and each document as a discrete distribution on a set of topics [3]. The most widely used method of topic modeling is the Latent Dirichlet Allocation (LDA), proposed in [4]. LDA greatly influenced the field of natural language processing and statistical machine learning and inspired a number of research papers in this direction. In particular, authors consider using word associations [5] and topic correlations [6]. The composition of probabalistic models and LSI is considered in [7], where probabilistic latent semantic analysis is introduced. Ambiguity is a distinctive feature of probabilistic models and researchers propose various methods of regularization to reduce this effect [8,9].

Algorithms based on matrix decompositions, such as NMF, ICA and PCA were also effective in detecting the main topics in a corpus of texts [10,11].

There are different approaches to modeling the evolution of topics over time. Here, two basic ideas should be distinguished: (a) models that assume topics to be static semantic concepts that are used uniquely over the period of analysis and (b) models that allow for a dynamic change of topics by modeling changes in the word sets describing the topic over time. We are more interested in models that fall in the second category.

The Dynamic Topic Model (DTM) introduced in [12] is the work to which we compare our research. Here, topics cease to generalize semantic concepts that undergo some change. Other related work that is based on this assumption was done by [13,14]. The approach proposed by [15] uses a parametric model, which allows us to find topics by linking them to timestamps. Here each topic is associated with a continuous distribution over timestamps, and for each generated document, the mixture distribution over topics is influenced by both word co-occurrences and the document's timestamp.

It was noted that there were few publications dedicated to dynamic topic models based on simpler methods such as LSI, PCA, ICA, NMF. The authors of [16] propose two-layer NMF methodology for identifying topics in large political speech corpora over time and apply it to a corpus of speeches of Members of the European Parliament. The obtained results proved to be semantically more coherent when compared with LDA. The approach proposed in this paper allows to track the evolution of topics over time in a sequentially organized set of documents. This approach was introduced in our work [17] but the results were not compared to appropriate baselines and such matrix decompositions as PCA and ICA were not considered as well.

## 2   Approach

### 2.1   Methods Based on Matrix Decompositions

In the paper we consider four methods LSI, PCA, ICA and NMF. All methods take as input a bag of words matrix (i.e. each document represented as row, with each column containing the word frequency in the collection). TF-IDF term weighting and document length normalization is applied to the bag of words matrix to filter frequent words that provide the most information about the document The mentioned decomposition methods are applied to document collections from non-overlapping time windows.

PCA is based on second-order statistics and ICA exploits inherently non-Gaussian features of the data and employs higher moments. PCA minimizes the covariance of the data, while ICA minimizes higher-order statistics such as fourth-order cummulant, thus minimizing the mutual information of the output. LSI is very similar to PCA, but differs in that it works on sample matrices directly instead of their covariance matrices. NMF is an alternative approach to decomposition that assumes that the data and the components are non-negative. Unlike PCA, the representation of a vector is obtained in an additive fashion, by superimposing the components, without subtracting.

### 2.2   Two-Pass Algorithm

First of all, for the purposes of the present paper the following definitions are used. The entire time interval is a sequence of disjoint time windows. Each window contains related documents. Each document may reflect one or more topics. Each topic is represented by its top-terms. Top-terms are terms that have the highest frequency (on average) in those documents that contain the topic. The number of top-terms for all topics, regardless of the time window, is the same and is assigned by the user (for example, 10, 20, 30, etc.). When applying matrix decompositions to each time window the user must specify the number of topics. One of the quality measures that allows us to choose the best number of topics is the so-called coherence measure.

The main hypothesis of the approach is that topics from different time windows, which share the same general topic, will have similar sets of top-terms describing them. So by reapplying matrix decompositions to an aggregated Topic-Term matrix from all time windows we obtain dynamic topics, which are related to a set of window topics.

The approach is represented by the following algorithm:

First pass. One of the indicated methods (LSI, PCA, ICA or NMF) is applied to each time window. As a result, for each window a set of $k$ topics is obtained, where $k$ is defined by the user. Topics are described by a user-specified number of top-terms $t$ and a set of all related documents.

Data transformation. Using the topic models obtained after the first pass we construct a new compressed representation, looking through the rows of each Topic-Term matrix of each window topic model. Each row contains weights of all the terms of a particular topic of the time window under consideration. We construct the new Topic-Term matrix with two subsequent procedures:

(1) In each topic from each window topic model, the top-t terms are taken from the appropriate topic-term matrix, all weights for the remaining terms are set to 0.
(2) The obtained vectors for all window topic models from all time windows are combined into one matrix.

Second pass. The considered topic modeling methods are re-applied to the transformed data, outputting a set of dynamic topics, each of which has a set of window topics associated with it. Applying matrix decompositions in this step, we identify $k'$ dynamic topics that potentially span several time windows. The number of dynamic topics $k'$ to be found in this step is specified by the user.

The matrix has the size $m \times n$, where $m$ is the total number of topics in all time windows, and $n$ is the subset of the terms remaining after the data transformation. By using only the top-t terms in each topic we include only the terms that were important in any time window and exclude the terms that never figured in any window topic. This reduces computational costs.

## 2.3   Quality of Modeling

Coherence measures evaluate the interpretability of the automatically generated topics and find the best number of topics. The higher the coherence score, the better the topic model. In the paper we have applied three most widely used coherence measures to determine the optimal number of topics in each time window and the optimal number of dynamic topics, such as $UCI$ [18], $NPMI$ [19], $C_v$ [20].

In [18] the authors propose the UCI coherence measure based on pointwise mutual information (PMI). It is based on the assumption that the co-occurrence of words within documents in the corpus can indicate semantic relatedness.

Th authors of [20] introduced topic coherence based on word co-occurrence counts determined using context windows that contain all words located 5 tokens around the ocurrences of a specific word. Additionally, [20] showed that the UCI coherence performs better if the PMI is replaced by the normalized PMI (NPMI) [19].

## 3   Data

The proposed algorithm was applied to the data collected from the Russian news resource RosBusinessConsulting from the "Political News" section [1]. The key statistics for this corpus are presented in Table 1. The data was divided into a set of consecutive disjoint sections or time windows - in particular, 12 monthly windows from January 2016 to December 2016. We chose 1 month as the length of the time window to ensure that there is enough data in each time window for topic modeling. Every article from the dataset went through the following preprocessing procedures:

- removal of stopwords
- removal of short words (less than 3 characters)
- lemmatization.

Also TF-IDF term weighting and document length normalization is applied to the Document-Term matrices for each time window.

**Table 1.** Key statistics of the RBC corpus

| Dataset size | |
|---|---|
| Num. of articles | 14725 |
| Average num. of articles per month | 1500 |
| Article size | |
| Average num. of words per article | 331 |

## 4   Experiments, the First Pass

In this section we consider the results of the first pass of the presented approach obtained for each time window. We compare the algorithms by varying the following settings:

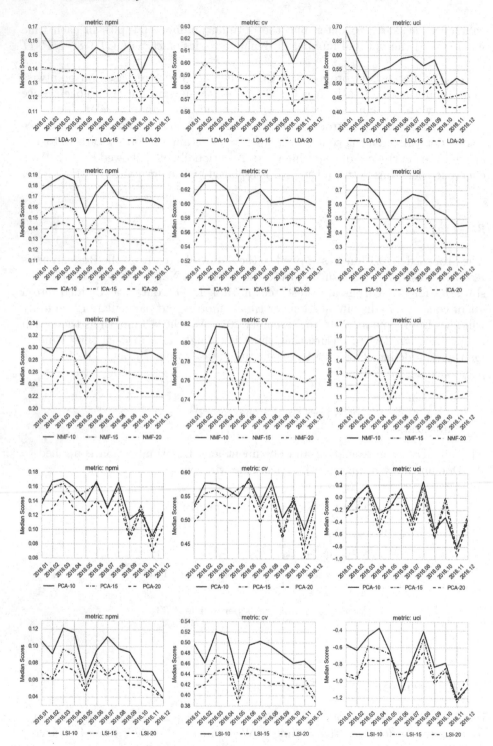

**Fig. 1.** Changes in the coherence scores depending on modeling method and number of top terms for different coherence measures

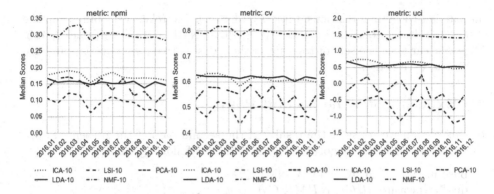

**Fig. 2.** Coherence scores of static topics

- base method (LSI, ICA, PCA, NMF)
- quality measure ($UCI$, $NPMI$, $C_v$)
  preprocessing (number of top-terms: 10, 15, 20)

### 4.1  Evaluation of Static Topic Coherence

Figure 1 shows the median coherence scores of topics for all 12 time windows for topic models created by LSI, ICA, PCA, NMF and LDA depending on the number of top terms. We compare median scores to provide a more robust evaluation. Regardless of the topic modeling method, the highest coherence score is achieved with the number of terms $t = 10$.

Figure 2 allows comparison of the mentioned topic models. The results show that the NMF achieves higher topic coherence scores in each of the time windows examined for any coherence measure. The results obtained by using ICA are comparable to those found by LDA in terms of coherence.

### 4.2  Evaluation of Static Topics Descriptors

The results of the first pass of topic modeling are shown in Tables 3, 4, 5, 6, 7 of Appendix A. All terms were translated to English and all topics were manually labeled by experts for better interpretation of results. In these tables, the month and topic number are indicated in the first column. The second column contains the topic label and the top-10 terms that represent the topic.

Tables 5 and 6 show the top-10 terms of topics from the month of January that were obtained with LSI and LDA, respectively. It can be observed, that LSI is less sensitive to more narrow topics and is able to distinguish only broader general topics. For example, it can be seen, that LSI distinguished the following topics: international politics, Iran-Saudi relations, rallies in Chechnya and Kadyrov, events in Syria, the Litvinenko case and nuclear tests in North Korea.

Comparing the mentioned topics with the results obtained by the LDA, it can be noted that the LDA has a wider range of topics, in particular, one should mention the diversity of topics on international politics, for example, topic 6 on Russian-Ukrainian relations, topic 7 on US-Russian relations. Comparing the topics and descriptors obtained with ICA, PCA, NMF and LDA (Tables 3, 4, 5, 7), it is clear that the sets of topics and their descriptive terms overlap and are similar to each other.

## 5    Experiments, the Second Pass

In this section we consider the results of the second pass of the presented approach. We compare the algorithms by varying the following settings:

- base method (LSI, ICA, PCA, NMF)
- quality measure ($UCI$, $NPMI$, $C_v$)
- preprocessing (number of top-terms: 10, 15, 20)

### 5.1    Evaluation of Dynamic Topic Coherence

Analyzing the influence of the number of top terms on the interpretability of dynamic topics (Fig. 3), it is noticeable that regardless of the model under consideration, the highest coherence score is achieved with the number of terms $t = 10$. In Fig. 4 it is shown that the two-pass NMF achieves higher topic coherence scores for any coherence measure. In Table 2 the optimal numbers of dynamic topics sorted by coherence scores are presented. It can be seen that PCA, ICA and NMF find more dynamic topics, this is because the methods are more sensitive to narrower topics.

**Table 2.** Number of Topics with highest coherence scores for top-10 terms

| Coherence measure | LSI | PCA | ICA | NMF | LDA |
|---|---|---|---|---|---|
| $UCI$ | 10, 11, 12 | 48, 47, 29 | 27, 12, 26 | 39, 38, 42 | 11, 13, 10 |
| $NPMI$ | 10, 12, 11 | 35, 30, 45 | 10, 31, 14 | 48, 49, 26 | 13, 15, 11 |
| $C_v$ | 10, 11, 12 | 33, 44, 22 | 10, 31, 42 | 27, 33, 29 | 14, 20, 18 |

### 5.2    Evaluation of Dynamic Topics Descriptors

Analyzing descriptor sets, you can track dynamic theme changes in time and get a brief overview of events. It should be noted that in one month, within a single dynamic topic, several topics can be found (in this case they are assigned sequential numbers). Examples of obtained dynamic topics are shown in Tables 8, 9, 10, 11 of Appendix B.

Tables 8, 9, 10 show examples of the evolution of the dynamic topic "War in Syria" obtained using the two-pass model based on NMF, ICA, PCA. All terms were translated to English. It can be seen that the NMF method within one general topic is able to identify narrower subtopics, for example, in Table 10 in February 2016, two topics related to Syria are found, one of which describes news articles related to the ceasefire, and the second - airstrikes on hospitals.

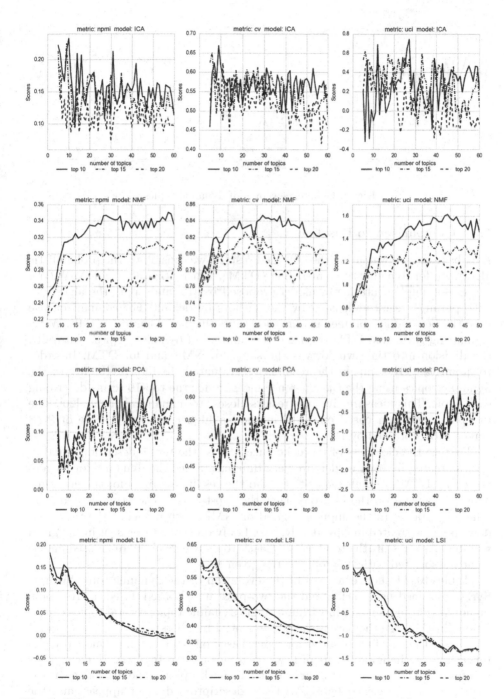

**Fig. 3.** Coherence scores depending on modeling method and number of top terms for different coherence measures

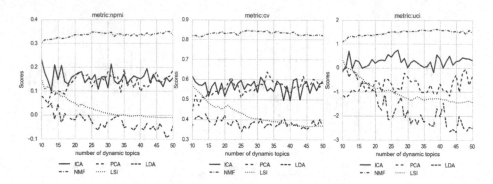

**Fig. 4.** Coherence scores of dynamic topics

## 5.3   Comparison to Baseline

As a baseline for evaluating the obtained results, we considered the probabilistic algorithm for dynamic topic modeling (DTM), which is based on LDA. We use the C ++ implementation of model proposed by [12] and apply the algorithm with parameters recommended by the authors by default. For comparison, we used the best model obtained in our study - it is the model based on NMF. When comparing NMF and DTM, we fixed the number of dynamic topics. Naturally, the division into time windows is the same for NMF and for DTM. In order to quantitatively compare the results, we evaluated the interpretability of the dynamic topics using the $C_v$ coherence measure for the top-10 terms describing each topic. This measure gives the results closest to human judgments [20]. The two-pass algorithm based on NMF method a higher coherence score of **0.78** versus **0.67** obtained by DTM.

Despite the closeness of the coherence scores, the terms describing window topics created by each model, are very different. Since the dynamic topics generated by DTM are built sequentially and the results obtained for the new time windows depend on the previous ones, the top-terms in each time window are relatively stable. In the approach based on NMF, each model of the time window theme is created independently, based only on the data present in the given window. As a result, the top terms for each topic are much more focused on the trends associated with this topic at the given time.

Tables 10, 11 show examples of the evolution of the dynamic topic "War in Syria" obtained using DTM and the two-pass model based on NMF. It should be noted that in one month, within a single dynamic topic, several topics can be found (in this case they are assigned sequential numbers).

We see that the first 10 terms for topics based on NMF are much more diverse, reflecting the changing nature of news on topics related to Syria. Namely, there is information about the ceasefire, airstrikes on hospitals, the armistice. In the dynamic topics received by DTM, these descriptors did not appear, and the lexical diversity, in general, is much lower.

# 6   Conclusions

In the paper we compare the performance of four methods of topic modeling (LSI, PCA, ICA and NMF) in the framework of the two-pass algorithm, which was recently developed for dynamic topic modeling. The comparison has been made using different coherence measures and different numbers of topic descriptors. The results showed that the proposed method based on NMF obtains topics with higher cohesion scores and the median scores for topics with the number of descriptors $t = 10$ is higher regardless of the method.

Comparing the proposed method to DTM, the two-pass algorithm based on NMF outperforms DTM. Although the considered dynamic topic models are relatively similar in terms of their cohesion scores, the two-pass approach based on NMF provides a greater lexical variety/diversity than DTM. Obviously, this improves the interpretability of topics and thereby enhances the quality of the analysis of the evolution of topics in time.

# APPENDIX

# A   Static Topics with Top-10 Descriptors

Table 3. Window topics found in January 2016 using NMF

| Time window | Descriptors |
| --- | --- |
| 2016.1-01: | *Government of Russia*: putin, president, year, russia, party, head, vladimir, choice, government, country |
| 2016.1-02: | *Iran-Saudi relations*: arabia, saudi, nimir, iran, saudian, al, penalty, embassy, shiite, tehran |
| 2016.1-03: | *Chechnya*: kadyrov, chechnya, opposition, people, enemy, ramsan, rally, statement, head, senchenko |
| 2016.1-04: | *Terrorist act in Istanbul*: explosion, terrorist attack, istanbul, happen, terrorist, victim, suicide bomber, perish, terrorist, police |
| 2016.1-05: | *Nemtsov murder case*: court, case, year, ruble, criminal, attorney, investigation, million, bulk, nemtsov |
| 2016.1-06: | *Nuclear weapon in North Korea*: test, dprk, korea, nuclear, bomb, hydrogen, pyongyang, northern, northern, rocket |
| 2016.1-07: | *Litvinenko murder case*: litvinenko, meadow, koktun, judge, fsb, owen, murder, london, case, report |
| 2016.1-08: | *Russian-Ukrainian relations*: ukraine, crimea, ukrainian, kiev, poroshenko, gryzlov, donbass, minsk, russia, negotiations |
| 2016.1-09: | *War in Syria*: syria, negotiations, extremist, military, syrian, us, russia, islamic, operation, isis |
| 2016.1-10: | *Nuclear program of Iran*: iran, usa, sanction, iranian, tehran, american, nuclear, sailor, magate, program |
| 2016.1-11: | *Downed aircraft in Turkey*: turkey, turkish, sukhoi, air, space, airplane, ankara, russia, border, russia |

**Table 4.** Window topics found in January 2016 using PCA

| Time window | Descriptors |
|---|---|
| 2016.1-01: | *Nemtsov murder case*: nemtsov, murder, dadaev, gubashev, ruslan, boris, goremeis, anzor, business, bastrykin |
| 2016.1-02: | *Chechnya*: kadyrov, chechnya, opposition, people, enemy, ramzan, statement, meeting, extra-systemic, senchenko |
| 2016.1-03: | *Litvinenko murder case*: litvinenko, meadow, kovtun, kadyrov, judge, fsb, owen, murder, london, case |
| 2016.1-04: | *Iran-Saudi relations*: arabia, saudi, iran, nimir, saudian, penalty, al, shiite, kadyrov, tehran |
| 2016.1-05: | *Nuclear weapon in North Korea*: test, dprk, korea, bomb, nuclear, hydrogen, pyongyang, northern, northern, rocket |
| 2016.1-06: | *Nuclear weapon in North Korea*: commodity, test, dprk, import, korea, embargo, product, ukraine, nuclear, bomb |
| 2016.1-07: | *Russia, corruption*: putin, million, shubin, president, ministry of finance, film, usa, wealth, corruption, thousand |
| 2016.1-08: | *War in Syria*: bbc, action, syria, turkey, shubin, united states, explosion, statement, military, syrian |
| 2016.1-09: | *Russian-Ukrainian relations*: negotiations, syria, ukraine, united states, russia, minsk, sanction, marmots, gryzlov, meeting |
| 2016.1-10: | *War in Syria*: syria, state, strike, islamic, country, turkey, bill, sirian, isis, party |
| 2016.1-11: | *Problems of migrants in Germany*: cologne, police, woman, germany, assault, migrant, harassment, refugee, merkel, sexual |
| 2016.1-12: | *Turkey, downed aircraft*:iran, turkey, turkish, space, sukhoi, air, airplane, sailor, anchor, sanction |

**Table 5.** Window topics found in January 2016 using LDA

| Time window | Descriptors |
|---|---|
| 2016.1-01: | *Iran-Saudi relations*: iran, arabia, saudi, nimir, saudian, tehran, al, penalty, embassy, iranian |
| 2016.1-02: | *Elections in Russia*: party, choice, deputy, parliament, rbk, state duma, talk, candidate, elections, question |
| 2016.1-03: | *Russian-Ukrainian relations*: ukraine, ukrainian, russia, year, crimea, kiev, january, poroshenko, donbass, president |
| 2016.1-04: | *Chechnya*: kadyrov, russia, litvinenko, chechnya, name, head, statement, word, opposition, call |
| 2016.1-05: | *Government of the Russian Federation*: putin, president, vladimir, russia, declare, sand, head, press, call, kremlin |

*(continued)*

**Table 5.** (*continued*)

| Time window | Descriptors |
|---|---|
| 2016.1-06: | *Russian-Turkish relations*: russia, country, united states, year, declare, president, turkey, own, sanction, russian |
| 2016.1-07: | *War in Syria*: military, russia, russian, airplane, syria, ministry of defense, strike, sukhoi, air, force |
| 2016.1-08: | *Corruption in Russia*: year, million, ruble, russia, thousand, court, head, law, decision, billion |
| 2016.1-09: | *Problems of migrants in Germany*: germany, refugee, migrant, eu, cologne, woman, country, merkel, border, attack |
| 2016.1-10: | *Terrorist acts in the world*: police, january, action, detain, report, action, report, employee, terrorist act, information |
| 2016.1-11: | *Terrorist act in Istanbul*: explosion, terrorist attack, victim, perish, happen, russian, among, istanbul, reuters, embassy |
| 2016.1-12: | *War in Syria*: syria, negotiations, test, islamic, dprk, military, united states, un, iraq, january |
| 2016.1-13: | *Nemtsov murder case*: case, court, criminal, investigation, lawyer, murder, crime, nemtsov, investigation, year |
| 2016.1-14: | *USA, elections*: president, usa, trump, post, state, candidate, party, donald, billionaire, presidential |

**Table 6.** Window topics found in January 2016 using LSI

| Time window | Descriptors |
|---|---|
| 2016.1-01: | *International relations*: russia, year, president, united states, ukraine, country, putin, state, iran, syria |
| 2016.1-02: | *Iran-Saudi relations*: iran, arabia, saudi, nimir, saudian, al, tehran, execution, embassy, shiite |
| 2016.1-03: | *Chechnya, Islamic world*: kadyrov, chechnya, iran, opposition, people, enemy, arabia, ramzan, rally, saudi |
| 2016.1-04: | *Chechnya, war in Syria*: kadyrov, syria, turkey, terrorist, explosion, islamic, terrorist attack, chechnya, isis, military |
| 2016.1-05: | *Litvinenko murder case*: litvinenko, case, court, murder, meadow, fsb, judge, koltun, investigation, criminal |
| 2016.1-06: | *Nuclear weapon in North Korea, Litvinenko murder case*: test, dprk, korea, nuclear, bomb, litvinenko, hydrogen, missile, pyongyang, united states |

**Table 7.** Window topics found in January 2016 using ICA

| Time window | Descriptors |
|---|---|
| 2016.1-01: | *War in Syria*: nimir, al, arabia, saudi, penalty, crime, party, putin, shiite, protest |
| 2016.1-02: | *War in Syria*: negotiations, syria, geneva, en, delegation, rebel, opposition, syrian, carrie, meeting |
| 2016.1-03: | *Nuclear weapon test in North Korea*: test, dprk, korea, nuclear, bomb, hydrogen, pyongyang, northern, northern, rocket |
| 2016.1-04: | *Litvinenko murder case*: litvinenko, meadow, koltun, judge, killing, fsb, owen, london, case, putin |
| 2016.1-05: | *Undefined*:terrorist, town, bbc, al, assault, united states, dagestan, police, hostage, woman |
| 2016.1-06: | *Undefined*: putin, year, ruble, syria, court, russia, president, business, million, russian |
| 2016.1-07: | *Russian-Ukrainian relations*: ukraine, crimea, ukrainian, poroshenko, kiev, gryzlov, donbas, goods, minsk, contact |
| 2016.1-08: | *War in Syria*: syria, action, military, isis, islamic, operation, al, strike, iraq, zorah |
| 2016.1-09: | *Iran-Saudi relations*: arabia, saudi, nimir, saudian, iran, al, penalty, shiite, embassy, raqqa |
| 2016.1-10: | *Nemtsov murder case*: court, case, nemtsov, criminal, attorney, investigation, bulk, murder, crime, detain |
| 2016.1-11: | *Undefined*: year, ruble, government, refugee, minister, prime minister, billion, choice, candidate, court |

# B    Dynamic Topics with Top-10 Descriptors

**Table 8.** "War in Syria" Topic Evolution - ICA

| | Feb 2016 | May 2016 | Jun 2016 | Aug 2016 |
|---|---|---|---|---|
| 1 | Aleppo | Syria | Syria | Syria |
| 2 | Army | Aleppo | Aleppo | Operation |
| 3 | Town | Mode | Terrorist | Aleppo |
| 4 | Offensive | Ceasefire | Strike | Turkey |
| 5 | Strike | Fire | An | Turkish |
| 6 | Asad | Nusra | Nusra | Syrian |

(*continued*)

**Table 8.** (*continued*)

|    | Feb 2016 | May 2016 | Jun 2016 | Aug 2016 |
|----|----------|----------|----------|----------|
| 7  | Hospital | An | Syrian | Town |
| 8  | Syria | Silence | Ministry of defense | Strike |
| 9  | Aviation | Province | Gunning | Jarabulus |
| 10 | Province | Organization | Fire | Kurdish |

**Table 9.** "War in Syria" Topic Evolution - PCA

|    | Jan 2016 | Feb 2016 | Mar 2016 | Apr 2016 |
|----|----------|----------|----------|----------|
| 1  | Syria | Admiral | Aleppo | Aleppo |
| 2  | Aleppo | Strike | Terrorist | Syria |
| 3  | Mode | Kuznetsov | Syria | Terrorist |
| 4  | Fire | Aleppo | Town | Town |
| 5  | Ceasefire | Syria | Ministry of defense | Syrian |
| 6  | Military | Cruiser | Army | Strike |
| 7  | Province | Plane | Plane | Humanitarian |
| 8  | An | Ministry of defense | Eastern | Army |
| 9  | Terrorist | Military | Palmira | UN |
| 10 | Plane | Ukraine | Military | Military |

**Table 10.** "War in Syria" Topic Evolution - NMF

|    | Jan 2016 | Feb(1) 2016 | Feb(2) 2016 | Mar 2016 |
|----|----------|-------------|-------------|----------|
| 1  | Syria | Syria | Aleppo | Syria |
| 2  | Aleppo | Ceasefire | Syria | Palmira |
| 3  | Military | Armistice | Army | Russia |
| 4  | Isis | Fire | Town | Military |
| 5  | Islamic | USA | Strike | Russian |
| 6  | Iraq | Russia | Offensive | Military |
| 7  | Operation | UN | Assad | Aircraft |
| 8  | Town | Agreement | Hospital | Syrian |
| 9  | State | Mode | Aviation | Assad |
| 10 | Beat | Assad | Russia | Operation |

**Table 11.** "War in Syria" Topic Evolution - DTM

|    | Jan 2016  | Feb 2016  | Mar 2016  | Apr 2016  |
|----|-----------|-----------|-----------|-----------|
| 1  | Operation | Operation | Town      | Town      |
| 2  | Town      | Town      | Operation | Terrorist |
| 3  | Mosul     | Mosul     | Terrorist | Operation |
| 4  | Iraq      | Extremist | Isis      | Syria     |
| 5  | Isis      | Isis      | Syria     | Army      |
| 6  | Iraq      | Iraq      | Islamic   | Isis      |
| 7  | Islamic   | Islamic   | Mosul     | Islamic   |
| 8  | State     | Syria     | Army      | State     |
| 9  | Syria     | State     | State     | Palmira   |
| 10 | Army      | Army      | Iraq      | Iraq      |

# References

1. RosBusinessConsulting. (http://www.rbc.ru/). Accessed 01 May 2017
2. Deerwester, S., Dumais, S., Furnas, G., Landauer, T., Harshman, R.: Indexing by latent semantic analysis. J. Am. Soc. Inform. Sci. Technol. **41**, 391–407 (1990)
3. Steyvers, M., Griffiths, T.L.: Probabilistic topic models. In: Tang, Z., MacLennan, (eds.) Latent Semantic Analysis: A Road to Meaning, pp. 1–6. Laurence Erlbaum, Mahwah, NJ (2006)
4. Blei, D.M., Edu, B.B., Ng, A.Y., Edu, A.S., Jordan, M.I., Edu, J.B.: Latent Dirichlet allocation. J. Mach. Learn. Res. **3**, 993–1022 (2003)
5. Wei, X., Croft, W.B.: Modeling term associations for ad-hoc retrieval performance within language modeling framework. In: Amati, G., Carpineto, C., Romano, G. (eds.) ECIR 2007. LNCS, vol. 4425, pp. 52–63. Springer, Heidelberg (2007). https://doi.org/10.1007/978-3-540-71496-5_8
6. Blei, D.M., Lafferty, J.D.: Correlated topic models. Adv. Neural Inf. Process. Syst. **18**, 147–154 (2006)
7. Daud, A., Li, J., Zhou, L., Muhammad, F.: Knowledge discovery through directed probabilistic topic models: a survey (2010)
8. Vorontsov, K., Potapenko, A.: Tutorial on probabilistic topic modeling: additive regularization for stochastic matrix factorization. Commun. Comput. Inf. Sci. **436**, 29–46 (2014)
9. Vorontsov, K., Potapenko, A.: Additive regularization of topic models. Mach. Learn. **101**, 303–323 (2014)
10. Wang, Q., Cao, Z., Xu, J., Li, H.: Group matrix factorization for scalable topic modeling. In: Proceedings of 35th SIGIR Conference on Research and Development in Information Retrieval, pp. 375–384 (2012)
11. Grant, S., Skillicorn, D., Cordy, J.R.: Topic detection using independent component analysis. In: Proceedings of the Workshop on Link Analysis, Counterterrorism and Security (LACTS 2008), pp. 23–28 (2008)
12. Blei, D.M., Lafferty, J.D.: Dynamic topic models. In: Proceedings of the 23rd International Conference on Machine Learning - ICML 2006, pp. 113–120 (2006)

13. Caron, F., Davy, M., Doucet, A.: Generalized Polya Urn for time-varying Dirichlet process mixtures. In: 23rd Conference on Uncertainty in Artificial Intelligence UAI'2007 Vancouver Canada, pp. 33–40 (2007)
14. Wang, C., Blei, D., Heckerman, D.: Continuous time dynamic topic models. In: Proceedings of the Twenty-Fourth Conference Annual Conference on Uncertainty in Artificial Intelligence (UAI-08), pp. 579–586 (2008)
15. Wang, X., McCallum, A.: Topics over time: a non-markov continuous-time model of topical trends. In: Proceedings of the 12th ACM SIGKDD International Conference on Knowledge Discovery and Data Mining, pp. 424–433 (2006)
16. Greene, D., Cross, J.P.: Exploring the political agenda of the europeanparliament using a dynamic topic modeling approach. Polit. Anal. **25**, 77–94 (2017)
17. Skitalinskaya, G.: Analysis of news dynamics using two-pass algorithms of dynamic topic modeling. Math. Methods Inf. Soc. Process., Publ. House KIAM-RAS **19**, 13 (2017)
18. Newman, D., Lau, J., Grieser, K., Baldwin, T.: Automatic evaluation of topic coherence. In: Human Language Technologies: The 2010 Annual Conference of the North American Chapter of the Association for Computational Linguistics, pp. 100–108 (2010)
19. Bouma, G.: Normalized (pointwise) mutual information in collocation extraction. In: Proceedings of German Society for Computational Linguistics (GSCL 2009), pp. 31–40 (2009)
20. Aletras, N., Stevenson, M.: Evaluating topic coherence using distributional semantics. In: Proceedings of the 10th International Conference on Computational Semantics (IWCS 2013)-Long Papers, pp. 13–22 (2013)

# Hermitian Laplacian Operator for Vector Representation of Directed Graphs: An Application to Word Association Norms

Víctor Mijangos$^{(\boxtimes)}$, Gemma Bel-Enguix, Natalia Arias-Trejo, and Julia B. Barrón-Martínez

Universidad Nacional Autónoma de México, Mexico City, Mexico
vmijangosc@ciencias.unam.mx, gbele@iingen.unam.unam.mx,
natalia.arias-trejo@sthughs-oxford.com, juliabbm@comunidad.unam.mx

**Abstract.** In this paper, we propose a spectral method for the analysis of directed graphs. For this purpose, a Hermitian Laplacian operator is proposed, that defines interesting properties for the embedding of a graph into a vector space. We use the notions of the Hermitian Laplacian operator to embed a directed graph structure, build over corpura of Word Association Norms, into a vector space. We show that the Hermitian Laplacian operator has advantages over a traditional Laplacian operator when the original structure of the graph is directed. Moreover, we compare the lexical relations obtained by a WAN graph with the connections the Hermitian Laplacian operator establishes between the words of the corpora.

## 1 Introduction

During the last decades natural language has been studied and represented by means of network structures [1–4] and statistical methods. The simplest way to build word networks is based on co-occurrences, linking every pair of words that appear together. There are two main types of co-occurrence networks: directed and undirected. Directed graphs are a good tool to study syntactic relations [5], collocations and lexicalizations [6]. Undirected graphs are useful for revealing some general properties of the vocabulary [4], like hubs, or indicate which words are more connected and under which conditions. Some authors have built co-occurrence networks for words sense discovery [7,8]. Moreover, semantic networks [9], which are graphs relating words [10], are being used not only to study the organization of the vocabulary, but also to approach the structure of knowledge.

Psycholinguistics has also approached the issue of the organization of lexicon from network theory. Ferret [11,12] and Zock et al. [13] suggested a matrix-based model to deal with topical detection and collocation links; i.e., syntactic and semantic contexts in which a single word appeared. Another classical approach

© Springer Nature Switzerland AG 2018
F. Castro et al. (Eds.): MICAI 2017, LNAI 10633, pp. 44–56, 2018.
https://doi.org/10.1007/978-3-030-02840-4_4

to deal with the mental organization of the lexicon is the building of Word Associations, that have been used by psychologists of various schools to understand the human mind. Corpora of Word Association Norms (WAN) are obtained by a stimulus-response procedure [14,15]: i.e., a word is given to a subject who responds the first word that comes to his/her mind. In free word associations, a person typically hears or reads a word, and then is asked to produce the first other word coming to mind. Up to now, the only way to achieve a repertory of these is experimentally. One of the first examples is provided by [16], who used this method for comparisons of words, introducing 100 emotionally neutral test words. They conducted the first large scale study with 1,000 test persons, and concluded that there was uniformity in the organization of associations and people shared stable networks of connections among words. In recent years, the web has become the natural way to get data to build such resources. Jeux de Mots provides an example in French[1] [17], whereas small world of words deals with nine different languages[2].

Graphs have been used to study the properties of lexical relations obtained from a WAN [18]. In Natural Language Processing, the Distributional Space Model (DSM) proposes a method that is different in conformation, but similar in essence [19]. The DSM proposes to generate a matrix of co-occurrences of words that are weighted in many different ways [20]. This matrix is equivalent to an adjacency operator of a graph; in other words, the DSM method generates a weighted graph [21].

The main difference between DSM and graph-based procedures is that the first gives an undirected graph, while the latter retrieves a non necessarily undirected one (it can be directed or mixed[3]). This difference is crucial; it manifests different data structures that are not necessarily comparable.

In linguistics terms, a directed graph represents better the relations between words; for example, in a taxonomy or a syntactic tree. Nevertheless, a method for spectral analysis of directed graphs has not been clearly developed. Algorithms of Spectral Clustering focus on undirected graphs [22–24]. These algorithms are not easy to adapt into directed structures: it becomes necessary to turn the directed graph into an undirected one; or it can be computed an adjacency operator into the directed structure, but without guarantee of full functionality.

In this paper we propose a method for analysis of directed (or mixed) graphs, using techniques for spectral analysis through the introduction of Hermitian operators [25]. Then, we apply Laplacian and Hermitian Laplacian operators to two WAN graphs for Spanish in order to compare the word vector representations retrieved by both methods with the ones offered by the WAN corpora. We have as an objective to study the lexical relations, that are highlighted by each one of

---

[1] http://www.jeuxdemots.org/.

[2] http://www.smallworldofwords.com.

[3] In this paper, we focused in directed graphs; nevertheless, a directed graph is just a special case of a mixed graph. Therefore, when we refer to mixed graphs, it necessarily implies directed graphs.

the procedures, and the meaning they can have to explain the structure of the Lexicon.

In Sect. 2 we present the necessary theory to understand the proposal; Sect. 3 shows the experiment over Words Association Norms corpora [14,15]; Sect. 4 shows the results and finally Sect. 5 presents the conclusions and future work.

## 2   Prerequisites

In this section we present the basic theory to understand the experiments described here. This theory is about the Hermitian adjacency and Hermitian Laplacian operators of a not necessarily undirected graph. It is pointed that when the graph is undirected this operators are the traditional Adjacency and Laplacian operators [22–24].

### 2.1   Hermitian Operator of Directed Graphs

Being $G = (V, E, \phi)$ a weighted graph; in the general case, there are edges in $E$ such that they are directed and undirected. We represent an undirected relation as $v_j \leftrightarrow v_k$ with $v_j, v_k \in V$; a directed relation can be represented as $v_j \to v_k$ or $v_j \leftarrow v_k$, depending if the direction of the connection is from $v_j$ to $v_k$ or from $v_k$ to $v_j$, respectively. An example of a directed graph in the Natural Language Processing area is a taxonomy: the relationships in this kind of structures is always from the higher hierarchical elements to the lower ones. In this case, if $v_j > v_k$ in the hierarchy, the edges are represented as $v_j \to v_k$.

Frequently a graph $G$ is represented with an adjacency operator $A(G) = (a_{jk}) = \phi(v_j, v_k)$, that codifies the connections between the nodes in the graph. When the graph is undirected, it happens that $\phi(v_j, v_k) = \phi(v_k, v_j)$. This means that the operator is symmetric and therefore the existence of a spectral basis is guaranteed [26,27]. However, if the graph is directed $A(G)$, it is not symmetric and the existence of a spectral basis is not clear by failing in the spectral theorem hypothesis. Liu and Li [25] propose a Hermitian Adjacency matrix for mixed graphs which we adapt to represent weighted directed (and mixed) graphs:

**Definition 1.** *Let $G$ be a mixed graph. The Hermitian Adjacency operator $H(G)$ is defined as follows*[4]:

$$H(G) = (h_{jk}) := \begin{cases} \phi(v_j, v_k) & \text{if } v_j \leftrightarrow v_k \\ i \cdot \phi(v_j, v_k) & \text{if } v_j \to v_k \\ -i \cdot \phi(v_j, v_k) & \text{if } v_j \leftarrow v_k \end{cases} \qquad (1)$$

This definition give us an adjacency operator for which $H(G) = H(G)^*$, where $H(G)^*$ is the conjugate transpose $\overline{H(G)^t}$ of the operator $H(G)$. In other words, $H(G)$ is a hermitian operator. Therefore, there exists a positive spectra

---

[4] It is pointed that when the graph is undirected this operators are the traditional Adjacency and Laplacian operators [22–24].

and its spectral basis [26, 28]. However, this Hermitian Adjacency operator is not positive semi-definite, all the entries in the diagonal are zeros. In the next section, we define a hermitian positive semi-definite operator: the Hermitian Laplacian operator associated with a directed graph.

It must be pointed out that the Hermitian Adjacency operator does not precisely codifies the weights in the graph. Therefore, the degree of a node $v \in V$ is not the sum of the entries related with $v$ in the hermitian adjacency matrix. For our purposes, the degree of $v$ is the sum of the original weights of the neighbors nodes in the graph. To clarify this fact, we give the next definition:

**Definition 2 (Degree operator).** *Let $G = (V, E, \phi)$ be a weighted directed graph. The degree operator associated with $G$ is defined as:*

$$D = (d_{ij}) := \begin{cases} \sum_k \phi(v_i, v_k) & \text{if } i = j \\ 0 & \text{if } i \neq j \end{cases} \tag{2}$$

As can be seen in the definition, the degree operator is a diagonal operator and it does not have any complex entry, as the weights in the graph are real.

## 2.2   Hermitian Laplacian Operator of Directed Graphs

The Laplacian operator of a undirected graph is defined as $L = D - A(G)$ where $A(G)$ is the symmetric adjacency operator and $D$ the degree operator of the graph. It is clear that $L$ is also symmetric and positive semi-definite. Thus, by the spectral theorem [26], there exists a positive spectra and a spectral basis of eigenvectors of $L$.

However, when we are working with directed graphs, $L$ is not symmetric and the existence of a spectral basis can not be guaranteed. To solve this problem, the use of a Hermitian Laplacian operator instead of a simple Laplacian operator is proposed. This Hermitian Laplacian operator is defined as follows:

**Definition 3.** *Let $G$ be a directed graph with associated degree operator $D$ and Hermitian Adjacency operator $H(G)$. The Hermitian Laplacian operator associated with $G$ is:*

$$LH = D - H(G) \tag{3}$$

In this definition, the symmetric adjacency matrix is replaced with the Hermitian adjacency matrix. The degree operator remains the same. Then, the Laplacian operator reflects the directionality of the graph. This means that the entries in the diagonal of $LH$ are real, while the other entries are complex, where if $v_j \rightarrow v_k$ then $LH_{jk} = i\phi(v_j, v_k)$ and $LH_{kj} = -i\phi(v_j, v_k) = \overline{i\phi(v_j, v_k)}$. This means that in general $LH = LH^*$. This properties tell us that $LH$ is a hermitian positive semi-definite operator. It is clear, however, that $LH$ and $L$ are different operators [29]. $LH$ have complex entries while in $L$ all the entries are real.

Being $LH$ a hermitian positive semi-definite operator we can guarantee the existence of a real spectra and its associated spectral basis. So, let's denote the spectrum of $LH$ as $\sigma(LH) = \{\lambda \in \mathbb{R} : LH - \lambda I \notin GL_n(\mathbb{C})\}^5$. Also, we can denote the eigenvectors of $LH$ as $\beta_\sigma = \{x_{\lambda_i} \in \mathbb{C}^n : LHx_{\lambda_i} = \lambda_i x_{\lambda_i}, \lambda_i \in \sigma(LH)\}$. $\beta_\sigma$ conforms a orthogonal basis; an orthonormal basis can be easily obtained with a Gram-Schmidt procedure [30].

Even if the theory of Hermitian Laplacian operators has not been fully developed, we can state some helping properties for the description of graphs [31] that we present in the next Proposition:

**Proposition 1.** *Let $G$ be a directed graph and $LH$ the associated Hermitian Laplacian operator, then $LH$ satisfies:*

1. *If $G_1$ and $G_2$ are two directed graphs with Hermitian adjacency matrix $H_1$ and $H_2$, respectively, and such that $G_1 \equiv G_2$, then $\sigma(H_1) = \sigma(H_2)$.*
2. *$\lambda_1 \le 2 \cdot \max_k deg(v_k)$ with $\lambda_1 \in \sigma(H)$ and $v_k \in V, k = 1, ..., n$.*

The first property explains that if two graphs are related such that $H_1 = U^{-1} \cdot H_2 \cdot U$, $U \in GL_n(\mathbb{C})$ then its respective spectra are equal. This looks obvious in a first sight even for simple Laplacian operators. However, we must to take into consideration that when the graphs are not symmetric or hermitian, we can say nothing about its spectra. The Laplacian Hermitian operator allows us to compare graph structures that are not necessary undirected. The second property shows that the smallest eigenvalue is related with twice the maximum degree of the graph. As we will explain later, in the experiments, the eigenvector associated with this eigenvalue resulted real. Then, we can take advantage of this property to represent the data in a vector space.

## 3    Experiment

### 3.1    Corpora

For the experiments, two Spanish corpora were used two corpora: The Corpus of Word Association Norms for Mexican Spanish (WAN) [15]. It was elaborated with a sample of 578 young adults, males (239) and females (339), with ages between 18 and 28 years, and at least 11 years of education. All of them were monolingual with Mexican variant of Spanish as a mother tongue. In order to avoid bias in the type of response given by the participants, students from different areas were considered. They came from different universities of Mexico. For the task, 234 stimuli words were used taken from Jackson-Maldonado et al. [32]. The selection was made according to two criteria: (a) all of them should be concrete nouns; (b) they should be able to be visually represented; and (c) familiar to children.

The other corpus was the Corpus of Word Association Norms from children population [14]. It is a corpus composed by 60 stimulus words; 54 of these words

---

[5] Two things need to be noted: (1) As $LH$ is hermitian all the eigenvalues in the spectrum are real; (2) $GL_n(\mathbb{C})$ is the General Linear Group of matrices of $n \times n$ in $\mathbb{C}$, this is, not invertible matrices.

are a subset of the words in the WAN corpus. They were obtained from Jackson-Maldonado et al. [32]. The corpus was elaborated with a sample of 464 children from public and private primary school between 6 and 12 years.

For the corpora, the words connected with weight 1 were removed in order to avoid *hapax legumena* that could affect the computation of the data. Further, these words had little appearance and did not affect the final results. As the corpora was established in terms of stimulus-response, we created the graphs with the data of the relations. Both graphs are not easily comparable because of its difference in size. However, the graphs have properties in common that can be exploited for their analysis.

The statistics of both graphs are presented in Table 1. The diameter of both graphs is 6, so that the networks are small worlds [33]. The entropy[6] is almost the same, which tell us that the transition between nodes is almost equally predictable in both graphs.

**Table 1.** Comparison between the statistical information of the analyzed graphs.

|  | Adults | Children |
|---|---|---|
| Activation words | 234 | 54 |
| # Nodes | 2288 | 783 |
| Diameter | 6 | 6 |
| Entropy | 3.51 | 3.99 |
| Hermitian energy | 35434.3 | 5482.5 |

The Hermitian Energy was computed with the Eq. [36,37]:

$$\mathcal{E}_H(G) = \sum_{j=1}^{n} |\lambda_j| \tag{4}$$

Here $\lambda_j \in \sigma(H)$. This formula can be regarded as a variant similar to graph energy [38,39]. In this case, the adults graph reports higher graph energy. This can be interpreted as higher weight connections in the graph; this is because the adults graph is larger than the children graph. Unlike the other statistics, the Hermitian Energy is obtained from the Hermiatian Laplacian operator.

## 3.2 Description of the Experiment

With the graphs described above, we look for representing the 54 coincident stimulus-words into a vector space. By taking a sub-sample of the WAN graph, the comparison becomes more feasible. The difference in size, however, prevails. We compared the results obtained with the simple Laplacian operator and the

---

[6] The entropy was determined through a random walk in the graph [34,35].

results obtained with the Hermitian Laplacian operator, which we claimed is better for representing directed relations in a semantic network.

The algorithm of Laplacian Eigenmaps also can be found in [40,41] and it is used for Spectral Clustering in [42,43]. Nevertheless, we claim that this algorithm can be overpassed with taking the Hermitian Laplacian operator when the graph is directed. Given that the construction of the corpora was by the method of stimulus-response, the graphs obtained are originally directed. Taking into account this structure, the results must be improved. The methodology used is as follows [31,44]:

1. The Hermitian Laplacian operator $LH$ of $G$ is computed. Then, the spectra, $\sigma(LH)$, and spectral orthonormal base of $LH$ were obtained.
2. We choose the $k$ eigenvectors associated with the $k$ smallest eigenvalues (all eigenvalues were real, but some of them were negative). By property 2 of Proposition 1 the eigenvector associated with the smallest eigenvalue codifies information about the graph. We constructed the basis matrix $W \in \mathbb{C}^{n \times k}$ with this $k$ eigenvectors.
3. We described the column vectors of $H(G)$ represented the words into the spectral basis of $k$ eigenvectors by taking the projection of $v \in H(G)$ into $w_k \in W$. The $k$th component of the new low-dimension vector $\hat{v}$ is defined as $\hat{v}^k = \langle w_k, v \rangle$.

It is clear that this algorithm is very similar to the Laplacian Eigenmaps one [40,41]. Nevertheless, in the Hermitian Laplacian algorithm there is no need of turning the graph into undirected, conserving the original properties untouched. Similarly, when selecting the Hermitian Laplacian operator, most of the eigenvectors are complex. This does not happen with the simple Laplacian operator. In this cases, a complex vector can be represented as two real vectors, given the isomorphism $\mathbb{C} \equiv \mathbb{R}^2$.

We obtained different vector representations for these words by varying the $k$ eigenvectors of the spectral basis in both the Laplacian and Hermitian Laplacian procedures. The number $k$ represents the dimensions of the obtained vector space.

## 4    Results and Evaluation

Two vector spaces $V_1 \cong G_1$ and $V_2 \cong G_2$, representing each graph, were obtained with the Hermitian Laplacian and Laplacian procedure. The evaluation consist in determine how well the words are represented in the vector space obtained by the proposed method. To evaluate the methods, we took 54 control words in the corpora. We took the closest vector point to each of these 54 words. If this word vector is a node directly connected to the control word in the graph (in other words, if the word vector is a response to the stimulus word in the experiment), then we take it as a correct prediction. This procedure defines the so called

Precision at $1^7$. Table 2 shows the Precision at 1 obtained by this strategy. We evaluate over the children graph, taking two dimensions.

**Table 2.** Precision at 1 for the Laplacian and Hermitian Laplacian methods.

| Method | P@1 |
|---|---|
| Laplacian | 0.059 |
| Hermitian Laplacian | **0.208** |

Table 3 shows some of the closest vector points to stimulus words for both methods. It can be seen that most of the closest neighbors are semantically related when using Hermitian Laplacian procedure, while semantic relations are not clear when the simple Laplacian procedure is used. In general, the method proposed here represents the data in low dimensions conserving the directed structure of the original data. Therefore, from the semantic point of view, we consider that the Hermitian Laplacian procedure performs better.

**Table 3.** Closest neighbor for some example words obtained with the Hermitian Laplacian (HL) and Laplacian (L) procedures in the children graph.

| Stimulus | HL | L |
|---|---|---|
| globo (ballon) | niño (kid) | araña (spider) |
| zapato (shoe) | calcetín (sock) | chocolate (chocolate) |
| refresco (soda) | vaso (glass) | libro (book) |
| carro (car) | muñeca (doll) | manzana (apple) |
| jabón (soap) | mano (hand) | luna (moon) |
| oreja (ear) | gato (cat) | tv |
| pato (duck) | pollito (chiken) | bebé (baby) |
| tortilla | plato (dish) | cepillo (brush) |

Next step is analyzing the relationship between the results obtained by the HL graph and the ones retrieved by the WAN corpus. Table 4 shows the place in the original graph of the predicted closest neighbors in the vector space (third column). The value represents the range of the word in the relationship with the stimulus. The higher the range the more related in the stimulus-response experiment. This shows that even if a word is directly connected with the stimulus, the semantic relationship is not necessarily strong.

---

[7] Precision at $k, k = 1, 2, \ldots$ is a common method in machine translation literature; for example, [45]. In here, we adapt it to evaluate the semantic quality of the embedding word vectors.

**Table 4.** Closest neighbor to the children HL graph and its place in the original graph structure (NC is for not direct connection).

| Stimulus | Children | Place in graph |
|---|---|---|
| globo (ballon) | niño (kid) | 85 |
| zapato (shoe) | calcetín (sock) | 5 |
| refresco (soda) | vaso (glass) | 11 |
| carro (car) | muñeca (doll) | NC |
| jabón (soap) | mano (hand) | 2 |
| oreja (ear) | gato (cat) | NC |
| pato (duck) | pollito (chiken) | 8 |
| tortilla | plato (dish) | 26 |

When comparing the PR of every stimulus in WAN with the outcome of the HL operation, the results are the ones shown in Table 5. First, it can be seen that, while in WAN corpus there are some responses that do not have the same grammatical category than the stimulus (globo-volar, jabón-lavar, oreja-oir), this never happens in the HL representation. This can be either the cause or the effect of the fact that the relation of functionality is not represented in the words suggested by Hermitian Laplation procedure. It is also clear that the HL retrieves words that are almost only related by metonymy or cohyponymy.

**Table 5.** Closest neighbor for some example words obtained with the Hermitian Laplacian (HL) and Laplacian (L) procedures in the children graph.

| Stimulus | WAN | Lex. Rel. | HL | Lex. Rel. |
|---|---|---|---|---|
| globo (ballon) | volar (to fly) | functionality | niño (kid) | metonymy |
| zapato (shoe) | pie (foot) | metonymy | calcetín (sock) | metonymy |
| refresco (soda) | agua (water) | hypernymy | vaso (glass) | metonymy |
| carro (car) | moto (motorcycle) | cohyponymy | muñeca (doll) | cohyponymy |
| jabón (soap) | lavar (to wash) | functionality | mano (hand) | metonymy |
| oreja (ear) | oir (to hear) | functionality | gato (cat) | holonomy |
| pato (duck) | ganso (goose) | cohyponymy | pollito (chiken) | cohyponymy |
| tortilla | maiz (maize) | made of | plato (dish) | meronymy |

All these results should be confronted with psychological theories about the structure of the lexicon in the mind. According to [46] the ranking of the most frequent lexical relations in an adult WAN corpus are metonymy (12.29%), meronymy (10.19%), funcionality (7.88%), cohyponymy (4.24%), qualification (2.0%), made of (0.55%) and synonymy (0.37%). What has been obtained here corresponds to the children WAN corpus, so that the numbers are indicative.

Finally, to compare the different behaviour of HL when applied to each one of the graphs, Fig. 1 shows the spectra $\sigma(HL)$ of the children and adults graphs. As can be seen, all the spectra is real, but, unlike the spectra of the Laplacian operator, not all eigenvalues are positive. Likewise, the spectra for both graphs have a similar behaviour. The most obvious difference is the scale; however, they look very similar in shape. This can tell us that the behaviour of the semantic network between adults and children have similarities. It is clear that the network for the adults is larger because of the bigger vocabulary.

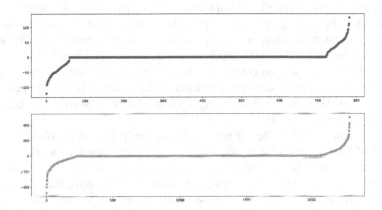

**Fig. 1.** Comparison of the spectra between children's graph (above) and adult's graph (below).

Even if we do not go deep in the similarities between children and adults graph, we present Fig. 1 in order to show the advantages of the Hermitian Laplacian method. The procedure allows us to look at similarities in the spectra of two or more directed graphs, preserving the directed structure. We consider this an advantage in that with the traditional Laplacian method the directed information is lost.

In this sense, the Hermitian Laplacian method, as has been shown, allows us to look for properties of graphs preserving their directed connections. Also, the proposal has shown that is has better performance in embedding the topology of a graph into the vector space when the graph is directed.

## 5 Conclusions

In this paper, we proposed a method of vector representation of directed graphs using the Hermitian Laplacian operator associated with the graph. We show that this method promises good results when original data is not necessarily undirected. This is the case for semantic networks, taxonomies, transition relations, and WAN corpora. The proposed method, here tested for directed graphs, preserves the original structure of the data. As the preliminary results show, when the original data is directed, the Hermitian Laplacian procedures perform better than the Laplacian procedure. For embedding graph structures into vector spaces, the Hermitian Laplacian procedure overpasses the embedding made by a simple Laplacian Eigenmaps algorithm. The semantic relations established by the Hermitian Laplacian method seem to be more coherent than the relations predicted by the Laplacian procedure. We believe that, when preserving the directed information of the edges in the graph, the spectral methods will capture this information. Being this way, the low-dimensional vector representation obtained from the spectrum will be better.

Furthermore, the Hermitian Laplacian method proposed here can be useful for comparing directed graph structures. We believe that further research on this topic can generate relevant results for the study of semantic networks and language graphs as its structure tends to be directed. The main application of our system is the comparison between linguistic resources that are not relatable in terms of size. Semantics and syntagmatic relations of words can be approached by this method, that can capture some lexical connections that are not easily seen with standard methods.

However, the theory of Hermitian Laplacian operators of graphs is not fully developed at the time. As far as we know, there are no current works on Spectral Clustering using Hermitian Laplacian operators. In here, we show a first approximation to this theory for spectral analysis of graphs. But this work is merely a beginning and needs to be extensively tested. In future works, we plan to develop a more complete method for clustering, taking into account a more detailed theory of Hermitian Laplacian operators of graphs.

Finally, we need to preform more tests in order to explain the different lexical relations expressed by the HL operators and the WAN graphs. The results of the research can be very fruitful for the development of the theories about the structure of the lexicon.

**Acknowledgements.** Thanks to the project PAPIIT IA400117 "Simulación de normas de asociación de palabras mediante redes de coocurrencias".

# References

1. Bollobás, B.: Modern Graph Theory. Springer, Heidelberg (1998). https://doi.org/10.1007/978-1-4612-0619-4
2. Newman, M.: The structure and function of complex networks. SIAM Rev. **45**, 167–256 (2003)
3. Boccaletti, S., Latora, V., Moreno, Y., Chavez, M., Hwang, D.U.: Complex networks: structure and dynamics. Phys. Rep. **424**, 175–308 (2006)
4. Albert, A., Jeong, H., Barabási, A.L.: Error and attack tolerance of complex networks. Nature **406**, 378–382 (2000)
5. Kayne, R.: The Antisymmetry of Syntax. MIT Press, Cambridge (1994)
6. Steyvers, M., Tenenbaum, J.B.: The large-scale structure of semantic networks: statistical analyses and a model of semantic growth. Cogn. Sci. **29**, 41–78 (2005)

7. Widdows, D., Dorow, B.: A graph model for unsupervised lexical acquisition. In: 19th International Conference on Computational Linguistics, 24 August–1 September, Taipeh, Taiwan (2002)
8. Rapp, R.: Word sense discovery based on sense descriptor dissimilarity. In: Proceedings of the Ninth Machine Translation Summit, pp. 315–322 (2003)
9. Sowa, J.F.: Semantic networks. In: Encyclopedia of Cognitive Science (2006)
10. Aitchison, J.: Words in the Mind: An Introduction to the Mental Lexicon. Wiley, Hoboken (2012)
11. Ferret, O.: Using collocations for topic segmentation and link detection. In: COLING 2002, pp. 260–266 (2002)
12. Ferret, O.: Building a network of topical relations from a corpus. In: LREC 2006 (2006)
13. Zock, M., Ferret, O., Schwab, D.: Deliberate word access: an intuition, a roadmap and some preliminary empirical results. Int. J. Speech Technol. **13**, 201–218 (2010)
14. Arias-Trejo, N., Barrón-Martínez, J.B.: Base de datos: Normas de asociación de palabras para el español de méxico en escolares (2014)
15. Arias-Trejo, N., Barrón-Martínez, J.B., Lopez-Alderete, R., Robles-Aguirre, F.: Corpus de normas de asociacion de palabras para el espanol de Mexico [NAP]. Universidad Nacional Autonoma de Mexico (2015)
16. Kent, G.H.: Emergency battery of one minute tests. J. Psychol. **13**, 141–164 (1942)
17. Lafourcade, M.: Making people play for lexical acquisition with the JeuxDeMots prototype. In: 7th International Symposium on Natural Language Processing, p. 7 (2007)
18. Enguix, G.B., Rapp, R., Zock, M.: A graph-based approach for computing free word associations. In: Proceedings of the Ninth International Conference on Language Resources and Evaluation (LREC 2014), 26–31 May 2014, Reykjavik, Iceland, European Language Resources Association (ELRA), no. 1150, pp. 3027–3033 (2014)
19. Baroni, M., Bernardi, R., Zamparelli, R.: Frege in space: a program of compositional distributional semantics. LiLT (Linguist. Issues Lang. Technol.) **9** (2014)
20. Brychcín, T., Konopík, M.: Semantic spaces for improving language modeling. Comput. Speech Lang. **28**, 192–209 (2014)
21. Biemann, C.: Vectors or graphs? On differences of representations for distributional semantic models. In: COLING 2016, p. 1 (2016)
22. Fiedler, M.: Algebraic connectivity of graphs. Czechoslovak Math. J. **23**, 298–305 (1973)
23. Anderson Jr., W.N., Morley, T.D.: Eigenvalues of the Laplacian of a graph. Linear Multilinear Algebra **18**, 141–145 (1985)
24. Mohar, B., Alavi, Y., Chartrand, G., Oellermann, O.: The Laplacian spectrum of graphs. Graph Theory Comb. Appl. **2**, 12 (1991)
25. Liu, J., Li, X.: Hermitian-adjacency matrices and Hermitian energies of mixed graphs. Linear Algebra Appl. **466**, 182–207 (2015)
26. Halmos, P.R.: What does the spectral theorem say? Am. Math. Mon. **70**, 241–247 (1963)
27. Mantoiu, M., Raikov, G., de Aldecoa, R.T.: Spectral Theory and Mathematical Physics. Operator Theory: Advances and Applications, vol. 254. Springer, Heidelberg (2016). https://doi.org/10.1007/978-3-319-29992-1
28. Birman, M.S., Solomjak, M.Z.: Spectral Theory of Self-adjoint Operators in Hilbert Space, vol. 5. Springer, Heidelberg (2012). https://doi.org/10.1007/978-94-009-4586-9

29. Zhang, X.D., Luo, R.: The Laplacian eigenvalues of mixed graphs. Linear Algebra Appl. **362**, 109–119 (2003)
30. Rice, J.R.: Experiments on gram-schmidt orthogonalization. Math. Comput. **20**, 325–328 (1966)
31. Yu, G., Qu, H.: Hermitian Laplacian matrix and positive of mixed graphs. Appl. Math. Comput. **269**, 70–76 (2015)
32. Jackson-Maldonado, D., et al.: MacArthur Inventarios del Desarrollo de Habilidades Comunicativas: User's Guide and Technical Manual. PH Brookes, Baltimore (2003)
33. Ferre-i-Cancho, R., Solé, R.V.: The small world of human language. Proc. Roy. Soc. Lond. B: Biol. Sci. **268**, 2261–2265 (2001)
34. Tamir, R.: A random walk through human associations. In: Fifth IEEE International Conference on Data Mining, 8-pp. IEEE (2005)
35. Burioni, R., Cassi, D.: Random walks on graphs: ideas, techniques and results. J. Phys. A: Math. Gen. **38**, R45 (2005)
36. Hu, D., Li, X., Liu, X., Zhang, S.: The spectral distribution of random mixed graphs. Linear Algebra Appl. **519**, 343–365 (2017)
37. Lu, Y., Wang, L., Zhou, Q.: Hermitian-Randić matrix and Hermitian-Randić energy of mixed graphs. J. Inequalities Appl. **2017**, 54 (2017)
38. Gutman, I., Li, X., Zhang, J.: Graph energy. In: Analysis of Complex Networks: From Biology to Linguistics, pp. 145–174 (2009)
39. Du, W., Li, X., Li, Y.: The energy of random graphs. Linear Algebra Appl. **435**, 2334–2346 (2011)
40. Belkin, M., Niyogi, P.: Laplacian eigenmaps and spectral techniques for embedding and clustering. NIPS **14**, 585–591 (2001)
41. Belkin, M., Niyogi, P.: Laplacian eigenmaps for dimensionality reduction and data representation. Neural Comput. **15**, 1373–1396 (2003)
42. Ng, A.Y., Jordan, M.I., Weiss, Y., et al.: On spectral clustering: analysis and an algorithm. NIPS **14**, 849–856 (2001)
43. Von Luxburg, U.: A tutorial on spectral clustering. Stat. Comput. **17**, 395–416 (2007)
44. Yu, G., Liu, X., Qu, H.: Singularity of Hermitian (quasi-) Laplacian matrix of mixed graphs. Appl. Math. Comput. **293**, 287–292 (2017)
45. Mikolov, T., Le, Q.V., Sutskever, I.: Exploiting similarities among languages for machine translation. arXiv preprint arXiv:1309.4168 (2013)
46. Mijangos, V., Barrón-Martínez, J.B., Arias-Trejo, N., Bel-Enguix, G.: A graph-based analysis of the corpus of word association norms for Mexican Spanish. In: Proceedings of the 2nd International Conference on Complexity, Future Information Systems and Risk - Volume 1: COMPLEXIS, INSTICC, pp. 87–93. ScitePress (2017)

# Evaluation of Information Retrieval Algorithms Within an Energy Documents Repository

Diego Márquez[1], Yasmín Hernández[1(✉)], and Alberto Ochoa-Ortiz[2]

[1] Instituto Nacional de Electricidad y Energías Limpias,
Gerencia de Tecnologías de la Información,
Reforma 113, 62490 Cuernavaca, Mexico
2155diego@gmail.com, myhp@iie.org.mx
[2] Maestría en Cómputo Aplicado, Universidad Autónoma de Ciudad Juárez,
Ciudad Juárez, Mexico
alberto.ochoa@uacj.mx

**Abstract.** The development of energy and electricity sectors have result in a cumulus of technical and scientific documents related with several topics. The large activity in these sectors results in a growing repository, where the search for information based on keywords is not sufficient. We need a way to find relevant documents given a need of information. Information retrieval is the process of finding unstructured documents to satisfy an information need from within large collections. Several information retrieval has been proposed, we have analyzed them. Base on this analysis, we are working on an information retrieval model according to specific needs of energy and electricity sectors. We have evaluated the vector Space algorithm, probabilistic algorithm and our proposal. Here, we present the results of the evaluation and our preliminary proposal.

**Keywords:** Information retrieval · Natural language processing
Artificial intelligence · Algorithms · Text retrieval · Energy documents

## 1 Introduction

Along the history, people has stored different kinds of useful objects for future use. Mostly, knowledge is stored in enormous repositories or libraries in the form of books, reports, journals, articles, newspapers, among other sources of information. To identify and use a relevant document, libraries have an organization system to know what there are in the library and where is it.

The advancement of information and communications technologies, particularly the internet, allows us to share, produce, store and retrieve an amazing volume of information in such as. Now, we retrieve relevant documents to current necessities in huge digital repositories.

On the other hand, electrical systems have played an important role on economic development of countries. Therefore, thousands or millions of documents have been

F. Castro et al. (Eds.): MICAI 2017, LNAI 10633, pp. 57–68, 2018.
https://doi.org/10.1007/978-3-030-02840-4_5

produced in the form of handbooks, specifications, technical reports, projects proposals, results and conclusions of projects, and scientific papers, among others.

We have stored by several decades a big amount of document. We have systems to retrieve documents by keywords, authors, etc., however now we want to retrieve documents according to relevance and pertinence according some topics.

Information retrieval is the process of finding material, usually documents, of an unstructured nature, usually text, that satisfies an information need from within large collections, usually stored on computers [1]. An information retrieval process begins when a user enters a query into the system. Queries are formal statements of information needs, for example search strings in web search engines. In information retrieval a query does not uniquely identify a single object in the collection. Instead, several objects may match the query, perhaps with different degrees of relevancy.

An object is an entity that is represented by information in a content collection or database. User queries are matched against the database information. However, as opposed to classical SQL queries of a database, in information retrieval the results returned may or may not match the query, so results are typically ranked. This ranking of results is a key difference of information retrieval searching compared to database searching [1].

We are in the initial process to develop an Information Retrieval system. Then we are evaluating the existent algorithms. In this paper we present preliminary results in this evaluation.

The rest of the paper is organized as follows: Sect. 2 briefly describes fundamentals of Information Retrieval, Sect. 3 presents recent work, Sect. 4 presents proposal and preliminary results. Finally, conclusions and future work are discussed in Sect. 5.

## 2  Information Retrieval

Information retrieval (IR) is the process of finding unstructured material (usually documents) to satisfy an information need within large collections (usually stored on a computer) [1]. The main purpose of an IR systems is to cover the information need that any user could have, from answering a simple question through a query, to generating similar results and matches with all available information. The most remote antecedent of IR is between the 30 s and 40 s and it is close to the work developed by the linguist George Kingsley Zipf (1902–1950), who declared a law which bears his name and which talks about the existing possibility of regularities detection and statistical patterns in large clusters of textual structures [2]. A collection of documents is classified by a set of common characteristics, in a text retrieval system; these characteristics can be or include topics, words, phrases, contexts, among other. In this repository it is automatized or manually assigned relationship elements, depending only on the system application domain [2]. The application scope of information retrieval is too extensive and it is often involved with efficiency improvement problems in lucrative spaces such as its application in web searches engines or data centers where operations are daily performed and requested services are executed around the world by billions of people, even in the most crowded sites like Facebook or Twitter, information retrieval is always present [3].

However, early information retrieval or retrieval systems used only logical comparison methods between the query of the user query and the available information, which resulted in a very low level of accuracy of response and this was further degraded if it was considered to be applied in very large information clusters, with millions of documents, for example as presented by Ponte [2]. The previous models that did not take into account important delimiting factors of the text, like the placements, the languages or even simple factors like the synonyms of the words among other more complex aspects.

The introduction of Natural Language Processing (NLP) in the area of artificial intelligence applied to traditional linguistics has significantly improved methods of information retrieval. With the use of NLP, it is possible to take into account factors that are very relevant and determinant in the text and information in general, for example, the levels in which the language is traditionally divided: phonetics, morphology, syntax, semantics, pragmatics, discourse.

The main objective of IR is to study and develop algorithmic or intellectual methods that facilitate as much as possible the following linguistics operations [4]:

1. Indexing
    a. Analysis: identification or assignment of the most relevant topics or document concepts.
    b. Standardization: Transformation of the most representative text in simple and generic terms.
2. Selection: (or recovery) is the process of identifying the most relevant documents in order to satisfy the information need. It is usually the most representative part of the process.
3. Ordering: Determine the best order of presentation for the user so, he can make use of the information (ranking).
4. Interconnection: Establish contextual relations between the document and its possible thematically related.
5. Categorization: Classify documents retrieved in sub-themes, taxonomy or ontology.
6. Abstraction: Produce an article summary or document useful and meaningful with the most relevant of the same that sometimes even replace the complete reading of it.
7. Display: Representation of the system in response to the user.

It is more understandable to say that the most important information retrieval goal is to automate and optimize the seven processes mentioned above with a good percentage of assertiveness and 100% of effectiveness.

To conceptualize an information retrieval system in general by a classic and generic model of how an IR system works, the following model was developed by Belkin Risjbergen [5]. A very abstract way of representing the base model of an information retrieval system regardless of the technique used is presented in Fig. 1.

**Fig. 1.** Generic information retrieval system. Basic processes in an information retrieval system are shown [5].

Figure 1 depicts the searching process of the model for the first moment as input to obtain the query or need for user information, then proceed to analyze the text, process that is necessary to unify the query representation with the available text in the same format, then a comparison is made, where the most appropriate information retrieval technique is used to generate a document ranking and finish with the system response to the user [4].

Although information retrieval has not become more precise or simple over time, it has improved significantly since its inception and the development of Natural Language Processing in the years 1950–1960 [6].

# 3   Recent Work

The constant growth of the web as the main communication and information means has developed over time the existence and need of information retrieval. In addition, web browsers are the main places where millions of internet users around the world spend most of their time daily besides to social networks and information sites.

The WebIR can be defined as the application of the methodologies and procedures of information retrieval within the World Wide Web, with that, the use of IR has become a fundamental part of the development of new technologies inside the internet.

Constant changes in site information, exponential growth of information, huge heterogeneous mix of themes, concepts and formats are basic examples of what WebIR models must face day by day and are challenged to overcome [7].

The summary of texts is the process of extracting relevant information from one or several textual sources. Usually, it is a tedious process for the human being to perform a summary of large text documents, techniques of language learning and interpretation are applied, which directly infer information retrieval techniques, such as the tree based method or the template based method. New methods of textual summary are constantly developed, with the aim to optimize the task of summarizing information and as a result, the summary is pretend to be more useful, understandable and truly meaningful to the human [8].

The information retrieval within opinion mining is a derivative of information retrieval, and it is concerned to retrieval of texts. With text mining we can find diverse applications, ranging from the extraction of statistical data, information classification, relevance of data to comments qualification and interpretation of them.

Opining mining has been done in order to obtain a comprehensive analysis of the statistical Internet user's opinion or users in relation to study domains, such as: entertainment, business, research and development, products, politics, health, general interest topics, among other. The opinion mining techniques have been refined taking as a base of execution the use of information retrieval techniques for further processing and cataloging [9].

Neural Information Retrieval and Machine Learning are within the main processes and methods of information retrieval and methods that are sought to optimize. They are concerned with the interpretation of the natural language to comply with the process of the user query analysis and tune into the same channel both the need of the user and the information available. Although it is usually limited, a similar situation happens in the specification of the query, it must be specific and within a domain of terms that can be found frequently and correctly within the textual corpus application of the information retrieval system [10].

As an example of the constant interest in developing a solution, a workshop has been held each year on the subject, where relevant scientific research articles and the most relevant advances are presented. New techniques of relation and processing of natural language with genetic algorithms and the application of the artificial intelligence in the field of the information retrieval are developed [11].

### 3.1  Boolean Information Retrieval Model

The Boolean recovery model is the simplest of all and it is also the one that initiated the concept of Information Retrieval in the area of computer science [12], In this model both the user query and the texts or the existing corpus are seen as a Boolean expression of terms, these terms are classically combined using logical operators AND, OR, NOT.

The main idea of this model is to generate logical vectors using the words of the texts, where each word is an element of the vector and the value can typically be only 1 or 0, where 1 means the presence of the word in the text and or the absence of it. The query process is based on performing logical operations between the query vector and the available information, where the best candidate for response to the user will be the one with the largest number of elements, so that the result of a Boolean search equation is the set containing the relevant documents for the user, of course if there are no matches, this set can be returned empty [4].

### 3.2  Vector Space Retrieval Model

In information retrieval, it is possible to implement a system using any kind of data structure imaginable, it depending on the execution requirements of the model and the hardware resources that are counted for execution. The vector space model offers a peculiar abstract way of representing the recovery process, far from depending on the system to be implemented or the type of document ranking, the model is based on understanding both the query and the documents as vectors of N dimensions, where N is the number of terms in the collection of texts [2]. The vector space recovery model calculates the similarity of the query with the documents by measuring the query distance, which can be measured in various ways, the model in general does not specify any particular way to calculate it [2].

This model uses the words frequency to determine the rarity of the same between all documents or all available information, it is determined by generating an array of terms where all terms in the corpus are available and comparable among them, classified by document or entry in the corpus, in the matrix of terms a weight is assigned to each one, which will essentially determine what is called the rarity of the term in documents [13]. It will determine in a certain way the importance that must be given to the search to each of the terms or words in the query entered by the user, thus it is possible to extract as a result of the query a ranking of documents that are more suitable to the user's query, this method despite taking into account different characteristics of the texts and a greater number of them compared to the previous model can work in some cases and in others it is usually not as effective, so each model user is able to add adaptations to the same to make an adaptation of the model to a specific search need. The Space Retrieval model for example is currently one of the most used IR model in web search engines [13].

### 3.3 Probabilistic Retrieval Model

In previous reference models, the ranking of documents is obtained by performing a formal logical comparison, with the information processed and meaningful for the information retrieval system. In the probabilistic recovery model, aggregate and calculated weights are added at the level of significance for the user and not only with the computed values, the weights are dynamic and kept in constant updating, using user comments to determine the level of relevance of each term, both within the user's query and in the relevant documents.

A mean significance level is established at the beginning, where each term of the query contains the same significant value for the system, so it can be said that the first query in a probabilistic model is very similar to the Boolean base recovery models, the process of change and adaptation to the context of relevance comes second with the outcome of information retrieval [1]. The probabilistic information retrieval model uses as a determinant both, the occurrence frequency query words in the text and a feedback of the user, where indicates the level of relevance that a set of documents has for him, mainly the recovered documents in consultation. This is how two sets of documents sorted by relevance for the user's query are created: relevant and non-relevant documents, taking into account individual terms within the full text. The weights of the terms are assigned in a standard way at the beginning, taking as the initial factor an intermediate value of relevance called "The greatest uncertainty" after that, the relevance value changes through the time due to the user's feedback.

### 3.4 Hybrids and Complex Models

In recent years, information retrieval probabilistic models have attracted attention in a very strong way. As a consequence, alternatives have been sought for the application and development of more efficient and effective methodologies for the processing of information retrieval, interpretation of results and human-computer interaction. Since the 1980s, intelligent systems have begun to be implemented in various areas of computer science and information retrieval is not the exception. Models based on the use of artificial intelligence are becoming more common and are found more frequently in all types of systems, as is the case of information retrieval models using: the connectionist Hopfield network, the symbolic ID3/ID5R, and Evolution-based genetic algorithms [14].

# 4 Proposal and Preliminary Results

Electrical and energy sectors are in constant development since they are detonating factor of economic sectors. For several decades we have stored knowledge and information in several types of documents that be use in the development of new projects and for training. As a result, we have a specialized repository with a big amount of documents. As a first step, we are working with the issues of a specialized journal (https://www.ineel.mx/publicaciones.html).

Currently, there is no information storage system and searches for information and knowledge are performed by keywords or name of authors, for example. However, relevance, classification and order are not included. In this search model, interested people spend a lot of time in their searches for relevant documents. To advance in the solution of this situation, we propose to build an Information Retrieval model for electricity and energy sector. A system based on this model would help to find relevant and information shortly.

Different models of information retrieval have been proposed and applied, we have evaluated them with the aim to determinate the suitable model to carry out the task that can solve with greater successful search of files within our domain.

To test and evaluate the existent information retrieval models, we worked with 100 electronic issues of the journal. These documents include scientific, technical and divulgation papers within energy and electricity field from years 2014–2016.

The queries that were used to test the information retrieval methods were ten basic examples of queries in energy articles sector, as mentioned in the beginning, the system works with texts in Spanish, Table 1 describes the queries used to perform the tests of the system.

The first model used in the evaluation of system functionality was the method of retrieval of Boolean information, in which results were obtained, although positive, not completely satisfactory, because of the strictly literal searches, one could not go beyond finding the words entered by the user within the textual corpus. In both, the boolean recovery model and all others, a text pre-processing must be performed in order to infer positively the results of the search and to ensure greater effectiveness in the comparative process of the model.

First, the texts of the desired location are obtained inside the computer, and then begin with the processing of the same. Using the Boolean information retrieval technique, first get both the user query and the information corpus where the query will be used. Subsequently, both the text and the query are tokenized, which means separating the text from sentences to words, this by using the NLTK (Natural Language Processing Toolkit) library in Python 3.4.0. It should be mentioned that the focus of both the texts and the queries is entirely in the Spanish language, as this changes drastically by all the adaptations of the language that it has, as well as the vocabulary used within NLTK methods. After that, once the tokens of all the information have been taken, stop words are eliminated, which are words that do not contribute any relevant meaning to the text, such as articles or conjunctions. When stop words are deleted, the remaining words are sent to their source format by a stemming method provided in the same way by NLTK in Python, with which we can generalize terms to avoid redundancy of

**Table 1.** Statements to evaluate the information retrieval models. The evaluate was conducted with Spanish queries, but its English translation is also shown.

| | Spanish query | English query |
|---|---|---|
| 1 | Energías renovables, alternativas sustentables | Renewable energy, sustainable alternatives |
| 2 | Almacenamiento de energía | Energy storage |
| 3 | Recursos humanos en el sector energético | Human resources in the energy sector |
| 4 | Técnicas de recolección de energía sustentable | Sustainable Energy Collection Techniques |
| 5 | Nanotecnología, aplicación, implementación, utilidad | Nanotechnology, application, implementation, utility |
| 6 | Alternativas verdes, uso y almacenamiento de energía | Green alternatives, use and storage of energy |
| 7 | Nuevas tecnologías en el sector energético | New technologies in the energy sector |
| 8 | Comunidad de innovación, tecnología e investigación | Community of innovation, technology and research |
| 9 | Recursos energéticos a través del agua y aire | Energy resources through water and air |
| 10 | Realidad virtual, sistemas de simulación de entornos reales | Virtual reality, real-world simulation systems |

information and to join terms whose etymological principle is the same. The stemming algorithm used is: snowball in Spanish language [15].

Then, after performing the stemming process, we proceed to compare texts already processed, both the available corpus and the query. This will retrieve only texts or articles that contain the query literally within its textual structure, which makes this type of recovery very limited. The results of the tests performed with the Boolean recovery model are in Table 2.

**Table 2.** Boolean information retrieval model results. Retrieved documents using the test queries in Table 1. Results of Boolean IR model.

| Queries | | | | | | | | | | |
|---|---|---|---|---|---|---|---|---|---|---|
| | 1 | 2 | 3 | 4 | 5 | 6 | 7 | 8 | 9 | 10 |
| Number of retrieved documents | 3 | 2 | 0 | 0 | 0 | 2 | 1 | 2 | 1 | 1 |

Next, we evaluate the vector space recovery method, which, unlike the Boolean recovery method, offers a greater comparative response between the query and the text within the corpus. In the process of implementing the vector space model, like the Boolean recovery model, the first step is to process the text, both the text of the articles and the requested text to the user as a query.

The first step of processing the text consists on the sentences separation into words, which is called Tokenizer, which process is similarly done using the tokenization method of the NLTK library in Python, then delete stop words as in the Boolean recovery method and finally the snowball stemming process is performed.

Subsequently, the linguistic diversity of the whole corpus is extracted, which consists of extracting all the different words in the text, with the purpose of building a lexical diversity header vector. Once the lexical diversity vector is present, each document or article of the corpus is interpreted as a vector of terms, which at the moment indicates the frequency of each term indexing within the lexical diversity vector. Then, once we have the frequencies of the terms in the vectors of the articles, we calculate the weight of each term in each article, this is done taking into account the "rarity" of the term both within the article and in the set of documents, so as to know which terms are the most representative within each article. It is also possible to discriminate those that are very common or that do not have significant meaning for the text within the set of them. Once the process of calculating weights is completed, the query is entered and a weight is obtained in relation to the lexical diversity within the corpus, when we have the weight of each term within the query, it proceeds to realize a scalar product that will determine which vectors of documents are the most similar to the query vector. The greater result of the products in the documents with those of the query, will be the one that has greater relation with what the user is looking for. As a result, we got a list of the most relevant articles or a ranking of those most similar to the user's query.

The most common and functional way of evaluating information retrieval systems is to calculate how many relevant documents are retrieved and how many of them are in place that should according to their relevance. The precision $p$ of a recovery method at a given point $r$ is the fraction of the ranking of documents that is important for the query (See Eq. 1).

$$P_r = \frac{Number\ of\ documents\ retrieved\ that\ are\ relevant}{Total\ number\ of\ documents\ retrieved} \tag{1}$$

The recall of a recovery method $R$ in the same manner at a given point $r$ is the proportion of the total of relevant documents that were recovered at the top of the document ranking (See Eq. 2).

$$R_r = \frac{Number\ of\ documents\ relevant\ that\ are\ retrieved}{Total\ number\ of\ documents\ relevant} \tag{2}$$

Because recall is a function that does not decrease with ranking, accuracy can be viewed more as a recall function than ranking. This relationship is represented in a diagram known as a recall-precision curve, in which the precision is plotted against the recall.

The results allow to graph the different models in a single graph and thus compare and ranking the algorithms. Which means that if one curve is higher than another, the algorithm has better results [16]. Thus, the vector space model and the probabilistic recovery model and the proposed model are evaluated in this way and finally compared using the graphic comparison method of recall-precision curve.

For purposes of testing and comparison, a maximum of ten documents retrieved using this model were established using each of the test queries and making an average of them in order to represent them in a graphical way.

The third model used as a measure of comparison of results is the model of recovery probabilistic information, which, unlike the vector space recovery model, adds the relevance characterized by the opinion of the user to the information returned, it is initialized with an intermediate value called "Maximum uncertainty value", which is modified through each query that the user makes, and the recovery model select the article with the content called relevant. Due to the above, the system is able to classify the articles into two groups: relevant documents and non-relevant documents, in a search evidently it will determine which are the papers with most probable relevance by the user, hence their name "probabilistic".

In the same way as the two previous models, the first step to begin to use this model is the text processing, which begins with the tokenization of the text, followed by the elimination of the stop words and ending with the stemming process using Snowball in Spanish, all included in the NLTK library in Python 3.4.0. After processing the text, the following is to create an array of terms in adjacency with the document in which it is contained, in order to determine the initial weights of the relevance values of the same, as mentioned at the beginning, initially are mean probability values, (0.5) and are modifiable by the user through the queries.

Once you have the matrix of terms with articles correctly related and structured, you can proceed to the query, which is processed in the same way as the text of the articles and subsequently used as a means to compare the terms included in the texts are literally searched for the terms within the available textual structures and the documents are classified as relevant and not relevant. Then the system will result in the ranking of the relevant documents according to the weight value of each term in the query and texts. Once the ranking of documents has been released, the user is able to give feedback to the retrieval made, taking into account the documents recovered with greater relevance or more significant for the user, thus the system is able to update to some extent the weights of relevance and thus grant a new result with expected values more accurate relative to the user's requirements. Thus, with each query, the system becomes more specific in the retrieval and classification of its recovered documents, taking into account the query.

In the corresponding evaluation of the information retrieval methods used as a solution prospect, a model was proposed adapted to the analysis and observation of possible improvement to the results obtained previously with the purpose of finding a solution that suits the specific purpose of retrieving articles from the repository, a model with the following characteristics was proposed: It is a model that uses the initial ranking model of the vector space information retrieval model, in which the recovered documents are organized with the acquired weights of each term by its rarity degree in function with the document and the set of the same ones within the complete search space. With this, the documents that are of priority for the model are initially obtained with the query of the user.

Subsequently, a filtering process of the recovered documents is conducted using the probabilistic recovery model, so it is possible to reorder the priority documents for the user and not for the system, thanks to the feedback that the user is able to perform in the system in each recovery (the option of feedback is optional, it is advisable to improve the searches, however, you can perform searches without using it). In this proposed model, the storage of previously processed data and information is retained to ensure its efficiency, as well as the implementation of previous models (Fig. 2).

**Fig. 2.** Proposed information retrieval model. It is based on the basic processes of the generic information retrieval model.

Finally, by graphically evaluating the three ranking models used, we can deduce significantly the efficiency of the operation of each model and compare them (See Fig. 3).

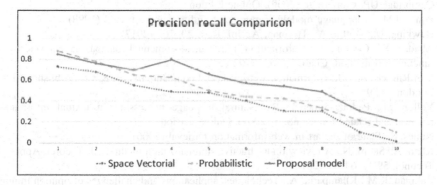

**Fig. 3.** Precision-recall curve for all models. It is presented the evaluation results of basic information retrieval models, Probabilistic and Vector Space, and the proposal model.

## 5   Conclusions and Future Work

In this work, a specific solution is formulated and implemented for an information retrieval problem of a particular scope articles. The proposal is an approach to how specific information retrieval problem can be solved taking into account all the worked and studied resources. Main purpose is to find the model that best suited to the recovery of popularization articles, including the researching and the diversity of existing recovery techniques. An information retrieval model with a greater precision of work was developed. This model allows to emphasize that probably there is not an existing perfect method or information retrieval technique, but through the time it has been improving and implementing new linguistic algorithms with which we can work in a more effective measure and efficient as well.

As future work, we plan to develop and implement new hybrid information retrieval models, which through the evaluation of the same in a general overview, it is possible to adapt each of them to new workspaces. It also seeks to expand the purpose of information retrieval systems. Also, we plan to involve techniques of retrieval in articles or printed information, to digitize them and also to expand the descriptive panorama, to give a focus of dissemination as much scientific as technical and educational, with the purpose of improving the performance of information retrieval systems.

**Acknowledgments.** Authors would like to thank to Publication Department of the Instituto Nacional de Electricidad y Energías Limpias for its support in the development of this research.

# References

1. Manning, C.D., Raghavan, P., Schütze, H.: Introduction to Information Retrieval. Cambridge UP, Cambridge (2009). Online Edition
2. Ponte, J.M.: A language modeling approach to information retrieval (1998)
3. Hawking, D., Moffat, A., Trotman, A.: Inf. Retr. **20**, 169 (2017)
4. Abadal, E., Codina, L.: Information retrieval, documented databases: characteristics, function and method, Chap. 2, pp. 29–92 (2005)
5. Van Rijsbergen, C.J.: Information Retrieval, 2nd edn. Butterworth & Co (Publishers) Ltd., London (1979)
6. Vallez, M., Pedraza-Jimenez, R.: Natural language processing in textual information retrieval and related topics, no. 5 (2007). Online version
7. Nunes, S.: State of the art in web information retrieval (2006)
8. Khan, A., Salim, N.: A review on abstractive summarization methods. J. Theoret. Appl. Inf. Technol. **59**(1), 64–72 (2014)
9. Rahman, K.M., Khamparia, A.: Techniques, applications and challenges of opinion mining. IJCTA **9**(41), 455–461 (2016)
10. Hui, K., Yates, A., Berberich, K., De Melo, G.: Position-aware representations for relevance matching in neural information retrieval (2017)
11. Craswell, N., Croft, W.B., Guo, J., Mitra, B., De Rijke, M.: Report on the SIGIR 2016 Workshop on Neural Information Retrieval (Neu-IR) (2016)
12. Steven, W.: Boolean operations, Information Retrieval Data Structures and Algorithms. Prentice-Hall, Upper Saddle River (1992)
13. Méndez, F.J.M.: Recuperación de información: modelos, sistemas y evaluación. KIOSKO JMC, Murcia (2004)
14. Chen, H.: Machine learning for information retrieval: neural networks, symbolic learning, and genetic algorithms (1995)
15. Porter, M. F.: Snowball: a language for stemming algorithms (2001)
16. Greenwood, M.A.: Implementing a vector space document retrieval system (2002)

# An Agent-Based System to Assess Legibility and Cognitive Depth of Scientific Texts

Omar López-Ortega[1], Obed Pérez-Cortés[1], Félix Castro-Espinoza[1(✉)],
and Manuel Montes y Gómez[2]

[1] Área Académica de Sistemas Computacionales, Universidad Autónoma del Estado
de Hidalgo, Carretera Pachuca-Tulancingo, km. 4.5, C. U., 42084 Pachuca,
Hidalgo, Mexico
{lopezo,obed_perez}@uaeh.edu.mx, fcastroe@gmail.com
[2] Laboratorio de Tecnologías del Lenguaje, Instituto Nacional de Astrofísica,
Optica y Electrónica (INAOE), Tonantzintla, 72840 Puebla, Mexico
mmontesg@inaoep.mx

**Abstract.** Knowledge transmitted through writing is suitable to be
refined by understanding, criticizing, reflecting upon, and using it.
Although several types of writings, from diffusion to highly specialized
texts, fulfill this purpose, they differ considerably in syntax, word selection and phrases length. It is widely accepted that proper scientific writings deploy facts with detail, rigor and legibility, for which scientists
acquire writing skills through experience, by following guidelines, by
obtaining feedback from fellow scientists or through a combination of
those approaches. We question whether scientific texts possess common
characteristics that can be determined through quantitative metrics. A
positive answer is confirmed by the fact that such writings in both languages, Spanish and English, display a normal probability distribution
for a metric called $\mu$ legibility. Moreover, by analyzing texts through a
new proposed metric called *cognitive depth*, scientific writings in Spanish display that *analysis* is the dominant Bloom's cognitive level. These
preliminary findings suggest that it is possible to evaluate and classify
new manuscripts through an agent-based human-computer interactive
system that informs writers if the ongoing text lies into the ranges discovered for published texts, and what is the prevalent cognitive level.
By having this feedback, writers can modify their manuscripts to make
them display good metrics.

**Keywords:** Text legibility · Cognitive level · Multi-agent systems
E-research

## 1 Introduction

Written knowledge constitutes the most reliable means for advancing in its refinement and further creation. Texts allow people to understand, use, analyze, crit-
icize, and re-arrange knowledge. However, there are several types of writings

© Springer Nature Switzerland AG 2018
F. Castro et al. (Eds.): MICAI 2017, LNAI 10633, pp. 69–81, 2018.
https://doi.org/10.1007/978-3-030-02840-4_6

that disseminate knowledge, ranging from general diffusion texts, such as news-
paper accounts of scientific discoveries, to highly specialized texts written for
specialized journals. Even though both types convey, in essence, the same facts,
their syntax, word selection, length of phrases differ considerably. Let us take,
for example, the writings that were produced to report the empirical evidence
of gravitational waves. The following passage is taken from Reuters [5].

> Scientists for the first time have detected gravitational waves, ripples in
> space and time hypothesised by Albert Einstein a century ago, in a land-
> mark discovery announced on Thursday that opens a new window for
> studying the cosmos. The waves were unleashed by the collision of the black
> holes, one of them 29 times the mass of the sun and the other 36 times the
> solar mass, located 1.3 billion light years from Earth, the researchers said.
> The scientific milestone was achieved using a pair of giant laser detectors
> in the United States, located in Louisiana and Washington state, capping
> a decades-long quest to find these waves. They detected remarkably small
> vibrations from the gravitational waves as they passed through the Earth.
> The scientists converted the wave signal into audio waves and listened to
> the sounds of the black holes merging.

The passage shown next is taken from the abstract of the article confirming
the existence of gravitational waves [1].

> On September 14, 2015 at 9.50:45 UTC the two detectors of the Laser
> Interferometer Gravitational-Wave Observatory simultaneously observed a
> transient gravitational-wave signal. The signal weeps upwards in frequency
> from 35 to 250 Hz with a peak gravitational-wave strain of $1.0 \times 10^{-21}$. It
> matches the waveform predicted by the general relativity for the inspiral
> and merger of a pair of black holes and the ringdown of the resulting
> single black hole. The signal was observed with a marched-filter signal-to-
> noise ratio of 24 and false alarm rate estimated to be less than 1 event
> per 203 300 years, equivalent to a significance greater that $5.1\delta$ ... These
> observations demonstrate the existence of binary stellar-mass black hole
> systems. This is the first direct detection of gravitational waves and the
> first observation of a binary hole merger.

To achieve the advancement of knowledge, scientific texts such as the latter example represent the proper way of communicating facts, even though the
nature of those texts make them challenging readings.

## 1.1  Writing Produces Anxiety in Scientists

Because scientists are expected to publish results through legible and accurate
texts, this sort of pressure leads them to experiment anxiety. For example, it is
documented the anxiety suffered by students who had written research proposals
[18]. Even though this suffering occurs not only in academic environments but
also in any form of writing [9], it is amplified in the case of writing scientific

reports [22]. It has also been found that PhD students are at risk of having or developing depression [14]. Among other determinant factors is the fact that PhD students are expected to publish [20] and to contribute considerably to the advancement of knowledge [13]. Anxiety is still present even after the manuscript is produced, because scientists are kept expecting the review outcome, which in turns leads to frustration in case the document is rejected or more demanding work when reviewers ask amendments. In both cases, the authors may wonder if the verdict has been *objective* [15] or biased.

On the other hand, several studies have shown that when writers receive feedback their manuscripts improve and the levels of anxiety decrease. Several ways to receive feedback exist, for instance, it can be done by audio feedback on written assignments [17], social collaborative revision [10], teacher-written direct vs. indirect feedback [11], or on line automated feedback [4]. Regardless the specific type of peer feedback, scientists perceive it favorably [22].

Given that feedback is desirable while scientists draft their texts, several computer-based tools have been developed to provide assistance. For example in [7] it is described a method for the automatic detection and correction of misspelling, grammar and vocabulary. Also, in [12] it is presented a computer-based system that provides feedback to writers who aim at producing cohesive texts [4].

## 1.2  The Long and Winding Road to Evaluate Scientific Manuscripts

The broadest question posed in this research is to determine how to evaluate scientific texts through a computer-based system. To solve this problem it is necessary to elucidate common aspects of scientific texts and then proceed to select the metrics to quantify such commonalities. This conflict is partially solved by the two metrics described next.

One of them is called *legibility*, for which several formulae have been already developed. The second metric is a new proposal which we name *cognitive depth*. We rely on the theory developed by Bloom to appraise the cognitive depth of a scientific text by assessing what cognitive level is predominantly conveyed: is the text aimed at listing facts? does it present a critique based on thorough evaluations? To determine the cognitive depth of a text we developed an algorithm to identify and quantify the cognitive actions within a text.

The next endeavor consists in determining the regions where legibility and cognitive depth reside for properly written documents. To do so, we characterize a sample of published scientific texts. This is the first time, to the author's best knowledge, that a characterization is carried for this class of manuscripts. Particularly novel is the evaluation of their cognitive depth.

The mentioned study is important because on these findings we created a preliminary version of an interactive system which is intended to function as a support tool for scientific writers. Once the regions for legibility and cognitive depth are established, the values of legibility and cognitive depth of ongoing manuscripts are shown to the writer and compared with those of properly written manuscripts (the regions found in the characterization stage). The application that we are constructing is also novel in the field of text processing, even though it requires refinement.

This article is organized as follows. Section 2 presents theory regarding legibility and cognitive valuation. Next, in Sect. 3 the statistical characterization of scientific texts written in Spanish and English is given. The intelligent agent-based system is described in Sect. 4, illustrating also how a new manuscript is evaluated through the system. Finally, conclusions and future work are outlined.

## 2   Theoretical Framework

### 2.1   Text Legibility

*Legibility* is one criteria to characterize texts. It is defined by the Oxford dictionary as *the quality of being clear enough to be read* or the *essential condition for the composition of a printed text to invite reading it and make it easy to understand.*

In written communication, *legibility* is one of the most important parameters. Its principles are taken from both linguistics and experimental psychology. However, to judge a text as legible or illegible is still subjective. Hence, it is vital to have tools that allow an objective quantification of text legibility. For this purpose we consider different studies that show that the difficulty to read a text, known as its *fluency*, depends on variables such as the number of words, the quantity of letters and syllables per word, and the total account of sentences. This conclusion is based on studies of the physiological process involved in reading, the so-called *saccadic movements* (abruptly eye movements). A great deal of saccadic movement provokes accumulated fatigue and makes it difficult to understand the symbols that must be interpreted.

Since the variables that are required to determine the *fluency* can be measured, different *formulae* have been proposed. In Table 1 it is shown a summary of them, all of which are based on different hypotheses [6,8,16,21]. The formulae are used to quantify the legibility of a text, and to map the numeric value to a linguistic interpretation ranging from texts that are *very difficult* to *very easy* to read.

However, the syntax of scientific writings is different from others. As we stated before, their nature makes them difficult readings per se and yet, they must fulfill the purpose of transmitting knowledge, so they must be understandable if read by experts in the field.

Consequently, in our analysis we consider that the first step to characterize scientific texts is to find the range of legibility values of documents that are *properly written.* To do so, we quantified the legibility of a sample of scientific texts using the metric called $\mu$ legibility. The purpose of this characterization is to discover the way in which a legibility index value of scientific writings can be determined objectively. Results of this characterization are given in Sect. 3.1.

**Table 1.** *Formulae* to compute legibility

| Spanish | | |
|---|---|---|
| *Formulae* | Equation | Notes |
| Fernández-Huerta | $L = 206.84 - 0.60P - 1.02F$ | **L**: rediability; **P**: syllable's average per word; **F**: word's average per phrase |
| Gutiérrez-Polini | $C = 95.2 - 9.7\frac{L}{P} - 0.35\frac{P}{F}$ | **C**: comprehensibility; **L**: letter's numbers; **P**: word's number; **F**: phrase's number |
| Szigriszt-Pazos | $P = 206.835 - 62.3\frac{S}{P} - \frac{P}{F}$ | **P**: perspicuity; **S**: syllable's total; **P**: word's number; **F**: phrase's number |
| $\mu$ | $\mu = \frac{n}{n-1}\frac{\bar{x}}{\sigma^2}$ | $\mu$: legibility index; **n**: number of words; $\bar{x}$: average number of letters per word; $\sigma^2$: standard deviation of number of letters |
| English | | |
| *Formulae* | Equation | Notes |
| Flesh-Kincadi | $L = 0.39\frac{P}{Sn} + 11.8\frac{S}{P} - 15.59$ | **L**: rediability; **P**: total words; **Sn**: total sentences; **S**: total syllables |
| Szigriszt | $RE = 207 - 84.6\frac{S}{P} - 1.02\frac{W}{F}$ | **RE**: reading easy; **S**: syllable's total; **P**: word's number; **F**: phrase's number |
| $\mu$ | $\mu = \frac{n}{n-1}\frac{\bar{x}}{\sigma^2}$ | $\mu$: legibility index; **n**: number of words; $\bar{x}$: average number of letters per word; $\sigma^2$: standard deviation of number of letters |

## 2.2   Cognitive Domain

The theory developed by Bloom, better known as Bloom's taxonomy, is widely accepted as a guide to set and evaluate academic objectives, and comprises three domains: cognitive, affective and psycho-motor. In particular, the cognitive domain is used to verify cognitive quality [3]. Bloom's cognitive domain consists of six cognitive levels: knowledge, understanding, application, analysis, synthesis and evaluation. A brief description of each cognitive level is presented in Table 2.

Each level can be described by a set of actions that individuals perform regarding a cognitive task, and each action is enunciated by a series of verbs. Table 3 shows a non-exhaustive list of verbs according to the corresponding cognitive level, as presented in [19].

It is predicted that scientific texts have a predominant cognitive level, which is evident by the prevalence of actions as expressed by the verbs in each level of Bloom's cognitive domain. For example, a scientific text can be aimed at *describing, identifying* or *observing* some phenomenon, while another can be aimed at *assessing* the potential benefits of the same phenomenon. In the first case the text would fit in the *knowledge* level, while the second would fit into the *evaluation* level.

Therefore, to prove that scientific texts contain a predominant cognitive level, the same sample of documents mentioned above is characterized according to the cognitive depth. This assessment is performed by identifying first, and then quantifying, the most predominant cognitive-level verbs within the text. Results of this characterization are given in Sect. 3.2. One disadvantage regarding the quantification of the cognitive depth of scientific texts is the absence of a standard list of verbs for each level; for this reason, the characterization results we present are solely based on the list of Table 3.

Table 2. Description of Bloom's levels of the cognitive domain.

| Cognitive level | Description |
| --- | --- |
| Knowledge | To remember or memorize facts. To recall knowledge previously acquired |
| Understanding | To grasp the meaning of information. The ability to interpret, translate, extrapolate or explain concepts |
| Application | To use a concept in a certain scenario |
| Analysis | To breakdown information. To distinguish elements from a whole. To subdivide in components and their relations |
| Synthesis | To integrate and combine ideas by re-arranging components into a new whole |
| Evaluation | To critique, judge, or support an idea or concept |

# 3   Characterization of Scientific Texts

We want to discover the values for legibility and cognitive depth of scientific texts already published, since they represent the convergence of opinions about properly written texts. This characterization is useful to further compare, objectively, how new scientific texts fare in these two metrics.

**Table 3.** Verbs of the cognitive domain according to Bloom's taxonomy.

| Knowledge | Understanding | Application | Analysis | Synthesis | Evaluation |
|---|---|---|---|---|---|
| Describe | Discuss | Change | Analyze | Create | Asses |
| Identify | Explain | Choose | Classify | Design | Choose |
| Recognize | Summarize | Apply | Research | Integrate | Evaluate |
| Record | Arrange | Assess | Compare | Construct | Prioritize |
| Recall | Demonstrate | Modify | Categorize | Combine | Predict |
| List | Distinguish | Operate | Distinguish | Develop | Justify |
| Observe | Translate | Develop | Examine | Compile | Critique |
| Detect | Comprehend | Prepare | Characterize | Re-arrange | Appraise |

## 3.1 Characterization by $\mu$ Legibility

In order to set the legibility range of scientific writings by means of the $\mu$ index, a sample of 72 scientific texts written in Spanish and 72 scientific texts written in English were analyzed. The documents written in English are published journal articles taken from Scopus, while the documents in Spanish were taken from the national repository of the Mexican Council of Science and Technology (CONACyT). Also, to verify that scientific texts possess indeed a distinctive signature, different than other types of writings, 72 texts written for entertainment purposes and 72 news reports, in Spanish, were also characterized.

Figure 1 displays box plots of the $\mu$ legibility for texts in Spanish written for entertainment purposes, news and scientific texts.

The graphic in Fig. 2 shows the resultant box plot of the $\mu$ legibility for scientific texts written in English and Spanish. Afterwards, the probability density function (PDF) was calculated for scientific texts written in Spanish and English. The resultant PDF's of the $\mu$ legibility are depicted in Fig. 3.

The PDF for Spanish writings has a quasi-normal distribution, as it can be observed from Fig. 3. This means that 68% of the *population* lies in the range of $44.3 \pm 4$.

Conversely, for scientific texts written in English the PDF shape has a resemblance of a bimodal PDF. The legibility range for English texts is $57.7 \pm 7.8$.

Then, measures of central tendency are computed: mean ($\bar{x}_z$) and the standard deviation ($\sigma_z^2$), where $z$ stands for either English or Spanish. Those values are shown in Tables 4 and 5. Also the same parameters for sample data are computed assuming that they display a normal distribution. This leads to discover the maximum and minimum values of the *sample*, and the relative difference between the normal-distribution numbers versus the sample. Nevertheless, data from Tables 4 and 5 suggest that the sample can be represented by a quasi-normal distribution.

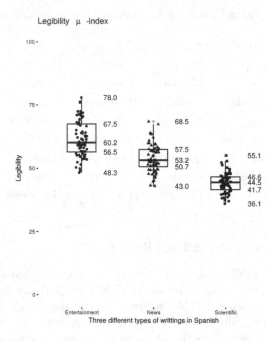

**Fig. 1.** Box plot of the $\mu$ legibility for entertainment texts, news reports and scientific texts written in Spanish

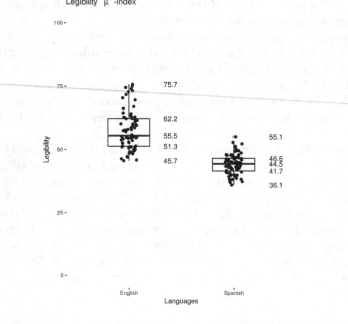

**Fig. 2.** Box plot of the $\mu$ legibility for scientific texts written in English and Spanish

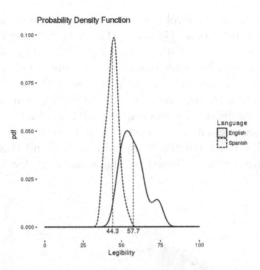

**Fig. 3.** Probability density functions of the $\mu$ legibility for scientific texts written in English and Spanish

**Table 4.** Comparison of values for $\bar{x}_z$ calculated from the sample and from the obtained normal distribution for scientific texts written in Spanish and English

| | $\bar{x}_z$ | | |
| --- | --- | --- | --- |
| Language | Value from sample | Adjusted value | Difference % |
| Spanish | 44.3 | 45.6 | 2.9 |
| English | 57.7 | 60.7 | 4.9 |

**Table 5.** Comparison of values for $\sigma^2$ calculated from the sample and from the obtained normal distribution for scientific texts written in Spanish and English

| | $\sigma_z^2$ | | |
| --- | --- | --- | --- |
| Language | Value from sample | Adjusted value | Difference% |
| Spanish | 4 | 5.6 | 28.6 |
| English | 7.8 | 8.9 | 12.4 |

## 3.2   Characterization by Cognitive Depth

To determine what cognitive level is mostly conveyed within a text we rely on the theory developed by Bloom. By doing this characterization it is possible to answer if the text is aimed at listing facts, in which case it will reside on the *knowledge* level or if, on the other hand, the text presents a critique based on thorough evaluations, fitting into the *evaluation* level.

The characterization by *cognitive depth* is carried by counting the frequency of occurrence of verbs belonging to each cognitive level over the total number of *Bloom verbs* appearing within the text (see in Table 3). Thus, after analyzing seventy-two scientific texts written in Spanish it is found that *analysis* is the predominant cognitive level, followed by the *application* level. The results are represented in Fig. 4.

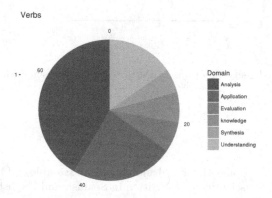

**Fig. 4.** Distribution of the cognitive levels found in the sample of seventy-two scientific texts written in Spanish.

## 4   Initial Design of the Agent-Based System

The agent-based application calculates both indices as writers produce new scientific texts and it indicates whether or not the ongoing manuscript lies within the values that have been determined (See Sect. 3). Three agents are needed to complete this task. First, an Interface Agent receives the text as it is being written and sends it to both, Legibility and Cognitive Agent. These two agents perform their own calculations in parallel and inform the results to Interface Agent., which post the conclusions on the Graphical User Interface (GUI). The agent-based system is being programmed on the JADE platform [2], which allows a smooth integration with the Java libraries that we also developed to calculate the $\mu$ and cognitive depth indices. When the agent-based system informs users that the manuscript displays legibility and cognitive depth values within the mentioned boundaries, they are certain that, at the very least, their document

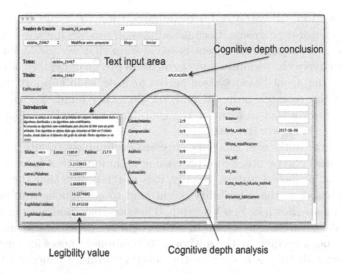

Fig. 5. Graphical User Interface of the agent-based interactive system.

has the same metrics that properly-written scientific documents display. A GUI of the agent system is shown in Fig. 5.

The metrics shown in Fig. 5 are obtained after analyzing an abstract of a PhD thesis in computer science written in Spanish. According to the agent-based system, the $\mu$ legibility is 46.86, which places the text within the acceptable range for scientific texts in Spanish. Also, the Bloom verbs found in the reports make it fall into the *application* cognitive domain. Despite being functional, confirmatory experimentation is needed to validate the metrics and their implementation on an agent-based system. The authors consider using a set of well-written documents and a set of bad-written documents (previously assessed by human experts) and contrast such results with the ones given by their proposal. At this regard, we are set to compare the resultant metrics of nine papers of a thematic issue on authorship analysis, four rejected papers versus five accepted papers. Moreover, to highlight the strengths of the proposed metrics and the weakness of previous ones the same corpus must be assessed with other metrics already proposed in the literature.

## 5   Conclusions

It is confirmed the existence of normal probability distributions for scientific texts written in Spanish and English, for the $\mu$ legibility. As for cognitive depth, it is confirmed the existence of a predominant cognitive level, *analysis*, for scientific texts written in Spanish. These findings lead to determine whether a scientific text legibility and cognitive depth are similar to already published scientific documents.

The implications are various, for example, during the evaluation process of prospects to doctoral programs. Because admission process includes the submission of a research proposal, the agent-based system that we developed allows to measure objectively the legibility and cognitive depth as indicators of its quality. In this sense, the agent-based system serves as a decision support tool for the evaluators of the research proposal and, on the other hand, for the prospects because they have a tool to monitor the legibility and cognitive depth as their manuscripts are being constructed.

Also, since the authors of this paper present preliminary results, it is imperative to assess and choose other text processing techniques that improve the performance of the proposed system. Finally, it is worth noting that the mere analysis of texts based on the $\mu$ legibility might lead to ambiguous results, because some of the values shown in Fig. 1 overlap. This possible ambiguity in the classification result is overcome by evaluating the cognitive depth of the manuscripts. This fact has been verified by the authors: entertainment notes and news report do not present a distinguishable cognitive level according to Bloom's theory.

# References

1. Abbott, B.P., et al.: Observation of gravitational waves from a binary black hole merger. Phys. Rev. Lett. **116**, 1–18 (2016)
2. Bellifemine, F.L., Caire, G., Greenwood, D.: Developing Multi-Agent Systems with JADE. Wiley, USA (2007)
3. Bloom, B.S.: Taxonomy of Educational Objectives. Handbook I. Cognitive Domain. Longman, London (1956)
4. Cheng, G.: The impact of online autometed feedback on students' reflective journal writing in an EFL course. Internet High. Educ. **34**, 18–27 (2017)
5. Dunham, W., Malone, S.: Einstein's gravitational waves detected in landmark discovery (2016). http://www.Reuters.com. Accessed 17 May 2017
6. Fernández Huerta, J.: Medidas sencillas de lecturabilidad. Consigna Revista Pedagóiga (1959)
7. Ferrero, C.L., Renau, I., Nazar, R., Torner, S.: Computer-assisted revision in spanish academic texts: peer-assessment. Procedia - Soc. Behav. Sci. **141**, 470–483 (2014)
8. Flesh, R.F.: Legibility. Teach. Coll. Rec. **6**, 422–423 (1944)
9. Grundy, D.: Writing-anxiety. Arts Psychother. **12**, 151–156 (1985)
10. Hanjani, A.M., Li, L.: Exploring L2 writer's collaborative revision interactions and their writing performance. System **44**, 101–114 (2014)
11. Jamalinesari, A., Rahimi, F., Gowhary, H., Azizifar, A.: The effects of teacher-written direct vs. indirect feedback on student's writing. Procedia - Soc. Behav. Sci. **192**, 116–123 (2015)
12. Lachner, A., Burkhart, C., Nückles, M.: Formative computer-based feedback in the university classroom: specific concepts maps scaffold student's writing. Comput. Hum. Behav. **72**, 459–469 (2017)
13. Larivière, V.: On the shoulders of students? The contribution of PhD students to the advancement of knowledge. Scientometrics **90**, 463–481 (2012)
14. Levecque, K., Anseel, F., Beuckelaer, A.D., der Heyden, J.V., Gisle, L.: Work organization and mental health problems in Ph.D. students. Res. Policy **46**, 868–879 (2017)

15. Michelle Cleary, J., Daly, G.W.: Dealing with peer-review: what is reasonable and what is not? Collegian **20**, 123–125 (2013)
16. Munoz y Munoz, J.: Legibilidad $\mu$, Chile (2006)
17. Nemec, E.C., Dintzner, M.: Comparison of audio versus written feedback on writing assignments. Curr. Pharm. Teach. Learn. **8**, 155–159 (2016)
18. Onwuegbuzie, A.J.: Writing a research proposal: the role of library anxiety, statistics anxiety, and composition anxiety. Libr. Inf. Sci. Res. **19**, 5–33 (1997)
19. Pierrakos, E.P.O., Nagel, R.: Using bloom's taxonomy to teach sustainability in multiple contexts. J. Clean. Prod. **48**, 54 64 (2014)
20. Sullivan, V.L.K.P.: Writing academic English as a doctoral student in Sweden: narrative perspectives. J. Second Lang. Writ. **35**, 20–25 (2017)
21. Szigrist Pazos, F.: Sistemas productivos de legibilidad del mensaje escrito: fórmula de perspicuidad. Universidad Politéncima de Madrid, Facultad de ciencias de la Información. Colección de Tesis Doctorales (2017)
22. Çinar Yastibaş, G., Yastibaş, A.E.: The effect of peer feedback on writen anxiety in Turkish EFL (English as a foreign language) students. Procedia - Soc. Behav. Sci. **199**, 530–538 (2015)

# Automatic Generation of Multi-document Summaries Based on the Global-Best Harmony Search Metaheuristic and the LexRank Graph-Based Algorithm

César Cuéllar$^{(\boxtimes)}$, Martha Mendoza, and Carlos Cobos

Information Technology Research Group (GTI), Universidad del Cauca,
Popayán, Colombia
{cmcuellar, mmendoza, ccobos}@unicauca.edu.co

**Abstract.** Recently, metaheuristic based algorithms have shown good results in generating automatic multi-document summaries. This paper proposes two algorithms that hybridize the metaheuristic of Global Best Harmony Search and the LexRank Graph based algorithm, called LexGbhs and GbhsLex. The objective function to be optimized is composed of the features of coverage and diversity. Coverage measures the similarity between each sentence of the candidate summary and the centroid of the sentences of the collection of documents, while diversity measures how different the sentences that make up a candidate summary are. The two proposed hybrid algorithms were compared with state of the art algorithms using ROUGE-1, ROUGE-2 and ROUGE-SU4 measurements for the DUC2005 and DUC2006 data sets. After a unified classification was carried out, the LexGbhs algorithm proposed ranked third, showing that the hybridization of metaheuristics with graphs in the generation of extractive summaries of multiple documents is a promising line of research.

**Keywords:** Multi-document extractive summarization · Metaheuristics
Global-Best Harmony Search algorithm · LexRank algorithm
Hybrid algorithms

## 1  Introduction

The growth in digital documents on the internet presents a real challenge. Users of the Net require to extract information that is as relevant as possible, related to a specific topic, and the time required to obtain that information constitutes one of the biggest problems, given the number of documents and the redundant information these inevitably contain. Therefore, it is necessary to have algorithms that identify the most representative sentences of a collection of documents in a summary. The automatic generation of document summaries addresses this problem, seeking to create using a range of different techniques, summaries that are most similar to those generated by humans. Some of the most common applications in the automatic generation of extractive text summaries are the summaries of one or multiple news items, news broadcast programs, email threads, medical information, scientific articles, recordings of meetings, spontaneous dialogues, voicemail, and video broadcasting, among others [1].

© Springer Nature Switzerland AG 2018
F. Castro et al. (Eds.): MICAI 2017, LNAI 10633, pp. 82–94, 2018.
https://doi.org/10.1007/978-3-030-02840-4_7

Summaries can be classified according to [2, 3]: *the sentences that make up the summary*, extractives that use original text sentences and abstractives that may include sentences that are not part of the original text, requiring the use of linguistic analysis tools; *the target audience*, generics that do not depend on the audience of the summary, based on queries that respond to a query, focused on the user that generate the summary according to the interests of a particular user and focused on topics that emphasize one topic in particular; *the number of documents processed*, of one or multiple documents; *the language*, monolingual or multilingual; and *genre*, such as news, blogs, scientific articles, etc.

In the automatic generation of summaries of multiple documents, the methods used have been based on [3]: *text connectivity* [4], which performs text segmentation and identifies lexical chains and their relationships in terms of WordNet[1] distance; *algebraic reduction* [5, 6], through latent semantic analysis and Non-negative matrix factorization to find the most significant sentences that represent documents, performing decomposition of non-negative matrices, or singular values decomposition; machine learning techniques [7, 8], using sentence grouping and assignment of scores based on the entropy of a reduced set of sentences; *graphs* [9–12], representing the set of sentences as an non-directed graph, in which the nodes are the sentences and the arcs the relation of similarity between pairs of sentences; *clustering and probabilistic models* [13, 14], which generate groups of sentences associated with a particular topic; *metaheuristics* (differential evolution, genetic algorithms and memory algorithms) [15–17], which seek to optimize an objective function to find the sentences that will form part of the summary. There are metaheuristics that have contributed to the solution of continuous and discrete problems, showing good results. These include Global-Best Harmony Search (GBHS) [18], but so far they have not been used to solve the problem of automatic generation of summaries for multiple documents; DESAMC+DOCSUM [17], is a proposal where the multi-document summarization process is solved as a p-medians optimization problem and the solution is searched with a new differential evolution algorithm based on self-adaptive mutation and crossover parameters. This approach expresses the relationship of sentence with sentence, summary to document and summary to subtopics; MA-MultiSumm [16], is a memetic algorithm that combines genetic operators (CHC) with a greedy local search, which is among the leading methods in the state of the art. However, an additional effort is required for the configuration of the operators of selection, crossover, mutation, replacement and local search; *Hybrids* [19, 20] where two metaheuristics cooperate and combine optimization methods to improve results that are obtained individually. Despite all these previous research, the quality of the obtained results can be improved, searching for summaries similar to those generated by humans.

This paper proposes two algorithms for automatic multi-document summarization that hybridize the GBHS metaheuristic with local search and the LexRank algorithm, Leveraging GBHS' strengths to explore and exploit search space on high dimensionality problems with presence of noise [21]; and on the other hand, Lexrank's strength in defining the degree of centrality of sentences with respect to the collection of documents (graph).

---

[1] WordNet is a lexico-conceptual database of the English language structured in the form of a semantic network, comprising lexical units and the relationships between them.

The rest of the article is organized as follows: Sect. 2 presents the representation of the document and the features of the objective function of the proposed algorithms. The base algorithms that form part of the proposed hybrid algorithms are found in Sect. 3. The proposed algorithms are described in the Sect. 4, while the results of the experimentation and evaluation, which include comparison and analysis with other methods of the state of the art, are found in Sect. 5, and finally Sect. 6 presents conclusions and future work.

## 2　Problem Statement and Its Mathematical Formulation

A document collection can be represented [22] as, $D = \{d_1, \ldots, d_j, \ldots, d_k\}$, where $k$ is the number of documents. Each document $d_j$ contains a set of sentences, therefore $d_j = \{s_1, s_2, \ldots, s_p\}$, where $p$ is the number of sentences in $d_j$. In this way the collection of documents can be represented as the set of all sentences in the collection, i.e. $D = \{s_1, \ldots, s_j, \ldots, s_n\}$, where $s_j$ denotes the $j$-th sentence in $D$, and $n$ is the number of sentences in the collection, $s_j \in D$ if and only if $s_j \epsilon d_j \epsilon D$. Likewise, sentences are represented by the set of terms that appear in $D$, $s_i = \{t_{i1}, t_{i2}, \ldots, t_{ik}, ..t_{im}\}$, where $t_{ik}$ is the k-th term of sentence $s_i$ and $m$ is the total number of terms in the sentence.

Given the above, considering the vector space model [22] to represent a sentence $s_j$, with $t_i$ terms that are weighted according to their importance ($w_{ij}$); then each sentence $s_j$ is represented by a vector as shown in Eq. (1).

$$s_j = \left(w_{j1}, ..w_{ji}, \ldots, w_{jm}\right) \tag{1}$$

where $m$ is the number of different terms in the document collection, $w_{ij}$ represents the weight of the $i$-th term of sentence $s_j$. $w_{ij}$ is calculated as the relative frequency of the term in the document [22], according to Eq. (2).

$$w_{ij} = (f_{ij}) * \log(N/n_j) \tag{2}$$

where $f_{ij}$ is the frequency of the term $i$ in sentence $j$, $N$ is the total number of sentences and $n_j$ is the number of sentences in which the term $i$ appears.

The purpose of generating a summary of multiple documents is to obtain sentences containing the most relevant information from the document collection, in this case, using features that enable the similarity between sentences to be measured, using cosine similarity [22]. Thus:

**Coverage:** Selects the most relevant sentences contained in the document collection with the least loss of information. This coverage is calculated by considering the cosine similarity between each sentence of the candidate summary and the sentences of the entire document collection, as shown in Eq. (3).

$$\text{Coverage} = \frac{\sum_{i=1}^{o} \text{sim}(D, s_i)}{o} \tag{3}$$

where $o$ is the number of sentences selected in the candidate summary, $D$ represents the centroid of the document collection, $sim(D, s_i)$ is the cosine similarity between the centroid vector of the document collection and the vector that represents the sentence.

**Diversity:** Seeks to avoid that the summary generated contains repeated information, given that the document collection deals with the same subject. Diversity is calculated by means of the average similarity of the sentences in the candidate summary. See Eq. (4).

$$Diversity = \frac{\sum_{i=1}^{n-1} \sum_{j=i+1}^{n} \left(1 - sim\left(s_i, s_j\right)\right)}{(n * (n-1)/2)} \tag{4}$$

where $s_i$ and $s_j$ are sentences in the candidate summary, $n$ is the number of sentences in the summary, and $sim(s_i, s_j)$ is the cosine similarity between sentences $s_i$ and $s_j$.

As such, the objective function to be maximized comprises the features of coverage and diversity, as can be seen in Eq. (5), which includes a restriction on the maximum number of words allowed in the summary (Eq. (6)) and a restriction where the sum of the weights must be equal to one (Eq. (7)).

$$\text{Maximize } (F(x)) = \alpha * Coverage + \beta * Diversity \tag{5}$$

Subject to:

$$\sum_{i=1}^{n} l_i x_i \leq L \tag{6}$$

$$\alpha + \beta = 1 \tag{7}$$

In Eq. (6), $x_i$ indicates one if the sentence $s_i$ is selected and zero otherwise; $l_i$ is the length of the sentence $s_i$ (measured in words) and $L$ is the maximum number of words allowed in the summary.

## 3 Base Algorithms

### 3.1 Global-Best Harmony Search

Global-Best Harmony Search (GBHS) [23] is a metaheuristic algorithm based on the musical process that seeks a perfect state of harmony. The improvisation process in musicians is comparable to the global and local search schemes of optimization techniques. The GBHS algorithm with local search [16] used in this research can be summarized in the following steps: (1) *Initialize the population*: The Harmony Memory (HM) is initialized randomly taking into account Harmony Memory size (HMS). In a harmony (vector solution) the sentences of the document collection are represented, where one indicates the presence of the sentence in the candidate summary and zero otherwise. When initializing each harmony, half of the sentences are placed in one (1) using a probability of 0.5 and then a repair process is applied, including knowledge of the problem to remove the sentences that contribute least to the summary (similarity between a sentence and document collection, divided by the length of the sentence), i.e. the sentences with less coverage to the collection of documents. This process is repeated until the maximum number of words in the summary restriction is fulfilled. (2) *Evaluate the initial population*: The fitness for each harmony in the memory is calculated based on Eq. (5). (3) *Optimize the initial population*: Each harmony in the initial population is optimized by means of a local search algorithm with a greedy approach, according to a probability of optimization. For each harmony to be optimized, a number of neighbours is created, defined by the maximum number of optimizations specified. A neighbour is generated by adding and removing sentences according to the coverage feature, i.e. the sentence with the greatest similarity to the document collection (from a list of the sentences ordered by this criterion) is added to the harmony (allocating a one) and from the same list the sentence with the least similarity is removed, controlling the number of sentences in the summary by means of the restriction in Eq. (6). The harmony is replaced by the neighbor only if the fitness value of the neighbor improves the fitness of the harmony. (4) *Improvise the new harmony*: The new harmony vector is generated taking into account the three rules defined in GHS [23]: consideration of HM, adjustment of tone based on Particle Swarm Optimization (PSO) concepts, and random selection of the space search. If necessary, the same repair process explained above is performed. Fitness is calculated for the new harmony and it is optimized according to a probability of optimization. Finally, the worst harmony in HM is replaced, by the new harmony, only if its fitness value is worse than the fitness of the new harmony.

### 3.2  LexRank

Erkan and Radev in [9], present the LexRank algorithm with a threshold, based on the "prestige"[2] concept of social networks, which is a map of relations between interacting entities and is commonly represented in the form of graphs, where the nodes represent the entities and the links represent the relationships between the nodes. A set of documents can be represented as a network of related sentences, some being similar to others, some sharing little information with the rest of the sentences. If a sentence is very similar to many of the other sentences, it is considered as the most central (outstanding) or representative of a topic. The algorithm determines the centrality of the sentences based on the similarity matrix of all the sentences of the documents, by means of cosine similarity. The LexRank algorithm can be summarized in the following steps: (1) *Calculate the cosine similarity matrix between the sentences in the document collection*: Representation of the weights of sentences is performed according to Eq. (2) and the sentences in the documents are represented as a graph by means of an adjacency matrix between sentences, where each value corresponds to the cosine similarity between the sentences in the document collection. (2) *Eliminate weak*

---

[2] Prestige and centrality in this proposal represent the same concept, with the difference that the first is usually defined for directed graphs, the second for undirected graphs.

*relations between sentences*: uses the threshold parameter to eliminate weak relationships between sentences, i.e. those nodes with a cosine similarity that does not exceed the threshold value. (3) *Normalize the matrix so that there is a stochastic matrix*: Each row is represented as a vector of changes of state with probabilities that add up to one. This is accomplished initially by adding each row of the similarity matrix to obtain the rank of each row and then dividing each element of the matrix by the degree of the row in which it is found. (4) *Ensure that the matrix is irreducible and aperiodic*: A Markov chain is irreducible if any state is accessible from any other state, i.e. for all $i,j$ exists $n$ such that $X^n(i,j) \neq 0$. A Markov chain is aperiodic if for everything $i$, $\gcd\{n : X^n(i,i) > 0\} = 1$. A damping factor is used, whose value is set between [0.0, 0.2] according to experience. Equation (8) shows how this factor affects the stochastic matrix, rendering it irreducible and aperiodic. (5) *Run the PowerMethod algorithm to find the resulting vector with the sentence scores*: The Markov chains convergence property provides a simple iterative algorithm, called PowerMethod, to calculate the stationary distribution. The algorithm begins with a uniform distribution where each sentence represented in the vector $P_0$ has equal weight (importance). In each iteration, the eigenvector is updated by multiplying it with the transpose of the stochastic matrix. To verify when the algorithm ends, the *error Tolerance* parameter is set at 0.01. (6) *Select the sentences that will form part of the summary*: Sentences are ordered from highest to lowest according to the value in the resulting vector. High-value sentences are included in the summary until maximum summary size is reached or stop criteria fulfilled.

$$Csm[i][j] = \left(\frac{dampingFactor}{n}\right) + (1 - dampingFactor) * Csm[i][j] \qquad (8)$$

## 4  The Proposed Hybrid Algorithms

### 4.1  LexGbhs

This proposed algorithm for the automatic generation of extractive summaries hybridizes LexRank [9] and GBHS [16], called LexGbhs (Fig. 1). This algorithm first executes the LexRank algorithm (see Sect. 3.2), from which a vector is obtained with the sentence weighting ordered from most relevant to least relevant. A modification was made to the iterative *PowerMethod* algorithm used by LexRank, where the initial vector $P_0$ with all sentences (nodes of the graph) no longer start with equal weight (relevance), but the initial weight of the sentences is based on the coverage (similarity between the sentence and the collection of the documents) divided by the sum of all similarities of the sentences. In LexGbhs a *Pruning* parameter is defined that allows to remove the least significant sentences and updates the cosine similarity matrix due to the reduced number of sentences. Then, with these sentences obtained from the pruning process, LexGbhs continues with running GBHS (see Sect. 3.1) and generates the summary with the sentences with the best harmony from the Harmony Memory, considering the restriction on the maximum number of words in the summary.

```
01    Hms=Harmony Memory Size, HM=Harmony Memory, Po=Probability of Optimization,
02    Csm=Cosine Similarity Matrix, Pruning=Rate of Sentence Removal
03    S(n)=Vector with sentences, P(n)=Vector resulting LexRank with the weights of sentences(relevance)
04    Neof=Number of evaluations of the objective function, Mneof=Maximum Neof
05    Begin                                    //Start LexGbhs
06    BeginLexRank                             //Start LexRank
07        For i=1 to n
08            sum=0
09            For j=1 to n                     //Calculate cosine similarity matrix
10                Csm[i][j] = idf-modified-cosine(S[i], S[j])
11                if Csm[i][j] > threshold     //Eliminate weak relationships
12                    sum += Csm[i][j]
13                else
14                    Csm[i][j] = 0
15                End if
16            End For
17            For j=1 to n                     //Normalize csm to stochastic matrix
18                Csm[i][j] = Csm[i][j] / sum;
19            End For
20        End For
21        For i=1 to n                         //Make the csm matrix irreducible and aperiodic
22            For j=1 to n
23                Csm[i][j] = (dampingFactor/n) + (1- dampingFactor) * csm[i][j];
24            End For
25        End For
26        P = PowerMethod (Csm, n, errorTolerance)    //Vector with the weights of sentences
27        Sort(P)                              //Sort from highest to lowest resulting vector
28    EndLexRank
29    //ApplyPruning
30    P = ApplyPruning (n,Pruning)             //Apply pruning to resulting vector of LexRank
31    UpdateMS(P)                              //Update the similarity matrix
32    BeginGbhs                                //Start Gbhs
33        InitializeHM (Hms)                   //Initialize the harmony memory
34        EvaluateHM ()                        //Evaluate the harmony memory
35        OptimizeHM (Po)                      //Optimize the harmony memory
36        Neof=1
37        While (Neof<Mneof)
38            CurrentPar = PAR (parmin, parmax, nofe, mnfe)
39            Do
40                NH.Longitud = 0;                     //Length of new harmony
41                while (NH.Longitud <= L)             //while not exceeding maximum # of words
42                    If (U(0,1) < hmcr)               //rule of memory consideration
43                        i = rand (hms)               //Select a random memory position
44                        If (U(0,1) < CurrentPar)     //Tone adjustment rule
45                            i=best                   //position of the best harmony
46                        End If
47                        dimension = rand(HM[i].SelectedSentences)
48                    Else                             //rule of random selection
49                        dimension = rand(n)
50                    End if
51                    If (NH[dimension] = 1) Continue While
52                    NH[dimension] = 1
53                    NH.Longitud += LengthSentence[dimension]
54                End While
55                NH.Evaluar ()                        //Calculate the fitness of the new harmony
56                NH.Optimizar ()                      //Try to optimize the new harmony
57                If (nofe >= mnofe) Exit While
58            While(HM.Exists(NH))
59            If (NH.Fitness > HM[HMS].Fitness)
```

**Fig. 1.** Diagram of LexGbhs hybrid algorithm

```
60                    HM[worse] = NH
61            End if
62        End While
63    EndGbhs
64    GenerateSummary (HM(0))              //select sentences from the best harmony
65    End
```

**Fig. 1.** (*continued*)

## 4.2   GbhsLex

This algorithm is also a hybrid between LexRank [9] and GBHS [16], called GbhsLex (Fig. 2). But in this case, the algorithm runs the GBHS first, obtaining as a result the last population of the harmony memory, from which non-repeated sentences are selected. GbhsLex then requires the similarity array to be updated due to the reduction in the number of sentences. Then, GbhsLex runs LexRank, which does not change with respect to the first algorithm proposed in Sect. 4.1, and when its run has finished, it also delivers a vector that contains the weighting of the sentences ordered from the highest to the lowest value of significance. Finally, GbhsLex generates the summary including the sentences that have the highest weighting until the maximum size of the summary is reached.

```
01    Hms=Harmony Memory Size, HM=Harmony Memory, Po=Probability of Optimization,
02    Csm=Cosine Similarity Matrix, Pruning=Rate of Sentence Removal
03    S(n)=Vector with sentences, P(n)=Vector resulting LexRank with the weights of sentenc-
es(relevance)
04    Neof=Number of evaluations of the objective function, Mneof=Maximum Neof
05    Begin                             //Start GbhsLex
06        Execute Gbhs                  //Code Lines 32 to 63 in LexGbhs (Figure 1)
07        S = GetDifferentPhrases (HM)  //Get Different phrases of the Harmony Memory
08        UpdateMS(S)                   //Update the similarity matrix
09        Execute LexRank               //Code Lines 6 to 28 in LexGbhs (Figure 1)
10        GenerateSummary (P)           //select sentences from P to maximum length of summary
11    End
```

**Fig. 2.** Diagram of GbhsLex hybrid algorithm

## 5   Experimentation and Evaluation

To evaluate the proposed hybrid algorithms LexGbhs and GbhsLex, the datasets of the Document Understanding Conference (DUC) were used for the years 2005 and 2006.

Before performing the process of automatic generation of summaries of multiple documents, pre-processing of the documents is performed, which includes linguistic techniques such as: *segmentation of sentences, stop word removal, removal of capital letters* and *punctuation marks, stemming process,* and *indexing.*

The metrics provided by the ROUGE [24] evaluation tool, version 1.5.5, are accepted by DUC and the academic community as official metrics for the evaluation of automatic summaries. To evaluate the quality of the summaries generated by LexGbhs and GbhsLex, the ROUGE-1, ROUGE-2 and ROUGE-SU4 measures were used.

The proposed algorithms were compared with the GBHS [21], LexRank [9], DESAMC+DocSum [17], SVR [7], LEX [14], TMR [8], Centroid [12], Hiersum [13], SNMF+SLSS [6], and MA-Multisumm [16] methods.

## 5.1  Parameter Tuning

Because the two proposed hybrid algorithms contain several parameters for their tuning, covering arrays [25] were used to obtain a smaller group of combinations of the parameters.

For the tuning process, a data set was created consisting of 15 randomly selected topics from the DUC2005 data set and 15 randomly selected topics from the DUC2006. Then we performed the experimentation through 30 runs per configuration (combination of parameters) and the 10 best configurations were selected. With these best configurations, the experiments were carried out on the entire DUC2005 and DUC2006 datasets to obtain the best parameter configuration shown in Table 1.

**Table 1.** The parameters for the best configuration of the LexGbhs and GbhsLex

| Parameter | LexGbhs | GbhsLex |
|---|---|---|
| Alpha | 0.35 | 0.30 |
| Beta | 0.65 | 0.70 |
| Threshold | 0.04 | 0.00 |
| dampingFactor | 0.12 | 0.12 |
| ToleranceError | 0.01 | 0.01 |
| Hms | 20 | 5 |
| Hmcr | 0.90 | 0.90 |
| Po | 0.90 | 0.50 |
| Nop | 10 | 10 |
| Pruning | 0.30 | 0.00 |
| Msle | 275 | 285 |

The parameters are harmony memory size (Hms), harmony memory consideration rate (Hmcr), probability of optimization (Po), number of optimizations (Nop), maximum summary length to evolve (Msle), LexRank threshold (Threshold), dampingFactor and Pruning. Likewise, the best combinations were selected for the weights of the objective function (alpha and beta). The number of evaluations of the objective function was set at 15.000, to make a comparison with the other metaheuristic algorithms under the same conditions. The tolerance error of the PowerMethod algorithm was set at 0.01. The maximum length of the summary measured in words was set at 250.

## 5.2   Results

Table 2 presents the results obtained in the ROUGE measurements for the proposed algorithms LexGbhs and GbhsLex, together with other state-of-the-art methods on the DUC2005 and DUC2006 datasets. The best solution is presented in bold, and the column after each ROUGE measurement indicates the classification of each method. The LexGbhs algorithm on the DUC2005 dataset is only outperformed by the MA-Multisum and DESAMC +DocSum methods in all ROUGE measurements. On the DUC2006 dataset, LexGbhs occupies third position in the ROUGE-1 measure, and sixth in the other two measures.

**Table 2.** Rouge values for methods on DUC2005 and DUC2006

| Method | DUC2005 | | | | | | DUC2006 | | | | | |
|---|---|---|---|---|---|---|---|---|---|---|---|---|
| | ROUGE-1 | | ROUGE-2 | | ROUGE-SU4 | | ROUGE-1 | | ROUGE-2 | | ROUGE-SU4 | |
| DESAMC +DocSum | 0.3937 | 2 | 0.0822 | 2 | 0.1418 | 2 | **0.4345** | 1 | **0.0989** | 1 | **0.1569** | 1 |
| MA-MultiSumm | **0.4001** | 1 | **0.0868** | 1 | **0.1434** | 1 | 0.4195 | 2 | 0.0986 | 2 | 0.1526 | 2 |
| LexGbhs* | 0.3899 | 3 | 0.0790 | 3 | 0.1363 | 3 | 0.4066 | 3 | 0.0889 | 6 | 0.1444 | 6 |
| SVR | 0.3849 | 5 | 0.0757 | 6 | 0.1335 | 6 | 0.4018 | 7 | 0.0926 | 3 | 0.1483 | 4 |
| GBHS | 0.3844 | 6 | 0.0774 | 4 | 0.1352 | 5 | 0.4023 | 6 | 0.0880 | 7 | 0.1438 | 7 |
| TMR | 0.3775 | 8 | 0.0715 | 10 | 0.1304 | 10 | 0.4063 | 4 | 0.0913 | 4 | 0.1504 | 3 |
| LEX | 0.3760 | 9 | 0.0735 | 9 | 0.1316 | 9 | 0.4030 | 5 | 0.0913 | 5 | 0.1449 | 5 |
| LexRank | 0.3868 | 4 | 0.0767 | 5 | 0.1354 | 4 | 0.4006 | 9 | 0.0848 | 11 | 0.1419 | 10 |
| HierSum | 0.3753 | 10 | 0.0745 | 8 | 0.1324 | 8 | 0.4010 | 8 | 0.0860 | 8 | 0.1430 | 8 |
| GbhsLex* | 0.3798 | 7 | 0.0755 | 7 | 0.1335 | 7 | 0.3946 | 11 | 0.0855 | 9 | 0.1404 | 11 |
| SNMF +SLSS | 0.3501 | 12 | 0.0604 | 12 | 0.1172 | 12 | 0.3955 | 10 | 0.0855 | 10 | 0.1429 | 9 |
| Centroid | 0.3535 | 11 | 0.0638 | 11 | 0.1198 | 11 | 0.3807 | 12 | 0.0785 | 12 | 0.1330 | 12 |

To identify which method obtains the best results on both datasets, a unified classification is presented taking into account the position of each of the methods for each measure. In Table 3, the *Rank* column indicates the position in the classification, a value which is calculated according to Eq. (9).

$$Rank(M) = \sum_{r=1}^{12} \frac{((12 - r + 1)R_r)}{12} \tag{9}$$

Where $R_r$ indicates the number of times that the method $M$ appears in the r-th rank and $M$ is each one of the methods. The number 12 corresponds to the number of methods with which the comparison was made.

Considering the results in Table 3, the following can be observed:

– LexGbhs is only outperformed by the methods based on metaheuristics, DESAMC +DocSum and MA-Multisum (these two occupy joint first place). However, LexGbhs does not require effort for the configuration of operators such as selection, crossover, mutation, replacement, and local search, as MA-Multisum requires.

**Table 3.** The resulting ranking of the methods

| Method | 1 | 2 | 3 | 4 | 5 | 6 | 7 | 8 | 9 | 10 | 11 | 12 | Rank |
|---|---|---|---|---|---|---|---|---|---|---|---|---|---|
| DESAMC+DocSum | 3 | 3 | 0 | 0 | 0 | 0 | 0 | 0 | 0 | 0 | 0 | 0 | 5.8 |
| MA-MultiSumm | 3 | 3 | 0 | 0 | 0 | 0 | 0 | 0 | 0 | 0 | 0 | 0 | 5.8 |
| LexGbhs* | 0 | 0 | 4 | 0 | 0 | 2 | 0 | 0 | 0 | 0 | 0 | 0 | 4.5 |
| SVR | 0 | 0 | 1 | 1 | 1 | 2 | 1 | 0 | 0 | 0 | 0 | 0 | 3.9 |
| GBHS | 0 | 0 | 0 | 1 | 1 | 2 | 2 | 0 | 0 | 0 | 0 | 0 | 3.6 |
| TMR | 0 | 0 | 1 | 2 | 0 | 0 | 0 | 1 | 0 | 2 | 0 | 0 | 3.3 |
| LEX | 0 | 0 | 0 | 0 | 3 | 0 | 0 | 0 | 3 | 0 | 0 | 0 | 3.0 |
| LexRank | 0 | 0 | 0 | 2 | 1 | 0 | 0 | 0 | 1 | 1 | 1 | 0 | 2.9 |
| HierSum | 0 | 0 | 0 | 0 | 0 | 0 | 0 | 5 | 0 | 1 | 0 | 0 | 2.3 |
| GbhsLex* | 0 | 0 | 0 | 0 | 0 | 0 | 3 | 0 | 1 | 0 | 2 | 0 | 2.2 |
| SNMF+SLSS | 0 | 0 | 0 | 0 | 0 | 0 | 0 | 0 | 1 | 2 | 0 | 3 | 1.1 |
| Centroid | 0 | 0 | 0 | 0 | 0 | 0 | 0 | 0 | 0 | 0 | 3 | 3 | 0.8 |

– LexGbhs occupies a better position than methods based on: metaheuristics, GBHS (fifth position); graphs, LexRank (eighth Position); algebraic reduction, SVR (fourth position), SNMF+SLSS (eleventh position) that uses non-negative symmetric matrix factorization to group sentences; clustering and probabilistic models, TMR (sixth position), to estimate the distribution of topics, LEX (seventh position) clustering of terms, Centroid (twelfth position) clustering of centroids.
– GbhsLex occupies a better position than Centroid and SNMF+SLSS; and obtains results equal to Hiersum (eighth position), which uses probabilistic models.

# 6   Conclusions and Future Work

This article proposes two hybrid algorithms for the automatic generation of extractive summaries of multiple documents. The first, LexGbhs, executes the LexRank algorithm, performs a pruning process on the set of sentences it delivers, executes GBHS with these sentences and generates the summary. The second, GbhsLex, executes GBHS first. The non-repeated sentences of the last population then form the input for LexRank, and it finally generates the summary.

The two proposed algorithms were evaluated using the ROUGE-1, ROUGE-2 and ROUGE-SU4 measures, along with other state-of-the-art methods, on the DUC2005 and DUC2006 datasets, resulting in the LexGbhs algorithm occupying third position and surpassed only by the MA-MultiSumm and DESAMC+DocSum methods (in joint first position). However, Lex-Gbhs does not require effort for the configuration of operators such as: selection, crossing, mutation, replacement, and local search, as MA-Multisum does.

Regarding the objective function, in the best results for the two proposed algorithms, LexGbhs and GbhsLex, diversity is the feature with the greatest weight, with values of 0.65 and 0.7, respectively. This indicates the importance of avoiding that the summary contains sentences that repeat the same information in the case of the automatic generation of multiple document summaries dealing with the same topic.

In terms of future work, it is expected: that experiments would be carried out with other local search algorithms, considering the specific features of the automatic generation of summaries. It is also hoped to include other features in the objective function, such as the position of the sentence in each document, the length of the sentences, and to allow sentences to be obtained that are more relevant to the content of the documents. In addition, it is hoped to carry out experiments with other datasets to explore other types of document generes.

# References

1. Nenkova, A.: Automatic summarization. In: Foundations and Trends® in Information Retrieval, vol. 5, pp. 103–233 (2011)
2. Lloret, E., Palomar, M.: Text summarisation in progress: a literature review. Artif. Intell. Rev. **37**, 1–41 (2011)
3. Becerra, M.E.M., Guzmán, E.L.: A review of the extractive text summarization. Revista Facultad de Ingenierías Fisicomecánicas UIS Ingenierías **12**, 7–27 (2013)
4. Chen, Y.-M., Wang, X.-L., Liu, B.-Q.: Multi-document summarization based on lexical chains. In: Proceedings of 2005 International Conference on Machine Learning and Cybernetics, vol. 3, pp. 1937–1942 (2005)
5. Park, S., Cha, B.: Query-based multi-document summarization using non-negative semantic feature and NMF clustering, pp. 609–614 (2008)
6. Wang, D., Li, T., Zhu, S., Ding, C.: Multi-document summarization via sentence-level semantic analysis and symmetric matrix factorization. Presented at the 31st Annual International ACM SIGIR Conference on Research and Development in Information Retrieval, Singapore (2008)
7. Ouyang, Y., Li, W., Li, S., Lu, Q.: Applying regression models to query-focused multi-document summarization. Inf. Process. Manag. **47**, 227–237 (2011)
8. Tang, J., Yao, L., Chen, D.: Multi-topic based query-oriented summarization. Presented at the SIAM International Conference on Data Mining, Nevada, USA (2009)
9. Erkan, G., Radev, D.R.: LexRank: graph-based lexical centrality as salience in text summarization. Artif. Intell. Res. **22**, 457–479 (2004)
10. Zhang, J., Cheng, X., Xu, H.: GSPSummary: a graph-based sub-topic partition algorithm for summarization. In: Li, H., Liu, T., Ma, W.-Y., Sakai, T., Wong, K.-F., Zhou, G. (eds.) AIRS 2008. LNCS, vol. 4993, pp. 321–334. Springer, Heidelberg (2008). https://doi.org/10.1007/978-3-540-68636-1_31
11. Ferreira, R., et al.: A multi-document summarization system based on statistics and linguistic treatment. Expert Syst. Appl. **41**, 5780–5787 (2014)
12. Radev, D.R., Jing, H., Budzikowska, M.: Centroid-based summarization of multiple documents: sentence extraction, utility-based evaluation, and user studies. Inf. Process. Manag. **40**(6), 919–938 (2004)
13. Haghighi, A., Vanderwende, L.: Exploring content models for multi-document summarization. Presented at the Conference of the North American Chapter of the ACL, Boulder, Colorado (2009)

14. Lei, H., Yanxiang, H., Furu, W., Wenjie, L.: Modeling document summarization as multi-objective optimization. In: Third International Symposium on Intelligent Information Technology and Security Informatics (IITSI), China, pp. 382–386 (2010)

15. Liu, D., Wang, Y., Liu, C., Wang, Z.: Multiple documents summarization based on genetic algorithm. In: Wang, L., Jiao, L., Shi, G., Li, X., Liu, J. (eds.) FSKD 2006. LNCS (LNAI), vol. 4223, pp. 355–364. Springer, Heidelberg (2006). https://doi.org/10.1007/11881599_40

16. Mendoza, M., et al.: A New memetic algorithm for multi-document summarization based on CHC algorithm and greedy search. In: Gelbukh, A., Espinoza, F.C., Galicia-Haro, Sofía N. (eds.) MICAI 2014. LNCS (LNAI), vol. 8856, pp. 125–138. Springer, Cham (2014). https://doi.org/10.1007/978-3-319-13647-9_14

17. Alguliev, R.M., Aliguliyev, R.M., Isazade, N.R.: DESAMC + DocSum: differential evolution with self-adaptive mutation and crossover parameters for multi-document summarization. Knowl. Based Syst. 36, 21–38 (2012)

18. Abdel-Raouf, O., Metwally, M.A.-B.: A survey of harmony search algorithm. Eng. Appl. Artif. Intell. 70, 17–26 (2013)

19. Meng, W., Xinlai, T.: Extract summarization using concept-obtained and hybrid parallel genetic algorithm. Presented at the 8th International Conference on Natural Computation (2012)

20. Fattah, M.A.: A hybrid machine learning model for multi-document summarization. Appl. Intell. 40, 592–600 (2013)

21. Cobos, C., Perez, J., Estupiñan, C.: Una revisión de la búsuqeda armónica. Revista Avances en Sistemas e Informática 8, 14 (2011)

22. Manning, C.D., Raghavan, P., Schütze, H.: An Introduction to Information Retrieval. Cambridge University Press, Cambridge (2009)

23. Omran, M.G.H., Mahdavi, M.: Global-best harmony search. Appl. Math. Comput. 198, 643–656 (2008)

24. Lin, C.-Y.: Rouge: a package for automatic evaluation of summaries. In: Proceedings of the ACL 2004 Workshop on Text Summarization Branches Out (2004)

25. N.I.O.S.A. Technology: NIST covering array tables—about these pages (2008). http://math.nist.gov/coveringarrays/coveringarray.html

# The Traffic Status and Pollutant Status Ontologies for the Smart City Domain

Miguel Gonzalez-Mendoza[1(⊠)], Nestor Velasco-Bermeo[1],
and Omar J. López Orozco[2]

[1] Tecnologico de Monterrey, Escuela de Ingeniería y Ciencias, Av Lago de
Guadalupe 3.5 Km, Margarita Maza de Juárez, 52926 Atizapán de Zaragoza,
Mexico
{mgonza,nestorvb}@itesm.mx
[2] Instituto Tecnológico Superior de Apatzingán, Computer Science Program,
Carr. Apatzingán-Aguililla Km. 3.5, Tenencia de Chandio, 60710 Apatzingán,
Michoacán, Mexico
omar@itsa.edu.mx

**Abstract.** Vocabulary must be well defined to promote Syntactical and
Semantic interoperability of cloud-based IoT (Internet of Things) architectures
in order to develop applications for Smart City environments. Ontologies are
used to represent knowledge within a domain, through them, it is possible to
define and classify things, actions, features and relations among other aspects.
This work describes the development of two ontologies, these are for traffic
status and pollution status.

**Keywords:** Ontology · Smart city · Interoperability · Cloud computing

## 1 Introduction

Interoperability in cloud-based IoT architectures, for smart cities, it can be categorized
as a key feature by providing seamless exchange of information [1] within various
systems or applications. Information can be used for enabling, create or compose
services, control or act over the environment, or simple to be processed and analyzed.
Lately, cloud computing application have been thriving throughout different domains.
[2, 3] From the perspective of knowledge representation, the Smart City domain
encompasses various domains such as environmental conditions, weather, transportation, traffic conditions, places, among others.

The key enabler that supports such seamless exchange of information resides on the
use of *Data Models*. Define Data models for interoperable systems within the Smart
City domain requires to identify the rough vocabulary of the things and entities, their
properties and relationships and then represent this knowledge through ontologies.
Ontologies should be developed using web-based languages to enable richer integration and interoperability, and therefore to provide a reference framework to obtain
machine readable *Data Models*. Some of the most used semantic languages to define
ontologies are RDF and OWL. RDF stands for Resource Description Framework and
OWL stands for Web Ontology Language. Both are standards defined and maintained
by the W3 Consortium [14].

© Springer Nature Switzerland AG 2018
F. Castro et al. (Eds.): MICAI 2017, LNAI 10633, pp. 95–101, 2018.
https://doi.org/10.1007/978-3-030-02840-4_8

Ontologies per se can be validated using reasoners and other tools [4], this is in order to check best practices aspects such as the relationships between classes and properties, well documented entities, among others. Aspects like validity and applicability of the knowledge represented in the ontologies can be checked using *Data Models* within the physical systems. In other words, by implementing the usage of *Data Models* in an interconnected application such as cloud-based applications can provide a better understanding if an ontology is "descriptive enough" for the smart city scenario.

This work is organized as follows. In section one, additional to the introduction it includes the problem description and the related work. Section two describes the methodology used to develop the ontologies following best practices. Final section includes conclusions and future work.

## 1.1 Problem Description

Interoperability as defined by [5] is *"the ability of two or more systems or components to exchange data and use information"*. In IoT cloud-based architectures interoperability faces its biggest challenge when generating data that further on will be consumed, processed or consolidated by other sources (applications or systems). By granting devices the capabilities of processing data right where it is being generated (at the computing edge level) thus gain the ability to recognize events and changes in the surrounding environment, and hence act autonomously [6].

In the Smart City domain, different projects and initiatives have been developed in form of architectures and testbeds [7], however, semantic and syntactic interoperability among different testbeds remains as an open issue [6]. Hence the importance of formally defining the vocabulary being used between applications and its logical structure by using ontologies and instantiating them as data models.

## 1.2 Related Work

Testbeds interact with the environment obtaining context information which is stored in their own proprietary format, this generates restrictive and unusable data. To avoid such cases Agarwal [8] proposes the usage of semantic-based technologies to describe the information exchanged by the platforms. Ontologies are important in IoT as well as in the smart city concept for which they may serve as explicit conceptual knowledge models that make domain knowledge available to systems and devices. They play a key role in the computing edge where they provide the semantic vocabulary used to communicate meaningfully and to achieve machine-to-machine understanding.

Some of the ideas and technologies used for the semantic web can be applied to one domain; transportation systems that address traffic safety, pollution status to classify contamination of air and water. The semantic web allows machines to interpret the meaning of data by using ontologies. An ontology is classification and description of the objects or beings, it formally represents knowledge as a set of concepts within a domain and the relations among them and their restrictions [9]. New ontologies can be either developed from scratch or as an extension of existing ontologies as the work done by Hamdaqa et al. in [10]. An ontology can be extended horizontally or vertically, a good ontology should be designed to support both types of extensions.

In any City under different circumstances alerts are the key element that an IoT based system possesses to communicate any interesting event to its surroundings or any other user. There are only a few solutions to generate alerts based on emergencies and accidents, for instance Kannan et al. [11] created an ontology modelling approach for helping vehicle driver with warning messages during time critical situations. CAOVA's structure was organized in four areas: Vehicle, Accident, Occupant and Environment [9].

## 2 Methodology

It is frequently recommended in the literature [4, 8] that ontology developers, before starting a new ontology, should think first in reusing ontologies or at least terms well defined previously within an ontology. Although it is a wise advice, in practice it is not always possible for different reasons (i.e. the external ontology does not include all terms needed for the domain of interest). In the domain of smart cities there are already some ontologies to be considered, at least to review the pertinence for the domain of Smart Cities and the requirements for the work in progress. Ontologies available online (among others) are:

- Fiesta IoT [21]
- IoT-Lite [17]
- Semantic Sensor Network [16].

Nonetheless there are always different ways to describe knowledge of domains that haven't been represented yet. For starters, knowledge representation of traffic and the environmental air conditions. Next, we'll describe the process to develop these two ontologies for the smart city concept.

According to [4], semantic interoperability refers to these three key aspects that must be observed when an ontology is being developed:

1. The structure of the ontology
2. The terms used to describe data
3. The meaning of the data according to the context (Fig. 1).

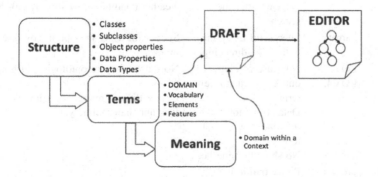

**Fig. 1.** Three key aspects to considered to develop an ontology first draft.

Paying attention to the best practices when defining the structure of the ontology helps towards homogeneity [reference]. Terms used to describe entities or elements of the domain are also a key aspect since different words may refer to the same thing (e.g., rain, rainfall, precipitation). The meaning of data or terms used must also be observed, i.e. humidity: humidity of the air (or relative humidity) and humidity of the soil (or soil moisture). For the proposed ontologies, Protégé was used to develop both Traffic Status (*TSO*) and Pollution Status (*PSO*) ontologies. Once the drafts were ready, it was used to test them based on the best practices recommendations for IoT proposed by Gyrard [4], some of them are illustrated in Fig. 2. These tools are free and available online.

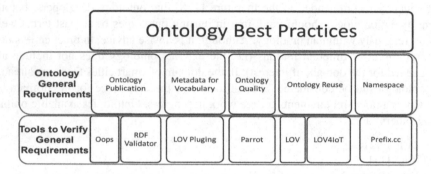

**Fig. 2.** Tools recommended to verify ontologies' general requirements. *Designed with information taken from* [4].

**Table 1.** Feedback from tools used to verify traffic status and pollution status ontologies' general requirements.

| Requirement | Tool | TSO | PSO |
|---|---|---|---|
| Ontology publication | Oops | Important: no license | Minor cases related with missing annotations |
| | RDF Validator [18] | Successful | The document was validated successfully |
| Metadata for vocabulary | LOV Plugin | LOV Recommendations. Appears after the search | LOV Recommendations appears in the search, but there were more related with weather conditions: **weather1, m3-lite** |
| Ontology quality | Parrot | Successful using the option "by direct input" | Successful using the option "by direct input" |
| Ontology and dataset reuse | LOV LOV4IoT | No reuse of entire ontologies, just a few terms Data set is not referenced with such tools No shared online yet | No reuse of entire ontologies, just a few terms Data set is not referenced with such tools It is not share online yet |
| Namespace | prefix.cc | Prefix **traffic** is no selected yet | |

Following such best practices, we verified the Ontology General Requirements using the free tools shown in Fig. 2, each tool was used over each ontology throwing feedback, results are shown in Table 1.

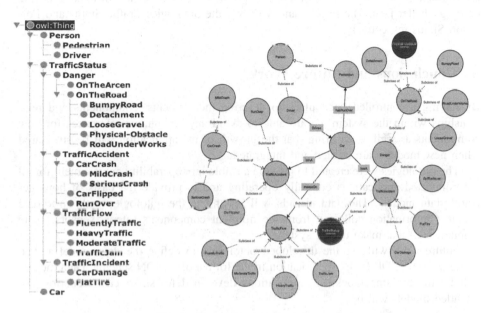

Fig. 3. The traffic status ontology.

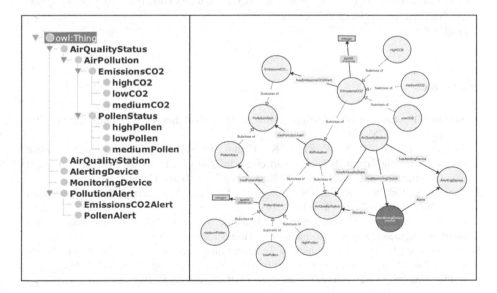

Fig. 4. The pollution status ontology.

Oops provides feedback using the following terms: critical, important and minor. For the critical aspect, it is recommended to correct the pitfall otherwise it could affect among others the ontology consistency and reasoning. For the important, although it is not critical for the ontology utilization, it is important to correct the pitfall. Finally, for the minor aspect, it will not represent any problem, but correct it will make look the ontology better [20]. The Figs. 3 and 4 shown the ontologies Traffic Status and Pollution Status respectively.

## 3   Conclusions and Future Work

By having a controlled vocabulary to describe the elements, components and relationships within the system we are able to avoid any ambiguous references for new components as well as ensuring that the growth of the application will be structured when new modules are created and integrated.

The ontologies were created to provide a stable interoperability environment for all the connected applications currently operating and to provide the basis of homogeneous data models. The data models will instantiate the ontologies with up-to-date instance information collected from the different components (alerts, sensors, route planner, etc.) that make up the system.

Future work will use the developed ontologies to define the data model and to implement the RDF JSON specification in the format of a JSON schema. Data models will be the building blocks of applications developed for smart city scenarios, the intended models will be:

- Device Data Models: (a) Device, (b) Device Model.
- Environment: (a) AirQualityObserved, (c) AirQualityThreshold, (d) WaterQualityObserved, (e) NoiseLevelObserved.
- Traffic Status.

## References

1. Murdock, P., et al.: Semantic interoperability for the web of things (2016). https://doi.org/10.13140/RG.2.2.25758.13122
2. Abberley, L., Gould, N., Crockett, K., Cheng, J.: Modelling road congestion using ontologies for big data analytics in smart cities. In: Third IEEE Annual International Smart Cities Conference (ISC2 2017), 14–17 September 2017, Wuxi, China
3. Zanella, A., Bui, N., Castellani, A., Vangelista, L., Zorzi, M.: Internet of things for smart cities. IEEE Internet Things J. 1(1) (2014)
4. Gyrard, A., Serrano, M., Atemezing, A.: Semantic web methodologies, best practices and ontology engineering applied to Internet of Things (2015)
5. Van der Veer, H., Wiles, A.: Achieving Technical Interoperability - the ETSI Approach, 3rd edn., ETSI (2008). Available at Online:http://www.etsi.org/images/files/ETSIWhitePapers/IOP%20whitepaper%20Edition%203%20final.pdf. (Accessed 30 July 2017)

6. Internet of Things-IoT Semantic Interoperability: Research Challenges, Best Practices, Recommendations and Next Steps. European research cluster on the Internet of Things. In: Serrano, M., Barnaghi, P., et al. (eds.) (2015)
7. Serrano, M., Gyrard, A., Boniface, M., Grace, P., Georgantas, N., et al.: Cross-Domain Interoperability Using Federated Interoperable Semantic IoT/Cloud Testbeds and Applications: The FIESTA-IoT Approach. Building the Future Internet through FIRE 2016 FIRE Book: A Research and Experiment based Approach, River Publishers, 2017, 978-87-93519-11-4
8. Agarwal, R., Fernandez, D.G., Elsaleh, T., Gyrard, A., Lanza, J., et al.: Unified IoT ontology to enable interoperability and federation of testbeds. In: 3rd IEEE World Forum on Internet of Things, December 2016, Reston, United States
9. Barrachina, J., Garrido, P., Fogue, M., Cano, J., Calafete, C., Manzoni, P.: CAOVA: A car accident ontology for VANETs. 2012 IEEE Wireless Communications and Networking Conference: Mobile and Wireless Networks
10. Hamdaqa, M., Tahvildari, L., LaChapelle, N., Cmpbell, B.: Cultural scene detection using Louvain optimization. Science of Computer Programming. Decembre 2014
11. Kannan, S., Thangavelu, A., Kalivaradhan, R.: An intelligent driver assistance system (I-DAS) for vehicle safety modelling using ontology approach. 1(3), pp. 1–13 (2010)
12. Strassner, J.: Knowledge engineering using ontologies. In: Handbook of Network and System Administration, vol. 4 (2008)
13. Consoli, S., Mongiovi, M., Nuzzolese, A., et al.: A Smart city data model based on semantics best practice and principles. In Proceedings of the 24th International Conference on World Wide Web (WWW '15 Companion). ACM, New York, NY, USA, pp. 1395–1400
14. World Wide Web Consortium: https://www.w3.org. Last accessed 16 Aug 2017
15. Time Ontology in W3C: http://www.w3.org/TR/owl-time/. Last accessed 16 Aug 2017
16. SSN Ontology: http://www.w3.org/2005/Incubator/ssn/ssnx/ssn#Event. Last accessed 16 Aug 2017
17. Iot-lite Ontology: http://iot.ee.surrey.ac.uk/fiware/ontologies/iot-lite. Last accessed 16 Aug 2017
18. RDF Validator: http://www.w3.org/RDF/Validator/rdfval. Last accessed 16 Aug 2017
19. Parrot Tool: http://ontorule-project.eu/parrot/parrot? Last accessed 16 Aug 2017
20. Oops Tool: http://oops.linkeddata.es. Last accessed 16 Aug 2017
21. FIESTA-IoT Ontology: http://ontology.fiesta-iot.eu/ontologyDocs/fiesta-iot/doc. Last accessed 20 Aug 2017

# Modelling and Simulating a Opinion Diffusion on Twitter Using a Multi-agent Simulation of Virus Propagation

Carlos Rodríguez Lucatero[✉]

Information Technologies Department, Universidad Autónoma Metropolitana
Unidad Cuajimalpa, Av. Vasco de Quiroga 4871, Col.Sta.Fe, Cuajimalpa, Torre III,
Cubiculo 609, Mexico City, Mexico
crodriguez@correo.cua.uam.mx

**Abstract.** Nowadays **Twitter** is one of most popular social communication network on the web. Because of that it is very important to try
to understand the phenomena of propagation of opinions that take place
in these media. A theoretical tool that allows the analysis of phenomena
in networks is the theory of graphs. So if we model a social network by
means of a graph we can make use of the solid theoretical concepts of
graph theory to try to explain phenomena such as the polarization of
opinions in social networks. Graph theory concepts as for instance centrality can be used to identify users, modelled as nodes of a graph, that
have more influence or popularity in a social network. That can be used
to classify users. Another useful graph parameter is the connectedness
that enable to know how robust is a given network topology. In this
article we will be interested in studying the impact of the topological
structure of a network as well as the conditions of probability of conta-
gion and recovery of the nodes that allow the polarization of an opinion
or on the contrary the extinction of this one. Given that the calculation
of exact values of the *fast extinction threshold* are hard to obtain even for
very simple versions of the problem, it is a good idea to apply simulation
to get a clue about the parameter values of the system that make the
information survive or get extinct in a network. For this end, based on
a virus propagation mathematical model, we are going to simulate the
opinion propagation using a multi-agent testbed known as **Netlogo** and
implement a opinion propagation mathematical model under a dynamical system approach using the **MATLAB** programming language.

## 1 Introduction

Recent work on information survival in human and P2P networks [1], try to
study how gossip or false information is spread or is preserved in a network
under the dynamical system approach. Some interesting solutions propose to
use non-linear dynamical systems and fixed point stability theorems, providing
closed form formulas that depend on the largest eigenvalue of the dynamic system
matrix. The speed with which a message is transmitted will depend on the type

© Springer Nature Switzerland AG 2018
F. Castro et al. (Eds.): MICAI 2017, LNAI 10633, pp. 102–119, 2018.
https://doi.org/10.1007/978-3-030-02840-4_9

of contact processes involved. Under our approach each person is represented by a vertex of a random graph with different connecting edges representing the contact of an individual with a group of neighbors. Each person, represented by a node, can reach different states depending on the messages that it receives. Many systems have been studied using structures called complex networks due to the number of its elements and their interaction. Each node in the network has associated a variable representing the state of the node. The edges that connect the nodes can be undirected or directed. The resulting graph is an undirected network or a directed network. The state of any node depends on the state of its neighboring nodes. Examples of such systems are the social networks, sensor networks, computer networks and the scientific collaboration networks. In all these types of networks the information must be stored, generated and retrieved. One of the issues that are important in this interconnection environment is the appearance of viruses that propagate quickly in a network causing performance degradation as well as loss of information. So under this new environments it can be very important to study and model how the information is spread or how to keep the spreading of a virus under control in such a way that the information still being useful under these vulnerable circumstances. In [1] the authors were interested in studying the problem of threshold information survival in both sensor networks and P2P networks. The authors of [1] model the problem as a non-linear dynamical system and use fixed point stability theorems for obtaining a closed form solution that depends on the largest eigenvalue of the dynamical system matrix. In many articles of conferences and magazines we can find very interesting and relevant results about the virus spread behavior in networks whose graph topology correspond to a *scale free or power law nets* such as is the case of the Web. In [2] the authors study the communication mechanisms for gossip based protocols. Another very recent and interesting work on how to distribute antidotes for controlling the epidemics spread is presented in [3]. In this research the authors analyze the problem under the approach of contact processes [4] on a finite graph and obtain very interesting and rigorous results. Concerning the properties that arise in the random graphs, such as the existence of a *giant component, percolation* phenomena, node degree distribution and *small world* phenomena, and that are the base of many recent works on virus spread on networks, we can mention [5–7] as well as [8–11]. Previous work concerning nonequilibrium transition induced by mass media in a model for social influence can be found in [12]. A previous work that refers to the study of the impact of the structure of a network in diffusion processes can be found in [13]. One of the most interesting previous works in terms of trying to determine influential Twitter users based on structural information of a social network such as the concept of centrality is the article [14]. In social networks as **Twitter** there can be messages that go from one place to another, and with some associated probability, and depending of the subject they can become *viral*. The question to answer is how and when a network message can become global or can be in extinction or at least confined in a fixed portion of the network.

# 2   The Mathematical Model of Virus Spread

In the case of P2P networks as well as the sensor networks it is very important the presence, availability and integrity of the information along the time even when the network is overloaded of messages. The mathematical tool that can help us to understand what are the conditions under which the information on a network can survive along some interval of time are the mathematical models that are used in *epidemiology*. So the mathematical models that can help us to know under what conditions an epidemic remains as an endemic disease can be used to know the conditions that ensure the permanence of the information in a network.

## 2.1   Relation of Virus Spreading and Opinion Spreading on Twitter

Many interesting stochastic models can be consulted in the *epidemiology* research literature where the spread and die-out of diseases in a population have been analyzed. The two emblematic virus spreading stochastic models are SIR and SIS ($S = Susceptible, I = Infected, R = Recovered$ and $S = Susceptible, I = Infected, S = Susceptible$). In the SIS model, a node becomes susceptible once it recovers from the disease and in the SIR model a node becomes immune once it recovers. The situation on **Twitter** that we will study in analogy with the SIS model is as follows. We will suppose that in a discussion about some subject in a social network the participants can have a neutral opinion but be exposed to the opinions on that subject, which would correspond to being in a state of susceptibility. After interacting with their contacts they can acquire consensus opinion, which would correspond to the transition to an infected state. After discussing a certain time the topic the user can lose interest on the subject and become indifferent which corresponds to transit to a state of recovery to return to be exposed to the opinion of consensus and become susceptible again. In this model a node is *susceptible* to a opinion when it is online. When the users of the social network lose interest on the discussion, they become *immune* during their indifference period, and later they become *susceptible* again when they are back to the discussion. The results obtained in [1] provide some elements to analyze the survival of an infection in a population. Similar results are mentioned in [6–8]. Using the model described in [1] it can be analytically calculated the *epidemic thresholds* for some topologies. The calculation *epidemic thresholds* are useful for knowing what are the conditions under which a fast extinction or epidemic spread takes place. In [15–17] *epidemic thresholds* have also been estimated. We assume that we have social network network of $N$ nodes and $E$ links between them. We also assume that we take very small discrete time steps of size $\Delta t$ where $\Delta t \to 0$. We know that the results of [1] can be also applied in the case of continuous systems. Within a $\Delta t$ time interval, each node $i$ has probability $r_i$ of trying to broadcast its information every time step, and each link $i \to j$ has a probability $\beta_{i,j}$ of being *up*, and thus correctly propagating the information to node $j$. Each node $i$ also has a node probability of leaving the discussion temporarily $\delta_i > 0$ (e.g., due to lose of interest in the discussion about the subject). Every dead node $j$ has a rate $\gamma_j$ of returning to the *up* state, but without any opinion. These and other symbols are listed in Table 1.

**Table 1.** Parameters of the mathematical model

| Symbol | Description |
|---|---|
| N | Number of nodes in a network |
| $\beta_{ij}$ | Probability that the link $i \to j$ is up |
| $\delta_i$ | Death rate: Probability that node $i$ dies |
| $\gamma_i$ | Resurrection rate: Probability that node $i$ comes back up |
| $r_i$ | Retransmission rate: Probability that node $i$ broadcasts |
| $p_i(t)$ | Probability that node $i$ is alive at time $t$ and has info |
| $q_i(t)$ | Probability that node $i$ is alive at time $t$ but without info |
| $1 - p_i(t) - q_i(t)$ | Probability that node $i$ is dead |
| $\zeta_i$ | Probability that node $i$ does not receive info from any of its neighbors at time $t$ |
| $p(t), q(t)$ | Probability column vectors |
| $f : \Re^{2N} \to \Re^{2N}$ | Function representing a dynamical system |
| $\nabla(f)$ | The Jacobian matrix of $f(.)$ |
| S | The $N \times N$ system matrix |
| $\lambda_S$ | An eigenvalue of the $S$ matrix |
| $\lambda_{1,S}$ | The largest in magnitude eigenvalue of the $S$ matrix |
| $s = |\lambda_{1,S}|$ | Survivability score = Magnitude of $\lambda_{1,S}$ |

Each node of the system can be modeled as a Markov chain having three states: *Has Info* (having an opinion), *No Info* (being neutral) or *Dead* (being temporarily out of the discussion), with transitions between them as shown in Fig. 1. The total number of possible configurations of the system at any instant that consist of $N$ nodes is $3^N$. Transitions out of the current system state depend only on the current state and not on any previous states. The Fig. 1 represents the possible state transition in each node.

Given that the number of different possible configurations of the system is $3^N$, the direct use of the Markov chain mathematical tools for obtaining the fast extinction condition becomes intractable. Is for that reason that in [1] it

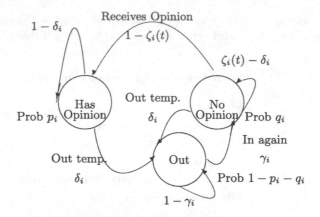

**Fig. 1.** Transitions on each node

is proposed as alternative analysis tool the non-linear dynamical systems approach. By using the non-linear dynamical systems model approach it can be
known under what conditions does the information survive for a long time, and
when will the information dies out quickly. These conditions can depend on the
values of the parameters or state transition probabilities, the kind and rate of
interaction between the nodes, and on the particular topological structure of the
network. In [1] the authors denote the expected number of *carriers* (nodes in
*Has Info* state) at time $t$ as $\overline{C}(t)$. The decay time of $\overline{C}(t)$ can be exponential,
polynomial or logarithmic if the system is working, below at or above a threshold
respectively [4]. The model proposed in [1] is a special case of a SIS model that
consist in a non-linear dynamical system of only $N$ variables. The heart of their
approximation is to consider the states of the two different nodes to be mutually
independent. From the model the probability at time $t$ that the node $i$ is at the
state *Has opinion* is $p_i(t)$, and at state *No opinion* is $q_i(t)$. Thus, the probability
of being out temporarily is $(1 - p_i(t) - q_i(t))$. If a node is in the state *No opinion* at time $t - 1$, node $i$ can receive this information (and move to state *Has
opinion*) by interaction with some neighbor node $j$. Let $\zeta_i(t)$ be the probability
that node $i$ does not receive the information from any of its neighbors. Then,
assuming that the neighbor's states are independent we can define the following
equation:

$$\zeta_i(t) = \prod_{j=1}^{N}(1 - r_j\beta_{ji}p_j(t-1)) \tag{1}$$

From Fig. 1 we can deduce the following equations that describe the transition
behavior of each node $i$ at time $t$ in terms of the state probabilities at time $t-1$.
(recall that we use very small time steps $\Delta t$, and so we can neglect second-order
terms):

$$p_i(t) = p_i(t-1)(1-\delta_i) + q_i(t-1)(1-\zeta_i(t)) \tag{2}$$

$$q_i(t) = q_i(t-1)(\zeta_i(t)-\delta_i) + (1-p_i(t-1)-q_i(t-1))\gamma_i \tag{3}$$

Eqs. 1, 2 and 3 are the base of the calculations that we have implemented in **MATLAB** and the simulations that we have implemented in **Netlogo**.

For the sake of completeness we will end this section by summarizing without proofs the main results about fast extinction obtained in [1].

**Definition 1.** *Define $S$ to be the $N \times N$ system matrix:*

$$S_{ij} = \begin{cases} 1 - \delta_i & if\ i = j \\ r_j \beta_{ji} \frac{\gamma_i}{\gamma_i + \delta_i} & otherwise \end{cases} \tag{4}$$

*Let $|\lambda_{1,S}|$ be the magnitude of the largest eigenvalue and $\widehat{C}(t) = \sum_{i=1}^{N} p_i(t)$ the expected number of carriers at $t$ of the dynamical system.*

**Theorem 1 (Condition for fast extinction).** *Define $s = |\lambda_{1,S}|$ to be the **survivability score** for the system. If $s = |\lambda_{1,S}| < 1$, then we have fast extinction in the dynamical system, that is, $\widehat{C}(t)$ decays exponentially quickly over time.*

Where $|\lambda_{i,S}|$ is the magnitude of the largest eigenvalue of $S$, being $S$ an $N \times N$ system matrix defined as $S_{ij} = 1 - \delta_i$ if $i = j$ and $S_{ij} - r_j \beta_{ji} \frac{\gamma_i}{\gamma_i + \delta_i}$ otherwise, and being $\widehat{C}(t) = \sum_{i=1}^{N} p_i(t)$ the expected number of carriers at time $t$ of the dynamical system. Two additional results that appears in [1] are the following

**Lemma 1 Fixed point.** *The values $(p_i(t) = 0, q_i(t) = \frac{\gamma_i}{\gamma_i + \delta_i})$ for all nodes $i$, are a fixed point of the Eqs. (2) and (3). Proved by a simple application of the Equations.*

**Theorem 2 (Stability of the fixed point).** *The fixed point point of Lemma 1 is asymptotically if the system is bellow threshold, that is, $s = |\lambda_{1,S}| < 1$.*

**Lemma 2.** *(From reference [8] of [1]) Define $\nabla(f)$ (also called the Jacobian matrix) to be a $2N \times 2N$ matrix such that*

$$[\nabla(f)]_{ij} = \frac{\partial f_i(v(t-1))}{\partial v_j(t-1)} \tag{5}$$

*where $v$ is the concatenation of $p$ and $q$. Then, if the largest eigenvalue (in magnitude) of $\nabla(f)$ at $v_f$ (vector $v$ valued at the fixed point) is less than 1 in magnitude, the system is asymptotically stable at $v_f$. Also, if $f$ is linear and the condition holds, then the dynamical system will exponentially tend to the fixed point irrespective of initial state.*

In [1] the authors apply (2) and obtain the following block matrix

$$\nabla(f)|_{v_f} = \begin{bmatrix} S & 0 \\ S_1 & S_2 \end{bmatrix} \tag{6}$$

The dimensions of each block matrix are $N \times N$ whose elements are

$$S_{ij} = \begin{cases} 1 - \delta_i & if\ i = j \\ r_j \beta_{ji} \frac{\gamma_i}{\gamma_i + \delta_i} & otherwise. \end{cases} \tag{7}$$

The others are

$$S_{1ij} = \begin{cases} 1 - \delta_i & \text{if } i = j \\ -r_j\beta_{ji}\frac{\gamma_i}{\gamma_i+\delta_i} & \text{otherwise} \end{cases} \tag{8}$$

and

$$S_{2ij} = \begin{cases} 1 - \gamma_i - \delta_i & \text{if } i = j \\ 0 & \text{otherwise} \end{cases} \tag{9}$$

So the question is *how can be obtained the fixed point of the system?*. In the following paragraph we will sketch, in an alternative way of the used in [1], how it can be done. In dynamical systems theory the *fixed point* is called *equilibrium point* of the system. In this very point the state probabilities become stable, then $p_i(t) = p_i(t-1)$ and $q_i(t) = q_i(t-1)$. Then simplifying the notation by dropping the subindex and the time parameter we can state the following equations system:

$$\begin{aligned} p &= p \cdot (1-\delta) + q \cdot (1-\zeta) \\ q &= q \cdot (\zeta - \delta) + (1-p-q) \cdot \gamma \end{aligned} \tag{10}$$

after algebraic simplification it can be obtained the following equations system

$$\begin{aligned} -\delta \cdot p + (1-\zeta) \cdot q &= 0 \\ \gamma \cdot p + (\zeta - 1 - \delta - \gamma) \cdot q &= q \end{aligned} \tag{11}$$

Expressing the equations system in matrix form we get

$$\begin{bmatrix} -\delta & 1-\zeta \\ -\gamma & \zeta - 1 - \delta - \gamma \end{bmatrix} \begin{bmatrix} p \\ q \end{bmatrix} = \begin{bmatrix} 0 \\ -\gamma \end{bmatrix} \tag{12}$$

Solving by Cramer's method we obtain

$$\begin{aligned} p &= \frac{\gamma \cdot (1-\zeta)}{\gamma \cdot (1-\zeta) - \delta \cdot (\zeta - 1 - \delta - \gamma)} \\ q &= \frac{\delta \cdot \gamma}{\gamma \cdot (1-\zeta) - \delta \cdot (\zeta - 1 - \delta - \gamma)} \end{aligned} \tag{13}$$

The expressions (13) can be simplified by observing that the stable state *No Info* is related with the desired *fast extinction* condition that is also related with Markov chain probability condition $(1-\zeta) \to 0$, that implies $p \to 0$. Taking into account this fact, we can rewrite (13) as follows:

$$\begin{aligned} p &= \frac{\gamma \cdot (1-\zeta)}{\gamma \cdot (1-\zeta) + \delta \cdot (1-\zeta+\delta+\gamma)} \\ &= 0 \\ q &= \frac{\delta \cdot \gamma}{\gamma \cdot (1-\zeta) - \delta \cdot (\zeta - 1 - \delta - \gamma)} \\ &= \frac{\delta \cdot \gamma}{\gamma \cdot (1-\zeta) + \delta \cdot (1-\zeta+\delta+\gamma)} \\ &= \frac{\delta \cdot \gamma}{\delta \cdot (\delta+\gamma)} \\ &= \frac{\gamma}{\delta+\gamma} \end{aligned} \tag{14}$$

Finally the authors state the following result.

**Lemma 3 (Homogeneous case).** *If* $\delta_i = \delta$, $r_i = r$, $\gamma_i = \gamma$ *for all* $i$ *and* $B = [\beta_{ij}]$ *is a symmetric binary matrix (links are undirected and always up or always down) then the for fast extinction is:*

$$\frac{\gamma}{\delta(\gamma + \delta)}\lambda_{1,B} < 1 \tag{15}$$

## 3   Simulations of the Dynamical System Model in MATLAB

As we mentioned in the abstract the exact calculation of the *fast extinction threshold* is hard even for very simple version of the problem. Because of that we propose the use of simulation for getting some clues about values of the parameters of the dynamical system that steer it to the state of extinction of the information or to the state of global presence of the information. For this end we are going to expose in this section the simulation that we implemented based on the mathematical model proposed in [1] and verify how their theoretical results are consistent with calculations made by our **MATLAB** program. In our **MATLAB** simulation we suppose the case where $\delta_i - \delta$, $r_i - r$, $\gamma_i - \gamma$ for all $i$. The algorithm used in our **MATLAB** simulation is illustrated in following pseudo-code:

### Algorithm 1: MATLAB simulation

```
A = generate adjacency matrix with some degree distribution of nodes
b=0.1*A; Matrix of betas
C = initilize randomly some carriers
z=zeros(n,1); inicialize vector of zetas

for t =1 to number of time steps
   for each node i from 1 to n
       z(i)=calculazeta(r,b,p(t,i),i);
       p(i,t+1)=p(i,t)*(1-delta)+q(i,t)*(1-z(i));
       q(i,t+1)=q(i,t)*(z(i)-delta)+(1-p(i,t)-q(i,t))*gamma;
       p(i,t)=p(i,t+1);
       q(i,t)=q(i,t+1);
   end
   C(t) = average on the number of carriers
end
```

Algorithm for the calculation of carriers C in the Chakrabarti's model [1].

In Fig. 2 we are running the Chakrabati's model [1] for a **Lattice4** network topology and in Fig. 3 for **Powerlaw Topology** giving the same values to the respective parameters. The reason why we compare the behavior of the simulations using the **Lattice4** and **Powerlaw** topologies is because in the first case the degree of the nodes is low and uniform, in the second case the graph follow

a degree distribution more heterogeneous and we want to see how these characteristics impact in the speed propagation and permanence of the information in
networks whose characteristics are very different. It can be noticed that in both
cases the messages becomes *viral* but it takes less time for that in the case of
the **Powerlaw Topology**. The reason for that behavior can be the higher connectivity of the **Powerlaw Topology** with respect to the **Lattice4 Topology**.
This situation maps to the case where in **Twitter** the opinion becomes the same
for almost all the users.

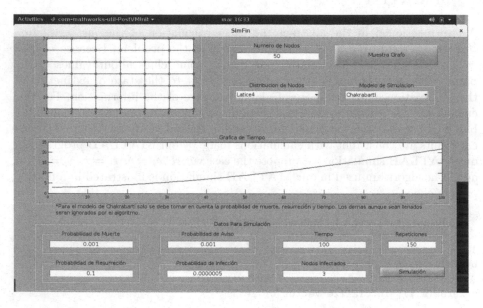

**Fig. 2.** MATLAB Simulation $\gamma = 0.1, \delta = 0.001, 1 - \sigma = 0.0000005$ lattice4 Network
Topology t = 100 time steps

In the following two figures we are going to illustrate the situation where the
information does not survive in the network after some time steps.

As can be noticed in the Figs. 4 and 5 the *fast extinction* behavior of bot
topologies is the same. This situation on **Twitter** corresponds to the case where
the users of that social network are no longer interested on that opinion or are
indifferent. If we calculate the eigenvalues of the dynamical system matrix and
apply the *fast extinction* results obtained in [1] and exposed in Sect. 2.1 we get
convinced of the fairness of our **MATLAB** simulation. In the following two
figures we are going to illustrate the situation where the information survive in
some portion of the nodes of the network after some time steps.

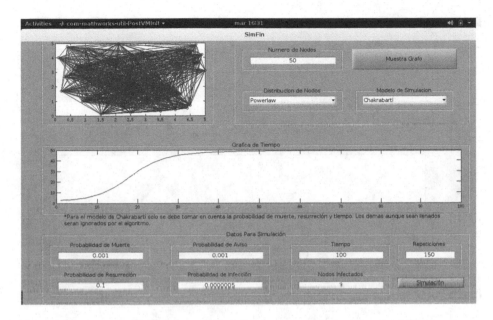

**Fig. 3.** MATLAB Simulation $\gamma = 0.1, \delta = 0.001, 1 - \sigma - 0.0000005$ Power law Network Toplogy t = 100 time steps

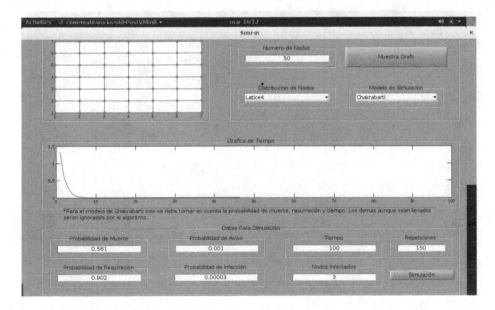

**Fig. 4.** MATLAB Simulation $\gamma = 0.902, \delta = 0.561, 1 - \sigma = 0.00003$ lattice4 Network Toplogy t = 100 time steps

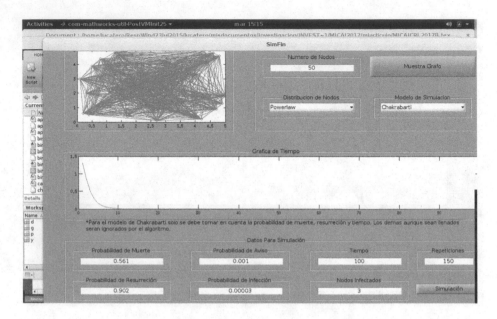

**Fig. 5.** MATLAB Simulation $\gamma = 0.902, \delta = 0.561, 1 - \sigma = 0.00003$ Power law Network Toplogy t = 100 time steps

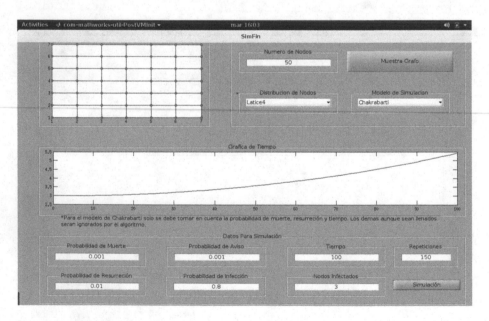

**Fig. 6.** MATLAB Simulation $\gamma = 0.01, \delta = 0.001, 1 - \sigma = 0.8$ lattice4 Network Toplogy t = 100 time steps

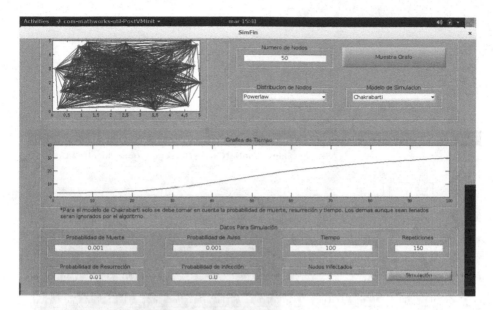

**Fig. 7.** MATLAB Simulation $\gamma = 0.01, \delta = 0.001, 1 \quad \sigma = 0.8$ Power law Network Toplogy t = 100 time steps

## 4  Simulations of a Multi-agent System in Netlogo

In this section we are going to show the results obtained by the use of the multi-agent testbed called **Netlogo**. The goal of this simulation is to illustrate the dynamic followed by the agents interacting in a given topology and see if an opinion get extincted or becomes viral. As it can be seen in Figs. 8 and 9 of the **Netlogo** simulation the *fast extinction behavior* is consistent with corresponding calculations of the **MATLAB** simulation shown in the Figs. 4 and 5. The figures associated with the simulations with **Netlogo** show a section where parameters of the simulation are set, a section where the final state to which all the nodes of the network arrive after a certain number of steps and a graph of the evolution in time of the number of nodes with opinion or without opinion. If all the nodes of the graph have green color means that the opinion is extinguished. If on the contrary all the nodes have red color means that the whole network is polarized with the opinion initially introduced. If they appear pink nodes means they are in a state of indifference. We can observe in the figures associated to the simulations with Netlogo that the graph structure has an impact on the speed with which a network is polarized also depending of course of the given parameters (Figs. 6, 7, 10 and 11).

In the next figures we are going to see that the diffusive behavior of the opinion simulated in **Netlogo** is consistent with corresponding calculation made in **MATLAB**.

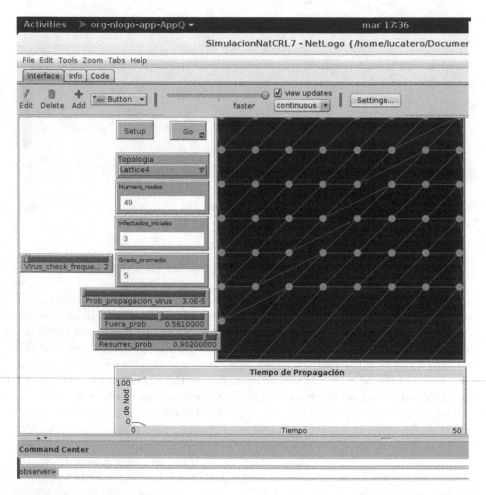

**Fig. 8.** Netlogo Simulation $\gamma = 0.902, \delta = 0.561, 1 - \sigma = 0.00003$ lattice4 Network Toplogy

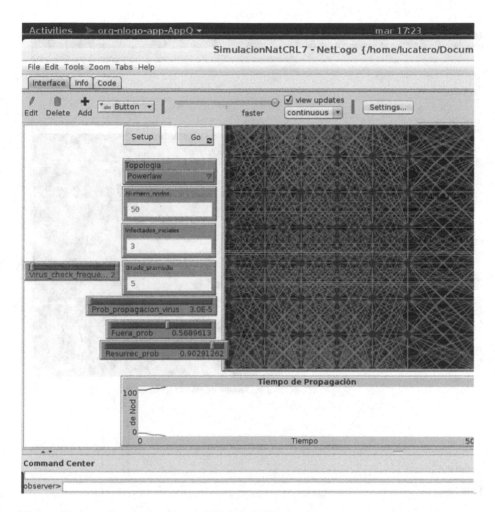

**Fig. 9.** Netlogo Simulation $\gamma = 0.902, \delta = 0.561, 1 - \sigma = 0.00003$ Power law Network Toplogy

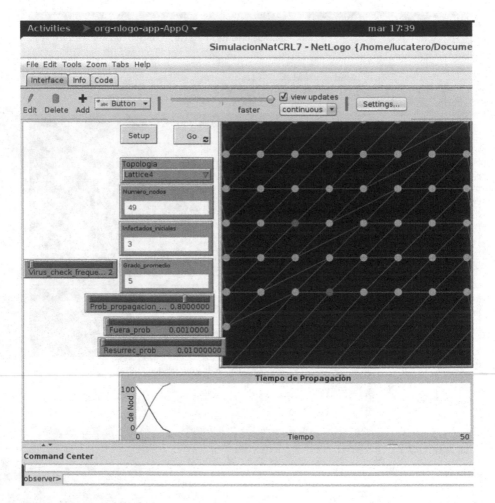

**Fig. 10.** Netlogo Simulation $\gamma = 0.01, \delta = 0.001, 1 - \sigma = 0.8$ lattice4 Network Toplogy

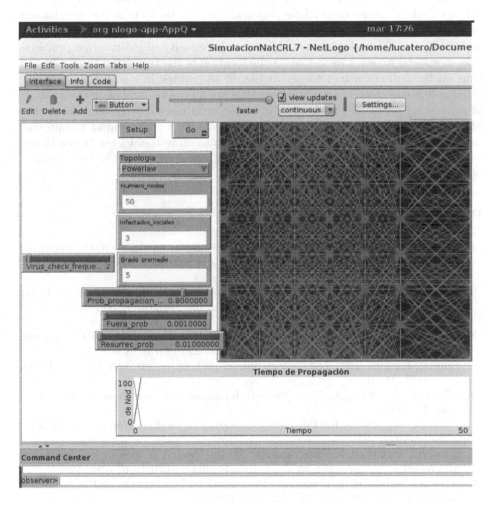

**Fig. 11.** Netlogo Simulation $\gamma = 0.01, \delta = 0.001, 1 - \sigma = 0.8$ Power law Network Toplogy

# 5 Conclusions and Future Work

As has been shown along the Sects. 3 and 4 of this article, the mathematical model simulation done in **MATLAB** as well as the multi-agent done in **Netlogo** can help us to get information about the behavior of the diffusion of information on complex systems, as is the case of the messages on **Twitter**, even when the exact calculations are hard to be obtained. As can be seen in the simulations of both **MATLAB** and **Netlogo**, the connectivity associated with the degree distribution of the nodes has an impact on the velocity of information propagation in a social network as well as on the location of the transition threshold and thus on the permanence or the extinction of an opinion in a social network. By other side it was shown how a mathematical model can be applied in the analysis of interesting problems and help us to understand more clearly the information phenomena that take place in such settings. A future extension of the present work will be the application of the simulations to more topologies. In the future we will apply this simulations for the case of the competition of two or more opinions in a social network.

# References

1. Leskovec, J., Chakrabarti, D., Faloutsos, C., Madden, S., Guestrin, C., Faloutsos, M.: Information survival threshold in sensor and P2P networks. In: IEEE INFOCOM 2007 (2007)
2. Kempe, D., Kleinberg., J.: Protocols and impossibility results for gossip-based communication mechanisms. In: Proceedings of the Symposium on Foundations of Computer Science, FOCS 2002 (2002)
3. Borgs, C., Chayes, J., Ganesh, A., Saberi, A.: How to distribute antidote to control epidemics. Random Struct. Algorithms **37**, 204–222 (2010)
4. Durrett, R., Liu, X.F.: The contact process on a finite set. Ann. Probab. **16**(3), 1158–1173 (1988)
5. Albert, R., Barabási, A.: Error and attack tolerance of complex networks. Nature **406**, 378 (2000)
6. Barabási, A., Albert, R.: Emergence of scaling in random graphs. Science **286**, 509–512 (1999)
7. Schwartz, N., Cohen, R., Ben-Avraham, D., Barabási, A.L., Havlin, S.: Percolation in directed scale-free networks. Phys. Rev. E **66**(1), 0151041–0151044 (2002)
8. Alon, N., Benjamini, I., Stacey, A.: Percolation on finite graphs and isoperimetric inequalities. Ann. Probab. **32**, 1727–1745 (2004)
9. Balister, P., Bollobás, B.: Bond percolation with attenuation in high dimensional Voronoi tilings. Random Struct. Algorithms **36**, 5–10 (2009)
10. Faloutsos, M., Faloutsos, P., Faloutsos, C.: On power-law relationships of the internet topology. In: Proceedings SIGCOMM 1999 (1999)
11. Radicchi, F., Ramasco, J.J., Barrat, A., Fortunato, S.: Complex networks renormalization: flows and fixed points. Phys. Rev. Lett. **101**, 1487011–1487014 (2008)
12. Gonzalez-Avella, J., Cosenza, M., Tucci, K.: Nonequilibrium transition induced by mass media in a model for social influence. Phys. Rev. E **72**, 0651021–0651024 (2005)

13. Nicosia, V., Bagnoli, F., Latora, V.: Impact of network structure on a model of diffusion and competitive interaction. Phys. Rev. E **67**, 0261201–0261206 (2003)
14. Riquelme,    F.:    Measuring    user    influence    on    Twitter:    a    survey. arXiv:cs.SI/1508.07951v1, pp. 1–24 (2015)
15. Pastor-Satorras, R., Vespignani, A.: Epidemic dynamics and endemic states in complex networks. Phys. Rev. E **63**, 0661171–0661178 (2001)
16. Pastor-Satorras, R., Vespignani, A.: Epidemic spreading in scale-free networks. Phys. Rev. Lett. **86**, 3200–3203 (2001)
17. Pastor-Satorras, R., Vespignani, A.: Epidemic dynamics in finite size scale-free networks. Phys. Rev. E **65**, 0351081–0351084 (2002)

# Criminal Events Detection in News Stories Using Intuitive Classification

Luis-Gil Moreno-Jiménez[1(✉)], Juan-Manuel Torres-Moreno[2,3],
Noé Alejandro Castro-Sánchez[1], Alondra Nava-Zea[1], and Gerardo Sierra[4]

[1] Centro Nacional de Investigación y Desarrollo Tecnológico,
Tecnológico Nacional de México, Cuernavaca, Mexico
{luismoreno,ncastro,anz}@cenidet.edu.mx
[2] LIA/Université d'Avignon et des Pays de Vaucluse, Avignon, France
juan-manuel.torres@univ-avignon.fr
[3] École Polytechnique de Montréal, Montreal, Canada
[4] Universidad Nacional Autónoma de México, Mexico City, Mexico
gsierram@iingen.unam.mx

**Abstract.** This paper proposes a model for the identification of criminal events through the analysis of journalistic news implementing classification mechanism. The classification process is composed of three subprocess: Information Extraction, Classification process and a Selection process of the classes with the best scores obtained after the classification. To obtain the harmonic mean between recall and precision (F-Score) of this classification model, a criminological corpus called CAD was used to simulate different scenarios. CAD is a corpus in spanish composed of news reporting crimes about homicide, assaults, kidnapping, sexual abuse, and extortion, called High Impact Crimes according to [1].

## 1 Introduction

The crime is a real problem in the society, which avoids the growth of vital areas for the development of countries, the impact that it provokes has become a motivating factor for the realization of this work. The purpose is detecting criminal activity, which allows to generate and constantly update a corpus of crimes that could be used in different applications.

This article proposes the creation of a news classifier model performing a Semantic Analysis (SA) module (Sect. 4), in order to analyze journalistic notes and detect important information, like the crime reported on it, the results of this model could be used to establish a statistical report about the frequency of crime per zone and establish mechanisms against delinquency.

To obtain an efficiency measure *F-Score* about this model, different scenarios were simulated using the news from the CAD corpus[1] and compared it with the efficiency achieved by conventional classifiers as Support Vector Machine (SVM)

---

[1] To get a copy of corpus CAD send a mail to *luismoreno@cenidet.edu.mx/ncastro@cenidet.edu.mx.*

© Springer Nature Switzerland AG 2018
F. Castro et al. (Eds.): MICAI 2017, LNAI 10633, pp. 120–132, 2018.
https://doi.org/10.1007/978-3-030-02840-4_10

and Naïve Bayes Model. Both, SVM and Bayes model were selected because of their high use in textual classification tasks.

In this work a predictive model with a Semantic Analysis (SA) was developed in order to infer crime reported in journalistic notes.

The paper is organized as follows. In Sect. 2, the related work is presented. Then, in Sect. 3 the CAD corpus is characterized. In Sect. 4 the methodology is described. In Sect. 5 the results obtained in the experimentation are presented. Finally, in Sect. 6 the conclusions and the perspectives are presented.

## 2 Related Work

In recent years different works on the use of Natural Language Processing (NLP) about Information Extraction (EI) on criminal matters have been developed, but the most of the investigations in this field are in English according to [2] Those ones that have been helpful to develop this work are described below.

In the paper [3], the authors have used IE techniques and cognitive models to increase the information obtained from interviews with criminal witnesses. [4] uses an automatic grouping method *(clustering)* based on *k-means* to find criminal patterns. [5] uses similarity measures and automatic learning to analyze and classify texts which describe the same kind of crimes, even if the texts are the same, similar or different. [6] uses Artificial Neural Networks (ANN) to find classification patterns in the police's criminal databases. The work developed by [7], criminal reports from Arizona Police in the US are processed to look for relevant elements such as names of people, drugs, weapons or criminal events.

In the work carried out by [2], a comprehensive study is done on different working environments or existing *Frames*, which analyze patterns to search of criminal tendencies. Although most of them use sensors to search for more specific elements such as firearms or weapons, there are some that work directly with NLP tools.

IE techniques are varied and are often based on the frequency of terms in the texts. [8] uses the TF-IDF model where the input texts are vectorized, terms with a high frequency as well as empty words are discriminated, and those with single frequency are considered as Named Entities (NE). For the Portuguese language, the authors of [9] use IE in order to automatically enrich the information about crimes present in the collaborative *WikiCrimes*[2].

After investigating the related work we found that in Spanish there are no works similar to our investigation.

The importance of automatic classification of criminal texts lies in the fact that it can be used in criminal analysis [10] and in the detection of criminal entities [11].

Even News classification can help find patterns in criminal reports or other criminalistic aspects [4].

---

[2] http://www.wikicrimes.org.

## 2.1   Features Used

For the development of this project, the conclusions obtained in [12] were considered. After multiple testing processes with classification models like Naïve Bayes and Support Vector Machine (SVM) was detected that the same journalistic news can report more than one kind of crime. This phenomenon induce to a low accuracy at the moment of classifying some journal news. Is this because of, standard classifiers as SVM and Bayes performs uniquely single classification, it means, just one kind of crime can be found in a journalistic news. Based on this observation, in this paper, a new intuitive classification model was developed. This model allows to perform a multi-classification and getting various kinds of crimes in a note.

To obtain a real comparative between the results expressed in [12] and those ones obtained in this work, the experimentation process was developed using the sames classifiers (SVM and Bayes) adding the model multi-classifiers described here.

## 3   Statistical Information of the CAD Corpus

This section details statistical information about the Annotated Crimes Corpus *(Corpus Anotado de Delitos)* in Mexico (CAD) [12], such as, the number of samples that constitute it, the sources of the samples, and the classes in which they are divided.

The samples are divided into periods of time: the first is from April 04 to June 25, 2016 and the second, from July 1 to September 05. 2016. They were all downloaded during 2016.

The corpus was constituted with Spanish news which were downloaded from the following mexican newspapers:

- *La Unión de Morelos*[3]
- *El Diario de Morelos*[4]
- *La Jornada de Morelos*[5]

A total of 1,000 news items were downloaded and stored in raw text using *utf8* encoding. The recovered documents meet the condition of reporting at least one of the following crimes:

1. Homicide
2. Assault
3. Kidnapping
4. Sexual abuse
5. Extortion

---

[3] http://www.launion.com.mx.
[4] http://www.diariodemorelos.com.
[5] http://www.jornadamorelos.com.

This corpus was distributed between four people[6] without repetition for the annotation process. The agreement for them, was to express the terminology that could be useful for anyone to annotate each news, in the Table 1 are detailed the terms expressed by them.

**Table 1.** Keywords of CAD corpus

| Class | Keywords |
| --- | --- |
| Assault | Theft, to subtract, to steal, to threaten, to strip, to intercept, to remove, to deprive, to dismantle, to surprise in possession, to hide |
| Homicide | Find lifeless, lynch, murder, run over, find dead, corpse, shoot, shot, bullet, rustle, attack shot, lifeless person, die, shoot |
| Abduction | Kidnapping, rising to force, struggling, freedom, lifting person, victim rescued, deprivation, releasing victim, carrying force, rescue |
| Sexual abuse | Rape, sexual assault, intimate, rape |

It was discovered that in several cases, one news can report more than one type of crime, the process of annotation is detailed in [12].

Below are two examples of news, the first one is reporting one crime and the second one is reporting more than one type of crime.

The following example reports kidnapping.

*"A kidnapped man was rescued at a security house, located on the private street Banco Ejidal, in the Colony Ampliación Chipitlán, Cuernavaca, where he was deprived of his freedom".*[7] The people who classified the news identified this news as a kidnapping report because the word "kidnapped" and the phrase "deprived of his freedom" was found in the text.

The following example reports two types of crimes: Homicide and Kidnapping:

*"Policeman of the 'Mando Único' of Xochitepec remains in custody for the crime of kidnapping equated to threaten a commander of said municipality, while another Element is investigated for attempted homicide to the detriment of a former municipal official."*

According to the people who classified the news, the words "kidnapping" and "attempted homicide" were useful to determining what kind of crimes were reported in this news.

In this case, it is important to mention that news with more than one type of crime must appear in all the categories where it belongs.

In the Table 2 statistical data about the CAD corpus are showed.

---

[6] Master Students.
[7] https://www.diariodemorelos.com/noticias.

**Table 2.** CAD corpus - statistical data

| Classes | La Unión de Morelos | El Diario de Morelos | La Jornada de Morelos | Total |
|---|---|---|---|---|
| Homicide | 139 | 130 | 125 | 394 |
| Assault | 145 | 160 | 136 | 441 |
| Kidnapping | 101 | 95 | 109 | 305 |
| Sexual abuse | 45 | 48 | 62 | 155 |
| Extortion | 36 | 69 | 45 | 150 |

## 4 Methodology

The methodology proposed in this paper is divided into three parts: the multi-classification model (Sect. 4.1), a model to select automatically terms or keywords (Sect. 4.2) and a hybrid classification model that was developed joining the conventional classifiers and that one elaborated in this work (Sect. 4.3).

In the Fig. 1 it is showed a summary about how this model works. The details of each process about this model is explained below.

### 4.1 Multiclass Intuitive Classifier

The motivation for the development of this news classification proposal, was born from the analysis of the results obtained by [12], in which conventional classification were evaluated: Vector Support Machine and Naïve Bayes, using the tools and configurations that provides the WEKA[8] platform.

After concluding the evaluation phase of [12], it was detected that the low percentage of precision obtained after the evaluation process was due to the classic classifiers works with a single classification, it means, just one class is detected in a journalistic note (news), but in several cases, more than one class of crime was detected during the manual classification, as mentioned in (Sect. 3), for that reason, a model considering the following premises is proposed:

- The keyword extraction model proposed in [12] will be reused, this model also calculates a score for the keyword extracted. The analysis that this model employs consists in the identification of Verbal Phrases and Nouns Phrases, then through an TF-IDF model adaptation the weight of each selected keyword is calculated.
- To create an automated keyword selection algorithm that does not sacrifice the classifier's precision and recall. Section 4.2 and giving more importance to the keywords according to their order of appearance in the news.

A keyword extraction model is going to be very useful because it is necessary to compare the keywords extracted between each news and each group of news that has be clustered by the type of crime Sect. 3 as described below.

---

[8] http://www.cs.waikato.ac.nz/ml/weka.

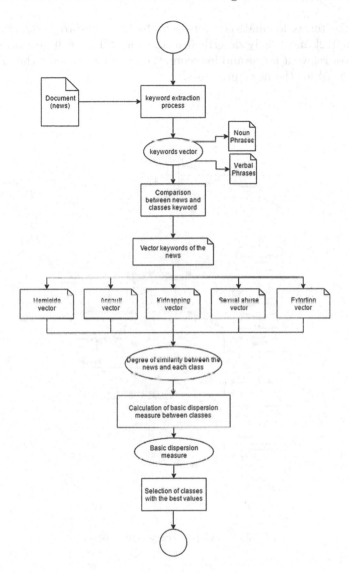

**Fig. 1.** Multi-classification process

First of all, the news in the CAD corpus are clustered by type of crime (assault, homicide, kidnapping and sexual abuse) to create profiles for each class of crimes.

Once the profiles are created, the new document or news to classify was analyzed one by one using FreeLing[9] in order to lemmatize the terms and to reduce the processing time.

---

[9] http://nlp.lsi.upc.edu/freeling/node/1.

Then, the terms lemmatized were sent to the keywords extraction model provided by [12] and briefly described in the Fig. 2 This will generate a vector with the most relevant terms and his score, the score will indicate the importance of that keyword for the news processed.

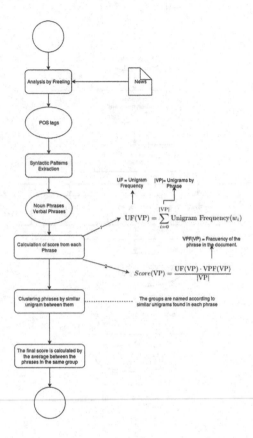

**Fig. 2.** Keywords extraction process

The same process is performed for each news on each profile created previously, the intention is to obtain a large vector with the most important keywords for each type of crime, that could be compared with the vector obtained after the single analysis news.

It is important to say, that the process of analysis each profile must be performed once, the results will be saved for the comparison process that will occur each time that a single news is processed.

It is noteworthy that the order of the terms appearance in the news must not be altered for any reason.

The above is derived considering that the reverse Pyramid Structure suggests that a journalistic note should answer in the first lines, 6 main questions: What?,

Who?, How?, When?, Where? and Why?. Therefore, in this work we prioritize the terms that have a primary order of appearance [13].

The comparison process between a single news and each profile works as follows.

A coincidence is detected when in two documents, in this case vectors are compared and found the same terms, so the term value is taken according to the profile it belongs to $P$. This value will be then divided by the position the term $i$ has in the Vector $VC$ obtaining thus the corresponding value of the term in the news as per the class or profile it belongs to $VC$ (see Eq. 1).

It should be mentioned that the same term could be in more than one profile, but possibly with different value.

$$VC_t = \frac{P}{i} \tag{1}$$

We will repeat the previous process with each keyword extracted from the news, and thus obtaining the total correspondence value $VTC$.

$$VTC = \sum_{n=1}^{i} VC_t \tag{2}$$

At the end, we will do the same process for all the classes, obtaining a similarity value for each profile (see Eq. 2).

For the multiclass selection, a basic dispersion measure was calculated among the five calculated values, this because there are five classes that are being analyzed in this investigation. The calculation consist in subtracting the lowest similarity value to the greatest similarity value. The lowest similarity value needs to be higher than 0. All classes with a higher VTC value than the basic dispersion measure calculated will be selected.

Consider the following example:

Suppose that after analyzing a journalistic note, we obtained the following correspondence values for each of the classes shows in the Table 3.

Table 3. Example of correspondence values obtained for each class

| Assault | Homicide | Kidnapping | Sexual abuse | Extortion |
|---------|----------|------------|--------------|-----------|
| 40      | 7        | 18         | 35           | 0         |

Our basic measure of dispersion would be 33, since $40 - 7 = 33$. Considering the obtained results, we would conclude that the news should belong to the assault and homicide class.

## 4.2  Automatic Selection of Terms

Up to this point, the selection of the best keywords of the profiles have been manually configured using the score calculated by the previous process; however, a model is now proposed for the automatic selection of keywords. This will provide to the classifier model a greater degree of autonomy and allow an efficient self-learning to update the profiles in the CAD corpus.

For that reason, a scheme of automatic selection of terms was established using the degree of dispersion of terms according to their weights.

Considering that the automatic selection will be made from the set of keywords extracted for the class "assault", proceed as follows:

The standard deviation is calculated considering the score obtained for each keyword.

Subsequently, the maximum weight of our set of keywords (max) is divided by the standard deviation $\sigma$. The result is then rounded, the quotient is taken and one is subtracted. This subtraction is done to reduce the acceptance threshold of the keywords, maintaining only the most significant ones (see Eq. 3).

$$X = \frac{\max}{\sigma} - 1 \tag{3}$$

Once calculated $X$, multiply by the standard deviation and obtain the lower limit (see Eq. 4).

$$\mathrm{li} = X \times \sigma \tag{4}$$

To obtain the upper limit, the lower limit (li) is multiplied by max (see Eq. 5).

$$\mathrm{ls} = \mathrm{li} \times \max \tag{5}$$

Experiments were performed considering the new CLIM classifier model and this automatic keyword selection model. The results of all evaluations are presented in the Sect. 5.

### 4.3   Hybrid Classifier

Observing the results obtained by the proposed classifier Sect. 4.1 and the two conventional classifiers (Naïve Bayes and SVM) [12], it was considered praiseworthy to create a model that would join the predictions of these three classifiers and present a result according to the confidence's degree each classifier calculates by analyzing the data.

The task consisted in adding the confidence's degree that each classifier gives. This sum is considered as 100% with the result that the collaboration percentage of each classifier is obtained. Subsequently, we add the percentages of the predictions that point to the same class to finally select the class with the highest score.

Consider the example values in the Table 4. The collaboration percentages were already calculated based on the confidence levels calculated by each classifier.

In this case the selected class would be Homicide, as it has a total of 73 % with both the results of Naïve Bayes and SVM compared to 27 % of the Assault class calculated by CLIM.

The results of this model were not as high as expected since sometimes the wrong predictions of the two conventional classifiers coincided. This prevented the results obtained by the CLIM classifier to influence in the final result.

**Table 4.** Example of values obtained for each classifier

|  | Naïve Bayes | Support vector machine | CLIM | Total |
|---|---|---|---|---|
| Prediction | Homicide | Homicide | Assault | – |
| Confidence's degree | 95 | 87.5 | 67.5 | 250 |
| Collaboration % | 38 | 35 | 27 | 100 |

## 5 Results and Evaluation

The proposed models were evaluated taking the CAD corpus. 70% of the corpus were used as training data and the remaining 30% as test data. Then the training data percentage was manually debugged, for an automatic keyword selection model is proposed in this work. All the tests performed in [12] were performed again but this time under the automatic scheme of keyword selection for the training data.

The class Extortion, was not evaluated because the number of news that report this crime was too low, it mean, of 150 news tagged in this crime, just 23 report uniquely this type of crime the others 127 are distributed between the other 4 classes, provoking inefficient results in the experiments performed by [12].

This time, tests were done processing complete news. On [12] different variants (title, first paragraph, and complete news) were used to perform the tests. This last one produced better results and for that reason it was selected to perform the evaluation process.

In all cases, the classical F-Score measure was used. This measure is defined by the Eq. 6.

$$\text{F-Score} = \frac{2 \times (\text{Precision} \times \text{Recall})}{\text{Precision} + \text{Recall}} \tag{6}$$

Table 5 shows the results obtained for the Vector Support Machine highlighting an average F-Score of 53%. Table 6 shows the results obtained for the Bayesian classifier which yields an average F-Score of 51%. These two experiments were carried out occupying WEKA (see footnote 8), a tool used for data mining, which facilitates the implementation of different classification models.

As mentioned previously, these classifiers were taken as *baseline*, because they are the best valuated ones in textual classification tasks, for that reason it was considered that experimentation with these algorithms could establish a good reference about the efficiency that could be reach by the model proposed in this work.

Table 8 shows the results obtained for the classifier proposed in this work which yields better results than the two previous with an average F-Score of 77.9%.

Table 7 shows the last experimentation that was carried out in an attempt to increase the percentages of precision. This objective was not reached given the low results obtained by the first two classifiers.

**Table 5.** Classification results (Full News - SVM)

| Classes | Assault | Homicide | Kidnapping | Sexual abuse | Average |
|---|---|---|---|---|---|
| Precision | 0.5137 | 0.7763 | 0.5937 | 0.9046 | 0.6973 |
| Recall | 0.5090 | 0.5412 | 0.1496 | 0.5106 | 0.4276 |
| F-Score | 0.5114 | 0.6378 | 0.2389 | 0.6530 | 0.5301 |

**Table 6.** Classification results (Full News - Naïve Bayes)

| Classes | Assault | Homicide | Kidnapping | Sexual abuse | Average |
|---|---|---|---|---|---|
| Precision | 0.5882 | 0.7368 | 0.5789 | 0.5789 | 0.6977 |
| Recall | 0.5454 | 0.5137 | 0.0866 | 0.0861 | 0.4114 |
| F-Score | 0.5660 | 0.6054 | 0.1506 | 0.6394 | 0.5176 |

**Table 7.** Classification results (Full News - Hybrid)

| Classes | Assault | Homicide | Kidnapping | Sexual abuse | Average |
|---|---|---|---|---|---|
| Precision | 0.6129 | 0.7375 | 0.5773 | 0.9387 | 0.7166 |
| Recall | 0.5181 | 0.5412 | 0.4409 | 0.4893 | 0.4974 |
| F-Score | 0.5615 | 0.6243 | 0.5 | 0.6433 | 0.5872 |

**Table 8.** Classification results (Full News - CLIM)

| Classes | Assault | Homicide | Kidnapping | Sexual abuse | Average |
|---|---|---|---|---|---|
| Precision | 0.7313 | 0.7857 | 0.7391 | 0.9516 | **0.7969** |
| Recall | 0.8909 | 0.7064 | 0.8267 | 0.6276 | **0.7629** |
| F-Score | 0.8032 | 0.7439 | 0.7692 | 0.7564 | **0.7795** |

Summarizing, in Table 9 it is presented the F-Score average obtained by all the classifiers models performed in this work, being CLIM the best one due to it was developed following the observations obtained over all experimentation and evaluation process Sect. 6.

**Table 9.** Classification results - Resume

| Classifiers | SVM | Naïve Bayes | Hybrid | CLIM |
|---|---|---|---|---|
| Precision | 0.6973 | 0.6977 | 0.7166 | **0.7969** |
| Recall | 0.4276 | 0.4114 | 0.4974 | **0.7629** |
| F-Score | 0.5301 | 0.5176 | 0.5872 | **0.7795** |

# 6    Conclusions

This article proposes a new method of textual classification (CLIM), based on the analysis of journalistic news, which was evaluated through the news that compose the (*Corpus Anotado de Delitos*) (CAD).

During the process of experimentations, some important elements were found and used to improve the model proposed and getting the best values of F-Score as showed in Table 9. For example, the news structure (inverse pyramid) was used to develop a best algorithm to extract the keywords and train the classifier, then to deal with the problem about various types of crimes exposed just in one note it was proposed a multi-classification method Sect. 4.1.

The areas in which this method could be employed are: police instances (reinforcement of security in strategic areas, implementation of new security schemes, etc.), decentralized organizations (human rights commissions) or non-governmental organizations (criminal censuses programs).

Some examples of possible tools in which this method can be used are: maps indicating the crimes detected by this model, criminal news search engines, documentation tools and the generation of crime synthesis [14] among others.

In the future, it will be studied whether this scheme of classical classifiers or others, including incremental type Artificial Neuronal Networks (ANN), could work with short texts (news summaries, tweets, Internet complaints, etc.).

We also plan to increase the number of news of the CAD corpus to cover different periods of time.

**Acknowledgments.** This work was supported by Mexican Government *(Tecnológico Nacional de México/CENIDET, Red Temática en Tecnologías del Lenguaje-Conacyt,* Conacyt scholarship 661101) and French Government *(Université d' Avignon et des Pays de Vaucluse/Laboratoire Informatique d' Avignon).*

# References

1. Observatorio Nacional Ciudadano Seguridad, Justicia y Legalidad: Reporte sobre delitos de alto impacto Junio 2016. Reporte Año 3, No. 5, México (2016)
2. Kumar, A.S., Gopal, R.K.: Data mining based crime investigation systems: taxonomy and relevance. In: 2015 Global Conference on Communication Technologies (GCCT), pp. 850–853. IEEE (2015)
3. Ku, C.H., Iriberri, A., Leroy, G.: Crime information extraction from police and witness narrative reports. In: International Conference on Technologies for Homeland Security, pp. 193–198. IEEE (2008)
4. Nath, S.V.: Crime data mining. In: Elleithy, K. (ed.) Advances and Innovations in Systems, Computing Sciences and Software Engineering, pp. 405–409. Springer, Dordrecht (2007). https://doi.org/10.1007/978-1-4020-6264-3_70
5. Ku, C.H., Leroy, G.: A decision support system: automated crime report analysis and classification for e-government. Gov. Inf. Q. **31**, 534–544 (2014)
6. Dahbur, K., Muscarello, T.: Classification system for serial criminal patterns. Artif. Intell. Law **11**, 251–269 (2003)

7. Chau, M., Xu, J.J., Chen, H.: Extracting meaningful entities from police narrative reports. In: Proceedings of the 2002 Annual National Conference on Digital Government Research, Digital Government Society of North America, pp. 1–5 (2002)

8. Lee, S., Kim, H.J.: News keyword extraction for topic tracking. In: Fourth International Conference on Networked Computing and Advanced Information Management, NCM 2008, vol. 2, pp. 554–559. IEEE (2008)

9. Pinheiro, V., Furtado, V., Pequeno, T., Nogueira, D.: Natural language processing based on semantic inferentialism for extracting crime information from text. In: International Conference on Intelligence and Security Informatics ISI, pp. 19–24. IEEE (2010)

10. Estivill-Castro, V., Lee, I.: Data mining techniques for autonomous exploration of large volumes of geo-referenced crime data. In: Proceedings of the 6th International Conference on Geocomputation, pp. 24–26 (2001)

11. Chen, H., Chung, W., Xu, J.J., Wang, G., Qin, Y., Chau, M.: Crime data mining: a general framework and some examples. Computer **37**, 50–56 (2004)

12. Moreno Jiménez, L.G., et al.: Creación y clasificación de un corpus criminológico en español usando características lingüísticas superficiales. Research in Computing Science (2016, accepted)

13. Associated Press: 2016 AP Stylebook. Spiral-Bound (2016)

14. Torres-Moreno, J.M.: Automatic Text Summarization. Wiley, Hoboken (2014)

# A New Corpus of the Russian Social Network News Feed Paraphrases: Corpus Construction and Linguistic Feature Analysis

Ekaterina Pronoza[1](✉), Elena Yagunova[1](✉), and Anton Pronoza[2](✉)

[1] St.-Petersburg State University, St.-Petersburg, Russian Federation
katpronoza@gmail.com, iagounova.elena@gmail.com
[2] Institute for Informatics and Automation of the Russian Academy of Sciences,
St.-Petersburg, Russian Federation
pronoza@gmail.com

**Abstract.** In this paper we present a new Russian paraphrase corpus derived from the news feed of the social network and conduct its primary analysis. Most media agencies post their news reports on their pages in social networks, and the headlines of the messages are often the same as those of the corresponding news articles from the official websites of the agencies. However, sometimes these pairs of headlines differ, and in such cases a headline from the social network can be considered a compression or a paraphrase of the original headline. In other words, such news feed from social networks is a rich resource of textual entailment, and, as it is shown in this paper, various linguistic phenomena, e.g., irony, presupposition and attention attracting markers. We collect the described pairs of headlines and construct the Russian social network news feed paraphrase corpus based on them. We test the paraphrase detection model trained on the other existing Russian paraphrase corpus, ParaPhraser.ru, collected from official news headlines only, against the constructed dataset, and explore its linguistic and pragmatic features.

**Keywords:** Paraphrase corpus · News headlines · Social network news feed
Text compression · Textual entailment · Linguistic phenomena
Loose paraphrase

## 1 Introduction

Natural paraphrases occur rarely in real texts which makes the task of paraphrase extraction far from trivial. Nowadays paraphrase corpora are constructed from various sources, from different translations of the same stories to different answers to the same questions. We have already addressed this problem as part of the ParaPhraser project[1] dedicated to the construction of the Russian paraphrase corpus from the stream of news headlines [15]. In this paper we present another Russian paraphrase corpus constructed using an alternative method of paraphrase extraction which is resource-cheaper than traditional news aggregating and does not demand human annotation.

---

[1] http://paraphraser.ru/about.

© Springer Nature Switzerland AG 2018
F. Castro et al. (Eds.): MICAI 2017, LNAI 10633, pp. 133–145, 2018.
https://doi.org/10.1007/978-3-030-02840-4_11

Our approach towards paraphrase extraction is based on the following tendency in web media: most media agencies duplicate their news headlines in social networks and microblogs, and many of them paraphrase these headlines instead of just copying them from their official websites. Since social network headlines are often aimed to attract the readers' attention, they often differ from the official headlines in style (e.g., they may be more informal or short/long, lack some details or vice versa). We believe that in terms of paraphrase classification such pairs of headlines can be mostly considered loose paraphrases, i.e., those conveying similar but not necessarily the same meaning. A corpus of such paraphrases can be used for such tasks as text style normalization and text summarization.

We also test our previously developed paraphrase detection model against the collected data and reveal the main characteristics of this corpus. It is found out that the corpus is full of complex linguistic phenomena like irony and presupposition. It is also notable for the abundance of attention attraction techniques in the social network news headlines (the unofficial ones). All these factors make it quite hard for us to automatically classify pairs of headlines as paraphrases. We explore the distribution of such (and many other) phenomena in the corpus analysis across different media sources.

## 2   Related Work

Research in the area of paraphrase extraction and detection started more than a decade ago. There are already a number of available paraphrase corpora and Microsoft Research Paraphrase Corpus (MSRP) is the most well-known of them [5]. It has become a gold standard for the task of English paraphrase identification: state-of-the-art results are currently monitored on ACL Anthology wiki-page, and the best results achieve accuracy of 80.4% and F1-score of 85.9%. It consists of 5801 pairs of sentences (3900 of them being paraphrases) collected from news clusters. MSRP is widely used in paraphrase detection task, and it is the very corpus which inspired the development of other paraphrase resources.

Paraphrase extraction methods can be classified into those based on "natural" or "artificial" sources. The former are used to construct parallel multilingual corpora and comparable monolingual corpora (different translations of the same texts, news texts, texts on similar topics, e.g., from the social networks or students' answers to the questions, social media, Wikipedia, different descriptions of the same videos). "Artificial" sources are texts paraphrased by humans.

Our approach is a sentential one, and we focus on the corresponding paraphrase extraction methods in this section.

In one of the oldest works known to us paraphrases are extracted by collecting pairs of texts together with their summaries [9]. Based on these pairs, a corpus of 1067 sentence pairs is constructed, with no negative instances.

Another approach is presented in [16]. Japanese Paraphrase Corpus for Speech Translation is constructed from sentences derived from travel conversation and versions of them paraphrased by humans.

Paraphrases can also be extracted from the human responses (paraphrases) to the target sentences: thus, User Language Paraphrase Corpus [10] is collected from student paraphrases of biology textbook sentences. It consists of 1998 sentence pairs.

A complex annotation scheme along 10 dimensions of paraphrase characteristics on a 6 points scale is also proposed.

In another project by Microsoft Research [3] paraphrases are collected from different descriptions of the same videos provided by humans on the Amazon Mechanical Turk platform. The constructed Microsoft Research Video Description Corpus includes 85 K sentences.

In some approaches paraphrases are extracted from multiple sources. For example, Turkish Paraphrase Corpus[2] [4] is derived from (1) Turkish translations of a famous novel, (2) Turkish subtitles of a foreign movie, (3) Turkish reference translations from an English-Turkish parallel corpus, and (4) Turkish articles from a news website. The corpus is annotated by 14 native Turkish speakers. Sentences from the news articles are paraphrased by 12 native speakers and sentences from bilingual sources are paraphrased using Moses. Another example of paraphrase corpus collected from several sources is Semantic Textual Similarity Corpus [1]. It is collected from the following sources: 750 sentence pairs from news, 189 from Framenet-Wordnet glosses, 561 from OntoNotes-Wordnet glosses and 750 using machine translation evaluation.

Another interesting approach towards paraphrase extraction is the collection of summaries of the same TV show episodes. The corpus collected in such way and described in [16] consists of 1992 pairs of sentences annotated by 2 experts. There are 4 paraphrase cases which are reduced to 2 in the evaluation phase.

Paraphrases can also be extracted from the answers to the questions as it is shown in [6]: Student Response Analysis Corpus, consisting of 14228 sentence pairs, is collected from students' answers to explanation and definition question.

Microblogs also offer a rich resource for paraphrase extraction. In [19] Twitter Paraphrase Corpus is collected from tweets corresponding to the same events: tweets referring to the same date and mentioning the same personalities are extracted. The corpus is not a sentential one: it consists of about 4 million phrase paraphrases (with no negative instances) which are obtained using a phrase-based statistical machine translation pipeline.

There also exists Russian Paraphrase corpus ParaPhraser [12] collected, as in the strategy initially proposed by [18], from pairs of news headlines. Headlines from different media agencies published the same day are compared to each other, and paraphrase candidates with similarity value above the threshold are included in the corpus and further annotated by naïve native speakers via an online crowdsourcing annotation interface. The similarity value is calculated as the extended matrix similarity metric proposed in [8], or a variant of soft cosine measure [17].

## 3 Data

We monitor news feed of the 13 Russian news media agencies in VKontakte (a Russian social network). The texts published by these agencies differ in style, and these differences are reflected in their headlines. For example, the style of RBC is purely formal,

---

[2] There also exists another recently collected Turkish Paraphrase Corpus [7].

business-like and laconic, and that of Gazeta.ru and L!FE – more informal, while the style of Kommersant, although a business media agency, is far from being laconic and official. RG, Russia Today and RIA are pro-government media, while Fontanka.ru and partly InoSMI (because it publishes translations of the foreign media) are the oppositional ones. In other words, we include various media sources to collect a representative corpus from the linguistic point of view.

The corpus collected from pairs of headlines published by these agencies currently includes 8463 paraphrases (only positive instances).

It can be seen that the corpus is comparable in its size with the ParaPhraser corpus (about 11 thousand sentence pairs) which consists of purely official news headlines. However, it is much more complex than the ParaPhraser corpus (from the point of view of automatic paraphrase detection) and richer in its linguistic phenomena. Another difference is that in ParaPhraser there are 3 classes of paraphrases: precise, loose and non-paraphrases, while the corpus in question consists of only positive paraphrase instances, precise and loose, most of which are expected to be loose (but there is no annotation).

## 4  Construction Method

Messages of the news feed of the 13 Russian media agencies in VKontakte are parsed in real time using Vkontakte API. News headlines and URLs leading to the corresponding articles are extracted. Web pages at these URLs are also parsed and the titles of the articles are extracted too. Then such pairs of headlines (a social network one and an official one) are included in the corpus which is constantly rising in size.

Raw headlines contain hashtags and rubrics of the media agencies which are irrelevant to our tasks, and so a few text preprocessing steps are needed. Hashtags, rubrics and phrases like "See also…" and "Continue…" are cut off. Some social network headlines consist of several sentences. In such cases we apply the following heuristics: if there are more than 2 sentences in the social network post, only the first one is chosen as a headline. If the official headline is also more than one sentence long, and the social network text was reduced to one sentence, this headline is also reduced to one (the first) sentence. If a social network headline consists of the official one plus one more sentence, such headlines are also cut off.

## 5  Paraphrase Detection Model

We explore and analyze the collected social network news feed paraphrase corpus by testing our existing paraphrase detection model against it. We focus on the misclassified paraphrases because, being the most complex ones, they are potentially richer of various linguistic phenomena and therefore are of the main interest for us.

Our paraphrase detection model is an SVM with two different types of features: shallow and semantic ones. The model is presented in [11], and in this section we only provide its brief description. The model is trained on the ParaPhraser[3] corpus [12], another Russian paraphrase corpus collected from pairs of official news headlines (without any social network texts). We selected this very model because it is our best one so far: we participated in the Russian Paraphrase Detection Shared Task 2016[4] with this model and took the 1st place in one of the standard runs. It obtained accuracy of 0.7448 in the binary paraphrase classification (paraphrase/non-paraphrase) task.

## 5.1  Classifier

The choice of a classifier in our existing model is quite traditional because the dataset is not large. We use an out-of-the-box SVM implemented in scikit-learn[5] with grid search optimization of its parameters.

## 5.2  Features

The two feature sets of the model from [11] correspond to the two types of sentences similarity measures: shallow measures are based on the surface overlap between the sentences on the phrase, word or character level, whereas semantic measures go deeper and compare the sentences using semantic relations between the words/phrases in the two sentences. Obviously, semantic measures usually require semantic resources. Details of the calculation of all the features described further in this paper can be found in [13].

**Shallow Features.** Shallow features of the described model include 13 features traditionally used in paraphrase detection community and 11 newly introduced ones. The former include BLEU, edit distance between the sentences, sentence length difference, longest common subsequence length, number of matching proper names and cardinal numbers, etc. The latter are calculated based on what is left in the two sentences after the removal of overlapping words (e.g., the portion of notional/capitalized words, the portion of over-lapping substrings left in the two sentences, etc.).

**Semantic Features.** Semantic features of the model include a metric which is the extension of the metric proposed in [8] or a variant of soft cosine distance [17] and a set of features based on what is left in the two sentences after the removal of overlapping words, synonyms and words with the same root (all in all, 11 features). To calculate features values, we employ two semantic resources: YARN – Yet Another RussNet [2] (roughly speaking, a Russian WordNet) and the dictionary of word formation by Tikhonov [20].

---

[3] http://paraphraser.ru/download.

[4] http://paraphraser.ru/contests/?contest_id=1.

[5] http://scikit-learn.org.

# 6  Results

We tested our paraphrase detection model described in Sect. 5 and previously introduced in [11] against the collected social network news feed corpus and obtained accuracy of 0.4043. Such poor results (compared to 0.7448 on ParaPhraser testing set) demand a closer look at the data.

We selected a sample of the misclassified paraphrases (i.e., of false negatives). The set of misclassified paraphrases is highly imbalanced in terms of the media agencies distribution, and to collect a balanced sample we selected $n$ paraphrases from each media agency where $n$ equals the minimal amount of paraphrases provided by an agency (across all our 13 media agencies; in our case $n$ equals 9.

We manually annotated the each paraphrase pair from the misclassified sample with special linguistic and pragmatic markers. We also selected a sample of correctly classified paraphrases of the same size (9 pairs per media agency) and annotated it with the same markers. Most markers[6] together with their description are shown in Table 1.

**Table 1.**  Linguistic (and other) markers

| Marker | Description |
| --- | --- |
| Different content | Sentences differ in words or phrases which carry additional information and make the sentences semantically different |
| Context knowledge | Sentences differ in the words or phrases, which do not make them semantically different given their context is known |
| Presupposition | Prior knowledge of the world is needed to prove that the sentences are semantically similar (or equivalent) |
| Metaphor | A metaphor takes place in one of the sentences |
| Irony | Irony takes place in at least one of the sentences |
| Attention attractor | At least one of the sentences is an uninformative news headline aimed to attract attention of the readers |
| Synonymy | Sentences differ in the synonymous word(s) |
| Phrasal Synonymy | Sentences differ in the synonymous multiword expressions |
| Syntactic synonymy | The same information is expressed in the sentences using different constituents or the same constituents with different grammatical characteristics |
| Reordering | Sentences consist of the same words in different order |

We Calculated the Portions of the Markers in the Selected Samples (Tables 2 and 3).

It can be seen from Tables 2 and 3 that different content is the most frequently occurring marker in both samples. It means that most paraphrase pairs in the collected corpus (we suppose that the samples reflect the main characteristics of the whole

---

[6] A full list of the markers is not provided in this paper because some of them are either not present in the selected sample of paraphrases or are currently not of our main interest.

**Table 2.** Percentage of markers in the misclassified paraphrase sample

| Marker | Portion, % |
|---|---|
| Different content | 87 |
| Attention attractor | 32 |
| Context knowledge | 18 |
| Irony | 16 |
| Presupposition | 13 |
| Syntactic synonymy | 13 |
| Metaphor | 11 |
| Phrasal synonymy | 7 |
| Synonymy | 6 |

**Table 3.** Percentage of markers in the correctly classified paraphrase sample

| Marker | Portion, % |
|---|---|
| Different content | 65 |
| Presupposition | 26 |
| Reordering | 16 |
| Syntactic synonymy | 15 |
| Phrasal synonymy | 11 |
| Attention attractor | 9 |
| Context knowledge | 9 |
| Synonymy | 4 |
| Irony | 3 |

dataset) are similar but not precise. The second most frequent marker among the misclassified paraphrases is the "attention attractor": almost one-third of the paraphrases in the sample contain attention attracting techniques (see examples #2–3 in Table 4). In the correctly misclassified sample, attention attraction marker occurs in a small portion of paraphrases. However, presupposition is a frequent marker, twice as frequent in the correctly classified sample as in the misclassified one (26% against 13%) – see examples #1–2 in Table 5.

It is also interesting to note that syntactic and phrasal synonymy which are expected in paraphrases (by the paraphrase detection model) are more frequent in the correctly classified sample than in the misclassified one. On the other hand, such phenomenon as irony is quite frequent in the misclassified sample and infrequent in the correctly classified one which means that our paraphrase detection model cannot handle irony[7] properly at the moment (see #1, #3, #6 in Table 6). Metaphor is also surprisingly frequent (for a news headline) in the misclassified sample (11%) (see #4–7 in Table 4). Moreover, metaphor, irony and attention attraction markers often occur together in the misclassified sample – see, for example, #3–6 in Table 4.

Word reordering does not occur in the misclassified sample at all while it is the third most frequent marker among the correctly classified paraphrases. Indeed, when news headlines are paraphrased by simply changing their word order, such paraphrases can be easily detected by the model.

By comparing the portions of the markers in Tables 2 and 3 we can conclude that pragmatic markers are perhaps the main reason of the model failure on the misclassified paraphrases. However, there is one exception: presupposition, according to the obtained results, does not complicate paraphrase detection task for our model. We believe that such phenomenon can be caused by the nature of the data: in the headlines paraphrased by journalists presupposition is often used to refer to some well-known person or event expressed in very few words, that is why a surface overlap-based model can still be

---

[7] There are, of course, other irony modifiers in the corpus, apart from irony itself (e.g., sarcasm), but they are beyond the scope of this paper.

**Table 4.** Examples of misclassified paraphrases from the Russian social network news feed corpus

| # | Social Network News Feed Title | Official Headline | Marker(s) |
|---|---|---|---|
| 1 | Выкатное поле стадиона оказалось не соответствующим требованиям ФИФА по показателям вибрации, превысив их в семь раз /Withdrawable field of the stadium did not satisfy the requirements of FIFA concerning vibration, exceeding them seven-fold/ | Для поля на «Зенит-Арене» разработали собственные стандарты вибрации /New vibration standards established for the field of "Zenit-Arena"/ | irony |
| 2 | Жителей Латвии традиционно поздравляют с Новым годом не только президент и премьер-министр. /Citizens of Latvia are traditionally congratulated on the New Year not only by the president and prime-minister./ | Территория котиков Territory of little cats | attention attractor |
| 3 | Мирно, по-семейному. /Peacefully, in the family./ | Серена Уильямс победила сестру в финале Открытого чемпионата Австралии /Serena Williams defeated her sister in the final of the Australian Open/ | attention attractor, irony |
| 4 | Иран планирует отменить визы для россиян и граждан еще 35 государств. /Iran plans to abolish visas for Russians and citizens of 35 other countries./ | Границ больше нет /No boundaries any more/ | attention attractor, metaphor |
| 5 | О вреде и бесполезности программ, которые призваны обеспечивать безопасность компьютеров /On the dangers and futility of programs that are designed to provide security for computers./ | Голый король. Почему вам не нужны антивирусы /Naked King. Why you do not need antivirus software/ | attention attractor, metaphor |
| 6 | Назначению петербуржца Романова на должность первого следователя России помогла студенческая дружба Медведева и раздражение академиками Путина. /Appointment of Romanov from St.-Petersburg as the first Russian investigator was helped by student friendship with Medvedev and the irritation by the academics of Putin./ | Зигзаги удачи генерала Романова /General Romanov's zigzags of luck/ | irony, presupposition, metaphor |
| 7 | Российские власти хотят ввести маркировку еды по степени вредности /Russian authorities want to introduce food labeling according to its degree of harmfulness/ | Иванов предложил ввести в России продуктовый "светофор" /Ivanov proposed to introduce food "traffic light" in Russia/ | metaphor |

**Table 5.** Examples of correctly classified paraphrases from the Russian social network feed corpus

| # | Social Network News Feed Title | Official Headline | Marker(s) |
|---|---|---|---|
| 1 | День отречения императора Николая Второго от престола должен стать памятной датой, считает Виталий Милонов. /The Day of Emperor Nicholas II's abdication from the throne should become a memorable date, said Vitaly Milonov./ | Милонов предлагает ввести новую памятную дату – День Февральской революции /Milonov proposes to introduce a new memorable date the Day of the February Revolution/ | presupposition |
| 2 | Леонардо Ди Каприо в роли итальянского Шерлока Холмса /Leonardo DiCaprio in the role of an Italian Sherlock Holmes/ | Леонардо Ди Каприо сыграет итальянского сыщика /Leonardo DiCaprio will play the Italian detective/ | presupposition |
| 3 | «Верните нам Россию»: кто и почему добивается в Бельгии отмены санкций /"Give us Russia back": who and why is seeking the lifting of sanctions in Belgium/ | «Верните нам Россию»: кто и почему добивается в Бельгии отмены санкций против Москвы /"Give us back Russia": who and why is seeking the lifting of sanctions against Moscow in Belgium/ | presupposition |

successful here. On the other hand, metaphor, irony and attention attraction usually occupy more space (in words) in a sentence and inevitably cause more surface difference between two sentential paraphrases which leads to poor performance of our model.

Since attention attractor, irony and presupposition markers are of the most interest to us in the considered samples, we also calculated the distribution of their occurrences among the different media agencies in both misclassified and correctly classified samples. The results together with schematic description of the media agencies are presented in Tables 6, 7 and 8. Oppositional media agencies are given in italics and the business ones are in bold. In Tables 6, 7 and 8, where there are several media agencies in the first column, the portion value refers to each of the listed agencies. InoSmi is

**Table 6.** Distribution of **attention attractor** markers among different media agencies

| Media agency | Portion, % |
|---|---|
| *InoSmi\**, L!FE | 16.7 |
| Gazeta.ru | 14.6 |
| *Lenta.ru, Fontanka.ru*, RIA | 10.4 |
| **Kommersant** | 6.3 |
| NTV, TASS | 4.2 |
| RG.ru, Russia Today, **RBC** | 2.1 |

**Table 7.** Distribution of **presupposition** markers among different media agencies

| Media agency | Portion, % |
|---|---|
| RG.ru | 13.0 |
| TASS, **Kommersant**, Russia Today | 10.9 |
| NTV, **RBC** | 10.9 |
| *Fontanka.ru* | 8.7 |
| RIA, *Lenta.ru, InoSmi\** | 6.5 |
| Interfax, Gazeta.ru | 2.2 |

**Table 8.** Distribution of **irony** markers among different media agencies

| Media agency | Portion, % |
|---|---|
| L!FE, *InoSmi\**, *Fontanka.ru* | 21.7 |
| *Lenta.ru*, **Kommersant**, Russia Today | 8.7 |
| Gazeta.ru, **RBC** | 4.3 |

marked by * since it can be considered oppositional only because it publishes translations of the foreign articles and not because its owners represent the opposition of the
current government (which is not true).

It is clear from the distribution of the markers in Tables 6, 7 and 8 that irony and
attention attractor markers mostly occur in the oppositional media. Indeed, in such
media government initiatives or politicians are often criticized (see, for example, #1
and #6 in Table 4). In business media headlines are usually quite straightforward and
formal and do not attempt to attract attention of the readers or to influence them
emotionally: such tendency is confirmed by low frequency of irony and attention
attraction markers among such media. Presupposition is, on the contrary, a frequent
phenomenon among the pro-government and business media with headlines referring
to the events or personalities presumably known to everybody. We believe that such
results are by no means surprising.

We also calculated the portions of correctly classified paraphrases among the different media agencies. The distribution of correct labels is shown in Table 9, oppositional media are given in italics and business media are in bold (Tables 6, 7 and 8).

**Table 9.** Distribution of correctly classified paraphrases among media agencies

| Media agency | Correct, % | Media agency | Correct, % |
|---|---|---|---|
| **RBC** | 83 | *Fontanka.ru* | 40 |
| Gazeta.ru | 77 | NTV | 34 |
| RIA | 74 | *Lenta.ru* | 33 |
| L!FE | 67 | **Kommersant** | 22 |
| Interfax | 55 | TASS | 16 |
| Russia Today | 48 | *InoSmi\** | 8 |
| RG.ru | 47 | | |

According to the results of our model prediction, RBC paraphrases are the easiest
ones to detect automatically: indeed, this business media agency is characterized by
laconic style and its headlines in the social network news feed and the official website
do not differ much. On the other hand, in InoSmi (a media agency which publishes
translations of the articles from foreign media agencies), headlines are full of various
linguistic phenomena which complicate the paraphrase detection task for paraphrase
detection task. In general, it seems that paraphrases from the pro-government media are

easier to detect for our model. We believe that the main reason for this is that they contain less pragmatic features like irony in them than the oppositional ones.

## 7 Conclusion

In this paper we have presented a new Russian paraphrase corpus: Russian social network news feed paraphrase corpus

The underlying paraphrase extraction method is based on the simple notion that a large number of media agencies alter their headlines when posting them at their social network page. At the same time, the headlines refer to the same event and such pairs of headlines (the official ones and the ones posted at the social network pages of the media agencies) can be considered paraphrases. Unlike other approaches towards paraphrase extraction and paraphrase corpora construction, ours is quite easy in its realization and does not demand any special linguistic resources or tools. Moreover, it allows us to collect a corpus of considerable size in a short period of time (we have already collected a corpus of about 8 thousand paraphrases in a month).

We have also taken a few steps exploring the collected data Firstly, we tested our previously developed paraphrase detection model against the data set. The model is trained on the other Russian paraphrase corpus: ParaPhraser, which consists of about 9 thousand sentence pairs (official news headlines, mostly quite formal) annotated as precise, loose or non-paraphrases. The model (which is actually surface-based) performs quite well on the ParaPhraser data (accuracy 0.7448) and poorly on the newly collected dataset (accuracy 0.4043). Such difference is caused by the complex nature of the new corpus: it is collected from both official and social network headlines.

Our second step included exploring various linguistic and pragmatic characteristics of the collected corpus. It turned out that our model mostly misclassified paraphrases which contain either irony, or metaphor, or attention attraction markers, all of which evidently complicate automatic text analysis. However, according to the results, presupposition does not complicate paraphrase detection task much. It is interesting to note that such conclusion is different from the one made in [14] where misclassification analysis is held on the ParaPhraser corpus (our training data).

The abundance of complex linguistic and pragmatic phenomena in the social network news feed corpus proves that it could be used not only for a standard paraphrase detection task but, for example, for irony detection, given that the appropriate annotation of the corpus is conducted.

Our analysis of the distribution of linguistic and pragmatic markers across different Russian media agencies revealed that oppositional agencies in general contain more pragmatic features than the pro-government ones.

We suppose that the collected corpus (which is also being collected at the moment) could be useful for natural language processing tasks such as paraphrase identification and irony detection as well as for the research of Russian media style.

# References

1. Agirre, E., Cer, D., Diab, M., Gonzalez-Agirre, A., Guo W.: SEM 2013 shared task: Semantic Textual Similarity. In: The Second Joint Conference on Lexical and Computational Semantics (2013)
2. Braslavski, P., Ustalov, D., Mukhin, M.: A spinning wheel for YARN: user interface for a crowdsourced thesaurus. In: Proceedings of the demonstrations at the 14th Conference of the European Chapter of the Association for Computational Linguistics, pp. 101–104. Gothenburg, Sweden (2014)
3. Chen, D.L., Dolan, W.B.: Collecting Highly Parallel Data for Paraphrase Evaluation. In: Proceedings of the 49th Annual Meeting of the Association for Computational Linguistics, pp. 190–200. Portland, Oregon, USA (2011)
4. Demir, S., El-Kahlout, l.D., Unal, E., Kaya, H.: Turkish paraphrase corpus. In: LREC 2012, pp. 4081–4091 (2012)
5. Dolan, W.B., Quirk, C., Brockett, C.: Unsupervised construction of large paraphrase corpora: exploiting massively parallel news sources. In: Proceedings of the 20th International Conference on Computational Linguistics, Geneva, Switzerland (2004)
6. Dzikovska, M.O., et al.: SemEval—2013 Task 7: the joint student response analysis and 8th recognizing textual entailment challenge. In: Proceedings of the 7th International Workshop on Semantic Evaluation (SemEval 2013), Atlanta, Georgia, USA. 13–14 June 2013
7. Eyecioglu, A., Keller, B.: Constructing a Turkish Corpus for Paraphrase Identification and Semantic Similarity. In: Gelbukh, A. (ed.) CICLing 2016. LNCS, vol. 9623, pp. 588–599. Springer, Cham (2018). https://doi.org/10.1007/978-3-319-75477-2_42
8. Fernando, S., Stevenson, M.: A semantic similarity approach to paraphrase detection. In: Proceedings of Computational Linguistics UK (CLUK 2008) 11th Annual Research Colloqium (2008)
9. Knight, K., Marcu, D.: Summarization beyond sentence extraction: a probabilistic approach to sentence compression. Artif. Intell. **139**(1), 91–107 (2002)
10. McCarthy, P.M., McNamara, D.S.: The user-language paraphrase corpus. In: Cross-Disciplinary Advances in Applied Natural Language Processing: Issues and Approaches, pp. 73–89 (2008)
11. Pivovarova, L., Pronoza, E., Yagunova, E., Pronoza, A.: ParaPhraser: Russian Paraphrase Corpus and Shared Task. In: Filchenkov, A., Pivovarova, L., Žižka, J. (eds.) AINL 2017. CCIS, vol. 789, pp. 211–225. Springer, Cham (2018). https://doi.org/10.1007/978-3-319-71746-3_18
12. Pronoza, E., Yagunova, E., Pronoza, A.: Construction of a Russian Paraphrase Corpus: Unsupervised Paraphrase Extraction. In: Braslavski, P., Markov, I., Pardalos, P., Volkovich, Y., Ignatov, Dmitry I., Koltsov, S., Koltsova, O. (eds.) RuSSIR 2015. CCIS, vol. 573, pp. 146–157. Springer, Cham (2016). https://doi.org/10.1007/978-3-319-41718-9_8
13. Pronoza, E., Yagunova, E.: Low-Level Features for Paraphrase Identification. In: Sidorov, G., Galicia-Haro, Sofía N. (eds.) MICAI 2015. LNCS (LNAI), vol. 9413, pp. 59–71. Springer, Cham (2015). https://doi.org/10.1007/978-3-319-27060-9_5
14. Pronoza E., Yagunova E.: Comparison of sentence similarity measures for Russian paraphrase identification. In: Artificial Intelligence and Natural Language and Information Extraction, Social Media and Web Search FRUCT Conference (AINL-ISMW FRUCT), pp. 74–82 (2015)

15. Pronoza, E., Yagunova, E., Kochetkova, N.: Sentence Paraphrase Graphs: Classification Based on Predictive Models or Annotators' Decisions? In: Sidorov, G., Herrera-Alcántara, O. (eds.) MICAI 2016. LNCS (LNAI), vol. 10061, pp. 41–52. Springer, Cham (2017). https://doi.org/10.1007/978-3-319-62434-1_4
16. Regneri, M., Wang, R., Pinkal, M.: Aligning predicate-argument structures for paraphrase fragment extraction. In: LREC 2014, pp. 4300–4307 (2014)
17. Sidorov, G., Gelbukh, A., Gómez-Adorno, H., Pinto, D.: Soft similarity and soft cosine measure: similarity of features in vector space model. Computación Sistemas 18(3), 491–504 (2014)
18. Wubben, S., van den Bosch, A., Krahmer, E., Marsi, E.: Clustering and matching headlines for automatic paraphrase acquisition. In: Proceedings of the 12th European Workshop on Natural Language Generation, pp. 122–125, Athens, Greece (2009)
19. Xu, W., Ritter, A., Grishman, R.: Gathering and generating paraphrases from twitter with application to normalization. In: Proceedings of the Sixth Workshop on Building and Using Comparable Corpora, pp. 121–128. Sofia, Bulgaria (2013)
20. Tikhonov, A.: Slovoobrazovatelnij slovar' russkogo yazika v dvuh tomah: Ok 145000 Slov. Russkiy Yazik, Moscow (1985)

# Prediction of User Retweets Based on Social Neighborhood Information and Topic Modelling

Pablo Gabriel Celayes and Martín Ariel Domínguez[✉]

Facultad de Matemática, Astronomía, Física y Computación
Universidad Nacional de Córdoba, Córdoba, Argentina
mdoming@famaf.unc.edu.ar

**Abstract.** Twitter and other social networks have become a fundamental source of information and a powerful tool to spread ideas and
opinions. A crucial step in understanding the mechanisms that drive
information diffusion in Twitter, is to study the influence of the social
neighborhood of a user in the construction of her retweeting preferences.
In particular, to what extent can the preferences of a user be predicted
given the preferences of her neighborhood.

We build our own sample graph of Twitter users and study the
problem of predicting retweets from a given user based on the retweeting behavior occurring in her second-degree social neighborhood (followed and followed-by-followed). We manage to train and evaluate user-
centered binary classification models that predict retweets with an average $F1$ score of 87.6%, based purely on social information, that is, without analyzing the content of the tweets.

For users getting low scores with such models (on a tuning dataset),
we improve the results by adding features extracted from the content
of tweets. To do so, we apply a Natural Language Processing (NLP)
pipeline including a Twitter-specific adaptation of the Latent Dirichlet
Allocation (LDA) probabilistic topic model.

**Keywords:** Retweet prediction · Social model
Social network analysis · Machine learning · LDA · SVM

## 1  Introduction

In the last years, social media sites (e.g., Twitter, Facebook, and YouTube)
have become increasingly massive. The Twitter application is an online real-time
social and information network that enables its users to post, read and share
messages of up to 140 characters, known as tweets. Every time a user writes
a tweet, Twitter attaches to it a unique identifier and a creation timestamp.
Another frequently used function on the bird net is the "retweet", which is the
action of reposting someone else's tweet inside your own message stream (the
"timeline").

© Springer Nature Switzerland AG 2018
F. Castro et al. (Eds.): MICAI 2017, LNAI 10633, pp. 146–157, 2018.
https://doi.org/10.1007/978-3-030-02840-4_12

This work addresses the central question of determining the influence of a user's social environment on her retweeting behavior. To this end, we train and evaluate classifier models that seek to predict retweets by a given user, considering the retweeting behavior of her second degree social neighborhood (followed users, and followed by followed). Additionally, we explore the possibility of improving these purely social models using Natural Language Processing (NLP) techniques to include content-based features.

The present work has been carried out in the following phases:

- Construction of a dataset of Twitter users, followers and tweets.
- Study of models to learn and predict retweeting preferences on this dataset, based on information about the social neighborhood of each user.
- Study of possible improvements to social prediction models, introducing Natural Language Processing techniques.

The work constitutes not only an interesting analysis of different algorithms and techniques, but also a way of understanding how users are influenced by their social environment.

The rest of this paper continues as follows· In Sect. 2 we compare our work with some relevant works in the area. Next, we provide a description of how we built the dataset for our experiments, both for purely social experiments and for those where we consider the content of tweets. In Sect. 4, we describe how we built the social model for retweet prediction, and also how we added content-based features to it: first, using the LDA probabilistic topic model [1], second, using the Twitter LDA variation proposed in [13]. Section 5 contains the analysis of the results obtained. We finish with Sect. 6, including conclusions and possible lines of research for future works.

## 2   Related Work

Over the last years, the topic of user recommendation in Twitter has been widely studied. Some examples of this interesting research topic are [3–5,7,10]. In particular, in [3], authors defined a measure between users called "Similar-to" and their framework focuses on discovering top similar users for each type of user in Twitter. Summarizing, these proposed works [3–5,7] show the recommender system currently implemented by Twitter to suggest new users to follow. They have ranked the relationships between users by using different techniques based on features, such as users' retweets, favorite tweets, email address and some historical data. In contrast, our approach is trying to predict a retweet, based on the structure of followed users (first and second degree followed) and the content of tweets.

Another interesting research topic in this area aims to predict if a given tweet will become a viral one, that is, trying to measure its "retweetability". This approach is very related to ours as it attempts to achieve this goal by predicting if a tweet will be retweeted. Some relevant works along these lines are [8,9,11,12]. In [8] the authors base their prediction in the content of tweets extracted from

CHOUDHURY-EXT dataset [2]. They use different features based on the text of the tweet, such as topics extracted by the LDA algorithm. They train a Logistic Regression model, and get to the following conclusion about Twitter users: As a general rule, a tweet is likely to be retweeted when it is about a general, public topic instead of a narrow, personal one. For instance, a tweet is unlikely to be retweeted when it is addressed to another Twitter user directly, while their topic analysis revealed that general topics affecting many users (e.g.: a general election or Christmas) are more likely to be retweeted.

In [9], the authors predict retweets in a dataset crawled using the Twitter Streaming API throughout October 2010. They adopt a machine learning approach based on the passive-aggressive algorithm, using social features such as the author of the tweet, the number of followers, friends, statuses, favorites, among others. They also used features related to the content of the tweet itself: number of hashtags, mentions, URLs, trending words, the length of the tweet, novelty, etc. They built a general model of prediction, and their best model obtained a 46.6% of $F_1$ score in average.

In contrast to the two works mentioned earlier, our approach to retweet prediction generates a different model for each given user. Also, while previous models employ social data in aggregated ways or combined with other kind of features, our initial models are based purely on specific social information about which neighbor users retweeted each given tweet. This makes our approach a more direct way of assessing the influence of social neighborhood behaviour in the retweet behavior of users.

This first approach achieves an average $F_1$ score of 88%. In cases where the pure social models performed poorly on a tuning dataset; we incorporated content-related features, obtained by including LDA topics from the tweets.

It is important to mention that although in [2] they study a more global concept of retweetability than the user-centered one we explore, our approach can be extended to have more general notions of retweetability as we explain in the last section.

# 3   Dataset

In this section, we describe how we build the datasets used in this work. First, we explain how we build the social graph used in the social based prediction. Second, we describe how we build the tweets dataset.

## 3.1   Social Graph

To the purpose of this work, we wanted to build a network where each user has a rich enough neighborhood of users, which would allow us to build social models for any user in the network.

To this end, we decide to build a homogenous network, trying to ensure that all users have similarly sized neighborhoods, by means of the following process:

First we built a large enough *universe graph* from which a homogenous sub-graph would be subsequently sampled. The universe graph is built as follows: starting with a singleton graph containing just the account of a specific Twitter user $\mathcal{U}_0 = \{u_0\}$, we perform 3 iterations of the following procedure: (1) Fetch all users followed by users in $\mathcal{U}_i$; (2) From that group, filter only those having at least 40 followers and following at least 40 accounts; (3) Add filtered users and their edges to get an extended $\mathcal{U}_{i+1}$ graph.

From this process, we obtain a universe graph $\mathcal{U} := \mathcal{U}_3$ with $2,926,181$ vertices and $10,144,158$ edges.

Since we want to fetch shared content for every user of our social graph and we also want it to be homogenous (note that users added in the last step will have no outgoing edges), we take a subgraph following this procedure:

- We start off with a small sample of seed users $S$, consisting of users in $\mathcal{U}$ having out-degree 50.
- For each of those, we add their 50 most socially affine followed users. The affinity between two users is measured as the ratio between the number of users followed by both and number of users followed by at least one of them.
- We repeat the last step for each newly added user until there are no more new users to add.

This procedure returns a graph $\mathcal{G}$ with $5,180$ vertices and $229,553$ edges. We call it the homogeneous $K$-degree closure ($K = 50$ in this case) of $S$ in the universe graph $\mathcal{U}$.

### 3.2  Content

For each user in the graph $\mathcal{G}$ from the previous section, we fetched their time-lines (i.e. all tweets written or shared) for one month, from August 25th until September 24th, 2015. Finally, we only kept the tweets written in the Spanish language –using the Twitter API tag for filtering–, resulting in a set $\mathcal{T}$ of $1,636,480$ tweets. We do so to be able to analyze the content of the tweets with LDA which we do only for Spanish.

## 4  Experimental Setup

In this work we aim to build models capable of predicting the retweeting pref-erences of a given user, based both on what we know of her social environment and the content she previously shared. This section describes how we build those models attempting to achieve this over a selection of users and tweets from the $(\mathcal{G}, \mathcal{T})$ dataset defined before. We start describing the predictive model based only on the social environment. Then, we analyze the possibility of improving these predictions using NLP techniques, which also take into account the text of the tweets.

## 4.1  Social Media Graph Information

The main focus of this work is to predict if a given user $u$ will share a given *tweet* based on information on who in user $u$'s neighborhood has shared it. Since the process of feature extraction, modeling, and parameter tuning is computationally expensive, these experiments are performed on a selected subset of users. We begin by describing the criterion with which this subset was selected. We then describe how we generate, for each user $u$, a neighborhood of users $E_u$ and a set $T_u$ of potentially interesting *tweets*. Then, we describe the feature extraction process based on $T_u$ and the partitioning into sets of *training, tuning,* and *evaluation*. Finally, we explain the process of training classifiers and tuning their parameters.

**User Selection Process.** The process of training classifier models is computationally expensive, so we decided to focus on a subset of selected users. It is desirable to work with users having enough shared content and also a rich enough level of social interactions. We took the 1000 users with highest Katz centrality [6] in $\mathcal{G}$, and on the other side, we picked the 1000 users with the highest number of retweets. We restrict our analysis to users belonging to both lists, which leaves us a set $U$ of 194 users, with an average number of 494 retweets per user.

It is important to remark that in our experiments the universe of users is still $\mathcal{G}$, with all its users and connections. $\mathcal{G}$ is used to generate the environments of each user in $U$ whose retweeting preferences we are trying to predict.

**Visible Tweets.** Using the Twitter API we do not have explicit information about whether or not a user saw a given tweet, but we can at least take a universe of *potentially viewed* tweets. This is simply the set of all the tweets written or shared by the users followed by $u$.

We exclude from this set those tweets *written* by $u$ herself, since our focus is in recognizing interesting external content, and not on studying the generation of content from a particular user. Formally this set is defined as:

$$T_u := \left( \bigcup_{x \in \{u\} \cup \texttt{followed}(u)} \texttt{timeline}(x) \right) - \{t \in T | \texttt{author}(t) = u\}, \qquad (1)$$

where $\texttt{followed}(u) := \{x \in G | (u, x) \in \texttt{follow}\}$ and $\texttt{timeline}(x)$ is the set of all tweets written or shared by $x$ for tweets fetched in $T$.

For some users, the set $T_u$ turned out to be too large, making the process of experimenting and model training too computationally intensive. We decided to prune each $T_u$ to a maximum of $10,000$ tweets. Since the retweeted tweets are the minority class, we decided to keep all positive examples and do the pruning by subsampling on the class of negative examples (non-retweets).

**User's Environment.** As the user $u$ can only see tweets shared by those users she follows, the information about her extended network can provide more indicators of the degree of interest of a tweet $t$. That is why we decided to take as a user's environment not only the users she follows, but also to continue one more step in the `follow` relation and include the users followed by them. This is, we take all users (other than $u$ herself) to 1 or 2 steps forward from $u$ in the directed graph $G$, formally:

$$E_u = \left( \bigcup_{x \in \{u\} \cup \texttt{followed}(u)} \texttt{followed}(x) \right) - \{u\} \qquad (2)$$

**Environment Features.** Now, we can build the set of vectors needed for the predictive model centered in user $u$. Given $E_u = \{u_1, u_2, \ldots, u_n\}$, we define for each tweet $t \in T_u$ the following vector of boolean features:

$$v_u(t) := [\texttt{tweet\_in\_tl}(t, u_i)]_{i=1,\ldots,n}, \qquad (3)$$

where $\texttt{tweet\_in\_tl}(t, u) := \begin{cases} 1 & t \in \texttt{timeline}(u) \\ 0 & \text{otherwise} \end{cases}$

Note that the content of tweet $t$ is not considered, we only include the information about who retweeted $t$. Gathering the vectors of all tweets in $T_u = \{t_1, ldots, t_m\}$ into a single matrix, our vectorized dataset is constructed as:

$$M_u := [\texttt{tweet\_en\_tl}(t_i, u_j)]_{\substack{1 \leq i \leq m, \\ 1 \leq j \leq n}} \qquad (4)$$

where the variable to be predicted for each tweet $t$ is $\texttt{tweet\_in\_tl}(t_i, u)$. Putting together all values of the target variable for user $u$, we obtain the following objective vector: $y_u := [\texttt{tweet\_in\_tl}(t_i, u)]_{1 \leq i \leq m}$.

**Splitting the Dataset.** As usual, to evaluate the performance of our models in unseen data, we separate a portion of the dataset for evaluation that won't be used by the algorithms in the training phase. On the other hand, in our process of extending models with additional features, we will need to make decisions based on the quality of the first family of models, but we don't want those decisions to influence the final evaluation. This leads us to create an additional partition of dataset, taking a subset that we call the *tuning* dataset. Summarizing, we decide, for every user $u$ to randomly split $M_u$ in training ($M_u^{tr}$), tuning ($M_u^{tu}$) and evaluation ($M_u^{te}$) datasets, containing 70%, 10% and 20% of $M_u$ dataset respectively. We denote the corresponding output labels for each of these datasets $y_u^{tr}$, $y_u^{tu}$ and $y_u^{te}$.

### 4.2  Adding Natural Language for Prediction

In this section, we present how we add information about the content of the tweet in the classifiers. We describe the process to transform the text into feature vectors. Then, we enumerate all stages in the transformation: the normalization and cleaning of the text, its tokenization, generation of *bag of words* feature vectors and the reduction of their dimensionality using LDA topic models.

**Selection of Users.** In this section we focus on improving the prediction quality for those users whose social model performs poorly. To this end, we take all users who have an $F1$ score lower than 0.75 in the tuning dataset $M_u^{tu}$. We are also interested in analyzing if there is any improvement in cases of better quality, so we extend the sample with a random selection of 10 more users.

This results in a $U_{NLP}$ set of 37 users, over which we will try NLP extended models, while keeping the purely social models for the remaining 157 users in $U$.

**Preprocessing.** In this section we enumerate the sequential transformations performed to turn a tweet into a vector of numeric features describing its content.

- **Normalization.** In the first step, we remove the following for normalizing purposes: URLs, lowercase, accents, unusual characters, vowel repetitions (e.g.: turn `goooooal` into `goal`) and blank spaces repetitions.
- **Tokenization.** Next, we proceed to split the text into tokens by means of: punctuation removal, word splitting, *stopwords* removal, stemming and removal of single characters words. For this purpose, we use the `NLTK`[1] package, that implements stopword removal and stemming for Spanish language.
- **Bag of words.** We keep only tokens occurring in at least 100 tweets and at most 30% of the entire corpus of tweets. This results in a vocabulary $V = \{t_1, \ldots, t_{11238}\}$ of $11,238$ terms, which we use to represent any tweet $t$ as a vector of integers containing the number of occurrences of each term from $V$ in $t$ ( the so-called *bag-of-words* representation):

$$v_{BOW}(tweet) := [count(t_i, tokens(tweet))]_{i=1}^{11238}, \tag{5}$$

where $count(t, tokens)$ counts the occurrence of term $t$ in the list *tokens*.
In the case of short texts like tweets, most terms occur 0 or 1 times, so $v_{BOW}$ can be regarded as a boolean vector.

- **LDA and TwitterLDA.** Training models with a large dimensionality leads to problems of both efficiency and overfitting. This is why we need to reduce bag-of-words vectors to a representation with fewer dimensions, but that still captures relevant information about the content of each tweet. To do so, we use the LDA model which discovers underlying topics within a given corpus and represents them as probability distributions of occurrence of terms. In turn, this algorithm can be applied to texts to model them as vectors of topical scores/probabilities.
  The short length of tweets and the fact that they normally cover just one main topic can lead to poor performance of classical LDA algorithm. That's

---

[1]  http://www.nltk.org/.

why we also experiment with `TwitterLDA`[13], a variation of LDA that modifies the underlying probabilistic model to group tweets by user and assign a single topic to each tweet. For both `LDA` and `TwitterLDA`, we experiment with models of 10 and 20 topics.

# 5 Results

In this section, we describe how the retweet prediction models were generated and evaluated. We compare our models to simple baseline models that predict retweets for a user based only on popularity of tweets, given by the number of "likes"[2] and the number of "retweets" for a given tweet. To build the baseline model, we use simple feature vectors with the number of retweets and the number of likes. Then we train a Logistic Regression Classifier for each user in $U$.

## 5.1 Social Models

We analyze now the results obtained from training and evaluating user-centered classifier models using the feature vectors described in Sect. 4.1. For each user in $U$ we trained an SVC[3] model from `scikit-learn`[4] on her training dataset $(M_u^{tr}, y_u^{tr})$, using the class `GridSearchCV` to perform a 3-fold cross-validated parameter search for the optimal configuration among all possible combinations of the following parameter choices:

```
{ "C":[0.01, 0.1, 1], "class_weight":["balanced", None],
"gamma":[ 0.1, 1, 10 ], "kernel":["rbf", "poly"]}
```

Finally, for each user $u$ in $U$ we evaluate the resulting classifier over the test set $(M_u^{te}, y_u^{te})$, obtaining an average $F1$-score of about 88% (Table 1), with a median score also around the same value. A more detailed analysis of the distribution of observed precision, recall and $F1$ scores over all users in $U$ can be seen in Fig. 1.

**Table 1.** Performance of models over $U$ on $M_u^{te}$.

| Model | Avg. $F1$ | Avg. Pr. | AVg. Rec. |
|---|---|---|---|
| Baseline | 23.57% | 21.1% | 44.9% |
| Social | 87.68% | 97.4% | 81.1% |
| Soc.+LDA(10) | 85.37% | 91.1% | 80.9% |
| Soc.+LDA(20) | 85.04% | 92.1% | 80.1% |
| Soc.+TW-LDA(10) | 87.99% | 98.1% | 80.9% |
| Soc.+TW-LDA(20) | 87.97% | 97.9% | 81.0% |

**Table 2.** Performance evaluations over $U_{NLP}$ on $M_u^{te}$.

| Model | Avg. $F1$ | Avg. Pr. | AVg. Rec. |
|---|---|---|---|
| Baseline | 23.96% | 20.4% | 38.9% |
| Social | 76.46% | 95.6% | 67.2% |
| Soc.+LDA(10) | 64.38% | 65.5% | 66.0% |
| Soc.+LDA(20) | 62.62% | 66.4% | 61.9% |
| Soc.+TW-LDA(10) | 78.12% | 97.9% | 66.2% |
| Soc.+TW-LDA(20) | 77.99% | 97.0% | 66.4% |

---

[2] Likes are represented by a small heart and are used to show appreciation for a tweet. The number of "likes" is the number of the users which express it for a given tweet.

[3] For *Support Vector Classifier*, name of classical Support Vector Machines (SVM) in `scikit-learn`.

[4] http://scikit-learn.org/.

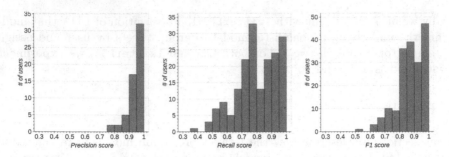

**Fig. 1.** Precision, recall and $F1$ score histograms of social model over $u \in U$ in $M_u^{te}$.

In Fig. 2 we compare the performance of our social prediction models with the baseline for users in $U$. We can see that the social models are in fact capturing the notion of social environment influence over each user, beyond what can be inferred from just looking at how popular a tweet is.

## 5.2   Social + NLP Models

In this section, we present some improvements on the purely social prediction by adding NLP features describing the content of tweets. We experiment with both classical LDA and TwitterLDA [13] models of 10 and 20 topics, on all selected 37 users in $U_{NLP}$. We use the same procedure as before to fit the classifiers, namely $SVM$ models with hyperparameters adjusted through a 3-fold cross-validated

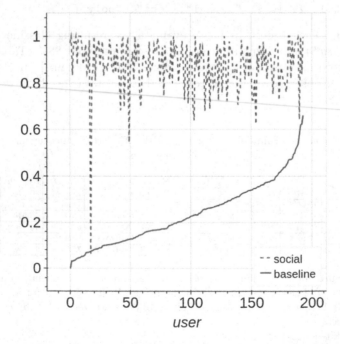

**Fig. 2.** $F1$ scores on baseline vs. social for $u \in U$ on $M_u^{te}$.

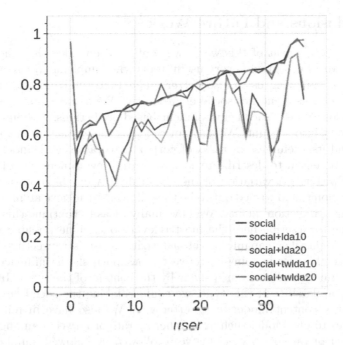

**Fig. 3.** $F1$ scores on soc vs. soc-LDA vs. soc-TwLDA for $u \in U_{NLP}$ on $M_u^{te}$.

search. To overcome convergence issues, in the case of classical LDA we apply scaling to all columns and impose a limit of $100,000$ iterations to the underlying numeric optimization algorithm.

We compare results with the models obtained in the previous section and the baseline, by analyzing performance over the test sets $(M_u^{te}, y_u^{te})$. It is important to remark that these datasets are not used in the training phase or in the selection of users in $U_{NLP}$. The latter were picked based on their performance on the tuning sets $(M_u^{tu}, y_u^{tu})$. In Table 2 we can see the results obtained over test sets of each user, restricted to users in $U_{NLP}$ for all models[5]. The best performing models are the ones that use `TwitterLDA` with 10 topics, attaining an average improvement of 1.7% over the purely social models.

From Table 2 we can also observe that classical `LDA` turns out to be very unsuitable for modeling Twitter content. Not only it doesn't attain an improvement, but it decreases the quality of models by more than a 12%, most likely due to overfitting on too descriptive topic probability features.

Only after switching to the `TwitterLDA` variation (which assigns a single topic to each tweet instead of a probability distribution over topics), we are able to obtain an improvement over the purely social model. These differences can be clearly observed in Fig. 3.

---

[5] We denote with `social+lda10` the models that combine social features and classical LDA features with 10 topics. Similar notation applies for 20 topics and the `TwitterLDA` variation.

# 6   Conclusions and Future Work

During the development of this work, we confirmed our idea that the analysis of social networks can provide very useful tools when implementing content recommendations, allowing us to also better understand the connections between the interests of a user and her social environment. We found it surprising to see the high performance of social environment-based predictions, without even taking the content into account. We also noticed that the extraction of topics with LDA, beyond its usefulness in tasks of corpus exploration and understanding, has enough potential to describe text content in a few dimensions of features. Using the TwitterLDA variation of the classical LDA model is of great importance at this point, and turned out to be the only way to achieve an improvement in the average prediction quality. We have many ideas to continue this work; we now continue to describe here the most relevant ones. One possible way is to try to infer a classifier capable of characterizing a user's retweeting behavior. This is, when the user is going to retweet, how much she is influenced by the social environment and how much she is by the content of the tweet. In the case of obtaining a classifier of this type, we could combine the social environment model and the content model in a better way. We also have in mind adding more features to our model such as number or rate of retweets among followed users, number or rate of retweets between followed by followed, number or rate of retweets between friendships (users who follow each other with the central user), among others. Finally, another interesting direction is to use our current user-centered retweet predictions to develop a notion of retweetability within groups or communities of users.

# References

1. Blei, D.M.: Probabilistic topic models. Commun. ACM **55**(4), 77–84 (2012)
2. Choudhury, M.D., Lin, Y.R., Sundaram, H., Candan, K.S., Xie, L., Kelliher, A.: How does the data sampling strategy impact the discovery of information diffusion in social media? In: ICWSM. The AAAI Press (2010)
3. Goel, A., Sharma, A., Wang, D., Yin, Z.: Discovering similar users on twitter. In: In 11th Workshop on Mining and Learning with Graphs (2013)
4. Gupta, P., Goel, A., Lin, J., Sharma, A., Wang, D., Zadeh, R.: WTF: The who to follow service at twitter. In: Proceedings of the 22nd International Conference on World Wide Web. International World Wide Web Conferences Steering Committee (2013)
5. Kamath, K., Sharma, A., Wang, D., Yin, Z.: RealGraph: user interaction prediction at twitter. In: In User Engagement Optimization Workshop @ KDD (2014)
6. Katz, L.: A new status index derived from sociometric analysis. Psychometrika **18**(1), 39–43 (1953)
7. Lin, J., Kolcz., A.: Large-scale machine learning at twitter. In: Proceedings of the 2012 ACM SIGMOD International Conference on Management of Data. ACM (2012)
8. Nasir, N., Gottron, T., Kunegis, J., Alhadi, A.C.: Bad news travel fast: a content-based analysis of interestingness on twitter. In: WebSci 2011: Proceedings of the 3rd International Conference on Web Science (2011)

9. Petrovic, S., Osborne, M., Lavrenko, V.: RT to win! predicting message propagation in twitter. ICWSM **11**, 586–589 (2011)
10. Yanar, A.: Combining topology-based & content-based analysis for followee recommendation on Twitter. Ph.D. thesis, Middle East Technical University, April 2015
11. Zaman, T.R., Herbrich, R., Van Gael, J., Stern, D.: Predicting information spreading in twitter. In: Workshop on computational social science and the wisdom of crowds, NIPS, vol. 104, pp. 17599–17601. Citeseer (2010)
12. Zhang, Q., Gong, Y., Wu, J., Huang, H., Huang, X.: Retweet prediction with attention-based deep neural network. In: Proceedings of the 25th ACM International on Conference on Information and Knowledge Management. ACM (2016)
13. Zhao, W.X., et al.: Comparing Twitter and Traditional Media Using Topic Models. In: Clough, P., et al. (eds.) ECIR 2011. LNCS, vol. 6611, pp. 338–349. Springer, Heidelberg (2011). https://doi.org/10.1007/978-3-642-20161-5_34

# Towards a Linguistic Corpus in Spanish with Personality Annotations

Yasmín Hernandez[1(✉)], Carlos Acevedo Peña[2], and Alicia Martínez[2]

[1] Instituto Nacional de Electricidad y Energías Limpias, Gerencia de Tecnologías de la Información, Reforma 113, 62490 Cuernavaca, Mexico
myhp@iie.org.mx
[2] Tecnológico Nacional de México, CENIDET, Interior Internado Palmira, 62490 Cuernavaca, Mexico
{carlos.acevedo,amartinez}@cenidet.edu.mx

**Abstract.** Personality is a combination of characteristics that determine the behavior of individuals in different situations, and it affects people interaction, relationships and environment. To know the personality can be useful to several tasks like marketing and personnel recruitment. Previous research indicates that personality can be predicted by text analysis. We are constructing a linguistic corpus with personality annotation for Spanish language with base on the DISC Model of personality. The corpus aim is to support personality prediction. As a basis for the corpus, we have conducted a study with 120 individuals, they answered a personality test and written some paragraphs. In this paper, we present our approach to construct the corpus base and the results of the study.

**Keywords:** DISC model · Linguistic corpus · Natural language processing
Personality recognition

## 1 Introduction

Personality is a combination of characteristics and behavior of an individual in dealing with different situations [1], it can influence on choices of people in several things such as websites, books, music and films [2]. Personality affects the way we interact with other people, our relationships and the environment around us. Personality has been shown to be relevant to many types of interactions; it has been shown to be useful in predicting job satisfaction, professional and romantic relationship success, and even preference for different interfaces [3]. The personality is important for several processes such as: personnel recruitment, psychological therapies conduction, tutoring o teaching students, and health advising, among others. Therefore, several applications could benefit from personality insights.

Previous work on personality and interfaces showed that users are more receptive and have more confidence in interfaces and information presented from the perspective of their own personality traits. Namely, introvert people prefer messages presented from the perspective of an introvert individual. If the personality of a user can be predicted from their social media profile, online marketing and other applications can use this to personalize their message and its presentation [3].

© Springer Nature Switzerland AG 2018
F. Castro et al. (Eds.): MICAI 2017, LNAI 10633, pp. 158–168, 2018.
https://doi.org/10.1007/978-3-030-02840-4_13

Several models of personality have been proposed, such as the Big Five model [4], the PEN model [5] or the DISC model [6, 7]. Typically, in order to identify personality, it is necessary for the individual to undergo a psychological assessment or a personality test based on a personality model.

Researchers have tried to obtain information about the personality of people through direct means such as the revised Eysenck personality questionnaire (EPQ-R) [8]. However, indirect methods, such as linguistic analysis, can be used [3]. The indirect methods use semi-supervised multi-label classification [9], data mining techniques, automatic learning, with demographic and text attributes [10].

Because personality is considered to be stable over time and throughout different situations, specialized psychologists are able to infer the personality profile of a subject by observing the subject's behavior. One of the sources of knowledge about the behavior of individuals is written text [8].

Much research in personality prediction has been conducted, however most of them are focused on English language and they are based on the Big Five model. In this research, we are interested in predict personality through Spanish text analysis and with base on the DISC model of personality.

We decided to use DISC model of personality because it is considered a simple model since needs short time to assess, the result can be obtained easily, and can provide adequate information regardless if the people conducting the survey are knowledgeable in psychology [11].

We are working on the construction of a linguistic corpus in Spanish annotated with the personality factors of the DISC model. This corpus will be useful in the identification of the personality through the analysis of texts. In order to build the corpus, we conducted a study of personality with 120 people participating. The study consisted on to have participants answering a general questionnaire and writing a text on a general topic they selected. Answers and text were handwritten.

The rest of the paper is organized as following: Sect. 2 presents background and related work, Sect. 3 describes briefly the DISC personality model, Sect. 4 presents our approach to build the corpus, Sect. 5 analyses preliminary results, and finally conclusions and future work are presented in Sect. 6.

## 2  Background and Related Work

Personality is a crucial aspect of social interaction. Under the computational perspective it can be very useful for marketing and for interesting tasks such as sentiment analysis [12]. There are several approaches and models of personality, such as the Big Five Model [4], PEN model [5] and DISC model [6, 7]. The Big Five model of personality has emerged as one of the most well-researched and well-regarded measures of personality structure in recent years [3], however there are interesting works using other personality models [8, 11, 13–17].

Social networks are an inexhaustible source of material to analyze several phenomena. Several studies with postings from social networks have been conducted to analyze personality of users.

In an study, a 45-question version of the Big Five Personality Inventory [18] was administered to Twitter© users. It was gathered public information from their profiles. After processing this data, many small correlations were found in the data. Using the profile data as a feature set, two machine learning algorithms were trained (ZeroR and Gaussian Processes) to predict scores on each of the five personality traits [3]. Another way of identifying the personality has been through the analysis of the behavior of social networks users. It was developed a set of measures based on the behavior of the Twitter© users towards their friends and followers, considering the intensity and the number of social interactions. This work identified personality with a statistically equivalent performance to the text analysis [19].

A research work was carried out using Italian language and the Big Five personality model. This approach identifies personality using linguistic characteristics and unsupervised machine learning. The study runs on a set of 1065 publications of 748 people [12]. Other techniques such as text mining and automatic learning have also been used to predict personality. A study was conducted considering demographic attributes and comments provided by the user [10].

In order to identify personality through the analysis of texts, the use of linguistic resources such as a linguistic corpus has been considered. A linguistic corpus can be defined as a collection of texts in electronic format, which become repositories of information from which to find, obtain, and therefore learn the multiple contexts in which a particular word may appear, becoming a fundamental source of information for several applications [20].

A research work was focused on the identification of personality and happiness, taking advantage of the dimension of the mobile network. An application was developed to acquire information in the form of written text from WhatsApp© application and SMS messages in Spanish. This work is still in early stages, however several tests have conducted with one public dataset with real messages and two datasets generated from messages collected from different websites. The public data set is a corpus of 63,017 tweets [8].

A different approach proposes the personality prediction as a multiple-label problem. It is based on the Big Five Model to predict personality in social media data, more specifically in tweets. A pre-processing is applied to extract the meta-attributes of the corpus and constructing a new one, a meta-base, using these data. The transformation process is responsible for converting each multi-label problem into a binary problem, and a classification process is responsible for the personality classification itself [9].

A recent study is focused on predicting personality from Chinese texts, using the Big Five personality model. It was found that extravert people seem to write more sentences and use more common words than introvert people. This indicates that extraverts are more willing to share their mood and life with others than introverts [21].

In another research based on text classification to predict personality used tweets in English and Indonesian. As result the MyPersonality corpus [22] was built, it consists of 10,000 updates from 250 users, which already are labeled into Big Five [4] personality dimensions [1].

Unlike most of aforementioned research works, which deal with texts in English and are based on the Big Five model of personality, this research work is based on the DISC model of personality and texts in Spanish to construct a linguistic corpus with annotations of personality. This corpus will be useful to predict personality from the text written in future work.

## 3   DISC Personality Model

The DISC model of personality [6, 7] states that there are four dimensions or unique characteristics of the personality. Although these traits represent existing characteristics in every person in some degree, it is important to know which of them is the predominant in a person in order to understand his or her personality. In this model personality is established by a test, which is answered by the individuals.

The four personality traits proposed by DISC Model are: *Dominance, Influence, Steadiness, Compliance* [23], and they denote the basic behavioral styles. The first axes represent assertiveness and receptiveness. The other axes represent openness and control. The personality of individual lies between the axes [7, 23]. Figure 1 shows the modern version of DISC model.

**Fig. 1.** DISC model. This model proposes four dimensions of personality: dominance, influence, steadiness, compliance [26].

When a set of DISC results shows a high *dominance factor*, they are describing someone with an independent attitude and a motivation to succeed on their own terms. High-D's people have the strength of will to work well under pressure, and are always ready to take on responsibility [7, 24, 25].

When *Influence* stands out as a major factor in a DISC profile, that profile describes someone with a positive attitude to other people, and the confidence to demonstrate that attitude. People of this kind are at their most comfortable in a social situation, and interact with others in an open and expressive way [7, 24, 25].

*Steadiness* is related to natural pace of a person and his reactions to change. This factor describes a comparatively reticent and careful type of person. Compared to Dominance or Influence, a person whose major factor is Steadiness will tend to be far less open or direct. Steady people more usually respond to events, rather than take pro-active steps themselves. As it implies, steady people are consistent and reliable in their approach. Indeed, they prefer to operate in situations that follow established patterns, and to avoid unplanned developments. Because of this, people with high steadiness tend to be quite resistant to change, and will take time to adapt to new situations [7, 24, 25].

*Compliance* factor is connected to accuracy, organization and attitudes to authority. A person who shows high compliance in their DISC profile has a concern for practicality and detail. The key to this factor lies in attitudes to authority. High-C's are concerned with working within the rules, and indeed are often described as rule-oriented. This applies in more general ways, they are also concerned with accuracy and structure, and understanding the ways things work [7, 24, 25].

## 3.1  Personality Test

The DISC personality test consists of 28 groups of four adjectives. In order to assess the personality, individuals have to choose the adjective that identifies them the most and the adjective that identifies them the less. Table 1 shows an example of adjectives group of DISC test.

**Table 1.** Example of adjectives group of DISC personality test.

|              | More | Less |
|--------------|------|------|
| Enthusiastic |      |      |
| Quick        |      |      |
| Logical      |      |      |
| Peaceful     |      |      |

As result of the DISC personality test, we have four graphs with a set of scores representing each dimension. The dominant DISC score is linked to a personality description system. Besides the dominant factor, the personality of an individual can be assigned to one of 15 classic personality combinations or patterns. Creative pattern can be assigned to both *Dominance* and *Compliance* dimensions of personality. These combinations are given because a person may have one or more dominant basic styles. Figure 2 shows four examples of the patterns presented in the graphs resulting in the DISC personality tests. Each graphics shows 4 points indicating the intensity of each personality factor. The points correspond to the score for each personality factor. The letters in the top corresponds to personality factors and numbers in the left corresponds to obtain score in the personality test. Points are joined by a line to form a pattern of personality. The height of each point indicates the intensity of corresponding personality factor.

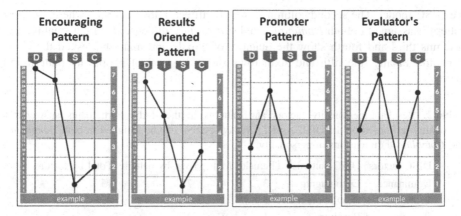

**Fig. 2.** Four of the fifteen classic patterns of the DISC personality test. The DISC model proposes four factors and fifteen classic patterns of personality. Each graphics is composed by four points corresponding to the four personality factors and corresponds to a pattern of personality.

## 4 Corpus Construction Approach

In this research work, we are interested in knowing personality from a written text, therefore we conducted a study for knowing personality and to relate it with writing features in order to build a linguistic corpus.

The study was organized in three stages. In the first stage, the participants answered questions about personal information, such as: gender, age, schooling, marital status, occupation, preferred social networks, and number of friends in such social networks. In the second stage, they filled out the questionnaire of the DISC personality model [6, 7]. In the third stage, the participants wrote some paragraphs about any subject. Some suggested subjects were: hobbies, what did you do yesterday, and so on. But they were free to choose any topic. These written texts are the basis to construct form our corpus.

In the study 120 college students participated, 49 females and 71 males, their age are between 20 and 30 years old. We asked for age range rather than exact age. The questionnaires and texts were hand written by participants. Texts were transcript to digital texts.

## 5 Study Results

After applying the personality test, we obtained the following results: Facebook and Twitter are preferred social networks of participants, with 105 participants and 15 participants. The average number of friends in the social networks of the participants is 531 people.

The most pronounced factor in each participant and the personality pattern are generated according to their responses. Table 2 shows the resultant personality and patterns of each person. In the first column we can see the four personality factors of the DISC model. The second column shows the fifteen DISC patterns, where *Creative* pattern is assigned to both *Dominance* and *Compliance* dimensions of personality. The columns third and fourth show the quantity of female and male that asked the questionnaire. Finally, the fifth and sixth rows show the total of people by pattern and factor.

**Table 2.** Resultant personality factors and patterns in the study. Participants answered a personality test based on the DISC model. Creative pattern can be assigned to both *Dominance* and *Compliance* dimensions of personality.

| DISC factors | DISC patterns | Female | Male | Total by pattern | Total by factor |
|---|---|---|---|---|---|
| Dominance | Encouraging | 3 | 4 | 7 | 15 |
| | Results oriented | 3 | 1 | 4 | |
| | Resolute | 1 | 1 | 2 | |
| | Creative | 1 | 1 | 2 | |
| Influence | Adviser | 6 | 9 | 15 | 25 |
| | Evaluator | 2 | 0 | 2 | |
| | Persuasive | 0 | 5 | 5 | |
| | Promoter | 1 | 2 | 3 | |
| Steadiness | Agent | 8 | 6 | 14 | 61 |
| | Specialist | 12 | 16 | 28 | |
| | Investigator | 4 | 8 | 12 | |
| | Producer | 1 | 6 | 7 | |
| Compliance | Objective | 1 | 1 | 2 | *19* |
| | Professional | 3 | 3 | 6 | |
| | Perfectionist | 2 | 5 | 7 | |
| | Creative | 1 | 3 | 4 | |

The results obtained from the applied surveys gave us the following results: the most frequent personality is the factor *Steadiness*, with a total of 61 people; the second most frequent factor was *Influence* with a total of 25 people; the next factor is the factor *Compliance* with 19 people; and the least frequent was the factor *Dominance* with 15 people.

Besides the personality of participants, we obtained a set of 120 texts written by participants in the survey. Texts have 90 words in average and a lexical richness of 0.19. To measure lexical richness, we used the Type-Token ratio (TTR) measure, this measure is expressed as the number of different words in a text divided by the total words in that text. Being type the repertoire of different words and token the number of total words. The lexical richness was measured by joining all the texts. In addition, we measured lexical richness eliminating the stopwords and obtaining a lexical richness of 0.39. In Table 3, an example of a text written by a participant is presented, also the translation to English is presented.

This set of texts will be the basis of the corpus. The set of texts was grouped into four groups based on the DISC personality factors.

**Table 3.** Example of a text of the corpus. The participants write a hand written Spanish text. The text is also presented in English only for clearness.

| Example of text in Spanish | Example of text in English |
|---|---|
| "Ayer me levanté con emoción me bañé y me cambié para andar en mi casa, terminé de construir un comedero para aves con un bote de plástico para reciclar, lo decoré con tronquitos de árbol y le coloqué alimento para pajaritos, después bajé a almorzar con mi familia y platicamos un rato, al terminar alzamos la mesa, mi mamá y mi hermana salieron a comprar, me quedé cuidando mi hermano menor, jugamos un rato y le dimos de comer a nuestra perrita, al bajar el sol subimos a ver la luna. Después de bajar de la azotea vimos un poco de televisión, nos reunimos en el comedor para platicar con la familia, terminamos de pintar unos útiles para colocarlos en la nueva cocina. Al terminar de cenar con mi familia estrenamos el lavadero, acompañé a lavar los trastes, cuando terminamos nos despedimos para dormir cada quien en su habitación y vernos al día siguiente." | "Yesterday I got up with excitement I took a shower and got dressed to stay at home, I finished the construction of a bird feeder with a recycled plastic bottle, I decorated it with tree trunks and I put food for little birds, then I go downstairs to have lunch with my family and we talked for a while, at the end we cleaned the table, my mother and my sister went shopping, I took cared for my younger brother, we played for a while and we fed our dog, when the sun set, we go up to see the moon. After getting off the roof we watch TV for a while, we met in the dining room to talk with the family, we finished painting some items to place them in the new kitchen. At the end of dinner with my family we opened the laundry room, I accompanied the washing of the dishes, when we finished we said goodbye to everyone and went to sleep in own room and see us the next day." |

A plain text file was created for each personality factor, and all the texts corresponding to the same type of personality were combined in the corresponding file, so that we could work with them in several ways.

After that, we performed a frequency counting of words to see if there is important information in the text that gives us some significant indicators about the prediction of personality. A spelling correction in the text was run out, then the stop words were deleted since they do not provide us with relevant information, finally the Freeling tool [27] was used to obtain the word root and thus to make a more effective count.

During the results analysis, we observed that most participants selected to write about suggested topics and most words were repeated in different sets of texts of the four personalities, and with different frequency. In addition, to the frequency with which the lemmas were used, a count of the number of people who used the lemma was also carried out to find out if they are really lemmas that are used more by people with a certain personality type. Table 4 shows the results of the most frequent lemmas in the four personality factors

Following with the analysis, we obtained the frequencies of each word and its percentage. For instance, the lemma "*yesterday*" is an adverb, and its frequency of use in the dominant personality group was 12. This represents 80% of people in this group who used this lemma, because the number of people in this group is 15. and presents this analysis, the texts corresponding to personality D (Dominance) was 73.3%, which, corresponding to the highest percentage in the use of adverbs. This factor is followed

**Table 4.** Results of text analysis, most frequent lemmas in the four-personality types. Where D: Number of occurrences in the Dominance factor; I: Number of occurrences in the Influence factor; S: Number of occurrences in the factor Steadiness; C: Number of occurrences in the factor Compliance.

| Tipo | English Word | Spanish Word | D | % | I | % | S | % | C | % |
|------|--------------|--------------|---|---|---|---|---|---|---|---|
| Adverbio | Yesterday | Ayer | 12 | 80.0% | 14 | 56.0% | 31 | 50.8% | 8 | 42.1% |
| Adverbio | After | Después | 10 | 66.7% | 12 | 48.0% | 10 | 16.4% | 7 | 36.8% |
| | | Total = | 22 | 73.3% | | 52.0% | | 33.6% | | 39.5% |
| Sustantivo | Day | Día | 12 | 80.0% | 24 | 96.0% | 38 | 62.3% | 13 | 68.4% |
| Sustantivo | Home | Casa | 10 | 66.7% | 10 | 40.0% | 20 | 32.8% | 8 | 42.1% |
| Sustantivo | Family | Familia | 8 | 53.3% | 21 | 84.0% | 17 | 27.9% | 8 | 42.1% |
| Sustantivo | Hobby | Pasatiempo | 7 | 46.7% | 14 | 56.0% | 19 | 31.1% | 8 | 42.1% |
| Sustantivo | Career | Carrera | 6 | 40.0% | 18 | 72.0% | 14 | 23.0% | 6 | 31.6% |
| Sustantivo | Life | Vida | 6 | 40.0% | 11 | 44.0% | 17 | 27.9% | 8 | 42.1% |
| | | Total = | 49 | 54.4% | | 65.3% | | 34.2% | | 44.7% |
| Verbo | Finish | Terminar | 11 | 73.3% | 19 | 76.0% | 37 | 60.7% | 8 | 42.1% |
| Verbo | Goal | Meta | 10 | 66.7% | 23 | 92.0% | 26 | 42.6% | 12 | 63.2% |
| Verbo | Like | Gustar | 5 | 33.3% | 15 | 60.0% | 18 | 29.5% | 9 | 47.4% |
| Verbo | Play | Jugar | 5 | 33.3% | 11 | 44.0% | 14 | 23.0% | 16 | 84.2% |
| | | Total = | 31 | 51.7% | | 68.0% | | 38.9% | | 59.2% |
| Adjetivo | Favourite | Favorito | 7 | 46.7% | 13 | 52.0% | 17 | 27.9% | 7 | 36.8% |
| Adjetivo | Principal | Principal | 5 | 33.3% | 14 | 56.0% | 14 | 23.0% | 5 | 26.3% |
| | | Total = | 12 | 40.0% | | 54.0% | | 25.4% | | 31.6% |

by the I factor (Influence) with a percentage of 52.0%, the next factor is C (Compliance) with 39.5% and finally S (Steadiness) with a percentage of 33.6%.

In the use of nouns, the factor that shows the highest percentage is the factor I (Influence) with 65.3%, followed by the factor D (Dominance) with 54.4%, followed by the factor C (Compliance) with a percentage of 44.7%, being the S factor (Steadiness) the lowest with a percentage of 34.2%. According to the analysis we could note that, the factor I (Influence) has the highest percentages in the use of verbs and adjectives. This could indicate that, in this type of personality, people write with a greater combination of grammatical elements. On the other hand, the S factor (Steadiness) showed lower percentages in the use of grammatical elements in all cases.

# 6    Conclusions and Future Work

The identification of personality traits is useful us to understand diverse aspects such as collective behaviors and preferences of people.

In this research, the approach to construct a linguistic corpus for Spanish language is presented. The corpus is annotated with personality traits as proposed by the DISC model [6, 7], and it will help us in the identification of the personality through the analysis of texts. To construct the corpus of texts, we conducted a study where 120 people participated. In this study the people was asked to answer a personality test and to write some paragraphs. In this study we gather texts and information of the participants. Until now, we use the set of texts to count the frequency of words using the techniques of spelling, frequency counting and lemming with the support of the Freeling tool [27]. Additionally, we identified the type of grammatical elements of each lemma. These processes were run out to try to figure out if there was important information in the text that would give us some significant indicator about personality prediction.

Also, after analyzing the results obtained, we can comment that, the factor with the highest average percentage of occurrence of adverbs is the D factor (Dominance) with a percentage of 73.3%. In the rest of the cases of use of nouns, verbs and adjectives the factor that showed the highest percentage was the factor I (Influence) with percentages of 65.3%, 68.0% and 54.0%. The S factor (Steadiness) is the factor that showed the lowest percentage in the use of grammatical elements in all cases. This indicates that people who have an I (Influence) personality have a tendency to write texts with a greater combination of grammatical elements.

This work is still in an early stage, there is a lot of work to be done in order to produce conclusive results. For example, the analysis of the patterns that are obtained from the personality tests since these are obtained when selecting adjectives in the surveys, one could find an important relation between the adjectives used in the test and the personalities. You could also gather more texts with a more varied group of people in terms of age or schooling to have a more varied set of lemmas in the results that tell us more about each personality.

It is planned in future research to find representative characteristics of each personality in the text and to carry out the personality detection through the analysis with the use of algorithms that allow us to reach that result.

# References

1. Pratama, B.Y., Sarno, R.: Personality classification based on twitter text using Naïve Bayes, KNN and SVM. In: 2015 International Conference on Data and Software Engineering (ICoDSE), pp. 170–174 (2015)
2. Cantador, I., Fernández-Tobías, I., Bellogín, A.: Relating personality types with user preferences in multiple entertainment domains. In: CEUR Workshop Proceedings, vol. 997 (2013)
3. Golbeck, J., Robles, C., Edmondson, M., Turner, K.: Predicting personality from twitter. In: 2011 IEEE Third International Conference on Privacy, Security, Risk and Trust (PASSAT) and 2011 IEEE Third International Conference on Social Computing (SocialCom), pp. 149–156 (2011)
4. Tupes, E.C., Christal, R.: Recurrent personality factors based on trait ratings. J. Pers. 60(2), 225–251 (1992)
5. Eysenck, H.J.: Dimensions of Personality. Transaction Publishers, Piscataway (1950)
6. Marston, W.M.: Emotions of normal people. Int. Libr. Psychol. Philos. Sci. Method 405, p. xiii (1928)
7. A. S. Ltd.: What is DISC? https://www.discusonline.com/disc/what-is-disc.php. Accessed 1 Jan 2017

8. Sáez Achaerandio, Y., Navarro, C., Mochón Sáez, A., Isasi Viñuela, P.: A system for personality and happiness detection. IJIMAI **2**(5), 8–16 (2014)
9. Lima, A.C.E.S., de Castro, L.N.: A multi-label, semi-supervised classification approach applied to personality prediction in social media. Neural Netw. **58**, 122–130 (2014)
10. Wald, R., Khoshgoftaar, T., Sumner, C.: Machine prediction of personality from Facebook profiles. In: 2012 IEEE 13th International Conference on Information Reuse and Integration (IRI), pp. 109–115 (2012)
11. Yuniar, I., Agung, A.A.G.: Personality assessment website using DISC. In: 2016 International Conference on Information Management and Technology (ICIMTech), pp. 72–77, Nov 2016
12. Celli, F.: Unsupervised personality recognition for social network sites. In: ICDS 2012 sixth International Conference on Digital Society, pp. 59–62 (2012)
13. Goh, J.X., Schlegel, K., Tignor, S.M., Hall, J.A.: Who is interested in personality? The interest in personality scale and its correlates. Personality Individ. Differ. **101**, 185–191 (2016)
14. Luyckx, K., Daelemans, W.: European language resources, "personae: a corpus for author and personality prediction from text". In: Sixth International Conference on Language Resource Evaluation LREC 2008, May 2017, pp. 2981–2987 (2008)
15. Liu, Y., Wang, J., Jiang, Y.: PT-LDA: a latent variable model to predict personality traits of social network users. Neurocomputing **210**, 155–163 (2016)
16. Anglim, J., Grant, S.L.: Incremental criterion prediction of personality facets over factors: obtaining unbiased estimates and confidence intervals. J. Res. Pers. **53**, 148–157 (2014)
17. de Vries, R.E., Tybur, J.M., Pollet, T.V., van Vugt, M.: Evolution, situational affordances, and the HEXACO model of personality. Evol. Hum. Behav. **37**(5), 407–421 (2015)
18. John, O.P., Srivastava, S.: Big five inventory (Bfi). Handb. Personal. Theory Res. **2**, 102–138 (1999)
19. Adali, S., Golbeck, J.: Predicting personality with social behavior. In: 2012 IEEE/ACM International Conference on Advances in Social Networks Analysis and Mining (ASONAM), pp. 302–309 (2012)
20. Taulé, M.: SENSEVAL, una aproximación computacional al significado, pp. 1–13 (2003)
21. Peng, K.-H., Liou, L.-H., Chang, C.-S., Lee, D.-S.: Predicting personality traits of Chinese users based on Facebook wall posts. In: 2015 24th Wireless and Optical Communication Conference (WOCC), pp. 9–14 (2015)
22. Celli, F., Pianesi, F., Stillwell, D., Kosinski, M.: Workshop on computational personality recognition: shared task. Proc. Work. Pers. Recogn. **2006**, 2–5 (2013)
23. I. Publishing: Research report. Technology, pp. 15–25 (2008)
24. D. Insight: The DISC Insights Web Development Team. https://www.discinsights.com/
25. D. P. 4U: DISC Behavioral Styles. http://www.discprofiles4u.com/
26. Bradberry, T.: El Codigo de La Personalidad. Editorial Norma, Bogotá colombia (2008)
27. Freeling. http://nlp.lsi.upc.edu/freeling/node/1

# Intelligent Tutoring Systems and Educational Applications

# Learning Models for Student Performance Prediction

Rafael Cavazos and Sara Elena Garza$^{(\boxtimes)}$

Facultad de Ingeniería Mecánica y Eléctrica, UANL,
San Nicolás de los Garza, Nuevo León, Mexico
rafael.cavazosm@uanl.mx, sara.garzavl@uanl.edu.mx

**Abstract.** Predicting student performance supports educational decision-making by allowing directives and teachers to detect students in special situations (e.g. students at risk of failing a course or dropping out of school) and manage these in a timely manner. The problem we address consists of grade prediction for the courses of a given academic period. We propose to learn a predictive model for each course. Two cases can be distinguished: historical grades are unavailable for prediction (first semester) and historical grades are available. For the first case, features that include selection test scores, socioeconomic information, and middle school the student comes from are proposed. For the second case, features that include past grades from similar courses are proposed. To test our approach, we gathered data from a Mexican public high school (three generations, 2,000 students, four semesters, and 24 courses). Our results indicate that features such as numerical ability, family, motivation, and social sciences are relevant for prediction without historical grades, while grades from the immediate previous semester are relevant for prediction with historical grades. Additionally, support vector machines and linear regression are suitable techniques for tackling grade prediction.

**Keywords:** Student performance · Machine learning
Educational data mining

## 1 Introduction

A common goal for educational institutions is to improve graduation rates. By predicting student performance, directives and teachers can handle, in a timely manner, students in special situations—such as those at risk of failing a course or dropping out of school. Furthermore, by acquiring knowledge about how well students will do in a given course, teachers are able to plan better and search for the most adequate learning strategies for their students. This can, in addition, foster technologies such as personalized intelligent tutors [1].

Student performance prediction is a problem that lies within the context of *educational data mining* [2–6]. This problem can be further subdivided into several tasks, such as grade prediction, dropout student prediction, and talent

© Springer Nature Switzerland AG 2018
F. Castro et al. (Eds.): MICAI 2017, LNAI 10633, pp. 171–182, 2018.
https://doi.org/10.1007/978-3-030-02840-4_14

student prediction. Moreover, predictions can be performed for several courses (institutional level) or a single course (classroom level), and can be performed a single time (e.g. before the course) or several times (e.g. at the beginning of the course and at mid-term). We specifically address *grade prediction* for the courses of a given academic period (semester, in our case); the prediction is done a single time before the courses begin. To predict grades, we consider two cases: (a) student historical grades are unavailable and (b) student historical grades are available. While the former refers to predicting first semester grades, the latter refers to predicting grades from second semester on (when the student already has grades from previous semesters).

Our approach consists of extracting features from the student's background to tackle the first case (historical grades unavailable) and using past grades from similar courses as features to tackle the second case (historical grades available); the aim is to generate one learning model per course. We explore different learning techniques (neural networks, support vector machines, and linear regression) to generate these models. Additionally, we use feature selection to discover the features that yield the best predictions.

To test our approach, we use data from a public technical high school in Mexico. The analyzed records belong to more than 2,000 students and span along three generations (2014–2017, 2015–2018, and 2016–2019); moreover, 24 subjects (courses) are analyzed for prediction. Our main results show that family and motivation are important features to consider when no historical grades are available; otherwise, grades from the previous academic period are the best grade predictors.

The remainder of this document is organized as follows: Sect. 2 presents related work. Later, Sect. 3 introduces our approach for student performance prediction and Sect. 4 describes experiments and results. Finally, Sect. 5 presents conclusions and future work.

## 2   Related Work

In recent years, the use of data mining and machine learning techniques for the field of education has increased [7]. Some of the different targets concern recommendations, analysis of student learning, and student performance prediction.

With regard to student performance prediction, Kotsiantis [8] analyzes an Informatics distance-based course with the aim of identifying dropout students. The approach uses student basic information (sex, age, marital status) and performance marks (e.g. *good*, *fail*) as features for machine learning techniques such as decision trees, neural networks, support vector machines (SVM), and naïve Bayes; a 63% of precision is reported with this last technique by the beginning of the course and an 83% by mid-term. A similar work [9] uses student information at registration and tutor history to predict if the student will finish the course or not and explores six learning techniques: C4.5, neural networks, naïve Bayes, 3-NN, logistic regression, and SVM. The most outstanding findings reveal that, since less data is available at the beginning of the course, prediction precision is lower; furthermore, precision can be improved by utilizing more training instances. To improve precision as well, Kotsiantis et al. [10] propose the use of online classifier ensembles for student performance prediction.

Márquez-Vera et al. [11] work with a case study that concerns high school student desertion from courses; in this case, a genetic algorithm based on grammar is proposed to evaluate learning evolution at different stages. Xing et al. [12] develop a model based on genetic programming to predict at-risk students by using data from the GeoGebra software in a sample of students from a Mathematics course. Desai et al. [13] use $k$-means to group students according to their performance for a specific course; the features used for clustering include selection test scores and teacher marks. Ramaswami and Bhaskaran [14] predict grades based on a series of features such as sex, weight, and visual capacity, which are used with a CHAID classification tree [15]. The reported accuracy for this approach is $\approx 45\%$.

Cortez and Silva [16], with information from the University of Minho in Portugal, carry out student performance prediction in three forms: using binary classes (success and failure), using five classes according to average, and using average. Four machine learning techniques are used: decision trees, random forests, neural networks, and support vector machines. The main conclusion states that it is possible to predict grades if historical grades from the previous academic period are available. Mishra et al. [17] classify student performance in one of five categories (*excellent, very good, good, acceptable, or poor*) using the J48 tree and the random tree, where both techniques yield a high precision. Ahmed and Elaraby [18] carry out this task as well using trees and a classification scheme of four classes (*below average, average, above average*, and *excellent*).

Daud et al. [19] analyze which factors have the greatest impact on Pakistani student performance by using learning algorithms such as support vector machines, bayesian networks, and naïve Bayes. The information is primarily focused on economic features, from which several are found to be significant (e.g. electricity bills).

## 3   Approach

The problem we address consists of predicting, for a given course, the student's final grade for a determined academic period (as we will see in Sect. 4, we predict grades for several generations, periods, and courses). There are two cases within this problem: the case when the student has just entered the school and therefore has no past grades (*historical grades unavailable*) and the case when the student is a re-entering one and therefore has past grades (*historical grades available*). The aim is to create one predictive model per course; however, each case requires a different set of features.

### 3.1   Features

While the features used for the *unavailable grades* case are more oriented towards mining the student's academic, geographical, and socioeconomic background, the features used for the *available grades* case are directed towards mining the student's academic record at the school. Our case study is focused on *high school grade prediction*. Consequently, several features are specific for this case, as well as for the high school we extract data from (see Sect. 4).

**Historical Grades Unavailable.** To tackle this case, we assume that student background can be used to create the predictive models. Based on experience and prior observations, we extract three basic features for our specific case study: current city of residence, middle school the student went to, and academic program where the student is currently enrolled. Furthermore, we extract several features from the high school selection test and a newcomer survey that is applied to all students since 2015 on the analyzed high school. Let us explain all features.

*City, Middle School, and Program.* Student city, middle school, and current program are managed as quartiles, where these are assigned according to historical records of past generation performance; for example, if secondary $j$ is assigned quartile 1, this implies that—historically—its students have obtained the best averages.

*Selection Test Features.* Six separate scores (ranging 1–100) can be obtained from this test: Verbal Ability, Numerical Ability, Mathematics, Spanish, Natural Sciences, and Social Sciences. Each of these is normalized and considered a feature.

*Socioeconomic Survey Features.* Since 2015, an online survey has been applied to all new students with the purpose of directing those students in need to specific instances, such as psychologists. The survey covers five sensible topics: family, health, motivation, economy, and nutrition (see Table 1 for a description of each topic), where each question ranges 1–100. Each of these is normalized and considered a feature.

**Table 1.** Survey description

| Topic | Questions | Aspect to evaluate | Problems to identify |
|---|---|---|---|
| Family | 4 | Environment for development | Family conflicts |
| Health | 5 | Medical background | Serious illnesses |
| Motivation | 15 | Self-perception | Low self-esteem |
| Economy | 7 | Socioeconomical status | Financial problems or transportation issues |
| Nutrition | 6 | Eating habits | Poor nutrition |

**Historical Grades Available.** To predict the grade of a course when the student has already historical information available, we use the most similar subjects the student has coursed. To determine the most similar courses, we rely on the *competency matrix* of our case study. This matrix contains *disciplinary competencies*, which group courses semantically into five clusters: Mathematics, Experimental Sciences, Social Sciences, Humanities, and Communications. A course is, consequently, related to the courses that are clustered in the same disciplinary competency. The related courses from previous semesters are considered to be the most similar. Table 2 presents an example of this matrix, where a 1 in a cell $a_{ij}$ indicates that the course in row $i$ belongs to discipline in column $j$ (a 0 indicates otherwise). Assuming that Calculus is taught in semester $k + 1$ and Mathematics II in semester $k$, Mathematics II would be used to predict the grade for Calculus, as both belong to the same discipline.

**Table 2.** Example of disciplinary competency matrix.

|                | Mathematics | Humanities | Social Sciences |
|----------------|-------------|------------|-----------------|
| Mathematics II | 1           | 0          | 0               |
| Calculus       | 1           | 0          | 0               |
| Arts           | 0           | 1          | 1               |

Because this competency matrix is specific for our case study, other feasible options can be considered for extracting the most similar courses. As our results will show (Sect. 4), a course dependency matrix could suffice to perform the predictions.

## 4    Experiments and Results

To test the proposed features and explore different learning techniques, we used a case study. Our case study consists of a Mexican public technical high school, where all courses follow a face-to-face scheme and are based on competencies [20]. The high school offers 17 technical programs. Students are accepted on a yearly basis, the stipulated academic period is a semester, and the program lasts three years (six semesters). Each semester, the students take two types of courses: general courses and specialization courses. While the former are the same across programs, the latter vary depending on the program.

From our case study, we gathered data comprising 24 courses and more than 2,000 students, who belong to the generations 2014–2017, 2015–2018, and 2016–2019. So far, we only predict grades for general courses, since—as previously stated—the program a student belongs to is used as a feature as well (in that sense, predicting grades for specialization courses is left as future work). In addition, we solely consider grades in "first opportunity"[1].

---

[1] In some institutions, students are granted several chances to pass a course during the same academic period. Each chance or "opportunity" has its own grade.

Our experiments include both the *historical grades unavailable* case and the *historical grades available* case, while the learning techniques explored comprehend neural networks, linear regression, and support vector machines (SVM). Because we treat grade prediction as a regression problem, several error measures—namely mean absolute error and root mean squared error—are reported. The experiments were performed using WEKA[2] with its default parameters and R.

## 4.1  Setup

We created a dataset per course. For the *unavailable grades* case, we used data from the generations 2015–2018 and 2016–2019, since the newcomer survey began to be applied since 2015. Features represented as quartiles were calculated using historical information from the generations 2014–2017, 2013–2016, and 2012–2015. The general courses for first semester are listed in Table 3. For the *available grades* case, we used data from the generation 2014–2017 for the third, fourth, and fifth semesters. The general courses for third semester are Mathematics II, English II, Biology II, Introduction to Scientific Methodology, Physics I, and Health III; for fourth semester, Art Appreciation, Health IV, Physics II, English III, Experimental Sciences, and Ethics Problems; for fifth semester, Calculus, Social Sciences I, English IV, Literature, and Orientation III.

Assuming that grades will tend to follow a normal distribution centered on the score needed to pass (70), our baseline consisted of random numbers that follow this distribution. We chose, based also on the previous assumption, a mean of 70 and a standard deviation of 15 (numbers above 100 where simply set to this upper bound).

## 4.2  Results

We present results for both cases (where we also performed feature selection) and present as well a brief comparison between approaching grade prediction with classification versus regression.

## 4.3  Historical Grades Unavailable

Table 3 presents the mean absolute and root mean squared errors for our datasets. As we can see, on one hand, the learned models are superior to the baseline; on the other hand, linear regression and support vector machines show a statistically significant advantage over neural networks for this specific task. Let us note that the Orientation and Health courses had the greatest error among all the predicted courses; we believe this is due to the particular evaluation method of the former, as the only grades possible are either 100 or 0.

By performing feature selection on each course dataset, we calculated the frequency with which each feature was selected. Figure 1 shows these frequencies,

---

[2] Available at: http://www.cs.waikato.ac.nz/ml/weka/.

**Table 3.** Results for the case of unavailable historical grades. MAE = Mean Absolute Error, RMSE = Root Mean Squared Error. LR = Linear Regression, NN = Neural Networks, SVM = Support Vector Machines. Results in bold indicate the smallest error, while the asterisk indicates a statistically significant difference ($p < 0.05$).

|  | MAE | | | | RMSE | | | |
|---|---|---|---|---|---|---|---|---|
|  | Baseline | LR | NN | SVM | Baseline | LR | NN | SVM |
| Biology | 17.47 | 10.00 | 11.46 | **9.36*** | 21.71 | **14.54*** | 16.89 | 15.01 |
| Chemistry | 16.91 | 10.52 | 12.46 | **9.67*** | 21.74 | **14.86*** | 18.44 | 15.48 |
| Health | 33.13 | 13.94 | 13.90 | **7.68*** | 37.45 | **26.18*** | 32.25 | 27.25 |
| Information Tech. | 18.83 | 13.41 | 15.56 | **12.59*** | 23.81 | **17.98*** | 22.51 | 18.61 |
| Mathematics | 18.7 | 12.09 | 14.39 | **11.57*** | 23.82 | **16.64*** | 21.72 | 17.05 |
| Orientation | 39.99 | 34.10 | 34.44 | **24.76*** | 45.71 | **41.22*** | 49.84 | 49.53 |
| Spanish | 18.05 | 13.00 | 15.86 | **12.12*** | 23.62 | **17.87*** | 24.03 | 18.58 |

where we may note that *numerical ability, motivation, family, and social sciences* were the most selected features along the subject datasets. Note that city had a frequency of 0.

Far from coming as a surprise, the first three features rather confirm previous intuitive knowledge: numerical skills are important for academic proficiency, motivation plays a key role in academic success, and behind a great student is a great family. The *social sciences* feature, however, could seem perplexing. With regard to this score in the admission test, it consists of 60 questions divided into three areas: History, Geography, and Civics and Ethics. We believe that, perhaps, general culture and values are correlated with academic results. However, testing this hypothesis is left as future work.

### 4.4 Historical Grades Available

Tables 4 and 5 present, respectively, the average mean absolute and root mean squared errors for grade prediction per semester using either the previous grades from the most similar courses or all previous grades. As we can see from these tables, results do not seem to vary substantially from one approach to the other.

**Table 4.** Mean absolute error for grade prediction using all previous grades (All) or only the grades from the most similar courses (MS). LR = Linear Regression, NN = Neural Networks, SVM = Support Vector Machines. Results in bold indicate the smallest error.

|  | Baseline | LR-MS | NN-MS | SVM-MS | LR-All | NN-All | SVM-All |
|---|---|---|---|---|---|---|---|
| 3rd semester | 18.87 | 8.9 | 13.99 | 8.19 | 7.53 | 10.29 | **7.17** |
| 4th semester | 19.53 | 8.01 | 9.32 | **6.15** | 7.76 | 10.73 | 6.37 |
| 5th semester | 20.15 | 10.24 | 11.85 | **8.71** | 10.14 | 14.87 | 8.75 |

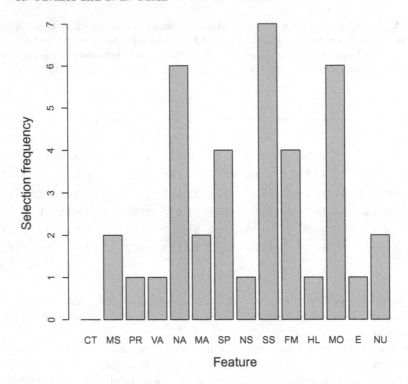

**Fig. 1.** Frequency for selected features. CT = city, MS = middle school, and PR = program. From the selection test: VA = verbal ability, NA = numerical ability, MA = mathematics, SP = spanish, NS = natural sciences, and SS = social sciences. From the survey: FM = family, HL = health, MO = motivation, E = economy, and NU = nutrition.

Similar to the previous section, we performed feature selection on each subject dataset. When grouping selection frequencies by semester (see Fig. 2), we can note that most of the features selected correspond to the immediate previous semester. In fact, for the third semester 58% of the selected features corresponds to the second semester; for the fourth semester, 55% corresponds to the third semester; and for the fifth semester 40% corresponds to the fourth semester.

## 4.5 Classification vs. Regression

Grade prediction can also be addressed as a classification problem if—at the end of the day—interest lies not in the specific amount of points but in the student passing or failing. In this case, we used a three-class scheme: *Excellent* (A), *Center* (C), or *Poor* (F), where F = 0–69, C = 70–89, and A = 90–100. We tested whether learning these classes would achieve a better F-score than predicting numerical grades using regression and then turning these grades into classes.

Our preliminary results are shown in Fig. 3, where F-score was calculated for third, fourth, and fifth semester courses. In this case, classification was performed

**Table 5.** Root mean squared error for grade prediction using all previous grades (All) or only the grades from the most similar courses (MS). LR = Linear Regression, NN = Neural Networks, SVM = Support Vector Machines. Results in bold indicate the smallest error.

|  | Baseline | LR-MS | NN-MS | SVM-MS | LR-All | NN-All | SVM-All |
|---|---|---|---|---|---|---|---|
| 3rd semester | 23.11 | 14.36 | 18.17 | 14.84 | **10.61** | 15.91 | 10.77 |
| 4th semester | 24.09 | 14.51 | 18.38 | 15.08 | **13.14** | 21.84 | 13.56 |
| 5th semester | 25.14 | 15.88 | 19.02 | 16.78 | **15.83** | 26.61 | 16.61 |

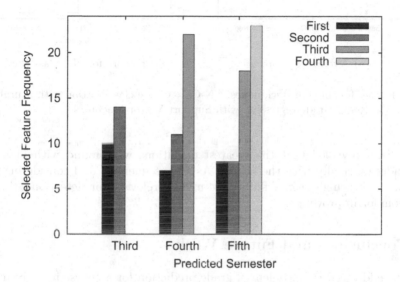

**Fig. 2.** Selected feature frequency grouped by semester

with neural networks, since techniques such as SVM and naïve Bayes were unable to detect the A and F classes due to the imbalanced class problem. As for regression, it was performed—given the results of the previous sections—with SVM. Even though neural networks seem to have a greater average F-score, as shown in Fig. 3a (and the inverse seems to hold for the F-score of the F class, as shown in Fig. 3b), we found there is no significant difference between the two approaches. There is a significant difference, nevertheless, with respect to the baseline, which consisted of a random class assignment that follows a normal distribution (C being the majority class).

## 4.6   Discussion

A first key point of discussion consists of the differences between the two cases. In that sense, we observed that the errors of the *unavailable grades* case were slightly greater. As a result, we believe prediction with historical information will tend to be more accurate. With respect to errors, a deeper analysis (not

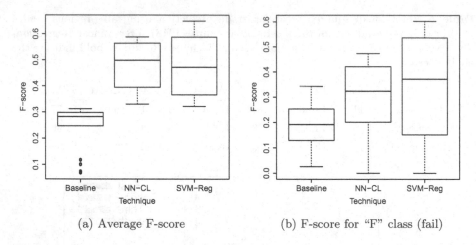

(a) Average F-score            (b) F-score for "F" class (fail)

**Fig. 3.** F-score for different techniques. NN-CL = Grade classification with neural networks, SVM-Reg = Grade regression with Support Vector Machines.

shown here) revealed that the greatest deviations were found with high and low grades (specially with the latter). As a consequence—and considering that students with a high risk of failing are usually relevant for detection—there is still room for improvement.

## 5    Conclusions and Future Work

We have addressed the problem of grade prediction for a course in a given academic period by learning a model for this course. We considered two cases: the case where the student counts with no previous grades and the opposite case. For the former case, we extracted features from the student's background, as to know: city, program, middle school, selection test features, and newcomer survey features. For the latter case, we used as features the grades from the most similar courses to the one being predicted.

Our main findings indicate that historical information, specially from the previous academic period is highly relevant. If this is not available, background information from numerical skills, family, and motivation could aid the prediction. While the overall task is still challenging, we believe that our methodology and main findings can shed some light on the current state of the art.

Future work includes school dropout prediction during different semesters; for this problem, data is readily available, but the challenge is overcoming the imbalanced class problem. Furthermore, since we have observed that grades from the previous academic period are relevant, an option is to incorporate the average from middle school into prediction for the unavailable grades case with the purpose of reducing error. Finally, within our case study, we were restricted in this work towards predicting general courses; consequently, a future line of exploration includes predicting grades for specialization courses.

# References

1. Klašnja-Milićević, A., Vesin, B., Ivanović, M., Budimac, Z.: E-learning personalization based on hybrid recommendation strategy and learning style identification. Comput. Educ. **56**(3), 885–899 (2011)
2. Baker, R.S., Yacef, K.: The state of educational data mining in 2009: a review and future visions. JEDM-J. Educ. Data Min. **1**(1), 3–17 (2009)
3. Siemens, G., Baker, R.S.J.d.: Learning analytics and educational data mining: towards communication and collaboration. In: Proceedings of the 2nd International Conference on Learning Analytics and Knowledge. LAK 2012, pp. 252–254. ACM, New York (2012)
4. Romero, C., Ventura, S.: Educational data mining: a review of the state of the art. IEEE Trans. Syst. Man Cybern. Part C (Appl. Rev.) **40**(6), 601–618 (2010)
5. Baker, R.S., Inventado, P.S.: Educational data mining and learning analytics. In: Larusson, J.A., White, B. (eds.) Learning Analytics, pp. 61–75. Springer, New York (2014). https://doi.org/10.1007/978-1-4614-3305-7_4
6. Dutt, A., Ismail, M.A., Herawan, T.: A systematic review on educational data mining. IEEE Access **PP**, 1 (2017)
7. Koedinger, K.R., D'Mello, S., McLaughlin, E.A., Pardos, Z.A., Rosé, C.P.: Data mining and education. Wiley Interdiso. Rev.. Cognit. Sci. **6**(4), 333–353 (2015)
8. Kotsiantis, S.B., Pierrakeas, C.J., Pintelas, P.F.: Preventing student dropout in distance learning using machine learning techniques. In: Palade, V., Howlett, R.J., Jain, L. (eds.) KES 2003 Part II. LNCS (LNAI), vol. 2774, pp. 267–274. Springer, Heidelberg (2003). https://doi.org/10.1007/978-3-540-45226-3_37
9. Kotsiantis, S., Pierrakeas, C., Pintelas, P.: Predicting students' performance in distance learning using machine learning techniques. Appl. Artif. Intell. **18**(5), 411–426 (2004)
10. Kotsiantis, S., Patriarcheas, K., Xenos, M.: A combinational incremental ensemble of classifiers as a technique for predicting students performance in distance education. Knowl.-Based Syst. **23**(6), 529–535 (2010)
11. Márquez-Vera, C., Cano, A., Romero, C., Noaman, A.Y.M., Mousa Fardoun, H., Ventura, S.: Early dropout prediction using data mining: a case study with high school students. Expert Syst. **33**(1), 107–124 (2016)
12. Xing, W., Guo, R., Petakovic, E., Goggins, S.: Participation-based student final performance prediction model through interpretable genetic programming: integrating learning analytics, educational data mining and theory. Comput. Hum. Behav. **47**, 168–181 (2015)
13. Desai, A., Shah, N., Dhodi, M.: Student profiling to improve teaching and learning: a data mining approach. In: 2016 International Conference on Data Science and Engineering (ICDSE), pp. 1–6, August 2016
14. Ramaswami, M., Bhaskaran, R.: A CHAID based performance prediction model in educational data mining. IJCSI Int. J. Comput. Sci. Issues **7**, 10–18 (2010)
15. Kass, G.V.: An exploratory technique for investigating large quantities of categorical data. Appl. Stat. **29**, 119–127 (1980)
16. Cortez, P., Silva, A.M.G.: Using data mining to predict secondary school student performance. Technical report, University of Minho (2008)
17. Mishra, T., Kumar, D., Gupta, S.: Mining students' data for prediction performance. In: 2014 Fourth International Conference on Advanced Computing Communication Technologies, pp. 255–262, February 2014

18. Ahmed, A.B.E.D., Elaraby, I.S.: Data mining: a prediction for student's performance using classification method. World J. Comput. Appl. Technol. **2**(2), 43–47 (2014)
19. Daud, A., Aljohani, N.R., Abbasi, R.A., Lytras, M.D., Abbas, F., Alowibdi, J.S.: Predicting student performance using advanced learning analytics. In: Proceedings of the 26th International Conference on World Wide Web. WWW 2017 Companion, Republic and Canton of Geneva, Switzerland, International World Wide Web Conferences Steering Committee, pp. 415–421 (2017)
20. Kelchen, R.: The landscape of competency-based education: enrollments, demographics, and affordability, pp. 1–20. American Enterprise Institute (2015)

# Bag of Errors: Automatic Inference of a Student Model in an Electrical Training System

Guillermo Santamaría-Bonfil[1,2]([✉]), Yasmín Hernández[1],
Miguel Pérez-Ramírez[1], and G. Arroyo-Figueroa[1]

[1] Gerencia de Tecnologías de la Información,
Instituto Nacional de Electricidad y Energías Limpias,
Reforma 113 Col. Palmira, 62490 Cuernavaca, Morelos, Mexico
{guillermo.santamaria,myhp,mperez,garroyo}@iie.org.mx
[2] CONACYT-INEEL, Mexico City, Mexico

**Abstract.** An indispensable element of any Intelligent Tutoring Systems is the student model since it enables the system to cope with student's particular needs. Furthermore, data accumulated by educational systems in bug libraries can be exploited to build a student model by data mining methods. In this work, we built a student model for a virtual reality system used by a Mexican utility to train electricians in operations with medium tension energized lines using its bug libraries. First, errors are mapped to features using a Bag-of-Errors scheme. Additional information about the courses, and the students is also incorporated. Then, a Decision Tree is employed to build the student model. Finally, several student models are built, and compared in terms of Accuracy, Sensitivity, and Specificity. Results show that the proposed model is able to identify trained/untrained students with high accuracy. Moreover, these models shed light on critical task knowledge components which may be used to improve the learning experience of technical operators.

**Keywords:** Student model · Bag of errors
Classification and regression trees · Variable importance

## 1 Introduction

An Intelligent Tutoring System (ITS) is a computer-based system with the solely purpose of enhancing human learning by aiding a user with correct, alas partial, information about the problem [1,2]. At the core of an ITS's lies the student model, which is a qualitative representation of the students knowledge of a specific domain [3,4]. It also models a large list of features for any given student such as its learning capacity, misconceptions, personality, emotions, and so on [4,5]. However, most of these features are not observable while there is a lack of formal frameworks to describe such phenomena [4]. Despite these, ITS have been quite

© Springer Nature Switzerland AG 2018
F. Castro et al. (Eds.): MICAI 2017, LNAI 10633, pp. 183–197, 2018.
https://doi.org/10.1007/978-3-030-02840-4_15

effective in providing support and enhancing human learning in several domains [1,3,6].

An ITS may be described by its computational utility rather than its structural cognitive fidelity using the proper terminology [3,6]. In this sense, a student model may describe a learner mindset within a domain in terms of the Knowledge Components (KC) of a specific topic, and determine aspects of the learner as the proficiency level for the given task. An example of this type of systems are the step-based models [2,7]. Basically, a step-based tutoring system provides educative material in a step by step fashion. Each step is elaborated by the student following the corresponding sub-steps and performing the corresponding actions in the user-interface. These ITS can provide assistance/feedback during each sub-step or once the step is completed [7]. Moreover, such systems have shown to be as effective in tutoring as its human counterparts [2,7,8].

A key component of any student model is the Bug Library (BL) [3]. The BL is the log where system stores errors committed during instruction through the interface by an user [9]. Typically, bugs are related to misconceptions, nonetheless, using the terminology proposed in [6], bug libraries can be employed to elucidate KC importance to determine the learning proficiency of a student (at least in a probabilistic sense). On the other hand, there are several limitations in working with bug libraries such as the required computational effort to compile them or performing poorly given new bugs [3]. Further, analysing bug libraries is far from trivial since error sequences are different (in elements and length) for every user, which hinders the similarity comparison among students' learning abilities. A typical approach used in text mining to compare texts similarity is called Bag-of-Words (BoW) [10]. This model has shown that linguistic similarity between documents of different lengths can be approximated by using their words distributions [10]. Thus, in this work we represent each student knowledge/misconceptions about a task in terms of the distribution of a Bag-of-Errors (BoE). More detailed information on how the errors were performed is coded using finer granularities (e.g. error type, step and sub-step, equipment id, and so on). This model also includes stereotype/profile information [3,11]. It is worth noting that, a fine BoE granularity is required to identify KCs that can be used to explain students' learning performance.

On the other hand, Machine Learning (ML) methods have proven to be useful for the design and construction of ITS [4,5,12]. Benefits range from reducing/improving the ITS construction effort [4], to the design of robuster student models that integrate different sources of information [1,3]. Decision Trees (DT) have been used to classify students proficiency [13,14], determine student characteristics associated with task success given a specific domain [15], and analyze students' errors to understand misconceptions, missing conceptions, and well-understood errors through the analysis of *Bug Libraries* [3,9].

Thus, in this work we build a student model for the ALEn$^{3D}$-MT system. A virtual reality system used to prepare human resources in maintenance and rescue procedures in energized lines [5,8,16,17]. In particular, we build and test a student model that discriminates trained from untrained students for a specific task given several performance thresholds. First, information from the BL is represented in the BoE + Stereotype space. Then, data is split into training/validation (80%) and the test (20%) sets. A DT model is trained using this feature space with a 5-fold cross-validation. Then, using the test set, the models' discriminatory ability is measured by employing Accuracy, Sensitivity, and Specificity metrics. Results show that students proficiency can be determined with high Accuracy and Sensitivity, and good Specificity. "High" and "good" will be clarified in the experimental section. Finally, variables importance of the resulting model are analysed to identify crucial information required to discriminate untrained from trained students. In particular, the feature importance analysis shows two things: (1) there are key KC/Bugs that can be used to determine between train and untrained students, whereas there are bugs and KC that statistically, do not contribute to proficiency at all; (2) stereotype information as jobs' responsibilities and course time are better for discriminating between trained and untrained studentsthan KC elements.

Concretely, the contributions of this work are:

- A BL representation as BoE.
- A model student built on a DT using BoE and Stereotype features.
- A DT variable importance analysis to identify key KC elements that discrim inate between train from untrained operators.

The remainder of this paper is organized as follows: Sect. 2 presents the virtual reality system for Electrical Training that we have used as study-case, and the corresponding KC behavior table. Section 3 describes the proposed model, and specifically, Bag-of-Errors and DT techniques employed to build it. Section 4 presents data pre-processing, model parameters, experimental results and feature importance analysis of the resulting model. Finally, conclusions and future work are presented in Sect. 5.

## 2 ALEn$^{3D}$ Medium-Tension System

ALEn$^{3D}$-MT® is a non-immersive Virtual Reality system designed to train Mexican utilities human resources in maintenance and rescue procedures in medium-tension energized lines. Such system is used within a blended-learning approach [16,17]. Thus, the VR system is just one of three parts that composes the instruction process: *VR training*, and traditional *theoretical/practical* training. For simplicity, from now on we will refer to the system simply by ALEn.

ALEn divides the domain into tasks called manoeuvre. These detail the operations in a step by step fashion. During each step, the system requires the student to provide intermediate steps to accomplish the step goal. Each maneuver is composed by three phases:

1. First, maintenance manoeuvre (MM) required equipment is selected (Fig. 1a), from four possible catalogues namely, *tools, equipment, safety gear* and *materials*. This is associated to the real process where workers will review that all the required material (tools and equipment) to perform a MM is in the bucket truck, before they travel to the working site.

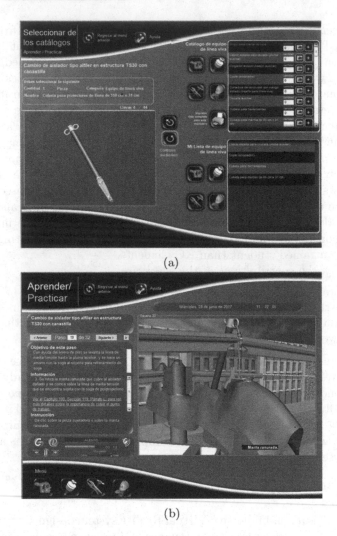

(a)

(b)

**Fig. 1.** ALEn's Interface. (a) Equipment selection interface where tools, equipment, safety gear and materials required for a MM are selected. (b) MM execution interface where the procedure, step by step, is displayed.

2. Second, the MM is performed per se (Fig. 1b). Here the system deploys information such as the objective of every step, an explanation of the MM, a link to the specific sections of the safety manual where all MMs are described, and the instruction/action that the student must perform through the system's interface. The events and actions are illustrated using a 3D environment.

3. Third, the students are evaluated (by a facilitator or even themselves). This process, in turn, is divided in two sub-phases, namely *practical evaluation* and *theoretical evaluation*. In the former the student is requested to perform a specific MM over the virtual environment without any aid. In the latter,

the instructor selects multiple questions from a questionnaire pool to create an exam automatically graded.

ALEn's KC content shown in Table 1 is described using the terminology proposed by [6]. Although, the ALEn system does not operates as a ITS, it is able to keep records of the students' progress. More importantly, since its content is organized in a step-based fashion, we can exploit this organization to pose the student model in terms of KC much like as a superposition student model.

## 2.1 Bug Libraries

Students instructed through the usage of the ALEn system can make errors, either during the material selection phase, or during the realization of the MM. Thus, for each maneuver there are two error logs: an Equipment Selection BL and the Maneuver Development BL. Moreover, for each phase distinct types of errors are recorded. For instance, when selecting the incorrect equipment for a maneuver, or indicating the incorrect amount of it. Another example is when user clicks the wrong element in the virtual environment. We refer the reader to [5], Tables 2 and 3, were error types have been already summarized. Every error is stored in a students' progress database during the practical evaluation mode. These altogether with the theoretical evaluation (exams) delineate the progress of each student for each MM. Nevertheless, for the time being, the performance evaluation of a given student is carried out by the human instructors, who have access to all the information related to students' progress.

# 3    The Proposed Student Model

The objective of this work is to develop a student model which will be employed to enhance ALEn$^{3D}$ instruction. Specifically, for each maneuver of the system a student model is built. Such models will be used to determine proficiency of students, and provide details about specific KC that students should take care of.

First, bug libraries are transformed to BoE, which also includes stereotype information. Then, users theoretical evaluations are employed to determine if they are Trained or Untrained. Several thresholds are considered to determine the training level of students, these are discussed in Sect. 4.1. Once this data is registered for each student, a student classifier can be built. In this work we employed Classification and Regression Trees (CART) [18] to build a student model. There are several reasons why we decided to employ a DT model, namely: (1) rule extraction can be performed over the DT model, (2) CART can manage nominal and continuous variables without additional effort, (3) the feature selection problem is already addressed by the DT model, and (4) Feature importance analysis can be performed over the resulting tree [18].

Below, we provide details on the Bag of Errors scheme, and the CART model.

**Table 1.** ALEn$^{3D}$ system elements.

| No. | ALEn$^{3D}$ | Term | Description |
|---|---|---|---|
| 1 | Maintenance operations in energized lines | Task domain | Skills and information corresponding to medium-tension maintenance/rescue maneuvers |
| 2 | Maneuver | Task | A several minutes activity composed by a sequence of steps to develop a maintenance/rescue procedure |
| 3 | Step | Step | A user-interface event required to complete a maneuver. Each step may correspond to one or more knowledge units and/or zero or more learning events |
| 4 | Substep | Substep | A step might be composed by one or more sub-steps. Thus, more specific knowledge units can be considered |
| 5 | Operations component | Knowledge component | An action, hardware selection, and/or application required to complete a maneuver |
| 6 | Maneuver process knowledge | Learning event | A non-observable mental event in the student mind consequence of the application of a knowledge component |
| 7 | ALEn$^{3D}$ Maneuver Loops | Outer and Inner Loops | In the current system setup, the outer loop is performed by a human facilitator while the inner is controlled by a proficiency score rule |
| 8 | Bug Library | Incorrect | Errors made during training are stored in two different bug libraries |

## 3.1   Student Behavior as a Bag of Errors

Bag-of-Words (BoW) is a simple model typically employed in Text Mining for several different tasks including the analysis of tutoring system texts [4,10,19,20]. This model has demonstrated that document's descriptors distribution (either text words or other key elements) are highly correlated to its meaning [10]. BoW maps any text to a term frequency probability distribution defined by key features (e.g. words), thus, it does not preserves semantic order [20].

In this work, we model any BL as a collection of documents, where a document corresponds to the errors made by a student during the execution of a given task. Each element of a document is an action parsed as text that contains features like the error type, the step and/or sub-step where error was made, and so on. More precisely, lets denote the total number of student-documents in the bug libraries by $N$, and by $\mathbf{x}_i = (x_1, \ldots, x_j)$ the collection of errors used to represent the student $\mathbf{x}_i$, where $x_j \in \mathcal{X}$, $j = 1, \ldots, f$ is a word in the error space $\mathcal{X}$. Thus, a BL is mapped into a BoE matrix of the following form:

$$
BoE = \begin{bmatrix} x_{11} & x_{12} & \cdots & x_{1f} \\ x_{21} & \ddots & \cdots & x_{2f} \\ \vdots & \vdots & \ddots & \vdots \\ x_{N1} & x_{N2} & \cdots & x_{Nf} \end{bmatrix} \tag{1}
$$

**BoE Granularity.** The granularity of words used to represent the BL can be as meager as only type errors, or more elaborated containing details about the step and even the sub-steps. In this work, we established three different levels of granularity which are shown in Table 2.

**Table 2.** ALEn BoE granularity.

| Word level | Maneuver development | | | Equipment selection | | |
|---|---|---|---|---|---|---|
| | Error type | Step | Sub-step | Error type | Hardware Id | Evaluation |
| 0 | ✓ | | | ✓ | | |
| 1 | ✓ | ✓ | | ✓ | ✓ | |
| 2 | ✓ | ✓ | ✓ | ✓ | ✓ | ✓ |

**Stereotype Information.** It is worth noting that not every $ALEn^{3D}$ student has made a mistake, nor every student that do not made an error (either in the task and/or in the equipment selection) have achieved a proficiency score in the theoretical evaluation. Thus, besides the BoE features obtained from the bug libraries, we included student stereotype information [3]. Stereotype data used in this work contemplates the following features:

1. Utility information
   - **Area:** The utility area where a user belongs which is a mix of the geographical and job responsibilities; values range from 1 to 52.
   - **Zone:** The geographical utility zones; values range from 1 to 10.
   - **User Type:** ALEn users can belong to three types of user: (1) administrator, (2) facilitator, and (3) student.
2. Courses information
   - **Course Time:** The total time assigned to each course; values range from 0 to $\infty$.
   - **Number of Maneuvers:** The total number of maneuvers that were imparted in each course; values range from 0 to 43.
   - **Number of Facilitators:** The total number of facilitators that were assigned to impart a course. For this data set, values range from 0 to 3.

### 3.2 Student Model Based on Decision Trees

Classification And Regression Trees (CART) were introduced by Breiman et al. in 1984, and is now considered a classical ML method [18,21]. Roughly speaking, CART builds a tree diagram that segments (in a binary fashion) the predictor space into a number of simple regions. Each region is assigned its most frequent class, thus, a new observation is classified by assigning it the class of the region where it lies [18]. In the following we briefly discuss splitting functions, and variable importance analysis used in this work. The reader is referred to [18, 21,22] for further details on DT's splitting criteria, feature importance analysis, and missing values handling.

To segment the feature space the two most preferred functions are the Gini Index (G) and Entropy (H) [18]: the former is a measure of how impure a node is (i.e. the purest node only has one class), while the latter measures the expected uncertainty of class distributions (the maximum entropy is obtained when all classes are equiprobable). On the other hand, variable importance is analysed intrinsically when constructing the tree [23]. An overall measure of variables importance is calculated as the summation of improvements for each split for which a variable was the primary variable. Since variable importance only provides a summarized impression, results are normalized to sum 100 [22].

## 4    Experimentation

In this section we describe how we build our student model using the students' information and DT, and how we evaluated the model. First, we describe the preliminary analysis, data set description, and features employed. Then, BoE and DT parameters are detailed. Then, performance measures employed in this work are described. Finally, an analysis of the results, and how to exploit features of the resulting model are discussed.

## 4.1   Preliminary Analysis

In the current blended-learning setup, a user is considered Trained or Untrained depending on his performance on three training stages, namely: the ALEn system, the theoretical, and practical evaluations. It is until a user achieves a *satisfactory* performance on the ALEn system, and a passing score in the theoretical evaluation, that the practical evaluation is performed. Thus, in this work a student is considered Trained if it achieves a passing score (at least of 70, 80, 85, or 90) in the theoretical evaluation, or Untrained otherwise. The proficiency scores along with the corresponding distribution of Trained/Untrained students are shown in the left hand side of Table 3. Observe that the approval rate of the students for all MM's is rather high (93% for a passing score of 80!), this depicts the class imbalanced data set. On the other hand, the most imparted tasks using ALEn are 1, 16, 17, 36 and 43. From these, maneuver 43 has the *most balanced* class distribution. Thus, we use it as benchmark to build and test our student model. Maneuver 43 class distribution is shown in the right hand side of Table 3. This maneuver requires the student to perform 17 steps, and to select 40 different types of equipment.

**Table 3.** ALEn class distribution. Percentage of students considered *untrained and trained* for all ALEn maneuvers (left), and just for maneuver 43 (right). As can be appreciated in this table, classes distribution is highly imbalanced.

| Proficiency score | All maneuvers | | Maneuver 43 | |
|---|---|---|---|---|
| | Untrained | Trained | Untrained | Trained |
| ≥70 | 3% | 97% | 7% | 93% |
| ≥80 | 7% | 93% | 17% | 83% |
| ≥85 | 14% | 86% | 26% | 74% |
| ≥90 | 27% | 73% | 41% | 59% |

**Data Set Description.** For the current data set, the total number of students that have received training from ALEn is 1,399. From these, a total of 89,402 errors have been recorded in the maneuver development BL, and 14,699 in the equipment selection BL. From the total pool of students, only 316 have been evaluated in the maneuver benchmark. For these, 1845 errors were registered in the task bug library, whereas 398 were registered in the equipment one.

## 4.2   Experimental Setup

In the following we provide details on the model parameters values such as BoE granularity level, the proficiency thresholds necessary to be considered trained, tree complexity parameter, the number of cross-validation (CV) folds for training a DT model, the minimum population required to perform a split, and the minimum population required by a node to be considered a leaf. In this work, the DT model construction do not consider surrogate splits. The mentioned parameters are summarized in Table 4.

On the other hand, one of the objectives of this work is to create a student model capable of identify key KC that can be used to provide feedback to any student, in particular, to untrained ones. However, DT models are typically pruned to avoid overfitting. While this approach improves the generalization of the model, the resulting tree lacks of enough detail to provide insight on KC. Thus, for every experimental configuration, a pruned and a complex DT model are obtained and compared.

In accordance to Table 4 for each proficiency score, there are 12 DT possible models (i.e. 3 BoE granularities × Pruned or Complex × G or H = 12). Thus, only best CV pruned and complex models are tested. For these Accuracy, Sensitivity, and Specificity CV results are averaged. All experiments where performed under the R 3.4.0 language, and the DT model was built using the RPART package [22].

**Table 4.** DT student model parameters.

| Parameter | Component | Values |
|---|---|---|
| Proficiency score | Student model | 70, 80, 85, and 90 |
| Error grain level | BOE | 0, 1, and 2 |
| Tree complexity | DT | cp = 0.001 |
| Cross-validation folds | DT | 10 |
| Split measure | DT | Gini or information |
| Minimum split | DT | Two elements, at least, are required to perform a split |
| Minimum bucket size | DT | Each leaf, at least, must contain two students |

### 4.3   Quality Measure

To test the discriminatory proficiency of our student model for maneuver 43, we used statistical binary classification measures, namely *Accuracy* (Acc), *Sensitivity or True Positive Rate* (TPR), and *Specificity or True Negative Rate* (TNR). The first is a typical measure of the overall performance of a classifier. It is the number of correct predictions made (in this case, the correct prediction of a student's maneuver proficiency) divided by the total number of predictions made. However, it weights equally correct identification of trained and untrained students. The second, measures how good the classifier identifies trained students, while the third measures its performance identifying untrained ones. These measures ranges $0 \leq Acc, TPR, TNR \leq 1$, where the worst classifier achieves a value of zero, and the best a value of 1 for the all three. We emphasize the use of TNR to evaluate the performance of the student model for the ALEn classifier, since real-world failures while performing any of these electrical maneuvers will carry lethal consequences. Acc, TPR, and TNR are defined as follows:

$$Acc = \frac{\sum TP + \sum TN}{Total\ Population}, \tag{2}$$

$$TPR = \frac{\sum TP}{\sum Condition\ Positive}, \tag{3}$$

$$TNR = \frac{\sum TN}{\sum Condition\ Negative}, \tag{4}$$

where $TP$ corresponds to the correct identification of true positive samples (i.e. true trained students identified as trained), $TN$ to the correct identification of true negative (i.e. true untrained students identified as untrained), *Condition Positive* and *Condition Negative* to all true positives (i.e. all trained students) and all true negatives (i.e. all untrained students), respectively.

### 4.4  Results and Analysis

Results for our student models measured by Acc, TPR and TNR are shown in Fig. 2. Model labels shall be read as "**proficiency threshold . BoE granularity . type of tree . split criterion**".

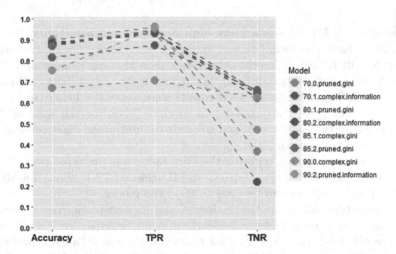

**Fig. 2.** Models performance. Train/Untrain results for Acc, TPR, and TNR in accordance to the proficiency scores previously detailed. Observe that for the $\geq 70$ threshold the pruned models obtained the best TNR, whereas for $\geq 90$ the overfitted model obtained better TNR. However, for the latter there is a larger trade-off in terms TPR and Acc.

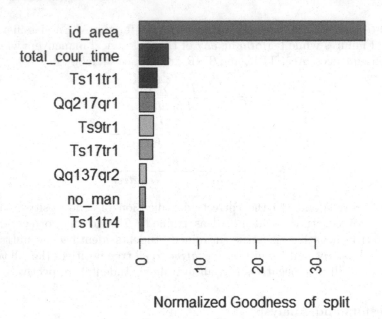

**Fig. 3.** DT variables importance. Observe that the most important variable to discriminate between proficiencies levels is the area, variable related to student job duties within a specific location of the utility. Nevertheless, KC elements associated to several steps of the maneuver development and equipment selection can be identified.

In general, all DT models achieve high Accuracy and Sensitivity, however, this is due the large classes imbalance, making trivial the classification of trained students. Specificity results, on the other hand, show that discrimination between untrained/trained students is difficult, in particular, for low proficiency threshold $\geq 70$. For $\geq 80, 85$ thresholds, all TNR results were above 0.6 being the best the complex DT. For $\geq 90$, the pruned tree sacrifice TNR for the sake of TPR, whereas the complex model is biased towards the untrained class reducing the identification of trained students.

In terms of the splitting criterion the Gini Index was preferred over Entropy by most of the models, however, both G and H achieved TNR above 0.6. Results show that either measure can be used to train the model.

It is interesting that for both, the lowest and highest proficiency scores, discrimination of untrained students is clearly difficult, whereas for $\geq 80, 85$ better results are obtained. Consequently, for this experimental setup the proficiency score that achieves the best discrimination rate between TPR/TNR is $\geq 85$, been the best model for this threshold the complex DT.

Consequently, the corresponding variable importance analysis for the complex tree, with a BoE grain level of 1, is shown in Fig. 3. It is worth noting that, features related to KC start with capital T (errors made during the MM execution) or Q (errors during the material selection), then, the step is coded by an 's' of 'q' (e.g. 's11' stands for step 11; q217 stands for the material identifier 217);

finally, the type of error is encoded by tr(MM execution error) or qr (material selection error).

The most important features identified on the learning performance of students are the area of the students within the utility, and the course duration time. A tutor that integrates this student model, can use these results to provide additional preparation or specific material for those students which comes from areas 29, 30, and 45. Moreover, it may also inform facilitators and course managers to improve/reduce course time. On the other hand, KC associated with maneuver realization steps 9, 11, and 17, and errors selecting material 217, and 137 can be identified as elements that have an impact on the student proficiency. Such information, can be used by a tutor to provide additional material related to these steps/materials to untrained students. These variables may also reflect inconsistencies in the tutoring system such as unclear instructions or bad interface design. Thus, a tutor should inform system administrators about these relevant bugs so they may address them in the best possible way.

## 5   Conclusions

In this work we proposed a student model using a Decision Tree for the ALEn system. First, the system bug libraries that registered previous trainees errors are mapped as a Bag of Errors. Stereotype information is also considered. Then, a DT classifier is trained in accordance to several proficiency thresholds which determine if a student can be considered trained or untrained. Results in terms of Accuracy, Specificity, and Sensitivity, reveal that the best proficiency score to discriminate between trained and untrained students is $\geq 85$. Special attention is put in Specificity for selecting the proper student model since bad execution of maneuvers in real world have fatal consequences. Variable importance shows that a student's area within the utility, or the course time spend teaching a maneuver have more impact on the students' learning performance than errors or KCs per se. However, due to the BoE granularity of best student model, key knowledge components related to important concepts, misconceptions, or system inconsistencies where detected. Thus, a intelligent tutors can use this information to provide the pertinent actions, whether is relevant information associated to these KCs or a message to the system administrator of a possible inconsistency.

Bug library analysis using BoE do not consider order of errors, thus, conditional information is lost. Moreover, it is common when using text mining to transform words frequency into its inverse to reveal relevant features otherwise hindered by high frequency irrelevant ones. Also, clustering algorithms may discover groups of learning proficiency within the bug libraries and students profile information, such grouping can be used to identify specific KC to address groups specific needs. Future work will be carried in these venues.

**Acknowledgments.** GS-B thanks the Consejo Nacional de Ciencia y Tecnología for the support provided under the Cátedra-Conacyt contract 969.

# References

1. Nkambou, R., Bourdeau, J., Mizoguchi, R.: Introduction: what are intelligent tutoring systems, and why this book? In: Nkambou, R., Bourdeau, J., Mizoguchi, R. (eds.) Advances in Intelligent Tutoring Systems. SCI, vol. 308, pp. 1–12. Springer, Heidelberg (2010). https://doi.org/10.1007/978-3-642-14363-2_1
2. Ranganathan, R., Vanlehn, K., Van de Sande, B.: What do students do when using a step-based tutoring system? Res. Pract. Technol. Enhanc. Learn. 9(2), 323–347 (2014)
3. Woolf, B.: Building Intelligent Interactive Tutors: Student-Centered Strategies for Revolutionizing e-Learning. Morgan Kaufmann Publishers, Burlington (2009)
4. Günel, K., Aşliyan, R.: Extracting learning concepts from educational texts in intelligent tutoring systems automatically. Expert Syst. Appl. 37(7), 5017–5022 (2010)
5. Hernández, Y., Cervantes-Salgado, M., Pérez-Ramírez, M., Mejía-Lavalle, M.: Data-driven construction of a student model using Bayesian networks in an electrical domain. In: Pichardo-Lagunas, O., Miranda-Jiménez, S. (eds.) MICAI 2016, Part II. LNCS (LNAI), vol. 10062, pp. 481–490. Springer, Cham (2017). https://doi.org/10.1007/978-3-319-62428-0_39
6. Vanlehn, K.: The behavior of tutoring systems. Int. J. Artif. Intell. Ed. 16(3), 227–265 (2006)
7. Vanlehn, K.: The relative effectiveness of human tutoring, intelligent tutoring systems, and other tutoring systems. Educ. Psychol. 46(4), 197–221 (2011)
8. Ayala-García, A., Galván-Bobadilla, I., Arroyo, G., Pérez-Ramírez, M., Muñoz-Román, J.: Virtual reality training system for maintenance and operation of high-voltage overhead power lines. Virtual Real. 20(1), 27–40 (2016)
9. Sison, R., Shimura, M.: Student modeling and machine learning. Int. J. Artif. Intell. Educ. 9(1), 128–158 (1994)
10. Cao, N., Cui, W.: Introduction to Text Visualization. Atlantis Press, Paris (2016)
11. Argotte, L., Hernandez, Y., Arroyo-Figueroa, G.: Intelligent e-learning system for training power systems operators. In: König, A., Dengel, A., Hinkelmann, K., Kise, K., Howlett, R.J., Jain, L.C. (eds.) KES 2011. LNCS (LNAI), vol. 6882, pp. 94–103. Springer, Heidelberg (2011). https://doi.org/10.1007/978-3-642-23863-5_10
12. Romero, C., Ventura, S.: Educational data mining: a survey from 1995 to 2005. Expert Syst. Appl. 33(1), 135–146 (2007)
13. Romero, C., Ventura, S., Espejo, P.G., Hervás, C.: Data mining algorithms to classify students. In: Educational Data Mining 2008, Proceedings of the 1st International Conference on Educational Data Mining, Montreal, Québec, Canada, 20–21 June 2008, pp. 8–17 (2008). http://www.educationaldatamining.org/EDM2008/uploads/proc/1_Romero_3.pdf
14. Ibrahim, Z., Rusli, D.: Predicting students' academic performance: comparing artificial neural network, decision tree and linear regression. In: Proceedings of the 21st Annual SAS Malaysia Forum, pp. 1–6 (2007)
15. Guruler, H., Istanbullu, A., Karahasan, M.: A new student performance analysing system using knowledge discovery in higher educational databases. Comput. Educ. 55(1), 247–254 (2010)
16. Hernández, Y., Pérez, M.: Open student model for blended training in the electrical tests domain. In: Lagunas, O.P., Alcántara, O.H., Figueroa, G.A. (eds.) MICAI 2015. LNCS (LNAI), vol. 9414, pp. 195–207. Springer, Cham (2015). https://doi.org/10.1007/978-3-319-27101-9_14

17. Hernández, Y., Pérez, M.: A B-learning model for training within electrical tests domain. Intell. Learn. Environ. **87**, 43–52 (2014)
18. Hastie, T., Tibshirani, R., Friedman, J.: The Elements of Statistical Learning: Data Mining, Inference, and Prediction. Springer, New York (2011). https://doi.org/10. 1007/978-0-387-84858-7
19. Piech, C., Sahami, M., Koller, D., Cooper, S., Blikstein, P.: Modeling how students learn to program. In: Proceedings of the 43rd ACM Technical Symposium on Computer Science Education - SIGCSE 2012, pp. 1–6 (2012)
20. Kwartler, T.: Text Mining in Practice with R. Wiley, Chichester (2017)
21. Loh, W.: Fifty years of classification and regression trees. Int. Stat. Rev. **82**(3), 329–348 (2014)
22. Therneau, T., Atkinson, B., Ripley, B.: rpart: Recursive Partitioning and Regression Trees. R package version 4.1-11 (2017)
23. Loh, W.: Classification and regression trees. Wiley Interdiscip. Rev.: Data Min. Knowl. Discov. **1**(1), 14–23 (2011)

# Linked Educational Online Courses
# to Provide Personalized Learning

Heitor Barros[1(✉)], Jonathas Magalhães[2], Társis Marinho[2], Marlos Silva[2],
Michel Miranda[3], and Evandro Costa[3]

[1] Instituto Federal de Brasília - IFB, Via L2 Norte, SGAN 610 (610 Norte),
Módulo D, E, F e G, Brasília, DF 70830-450, Brazil
heitor.barros@ifb.edu.br
[2] Federal University of Campina Grande - UFCG, Rua Aprígio Veloso, 885,
Bairro Universitário, Campina Grande, Brazil
{jonathas,tarsis,marlos}@copin.ufcg.edu.br
[3] Federal Univeristy of Alagoas - UFAL, Av. Lourival de Melo Mota,
Tabuleiro do Martins, Maceió, Brazil
{michel.miranda,evandro}@ic.ufal.br

**Abstract.** The emergence of MOOCs enabled students from around the
world engage in courses taught by professors from leading universities.
However, the relatively low completion rates of MOOC participants has
been a central criticism in the popular discourse. Some studies point to
up to 90% evasion in some courses. The lack of knowledge in relation to
course prerequisites (background gaps) is one of the reasons that reduce
the completion rate. To alleviate this problem, this paper proposes the
use of a Linked Courses structure to provide support to students. In this
proposal, before starting a course, the background gaps of each student
are identified and a personalized set of support courses is recommended
to help him. Results obtained so far indicate the effectiveness of this
approach.

## 1 Introduction

Massive Open Online Courses or MOOCs are online courses accessible to anyone
on the web. Hundreds of institutions have joined in an effort to make education
more accessible by teaming up with MOOC providers [9]. With this new approach, inquisitive learners from all over the world can participate in the lectures
of proven experts [5].

The relatively low completion rates of MOOC participants has been a central
criticism in the popular discourse [6]. Some studies point to up to 90% evasion in
some courses [5]. One of the reasons for these low completion rates is the static
nature of the courses that do not fit the needs of students. Often a student starts
a course without having the proper theoretical background. These **background
gaps** make he did not perform well and not finish the course [5].

This problem is common in e-Learning domain and happens not only
in MOOCs but in any Web-based Learning System. In this context, several

F. Castro et al. (Eds.): MICAI 2017, LNAI 10633, pp. 198–207, 2018.
https://doi.org/10.1007/978-3-030-02840-4_16

approaches have emerged in order to adapt the content of online courses according to user needs, creating techniques to provide personalized learning [2].

However, the construction of mechanisms that provide personalized learning involves activities such as predict possible needs of students during the execution of course and create educational resources for the different possibilities. Depending on the course, these activities can become very costly and make unfeasible the construction of the course.

Given this context, this paper presents an approach that links educational online courses aiming to use related courses as support resources for students. In other words, this approach identifies knowledge gaps of students and recommends courses that can help them overcome these gaps.

To evaluate our proposal, we conducted a preliminary study with a group of students trying to learn a course. This study showed that the proposed model is effective in detecting background gaps and recommending courses to help the students.

## 2   Related Work

The development of techniques and technologies to provide personalized learning has been one of the outstanding tasks in the Technology-Enhanced Learning (TEL) field. These work aims to identify the needs of students and guide them through the learning process.

Several techniques have been proposed, Chen [2] presents an approach for building personalized learning path guidance based on a **pre-test** that uses the incorrect responses of the learner to identify knowledge gaps. Lin et al. [7] proposes an approach based on the **data mining** technique of decision trees to provide personalized learning paths in a learning system focused on creativity skill.

Özpolat and Akar [8] proposed an automatic student modelling method that is based on a **clustering method** and **keyword mapping**. Fabio and Antonietti [4] presents an **intelligent agents** system with **machine learning** techniques to predict learners preferences or needs of students with attention deficit/hyperactivity disorder (ADHD).

Brinton et al. [1] proposes the Mobile Integrated and Individualized Course (MIIC). MIIC is a platform for personalized course delivery which integrates lecture videos, text, assessments, and social learning into a mobile native app. This approach collects **behavioural measurements** to update the learner model, which can in turn be used to determine the resources adaptation.

Henning et al. [5] presents an approach based on learning pathways and observation of learner behaviour to recommend the best resources for each step of the pathway.

Although there are techniques to enable personalized learning, one of the factors that hinder the widespread adoption of these techniques is the need to provide different paths and resources based on the characteristics of the students. In this context, our proposal has the advantage of the reuse of educational resources present in other online courses, facilitating the creation of personalized learning structure.

## 3    Linked Courses

Linked Courses structure aims to organize educational resources to facilitate their reuse. It takes into consideration the context in which these resources can be used within a course/discipline. In addition, Linked Courses structure allows to identify the required knowledge for a course, and also which courses can be used to support that required knowledge.

In the Sect. 3.1, we define the representation of a course structure through an Integration Ontology. In the Sect. 3.2, we present how different courses are linked, focusing on the precedence issues among courses. To present our approach we use some examples based on two online courses: Introduction to Programming in Java[1] and Java Web Programming[2].

### 3.1    Course Structure

As said before, the Integration Ontology is responsible for linking different courses structures. We define the course structure based on a model for knowledge representation. The Integration Ontology uses a strategy of **Course Models**. Course Models are used in steps of classification, structuring and alignment of educational resources. Besides, a Course Model specify the pedagogical units of a discipline in a structured way (*Hierarchical* and *Sequencing* structures). Hierarchical structure defines the notion of topics and subtopics and Sequencing structure determines the order in which the resources should be used in a course.

In the following, we present the definitions of the integration approach based on Course Models:

**D1** $\rightarrow$ A Course Model $M_a$ is composed by a set of Pedagogical Units (Topics) $U_a$ and it is related to a *Knowledge Domain* $D_x$.

**D2** $\rightarrow$ The set $U_a$ is given by a **Domain Specialist** in the step construction of the model $M_a$. He determines the pedagogical units according to his vision of how to structure an educational course in the domain $D_x$.

**D3: Sequencing Structure** $\rightarrow$ $\forall u_j \in U_a$ there is a set $N_j \subset U_a \setminus \{u_j\}$ that contains the *sequent* pedagogical units with respect to $u_j$. In the same way, $u_j$ is a *previous* unit to a unit $u_k \in N_j$.

**D4: Hierarchical Structure** $\rightarrow$ $\forall u_i \in U_a$ there is a set $S_i \subset U_a \setminus \{u_i\}$ that contains the pedagogical units that are *specializations* or *sub-topics* of $u_i$. In the same way, $u_i$ is a *generalization* or *super topic* of a unit $u_k \in S_i$.

---

[1] Available at: http://ocw.mit.edu/courses/electrical-engineering-and-computer-science/6-092-introduction-to-programming-in-java-january-iap-2010/.

[2] Available at: https://www.virtualpairprogrammers.com/training-courses/Java-Web-Development-training.html.

**D5** → To insert an **Educational Resource** to the model, the resource should be related to one or more Pedagogical Units. This way, it is defined the property $l(R, U)$, where $R$ is a set of Educational Resources and $U$ is set of Pedagogical Units. Given $r_e \in R$ and $u_i \in U$, so $l(r_e, u_i)$ indicates that the resource $r_e$ is related to the pedagogical unit $u_i$.

Following the presented definitions, the Listing 1.1 presents an OWL code snippet showing an instance of a Model Course related to the Java programming domain.

**Listing 1.1.** Course Model based on a Java programming presented in the Manchester OWL pattern..

```
1  Individual: <onto.owl#model_Java>
2
3    Types:
4      <onto.owl#CourseModel>
5
6    Facts:
7  <onto.owl#belongsTo> <onto.owl#Java_Programming>,
8  <onto.owl#hasTopic> <onto.owl#Variables_types>,
9  <onto.owl#hasTopic> <onto.owl#Operators>,
10 <onto.owl#hasTopic> <onto.owl#Methods>,
11 <onto.owl#hasTopic> <onto.owl#Loops_and_arrays>,
12 <onto.owl#hasTopic> <onto.owl#Access_control>,
13 <onto.owl#hasTopic> <onto.owl#Class_scope>,
14 <onto.owl#hasTopic> <onto.owl#Packages_and_Java_API>,
15 <onto.owl#hasTopic> <onto.owl#Inheritance>,
16 <onto.owl#hasTopic> <onto.owl#Interfaces>,
17 <onto.owl#hasTopic> <onto.owl#Exceptions>,
18 <onto.owl#hasTopic> <onto.owl#File_IO>
```

In Listing 1.1, line 1 defines the individual *model_Java*, line 4 defines that this individual is Course Model, line 7 uses the property *belongsTo* to relate this Course Model to the *Java_Programming* **Knowledge Domain**. Finally, lines 8 to 18 have the property *hasTopic* that defines the topics of this Course Model.

In Listing 1.2 the code of Topic *Exceptions* is presented. Line 4 defines the type of this individual. In line 7 this topic is linked with the *model_java* Course Model using the property *belongsToModel*. Line 8 uses the property *nextTopic* to define that the topic **File_IO** comes after the topic *Exceptions* in this Course Model.

**Listing 1.2.** OWL individual of Topic *Exceptions* that belongs to Course Model *model_Java*.

```
1  Individual: <onto.owl#Exceptions>
2
3    Types:
4      <onto.owl#Topic>
```

```
5
6      Facts:
7        <onto.owl#belongsToModel> <onto.owl#model_Java >,
8        <onto.owl#nextTopic> <onto.owl#File_IO >
```

## 3.2 Course Mapping

Our model also provides mapping properties to align common points in two distinct Course Models.

**D6** → Given $U_a$ and $U_b$ the sets of pedagogical unit of Models $M_a$ and $M_b$, respectively. A Course Model $M_a$ can be aligned to model $M_b$, using the following properties:

1. **Equivalence:** An unit $u_i \in U_a$ can be *equivalent* to a unit $u_m \in U_b$. It is defined the property $e(U, U)$, where $e(u_i, u_m)$ are equivalent units. This property is reflexive.
2. **Generalization:** An unit $u_i \in U_a$ can be *generalization* of a unit $u_n \in U_b$. It is defined the property $g(U, U)$, where $g(u_i, u_n)$ indicates that $u_i$ is a *generalization* of $u_n$ and $u_n$ is a *specialization* of $u_i$.
3. **Precedence:** An unit $u_j \in U_a$ can be a *precedent unit* of $u_o \in U_b$. It is defined the property $s(U, U)$, where $s(u_j, u_o)$ indicates that $u_j$ is a precedent unit of $u_o$ and $u_o$ is a sequent unit of $u_j$.

For example, the Listing 1.3 shows a fragment of a individual of Course Model that represents a course of Java Web Development. This Course Model belongs to *Java_Web_Development* domain.

**Listing 1.3.** Course Model of a Java Web Development course presented in Manchester OWL format.

```
1    Individual: <onto.owl#model_Java_Web>
2
3      Types:
4        <onto.owl#CourseModel>
5
6      Facts:
7    <onto.owl#belongsTo> <onto.owl#Java_Web_Development >,
8    <onto.owl#hasTopic> <onto.owl#Servlets >,
9    <onto.owl#hasTopic> <onto.owl#Web_Application_Deployment >,
10   <onto.owl#hasTopic> <onto.owl#Handling_Forms >,
11   <onto.owl#hasTopic> <onto.owl#GET_and_POST>,
12   <onto.owl#hasTopic> <onto.owl#Session_Management >,
13   <onto.owl#hasTopic> <onto.owl#Java_Server_Pages >,
14   <onto.owl#hasTopic> <onto.owl#Model_View_Control >,
15   <onto.owl#hasTopic> <onto.owl#Java_Standard_Tag_Library >,
16   <onto.owl#hasTopic> <onto.owl#Frameworks_and_Struts>
```

In this context, the student must have knowledge of Java language so that he can start the Java Web course. For this, it is necessary to use the properties **precedes** to link these courses.

Listing 1.4 shows the Topic *File_IO*. This topic is the last of Course Model *model_Java* and it uses the property **precedes** to link this model to the topic *Servlets*, first topic of *model_Java_Web*. Thus, the two course models are connected via *precedes* property.

**Listing 1.4.** OWL individual of Topic *File_IO* that belongs to Course Model *model_Java*.

```
1   Individual: <onto.owl#File_IO>
2
3       Types:
4           <onto.owl#Topic>
5
6       Facts:
7           <onto.owl#belongsToModel> <onto.owl#model_Java>,
8           <onto.owl#precedes> <onto.owl#Servlets>
```

## 4  Personalized Course Planning

Figure 1 illustrates the overview of personalized course planning. This process receive as inputs a learner, a linked courses graph and a goal course. The linked courses graph contains structured courses based on model defined in Sect. 3 and the goal course is the course that the student wants to study. The steps of this process are discussed below:

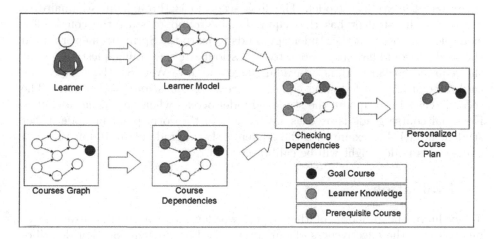

**Fig. 1.** Overview of personalized course planning

**Create Learner Model** - this step is responsible for create a Learner Model to describe the knowledge of the leaner. This process is described in Sect. 4.1.

**Define Course Dependencies** - this sub-process identifies the *goal course* prerequisites based on precedence links of Courses Graph.

**Check Learner Dependencies** - This step requires the Leaner Model and the prerequisites of *goal course*. In this sub-process the previous knowledge of the learner is compared with the *goal courses* dependencies. The purpose is to determine the dependencies that the learner has not learned.

**Create Course Plan** - the personalized course plan is based on the goal course dependencies that are not in the Learner Model.

## 4.1  Learner Model

We define a student model to represent the student's knowledge, using this model we can identify the student's background gaps in a determined course. We use Bayesian Networks (BN) to represent the student model, we follow a similar approach as proposed in [3]. The BN is constructed taking into account the hierarchical structure of Pedagogical Units presented in Subsect. 3.1. So, the BN contains just one type of node, a *Pedagogical Unit (PU)* that represents a skill of the learner. This node can be parent of a set of other *Pedagogical Unit* nodes. Every node has two values, mastered or not mastered, that measure the learner's knowledge.

The weights of the Bayesian Network are given by the Knowledge Engineer (responsible for modeling the domain knowledge). To set the prior probabilities, we established five degrees of knowledge: *No idea* = 0.05, *Basic* = 0.25, *Good* = 0.50, *Very good* = 0.75 and *Expert* = 0.95. To set the table of conditional probabilities, we follow the approach proposed by Zapata-Rivera and Greer [10].

We define two scenarios in which are collected evidence about the student to update the student model. The first scenario is through questionnaire to identify if the student has the required background to start the course. For example, suppose that the student pretends to learn the Spring framework, then the student would have to respond to a questionnaire containing questions about the required background, i.e., Java language and Java Web. So, the node can be calibrated using the following equation: *#correct_questions/#questions*. The second scenario to update the student model occurs when he finishes a course. Her final course grade is used as calibration to the correspondent node in her student model. For example, if the student takes a grade of 70/100 in the Java course, this node weight will be calibrated to 0.7.

## 5  Evaluation

To evaluate the proposal of this paper, we developed a running example to demonstrate the effectiveness of our approach. Initially, this Section describes the scenario of the running example, i.e. the courses and learners. Then, how our approach can provide recommendations to the students to help them in the process of learning. In this running example, we use the following courses:

**C1** - Java Programming (presented in Sect. 3).
**C2** - Java Web Development (presented in Sect. 3).
**C3** - Spring MVC Framework[3] (http://spring.io).

The Spring Framework is a widely-used MVC framework that provides a comprehensive programming and configuration model for modern Java-based enterprise applications. Listing 1.5 shows the Course Model code of Spring course. The Course Models of the other courses were presented in Sect. 3 (Listings 1.1 and 1.3).

**Listing 1.5.** Course Model of a Spring MVC Framework course presented in Manchester Owl format.

```
1   Individual: <onto.owl#model_Spring>
2
3     Types:
4       <onto.owl#CourseModel>
5
6     Facts:
7   <onto.owl#belongsTo> <onto.owl#Spring_Framework>,
8   <onto.owl#hasTopic> <onto.owl#Getting_Started>,
9   <onto.owl#hasTopic> <onto.owl#Autowiring>,
10  <onto.owl#hasTopic> <onto.owl#Wiring_with_Annotations>,
11  <onto.owl#hasTopic> <onto.owl#SPEL_Expression_Language>,
12  <onto.owl#hasTopic> <onto.owl#Web_Application_Basics>,
13  <onto.owl#hasTopic> <onto.owl#Web_Forms>,
14  <onto.owl#hasTopic> <onto.owl#Spring_Security>,
15  <onto.owl#hasTopic> <onto.owl#Logging_and_Testing>,
16  <onto.owl#hasTopic> <onto.owl#Hibernate>,
17  <onto.owl#hasTopic> <onto.owl#Spring_Webflow>,
18  <onto.owl#hasTopic> <onto.owl#JSON_and_AJAX>
```

In this scenario, a group of 14 students are involved in a project that uses the Spring Framework for application development. In this context, the chosen *goal course* is the Spring course (C3).

This is a heterogeneous group of students, some are undergraduate students and others are master's students, so they have different knowledge background. For this reason, we need to evaluate the individual knowledge of each student to identify potential knowledge gaps. Students that already known Spring Framework did not participate of this study.

First, it is necessary to identify Knowledge prerequisites of Spring course(C3). The development of applications with Spring Framework (C3) requires knowledge as Servlets and Java Server Pages that are topics of Java Web course (C2). Similarly, as shown in Sect. 3, Java Web course (C2) is dependent on the content of Java programming course (C1). This way, there is a dependence chain among these courses.

In this scenario, the student must have sufficient knowledge of the Java language and Java Web development to start the Spring course. Otherwise, the

---

[3] Available at: https://www.udemy.com/javaspring/.

student will start the course with background gaps that can result in poor performance in the course.

In other words, we need to to create the Learner Model of these students, as specified in Sect. 4.1. Thus, each student answered a questionnaire aiming to measure his knowledge related to background courses (C1 and C2). It is not possible that a student has knowledge of Java Web (C2) and he does not know Java (C1), whereas C1 is a prerequisite of C2.

The questionnaire classified the students into three groups as shown in Table 1. As expected, no group was empty. This proves the heterogeneity of the group.

**Table 1.** Students knowledge background and courses recommendation

| Group | Student knows Java programming? | Student knows Java web development? | Courses recommendation | Number of students |
|---|---|---|---|---|
| 1 | No | No | $C1 \rightarrow C2 \rightarrow C3$ | 3 |
| 2 | Yes | No | $C2 \rightarrow C3$ | 5 |
| 3 | Yes | Yes | $C3$ | 6 |

After running this case study we got the following conclusions:

- Students who participated in the case study showed the characteristic heterogeneity MOOCs students, even though a scenario on a much smaller scale.
- Given the goal of learning Spring, students were informed about the existence of knowledge gaps and what courses they should do. Without the use of this approach, students would start the course with knowledge gaps or would have to seek information and/or courses on their own.
- The proposed model was able to represent and connect the three courses. In addition this model identified the precedence order between them.
- The construction of this scenario not demanded much effort since the courses and educational resources were available on the web. The work came down to select these courses and use the Integration Ontology to annotate and connect these courses. This demonstrates that this approach encourages the reuse of educational resources.

## 6   Conclusion and Future Work

The emergence of MOOCs enabled students from around the world engage in courses taught by professors from leading universities in the world. This scenario increases the need for techniques that adapt these courses to students, providing personalized learning.

In this paper, we propose the use of a linked courses structure to identify knowledge gaps of students and use these courses to help students overcome these gaps. The main advantages of this approach are: (i) prevent students starting courses with background gaps, (ii) guide students so that they overcome these gaps and (iii) facilitate the reuse of educational resources.

To evaluate our proposal, we conducted a preliminary study that proved the effectiveness of the proposal in connecting related courses and use them to provide a personalized course plan for each student, based on his knowledge background.

As future work, we plan to evaluate the proposed model in a scenario with a higher number of students. Also, we will enhance the Learner Model and the course structure to enable the recommendation of a set of topics of a course for a student, not just a full course, in order to provide more accurate recommendations.

# References

1. Brinton, C., Rill, R., Ha, S., Chiang, M., Smith, R., Ju, W.: Individualization for education at scale: MIIC design and preliminaryevaluation. IEEE Trans. Learn. Technol. **PP**(99), 1 (2014)
2. Chen, C. M.: Intelligent web-based learning system with personalized learning path guidance. Comput. Educ. **51**(2), 787–814 (2008)
3. Costa, E., Silva, P., Magalhães, J., Silva, M.: An open and inspectable learner modelingwith a negotiation mechanism to solve cognitive conflicts in an intelligent tutoring system. In: Proceedings of the 2nd Workshop on Personalization Approaches for Learning Environments (PALE 2012). CEUR Workshop Proceedings, vol. 872. CEUR-WS.org (2012)
4. Fabio, R.A., Antonietti, A.: Effects of hypermedia instruction on declarative, conditional and procedural knowledge in ADHD students. Res. Dev. Disabil. **33**(6), 2028–2039 (2012)
5. Henning, P.A., et al.: Personalized web learning: merging open educational resources into adaptive courses for higher education. Personal. Approach. Learn. Environ. **55**, 55–62 (2014). ISSN: 1613-0073
6. Kizilcec, R.F., Piech, C., Schneider, E.: Deconstructing disengagement: analyzing learner subpopulations in massive open online courses. In: Proceedings of the Third International Conference on Learning Analytics and Knowledge, pp. 170–179. ACM (2013)
7. Lin, C.F., Yeh, Y.-C., Hung, Y.H., Chang, R.I.: Data mining for providing a personalized learning path in creativity: an application of decision trees. Comput. Educ. **68**, 199–210 (2013)
8. Ozpolat, E., Akar, G.B.: Automatic detection of learning styles for an e-learning system. Comput. Educ. **53**(2), 355–367 (2009)
9. Pappano, L.: The Rise of MOOCs. The New York Times Magazine, September 2013
10. Zapata-Rivera, J.-D., Greer, J.E.: Interacting with inspectable Bayesian student models. Int. J. Artif. Intell. Educ. **14**(2), 127–163 (2004)

# Emotion Recognition Using a Convolutional Neural Network

Ramon Zatarain-Cabada[✉], Maria Lucia Barron-Estrada,
Francisco González-Hernández, and Hector Rodriguez-Rangel

Posgrado en Ciencias de la Computación, Instituto Tecnológico de Culiacán,
Culiacán, Sinaloa, Mexico
rzatarain@itculiacan.edu.mx

**Abstract.** Learning-oriented emotions have not been studied by emotion recognition systems. These emotions have not been taken into account by other studies despite their importance in educational context. This work presents a recognition system which uses deep learning approach using convolutional neural network for solving that problem. A convolutional architecture was designed and tested with 3 different facial expression databases. The architecture is composed of 3 convolutional layers, 3 max-pooling layers, and 3 deep neural networks. The first database contains facial images on 6 basic emotions; the second and third databases contain images of learning-centered facial expressions. The tests show a 95% in the basic emotion database, a 97% for the first learning-centered emotion database and a 75% for the third database. We discuss about the differences in results among the three emotion databases.

**Keywords:** Deep learning · Artificial intelligence
Face expression recognition · Face expression database

## 1 Introduction

Picard defined some principles of affective computing in her most popular work [1] in the year 1999. Since then, several works focused on making systems able to recognize emotions in people. One the most used approach is the theory of Ekman which explains what are the basic emotions [2]. Basic emotions are defined as spontaneous short-duration feelings with clearly visible expressions which are presented in most cultures on the planet. Some emotions defined as basic affective states are anger, sadness, fear, happiness, and surprise. Intelligent Tutoring Systems (ITS) are programs built for helping, handling, and leading the training student. ITS work on different areas as psychology and pedagogy. The development of affective ITSs is still narrow, and there are a limited few works that face the issue [3, 4]. In these ITSs, emotions are used to choose the suitable action for students during their training or learning. The recognition of facial expressions is a common technique used by the ITSs. This technique locates the face in an image to extract a set of features which are used as inputs for a machine learning system. The features are used for training and using the machine learning system. However, evidence has been shown that there are other more important emotions involved during the learning activities of students. These emotions are known

© Springer Nature Switzerland AG 2018
F. Castro et al. (Eds.): MICAI 2017, LNAI 10633, pp. 208–219, 2018.
https://doi.org/10.1007/978-3-030-02840-4_17

as learning-centered emotions [5]. They contain features with longer time, are less expressive than basic emotions, and appear mainly during intellectual tasks [6]. Also, facial expression recognition has some important issues. For instance, features extraction uses some algorithm to obtain image pixels which are important. During this process some data is lost or accidentally ignored. This means that there is no certainty that all important data is selected. Another problem is to establish which extraction method is best. For example, factors such as illumination or face position affect the quality of extracted features. In addition to feature extraction, other issues related to feature selection are dimensionality reduction. This activity has also the possibility of losing important data during its performance. Our solution for all the previous issues or problems is applying the deep learning approach. Deep learning is composed of multiple processing layers to learn data representation with multiple levels of abstraction [7]. This approach has been used to solve problems such as speech recognition, object detection, and visual object recognition [8, 9]. The deep learning method has been proven with significant results in image processing [7]. The technique used is named convolutional neural networks (CNN) which connect layers sequentially. Image data is sent and processed through each layer. The approach identifies abstract patterns on objects automatically. Thus, the method does not necessarily perform feature extraction or feature selection. In this work, we first present a convolutional architecture which is tested with 3 different image databases. The first one is a database for posed facial expressions related to basic emotions. The second and third one are databases for spontaneous facial expressions related to learning-centered emotions. Then, we show an application of the emotion recognizer inside an Intelligent learning Environment for Java programming.

## 2   Related Work

This sections presents a review about the deep learning approach focusing in the facial expression recognition and databases with basic and non-basic emotions for posed and spontaneous facial expressions.

### 2.1   Convolutional Neural Network for Facial Expression Recognition

There are many works that have faced the challenge to recognize facial expressions. Usually, these works build a convolutional neural network combining some preprocessing method and modifying some features of the architecture. Next, related work to detect emotion expressions is presented. A proposal of identification of high-level features is presented in [10]. The authors introduces their new deep learning approach which consists of adding a new layer named *Deep hidden IDentity features* (DeepID). The goal of the DeepID Layer is identifying a large number of classes. The work follows a normal configuration of a convolutional network using four convolutional layers, three max-pooling layer, and one soft-max layer. The DeepID layer is located between the last convolutional layer and the soft-max layer. However, the previous authors are only focused on identifying people faces. In [11], the authors present a method for classifying 6 basic emotions and the neutral expression. The main goal is to reduce the complexity of the problem domain removing confounding factors. The authors used the feature extraction method *local binary pattern* (LBP). Also, the authors preprocessed the images transforming them in gray scale images and cropping the region of the face of the image. Some differences of other works which use LBP are that they are using a different LBP radius parameter (LBP uses two parameters, radius of the center point named as R and number of points around the center point named as P) in each image; LBP codes are mapped to a 3D space applying multi-dimensional scaling which is a code-to-code dissimilarity scores based on an approximation to the Earth Mover's Distance; another difference is that they not only use RGB original codes from the images as inputs for CNN; they also use the mapped codes obtained from LBP codes. In [12] is presented an interesting analysis of convolutional neural networks. The authors present a new pattern recognition framework. The pattern consists of a set of deep CNNs that are interconnected with various committee machines (also known as classifier ensembles). Each CNN is independently configured; this means that each CNN is an individual member inside of the framework; also, each CNN was trained using different datasets where each dataset is created using a distinct preprocessed for the original image dataset. A way of building different CNNs was configuring different weight initializations. Other important features is the use of methods to combine decision for committee levels from the individual members (CNNs) such as the majority voting, the median rule, and the simple average rule. They introduced a combination rule based on exponential weighting to give more weight on well-performed individual. Last, the authors introduce a hierarchical committee to divide a hard problem into easier ones where they constructed a procedure which consists in two expected merits; the first one is to organize each individual member in level sub-groups, and the second one is to collect all subgroups decision in the previous level. In [13] the authors presented a method to recognize static facial expressions where they use three techniques to detect faces in the SFEW 2.0 dataset: the joint cascade detection and alignment, the Deep-CNN-based, and the mixtures of trees. They applied a pre-processing over the images, each one is resized to 48 × 48 and transformed to grayscale. They propose a CNN architecture of five convolutional layers but instead of adding pooling layers in each connection among convolutional layers, they use stochastic pooling because it has proven giving a good performance with limited training data. The techniques used for building the CNN are the use of generating randomized perturbation in the dataset, the modification of the loss function for considering the perturbation, a pre-training of CNN using the FER dataset, a fine-tuning of the CNN using the SFEW dataset, and multiple networks for learning. They report good accuracies in emotions as happy, but most of the emotions were detected with less than 20% accuracy.

## 2.2 Face Expression Databases

The face expression databases are a set of images that are either an emotion, a situation, or an experience. There are several available databases. However, not all databases represent interesting emotions for this research. Next, the most important databases are presented and explained. Cohn-Kanade (CK) [14] is a dataset of 486 sequences from 97 positioned persons. The database seeks to represent the image sequence inside the

Facial Action Coding System (FACS). Each expression begins as a neutral expression and then move to a peak expression. Each time a neutral expression changes it is turned into a peak expression. In this way, each expression can receive an emotion label. CK includes basic emotions as well as Action Units (AU) annotations. Cohn-Kanade Plus (CK+) [15] as the name implies is an extension of original CK (version 2). This version includes in addition to posed expressions, non-posed (spontaneous) expressions recording from 84 novel subjects and more metadata information. Spontaneous expressions were taken at one or more times between tasks. A number of posed expression increased 22% with respect to initial version; the target of each expression is yet completing FACS coded. Radboud Faces Database (RaFD) [16] contains an image set of 49 models in two subsets: 39 Caucasian Dutch adults and 10 Caucasian Dutch children. All model expressed eight facial expressions (anger, happiness, fear, sadness, contempt, surprise, disgust, and neutral) with three gaze directions and five camera angles. They obtained a total of 120 images per model which had to comply various requisites like wearing a type of shirt or no hair on the face. The database reached the overall 82% agreement rate. Contempt was a complicated expression to detect. SEMAINE [17] is a database that includes high-quality, multimodal recordings. The recording was generated when people were talking to an automatic system which simulates emotions to observe whether participants had emotional reactions. The recordings showed people engaged with the system. In database-building, they investigated the concept known as dimensional emotions where six basic emotions were founded. The dimensions of an emotion are Valence, Activation, Power, and Anticipation/Expectation. M&M Initiative (MMI) [18] is a database of static images and image sequences of faces in frontal and profile view; also, MMI includes videos, the using of AU-coded as well as multiple AUs expressions. MMI contains more than 1500 samples and the database is contained in a web-based direct-manipulation application. Two FACS coders labeled the images and videos. At publication time two-thirds of the samples had been FACS coded when a disagreement was observed where the authors took the final decision whether a photo should be included or not.

# 3    Convolutional Neural Network for ITS

In this section the features of the CNN are presented. The preprocessing used to the image database and the CNN architecture are specified. The assembled parts are presented and explained.

## 3.1    Image Preprocessing

Preprocessing is not a formal part of the architecture. However, a CNN has the inconvenience of needing a powerful hardware. The use of filters in a large size set of images with multiple dimensionalities causes that the CPU has an important workload. Applying a preprocessing step was needed to achieve converging a CNN model adequately. The process consists of locating a region of interest (ROI) in every facial image. The viola-jones method [19] was used and OpenCV software supported that activity using the cascade architecture. After the ROI was located it is subtracted and the ROI is changed to a size of 75 × 75. The image is transformed to a grayscale image and saved into a new database (a special database for training and testing of the CNN).

## 3.2   Architecture Description

The architecture design contains 12 layers, each layer is shown in Fig. 1. The first section contains a representation of the preprocessing step previously explained. The second section contains the representation of the input for the network and the convolutional layers which transform the images in each layer. The convolutional layer has one dimension unlike other architectures where they use two or more dimensions. The reason is that the gray images obtained in the preprocessing step lose their three RGB channels becoming them in images of one dimension. The third section contains a representation of three densely-connected Neural Networks (NN). Also these NN are connected one after another.

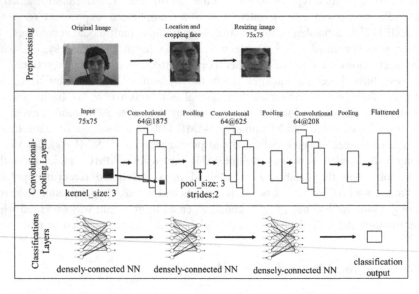

**Fig. 1.** The convolutional neural network architecture

## Convolutional Layers

The architecture is composed of three convolutional layers. These layers are the core of the architecture because they apply the learnable filters of the CNN. The parameters of the layer consist of a set of filters capable of learning. Each filter convolves across the width and height of the input volume, computing the dot product between the entries of the filter and the image (the input). As a result, the network learns filters that activate when it detects some specific type of feature. In a CNN a filter is called also kernel. Generally, the kernel refers to an operator applied to the whole image such that it transforms the information encoded in the pixels. Also, a kernel is a smaller-sized matrix in comparison to the input dimensions of the image, which consists of real valued entries. So, it is needed to define a kernel and its size and so to get the input image as a vector (or matrix) of pixels. Figure 2 shows an example on how to use the kernel with an input. The input is a matrix of pixels and the example shows only nine numbers to simplify the explanation. The process is as follows: first, the kernel is overlapped on top of the input image; second, the product between each number in the kernel and each number in the overlapped input is computed; third, a single number by summing these products together is obtained; fourth, the obtained number is set in a convolutional output; fifth and last, the kernel is moved to the next section in the input.

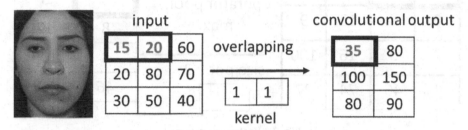

**Fig. 2.** The convolution operation

There are other important parameters as the strides and padding; the first one for establishing the amount of units to move the kernel inside the input; the second one establishes the amount of empty pixels used to fill zero padding of the input before overlapping the kernel. However, the architecture does not use these kind of parameters. The configuration of the convolutional layers is a kernel with a size of 3, 64 filters, and strides of size 1.

*Rectified Linear Units activation function*
Another feature is that the convolutional layers use a Rectified Linear Units (ReLU) activation function. This function increases the nonlinear properties of the decision function and the overall network without affecting the receptive fields of the convolutional layer. The ReLU function is defined by Eq. 1 where $x$ is a value in the layer and the function returns a 0 in case of having a value less than 0.

$$f(x) = \max(0, x) \tag{1}$$

**Max-Pooling Layers**
A pooling layer has the utility to reduce the spatial dimension of a convolutional layer for the next convolutional layer (or any layer). The pooling layer reduces the width and height of an input layer. The operation performed by this layer leads to loss information and it is known as *"down-sampling"*. However, losing information is beneficial for a neural layer: first, the decrease in size leads to less computational overhead for the upcoming layers; second, the losing of information works against over-fitting. The pooling divide the input image into a set of non-overlapping rectangles and for each sub-region, it gets the maximum value of each one. The goal is to reduce the number of features progressively. Figure 3 shows how the pooling operator works. The process is

as follows: first, a region is selected (represented as a black boundary); second, the max value inside the boundary is selected; third, the obtained number is set in a pooling output; fourth and last, the boundary area moves to the next section without overlapping a processed area.

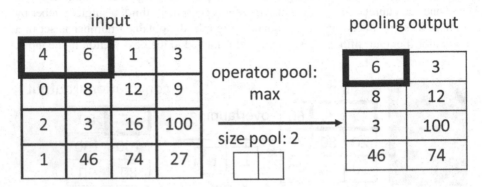

Fig. 3. Pooling operation

The architecture has three max-poling layers. Each one connected to a previous convolutional layer. The pool layers have a size of three units, a strides of two units, and the operator is a max-pooling.

**Classification Layers**
The convolutional and max-pooling layers have the function to identify the important features on the images automatically. A classification algorithm to identify what expression is showing the image by the processed features in convolutional and max-pooling layers was implemented. The architecture has three fully connected neural networks. A fully connected layer takes all units in the previous layer (no matter what type of layer is). Fully connected layers are not spatially located anymore, so it is no possible having convolutional layers after a fully connected layer. The first two neural networks use ReLU activation in their outputs, but the third neural network uses a softmax activation function to deal with the classification problem. The Softmax activation function distributes the output to be between 0 and 1, just like a sigmoid function. It also divides each output such that the total sum of the outputs is equal to 1. The architecture has three neural networks; the first and second network have 500 units to compute the output space and the third network has 15 units.

*Dropout connections*
There are dropout connections among the first two NN layers. The dropout connections work to reduce overfitting among NN layers because most of the parameters are sent layer by layer. Dropout consists in randomly setting a fraction rate of input units to 0 at each update during training time. The fraction rate used is 50%.

# 4  Using the CNN in an Intelligent Tutoring System for Java Programming

Java Sensei is an ITS to learn Java programming [20]. Java Sensei uses a module which uses fuzzy logic. The module contains fuzzy rules for managing pedagogic aspects of student. We adapted the module for integrating the learning-centered emotions of the first database. Two teaching experts built the rules considering the emotions and other aspects such as quality answer or global ability. As a result, we obtained a total of 495 rules. The rules are wrote using Fuzzy Control Language (FCL) and the implementation was supported with the library JFuzzyLogic [21]. Fuzzy logic needs to define fuzzy inputs and fuzzy outputs. The inputs for the fuzzy logic system are emotions and cognitive aspects of student. The emotional value is extracted from CNN. The cognitive values are generated by calculates of completed tasks and incorrect/correct answers in the ITS. The outputs variables are reactions and answers can do the tutor in the ITS; some of reactions are positive/neutral/negative feedback messages about the progress of the student or their level of care.

## 4.1  Fuzzification

Linguistic variables were established by two expert teachers in java and teaching. The variables are a representation of a state, in the case of cognitive states are bad or good; in the case of emotional states are a linguistic variable by each emotion. Table 1 shows the definition of linguistic variables.

**Table 1.** Linguistic variables

| Name | Type | Fuzzy Values |
|------|------|--------------|
| Currentemotion | Input | Engagement; excitement; frustration; boredom |
| Previousemotion | Input | Engagement; excitement; frustration; boredom |
| Abilityglobal | Input | Bad; good |
| Qualityanswer | Input | Bad; good |
| Expression | Output | Delighted; neutral; surprised; compassionate; skeptical |
| Feedback | Output | Positive; neutral; negative |
| Intervention | Output | Yes; no |

An example of a fuzzy logic rule is shown below. This rule is defined using FCL. It follows a structure typical of a fuzzy rule which contains number of rule, a section *if* with two types of conditions (and, or) and a section *then*.

```
RULE 1: IF lastemotion IS frustration AND currentemotion
IS engagement AND globalability IS bad AND qualityanswer
IS bad THEN feedback IS neutral;
```

## 5    Results and Discussion

This sections presents a validation process for knowing the accuracy of the recognizer. Three databases are used for the tests: RaFD, a posed facial expression database, and two different spontaneous facial expression databases created in our research laboratory [22]. The purpose of including RaFD is to compare the results of a database with basic emotions and posed expressions against databases with non-basic spontaneous emotions. Our first created database contains face expressions for 4 different learning-centered emotions (boredom, frustration, engagement, and excitement). The second created database contains face expressions for 6 different learning-centered emotions (boredom, engagement, excitement, focusing, interesting, and relaxing). Next, each database is described including the number of classes for each emotion and the obtained accuracy using the convolutional neural network.

The RaFD database originally includes eight emotional expressions and the neutral expression. In this work five emotions expressions (angry, happy, fear, surprise, sad, and neutral) were taken for an accuracy test. The final size of the used database was 1146 images. The global accuracy for the all classes was 95%. Table 2 shows a distribution of classes and the accuracy for each one.

**Table 2.**  Distribution of classes and the accuracy for RaFD

| RaFD | Angry | Happy | Fear | Surprise | Sad | Neutral |
|---|---|---|---|---|---|---|
| Number of instances | 191 | 191 | 191 | 191 | 191 | 191 |
| Accuracy | 96% | 95% | 94% | 96% | 92% | 97% |

The first spontaneous facial expression database created by our team includes four emotions related to an educational context. The emotions were obtained while students performed programming activities using the headset Emotiv Epoc which reports the emotional state [23]. These emotions are boredom, engagement, excitement, and frustration. The final size of the database is 322 images. The same convolutional neural network architecture was tested. The difference is the classes used for the training step. The global accuracy for the all classes was 97%. Table 3 shows a distribution of classes and the accuracy for each emotion.

**Table 3.**  Distribution of classes and the accuracy for first spontaneous facial expression database

| First database | Boredom | Engagement | Excitement | Frustration |
|---|---|---|---|---|
| Number of instances | 17 | 110 | 91 | 104 |
| Accuracy | 94% | 99% | 98% | 97% |

The second database includes five emotions related to an educational context. The database has the emotions boredom, engagement, excitement, focusing, interesting, and relaxing. These emotions were obtained from the headset Emovit Insight [24] while students performed designed activities to elicit a specific emotion. The global accuracy for all classes was 74%. The final version of the database contains a total of 5028 images. Table 4 shows results of the test.

**Table 4.** Distribution of classes an the accuracy for second database

| Second database | Boredom | Engagement | Excitement | Focusing | Interesting |
|---|---|---|---|---|---|
| Number of instances | 1040 | 1955 | 1661 | 222 | 150 |
| Accuracy | 79% | 82% | 78% | 65% | 66% |

We got satisfactory results in the three databases. In RaFD and our first database, the results overcome 90%, an important achieved accuracy for both databases. In our second database, the result is an accuracy of 74% where the result is still important because there are no works that face the problem with educational-centered facial expressions. For example, the work in [25] analyzed four emotions (boredom, engagement, delighted which is described like excitement, and frustration) and they got an accuracy of 64% or less for three classes (boredom, engagement, frustration) while the third test got results above 72%. Also, the analyzed expressions in this work are not posed, they are real expressions obtained during performing emotional tasks. The posed expressions are important for testing a classifier system, but in the real world the conditions are rarely optimal to take images. Also, students do not have exaggerated facial expression, but rather their expressions are very discrete.

## 6 Conclusions and Future Work

Detecting emotions is a complex task even for human beings. Using only the face to detect emotions is a very hard challenge so that this research needs to be continued. This work presents the building of a convolutional neural network architecture for detecting emotions related to an educational context. The tests validate that this work had successful results in three type of database: one for basic emotions and two for non-basic emotions. The results indicates that convolutional neural networks are a valuable choice in the recognition of basic and non-basic emotions. The architecture presented is a good beginning to recognize non-basic emotions and can be applied to recognize emotions from other different sources. In the future, we want to increase the size of the created facial expression databases and we will test them with different machine learning methods to increase the number of classifiers. Also, we will add different types of recognitions from other sources such as voice, text, and brain signals.

# References

1. Picard, R.W.: Affective Computing. MIT Press, Cambridge (1997)
2. Ekman, P.: An argument for basic emotions. Cogn. Emot. **6**, 169–200 (1992)
3. D'Mello, S.K., Graesser, A.C.: AutoTutor and affective AutoTutor: learning by talking with cognitively and emotionally intelligent computers that talk back? ACM **15**, 434–442 (2011)
4. Wiggins, J.B., et al.: JavaTutor: an intelligent tutoring system that adapts to cognitive and affective states during computer programming. In: Proceedings of the 46th ACM Technical Symposium on Computer Science Education - SIGCSE 2015, p. 599. ACM (2015)
5. Pekrun, R.: Emotions and learning. Harv. Educ. Rev. **25**, 95–104 (2014)
6. D'Mello, S., Graesser, A.: Dynamics of affective states during complex learning. Learn. Instr. **22**, 145–157 (2012)
7. LeCun, Y., Bengio, Y., Hinton, G.: Deep learning. Nature **521**, 436–444 (2015)
8. Glorot, X.: Domain adaptation for large-scale sentiment classification: a deep learning approach. In: Proceedings of the 28th International Conference on Machine Learning, pp. 513–520 (2011)
9. Hinton, G., et al.: Deep neural networks for acoustic modeling in speech recognition: the shared views of four research groups. IEEE Sig. Proc. Mag. **29**, 82–97 (2012)
10. Sun, Y., Wang, X., Tang, X.: Deep learning face representation from predicting 10,000 classes. In: Proceedings of the IEEE Conference on Computer Vision and Pattern Recognition, pp. 1891–1898 (2014)
11. Levi, G., Hassner, T.: Emotion recognition in the wild via convolutional neural networks and mapped binary patterns. In: Proceedings of the 2015 ACM on International Conference on Multimodal Interaction, pp. 503–510 (2015)
12. Kim, B., Lee, H., Roh, J., Lee, S.: Hierarchical committee of deep CNNs with exponentially-weighted decision fusion for static facial expression recognition. In: Proceedings of the 2015 ACM on International Conference on Multimodal Interaction - ICMI 2015, pp. 427–434. ACM Press, New York (2015)
13. Yu, Z., Zhang, C.: Image based static facial expression recognition with multiple deep network learning. In: Proceedings of the 2015 ACM on International Conference on Multimodal Interaction - ICMI 2015, pp. 435–442. ACM Press, New York (2015)
14. Kanade, T., Cohn, J., Tian, Y.: Comprehensive database for facial expression analysis. In: Automatic Face and Gesture Recognition, pp. 46–53. IEEE (2000)
15. Lucey, P., Cohn, J.F., Kanade, T., Saragih, J., Ambadar, Z., Matthews, I.: The extended Cohn-Kande dataset (CK+): a complete facial expression dataset for action unit and emotion specified expression. In: CVPRW, pp. 94–101. IEEE (2010)
16. Langner, O., Dotsch, R., Bijlstra, G., Wigboldus, D.H.J., Hawk, S.T., van Knippenberg, A.: Presentation and validation of the Radboud faces database. Cogn. Emot. **24**, 1377–1388 (2010)
17. McKeown, G., Valstar, M., Cowie, R., Pantic, M., Schroder, M.: The SEMAINE database: annotated multimodal records of emotionally colored conversations between a person and a limited agent. IEEE Trans. Affect. Comput. **3**, 5–17 (2012)
18. Valstar, M.F., Pantic, M.: Induced disgust, happiness and surprise: an addition to the MMI facial expression database. In: Proceedings of International Conference on Language Resources and Evaluation, Workshop on EMOTION, pp. 65–70 (2010)
19. Viola, P., Jones, M.: Rapid object detection using a boosted cascade of simple features. In: Proceedings of the 2001 IEEE Computer Society Conference on Computer Vision and Pattern Recognition. CVPR 2001, p. I-511–I-518. IEEE Computer Society (2001)

20. Cabada, R.Z., Estrada, M.L.B., Hernandez, F.G., Bustillos, R.O.: An affective learning environment for Java. In: 2015 IEEE 15th International Conference on Advanced Learning Technologies, pp. 350–354. IEEE (2015)
21. Cingolani, P., Alcala-Fdez, J.: jFuzzyLogic: a java library to design fuzzy logic controllers according to the standard for fuzzy control programming. Int. J. Comput. Intell. Syst. **6**, 61–75 (2013)
22. Zatarain-Cabada, R., Barrón-Estrada, M.L., González-Hernández, F., Oramas-Bustillos, R., Alor-Hernández, G., Reyes-García, C.A.: Building a corpus and a local binary pattern recognizer for learning-centered emotions. In: Advances in Artificial Intelligence and its Applications (2016)
23. Emotiv Systems: Emotiv EPOC. http://emotiv.wikia.com/wiki/Emotiv_EPOC
24. Emotiv Systems: Emotiv Insight. https://www.emotiv.com/insight/
25. Bosch, N., et al.: Automatic detection of learning-centered affective states in the wild. In: ACM (ed.) Proceedings of the 20th International Conference on Intelligent User Interfaces - IUI 2015, pp. 379–388 (2015)

# Courses Select Textbooks: Comparison of Two Methods

Dmitry Stefanovskiy[1], Mikhail Alexandrov[1,2(✉)], Angels Catena[2],
Vera Danilova[1], and Javier Tejada[3]

[1] Russian Presidential Academy of National Economy and Public
Administration, Moscow, Russia
dstefanovskiy@gmail.com, malexandrov@mail.ru,
maolve@gmail.com
[2] Autonomous University of Barcelona, Barcelona, Spain
angels.catena@uab.cat
[3] Catholic University of San Pablo, Arequipa, Peru
jtejadac@ucsp.edu.pe

**Abstract.** Let one need to select appropriate textbooks for a given course or
different parts of a course presented by their limited lists of keywords. When
such a selection is based only on correspondence between the contents of
textbooks and course description then the problem solution reduces to procedures of Information Retrieval. Here, the former can be considered as a database
of documents and the latter as a query. In the paper we show the possibilities of
two IR methods: (1) a spreading activation method (SAM) using semantic
network related to textbooks, and (2) a coverage-based method (CBM) using a
simple formal comparison of vocabularies. Unlike the usual applications of
SAM and CBM we use: the criterion of term specificity for building the
vocabulary of textbooks and the normalized measure of network activation. The
experimental data includes two examples from technical and humantitarian
sciences: the course of "Database Management" in the Catholic University of
San Pablo in Peru, and the course of "Spanish Lexicology" in the Autonomous
University of Barcelona in Spain. The results of the application of both methods
are compared to the manual assessments of experts. The presented research is a
Pilot study.

**Keywords:** Education · Information Retrieval · Spreading activation method
Term specificity

## 1 Introduction

### 1.1 Problem Setting

Our purpose is to assist professors, lecturers, librarians, etc. in the creation/correction of
the course-related bibliography contents. This work can also be potentially used in
digital libraries that collaborate with educational institutions to automatically
create/correct bibliographies related to different courses.

© Springer Nature Switzerland AG 2018
F. Castro et al. (Eds.): MICAI 2017, LNAI 10633, pp. 220–232, 2018.
https://doi.org/10.1007/978-3-030-02840-4_18

Let us have a course description (a lexicon) and a set of textbooks related to this course. These textbooks may cover the contents of the entire course or only certain sections. Therefore, the following questions should be answered: (1) Does a given textbook cover the whole course? (2) If it does not, what section(s) of the course is/are reflected better in a given textbook?

Obviously, textbook selection is a very subjective procedure taking into account not only the correspondence between contents of a given textbook and a given course but also the knowledge of course author, traditions of university, background of the students in a given area, and so on. In this paper we consider the problem of textbook selection only in the framework of relevance of textbook contents to course description. With this restriction the problem setting reduces to Information Retrieval (IR). In this case, the textbooks can be considered as documents to be explored and the keyword lists of courses as queries. Hereinafter by 'course' we mean both course itself and its sections as well.

At the moment IR suggests many methods and technologies, whose applications (realizations) depend on the form and size of a given document set and given queries [2, 9]. In our case the form of queries is fixed. It is a keyword list reflecting the contents of different sections of the course, and is further denoted as 'course vocabulary'. Its size varies from several tens to one-two hundreds words. Textbooks contain grammatically corrected text, whose size varies from tens of thousands to several hundred thousands words.

To present the contents of text we use 2 antipodal forms: a semantic network based on relations between textbook keywords and a simple lineal keyword list. The first form reflects internal relations in the text, which can be effectively used by the well-known spreading activation method (SAM). Its application consists in initial activation of nodes being the terms from the course vocabulary, and following propagation of this activation via the network. The summary activation can be an assessment of relevance of a textbook to a course. The second form allows to evaluate how the textbook vocabulary covers the course vocabulary. The assessment of relevance of textbook to course is defined by the intersection of these vocabularies with normalization on course vocabulary. In the paper this trivial method is named the coverage-based method (CBM).

The crucial point for both methods consists in building keyword lists for textbooks. For this we use the criterion of term specificity, which provides an easy scalable way for term extraction. This criterion takes into account the term frequency in any basic document corpus including the General Lexis of a given language.

In the paper we describe our experiments and give our proposals concerning term selection and text segmentation. The latter allows to calculate the mutual term occurrences and to build the network. We also describe SAM performance and introduce a normalized measure of network activation. This operation allows to make the results better correspond to expert opinions.

We test SAM and CBM on two examples from technical and humanitarian sciences: the course of "Database Management" in the Catholic University of San Pablo in Peru, and the course of "Spanish Lexicology" in the Autonomous University of Barcelona in Spain. The results of the application of both methods are compared to the manual assessments of experts.

The set of examples is limited for the following natural circumstance: each example needs careful manual assessment of correspondence between a textbook and all sections of a course. It is labour intensive and very time consuming. From the other hand we aim to demonstrate the possibilities of both methods on several real cases but not to collect statistics of SAM applications.

## 1.2   Related Work

As we have mentioned above the textbook selection is defined by many factors: program requirements, education and experience of course author, ideological and religious orientation of university, and so on. For this reason practically all publications related to this problem reduce to a set of advices for course authors. A good example is presented in paper [10], which contains recommendations on corresponding course curricula, existing visual materials, taking into account age of students, following Christian values, and so on. From the other hand the textbook selection as a problem of IR is not considered in the literature. The possible explanation is that this problem looks like a partial task of IR and doesn't need special attention. It is almost true but the devil is in the details related to concrete methods of IR.

First of all, we mention here the famous review [5], which surveys the use of SAM on semantic networks for associative IR. The major models of spreading activation are presented and their applications to IR are surveyed. The principal position here consists in the following: one presents a document or document corpus in the form of a network of its significant elements. The latter are nodes of this network. Some information about this document or the document corpus is known in advance. The correspondent nodes are activated and this activation step by step propagates via the network. When the process finishes the summary activation defines the level of relevance of a document or document corpus with respect to initial information introduced to the network.

A mining method based on SAM for egocentric and polycentric queries in multi-dimensional networks is proposed in the well-known paper [13]. The method allows fast search for objects in sufficient proximity of other object(s), where the proximity is defined in terms of multiple relationships between objects. Other potential uses of SAM are applications to collaborative filtering.

The authors of the short paper [12] use SAM for concept identification. They consider two examples related to medicine and social problems. The lists of keywords are built on the basis of the criterion of term specificity and these keywords are used for forming semantic networks for each example. SAM activates all nodes and this activation propagates via the network for several steps. When the contrast between the activated nodes achieves a given threshold we obtain several compact groups of nodes. Each group can be considered as a concept and taken together they form a topic reflected in the document.

The presented paper has the following differences from the examples described in [5, 13]: (1) we build semantic network on keywords reflecting specificity of a document and we use normalized network activation to evaluate the level of relevance. Although we repeat here some procedures from the paper [12], namely: forming semantic network, but unlike this paper we deal with Information Retrieval but not with Text Mining including concept and topic identification.

The criterion of term specificity was described and studied in detail in [8]. This criterion was successfully used in realization of the European project Riche concerning child healthcare [3] and the joint Spanish-Russian project on Internet sociology [1].

The rest of the paper is organized as follows. Section 2 presents lexical resources used in the experiments. Section 3 describes the SAM application. Section 4 explains the contents of CBM. Section 5 presents the results of experiments. Section 6 concludes the paper.

# 2 Lexical Resources

## 2.1 Experimental Data

For the purposes of the experiments, we use materials in Spanish related to two courses: (1) the course "Data Bases" being part of the curriculum of the Computer Sciences School at the Catholic University of San Pablo in Peru. It is composed of 4 sections, therefore, we have 5 lexicons: 1 per each section of the course and 1 for the entire course; (2) the course "Lexicology of Spanish language" being part of the educational program of the Philological Faculty at the Autonomous University of Barcelona in Spain. It is composed of 6 sections, therefore, we have 7 lexicons: 1 per each section of the course and 1 for the entire course.

For the course "Data Bases" the course author recommended the following two textbooks for the experiments: the well-known "Fundamentos de bases de datos" [11] and the special book related to Text Mining "Procesamiento automático del español con enfoque en recursos léxicos grandes" [6]. So, here we study the correspondence of 2 textbooks to 5 lexicons. For the course "Lexicology of Spanish language" the course author also recommended two textbooks for the experiments: "Curso de lexicología" [7] and "Apuntes de morfología y sintaxis del español" [4]. So, in this case we study the correspondence of 2 textbooks to 7 lexicons. The size of the mentioned textbooks are presented in the Table 1.

It should be said that the mentioned examples of textbooks are not perfect, but we aim to demonstrate the performance of the proposed methods on real examples – not to select the ideal textbooks. For this reason our examples reflect several typical situations, when a textbook covers well the entire course except one section, or covers well only one section from the course, or covers all sections but not very well.

**Table 1.** The textbooks and their size [words]

| No | Book names for the course "Data Base" | Size | Book names for the course "Lexicology…" | Size |
|----|----------------------------------------|--------|------------------------------------------|--------|
| 1 | Fundamentos de bases de datos | 162300 | Curso de lexicología | 83800 |
| 2 | Procesamiento automatico … | 67700 | Apuntes de morfología y sintaxis… | 17500 |

## 2.2   Keyword Lists of Textbooks

Both SAM and CBM use the same lexical model to describe the contents of a given textbook. It is a vocabulary of one-word topic-specific terms. For automatic term selection we use the utility LexisTerm [8].

LexisTerm selects terms according to the criterion of term specificity. 'Term specificity' with respect to a given corpus means a factor $K \geq 1$ that shows how much the word frequency in any given corpus (or a given document) $f_C(w)$ exceeds its frequency in any standard corpus $f_L(w)$: $K = f_C(w)/f_L(w)$. In the paper, we use the General Lexis of the Spanish language that reflects word frequencies in the Spanish National Corpus [http://www.iula.upf.edu/rec/corpus92/frecuencias.htm]. As we deal with stemmed words then we preliminary transformed the mentioned General Lexis to the stemmed form with corresponding correction of frequencies.

We compared the contents of lists that were built by the program for $K = \{2; 5; 10; 20; 50; 100\}$. This series of values reflects the logarithmic regularity between $K$ and the size of keyword list [8]. We found that: when $K \leq 20$ the lists include many insignificant terms, when $K \geq 50$ we lose many useful terms. So, we tested $K = \{25; 30; 35; 40; 45\}$ to find a compromise. It proved to be equal to $K = 40$ for all textbooks under consideration.

Table 2 shows the initial part of topic lexicons (ordered alphabetically) for the textbooks related to the course "Data Bases". Table 3 shows the initial part of topic lexicons (ordered alphabetically) for the textbooks related to the course "Lexicology...". We call "topic lexicons" those lexicons that are built on the basis of the criterion of specificity. The reason is that these words have a non-ordinary (increased) frequency that probably means their relevance to a specific topic.

**Table 2.**  Stemmed lexicons of textbooks for the course "Data Bases"

| No | Book names | Terms | Lexicon (first terms) |
|----|-----------|-------|-----------------------|
| 1 | Fundamentos de bases de datos | 55 | aislamient almacen alocacion aplic arbol archiv basic bibliograf ... |
| 2 | Procesamiento automatico ... | 84 | academic agrup algoritm alomorf altern ambigu anafor antonym ... |

**Table 3.**  Stemmed lexicons of textbooks for the course "Lexicología..."

| No | Book names | Terms | Lexicon (first terms) |
|----|-----------|-------|-----------------------|
| 1 | Curso de lexicología | 54 | acento afij amerindi casticismo consonante corpus cualitativ ... |
| 2 | Apuntes de morfología y sintaxis ... | 96 | adjetiv adverbio afij agrupa antonim auxiliar clasifica ... |

# 3 SAM Application

## 3.1 Preprocessing

At the preprocessing stage, we build a term-document matrix $TD$ for each textbook under consideration. To do so we complete the following steps:

1. Stemming a given textbook using Snowball Spanish stemming algorithm: [http:// snowball.tartarus.org/algorithms/spanish/stemmer.html];
2. Selection of specific terms (keywords) on the basis of criterion of word specificity. This procedure is described above;
3. Creation of document corpus by means of text fragmentation. Here, the text is split into fragments using the running window in order to reveal joint term occurrences. Each fragment is considered as a document;
4. Calculation of term occurrences in the documents and formation of matrix term-document.

To build a network of selected keywords one should determine the pairwise relations between them. The key-position here is text fragmentation, which allows to reveal the joint term occurrences in each fragment and calculate the correlation. To determine the optimal width of the running window we took into account the average density of keywords in textbooks. Namely, the window should include approximately 1 keyword from the list of keywords. It proved to be 6–7 sentences. Naturally, this is a very approximate assessment. To check the mentioned value we tested windows of length of 3, 5 and 7 sentences. With window of length 3, we lost many useful links, while with window of length 7, there were redundant links between terms in the network. Windows of length 5 has been taken as a compromise.

We prefer to use sentence as a unit for the length of step and for the width of window instead of word because sentence is the minimum semantic unit of a text. We can do so as we deal with grammatically corrected text but not with blogs and posts in social networks, where punctuation marks are often absent.

Having calculated the matrix $TD$ we multiply $TT = TD \times TD^T$. The resulting $TT$ matrix encodes the term co-occurrence in the corpus. Obviously, the elements of $TT$ matrix are the coefficients of co-variation with respect to the vectors reflecting the term distribution between documents. After normalization on vector lengths these elements become the coefficients of correlation. Their values change in the range [0, 1], where 0 refers to term pairs that do not occur together in the documents and 1 - to term pairs that always occur together in the documents.

$TT$ matrix can be considered an adjacency matrix that represents a graph with edges of variable length. To improve the SAM performance one needs to set a threshold $T \subset (0, 1)$ and remove all weak links from $TT$ matrix. A well-known approach here is based on the hypothesis about the relatively small number of significant links between terms in the same collection. To use this hypothesis it is necessary to build the dependence of the number of links on the thresholds and to set the transition point on the corresponding diagram. In our experiments, we considered several $T$ values ($T = 0.2, 0.5, 0.8$) with respect to the maximum value in $TT$ matrix. The results prove to be almost equal for $T = 0.2$ and $T = 0.5$ after network activation, which makes us select $T = 0.5$ with a smaller number of links.

## 3.2   Activation Algorithm

In the paper we use a simplified version of SAM having in view an undirected graph, no firing threshold, no decay factor. Only one or two iterations are performed. In the first iteration, the activation is propagated from the initially activated nodes to other nodes. In the second iteration, the activation is propagated from all the nodes activated in the first iteration to all other nodes. Usually in case of more than two iterations, all nodes get activated. This proved to be useful in social-semantic analysis, because it allows to consider the graph activation as a measure of news spread through social media. When analyzing individual documents, we need to extract groups of strongly connected terms. These groups constitute cliques or almost cliques. Such groups are distinguishable just after the first two iterations.

In order to measure the coverage of the course by textbooks, we activate only the terms of the course/course section lexicon. Naturally, these terms are the common for a given textbook and a given course/course section lexicon.

Network activation is commonly defined as the sum of activations of all its nodes. However, it turns out that this measure is not appropriate for revealing the connections between the course/course section lexicon and textbook. Namely, the results differed significantly from the expert opinion. Therefore, we have introduced a normalized measure of network activation: sum of activations divided by the activated nodes.

A node is considered activated, if its activation exceeds 1% of the maximal possible activation. As the maximal activation is equal 1.0 then this value is equal to 0.01. The level 1% is taken having in view the accepted level of precision. In reality, the summary activation changes insignificantly up to the level of 3% that is considered as a transition point.

Tables 3 and 4 give brief descriptions of the contents of each section of the mentioned courses and present the first terms from their lexicons. All terms are stemmed.

**Table 4.**  A partial description of the course "Data Bases"

| No | Section name | Terms | Lexicon (first terms) |
|----|--------------|-------|-----------------------|
| 1 | Physical development of data base | 40 | almacen arbol archiv benefici busqued clusteriz coloc … |
| 2 | Processing transactions | 22 | aislamient compromis concept concurrent control escog fall … |
| 3 | Storing and recovering information | 77 | almacen altern analisis arbol archive basic bibliograf bibliometri … |
| 4 | Distributed data base | 34 | acces almacen alocacion bas cantid cliente-servidor commit … |

**Table 5.** A partial description of the course "Lexicology..."

| No | Section name | Terms | Lexicon (first terms) |
|---|---|---|---|
| 1 | Lexicon and its study | 10 | combinatori form fraseolog lexem lexic locucion mental occuren... |
| 2 | Words with internal and external structure | 27 | actant adjet adverbial afij alomorf colocacion composicion ... |
| 3 | Meaning of words and relations among words | 18 | antonimi archisemem componencial hiperonim hiponim homonimi... |
| 4 | Change of lexicon: neology and lexical losses | 22 | acronimi arab arcaism calc cultism desmotivacion doblet etimologi... |
| 5 | Lexical variation: technical and special lexicon | 17 | cientif diafas dialect diames diastrat especial extraccion geograf... |
| 6 | Dictionaries: types, macro- y microstructure | 20 | acepcion actant analit aristotel bilingu definicion diccionari... |

## 4  CBM Application

As already mentioned in the Introduction CBM is a simple way to detect the relation between a pair of documents only by the comparison of their lexicons. In our case one document is a textbook and the other document is the course/course section lexicon. At the initial stage we build lexicon of a given textbook. The corresponding procedure is described above in p. 2. Besides we transform the course/course section lexicon to its stemmed form.

At the next stage, we measure the coverage of the course lexicon by the textbooks' lexicons. Let us have two topic lexicons with $n_1$ and $n_2$ terms respectively. Let $m$ be the amount of terms that these lexicons have in common. Then $m/n_1$ is the coverage of the lexicon-1 by the lexicon-2 and $m/n_2$ is the coverage of the lexicon-2 by the lexicon-1. In our case, lexicon-1 is represented by the lexicon of the course or its sections, and lexicon-2 is represented by the textbook lexicons.

Table 6 shows the intersection of the lexicons of the course "Data bases" and its textbooks. The 2-nd column contains the number of terms per each course section and in the whole program. The section lexicons have intersections, so the course lexicon is smaller than the sum of the section lexicons. The 3-rd column contains the number of terms shared by the textbook "Fundamentos de bases de datos" (DB, database) and the corresponding course section/entire course. The 4-th column contains similar values that refer to the textbook "Procesamiento automático del español con enfoque en recursos léxicos grandes" (TP, text processing). This data is used to calculate the coverage as follows: the number of terms shared by the course (course section) and a textbook is divided by the size of the course (course section) lexicon. These results are presented in the next section of the paper.

Table 7 shows the intersection of the lexicons of the course "Lexicology..." and its textbooks. The contents of columns are similar to those of the Table 6. Here the 3-rd column refers to the textbook "Curso de lexicología" (CL, course on lexicology) and 4-th columns refers to the textbook "Apuntes de morfología y sintaxis del español" (MS, morphology and syntax).

**Table 6.** The amount of terms shared by the course "Data Bases" and textbooks. DB denotes "Fundamentos de bases de datos". TP denotes "Procesamiento automático del español con enfoque en recursos léxicos grandes"

| Section | Terms | DB | TP |
|---------|-------|----|----|
| 1 | 40 | 17 | 2 |
| 2 | 22 | 6 | 2 |
| 3 | 77 | 26 | 11 |
| 4 | 34 | 14 | 2 |
| All | 142 | 48 | 13 |

**Table 7.** The amount of terms shared by the course "Lexicology..." and textbooks. CL denotes "Curso de lexicología". MS denotes "Apuntes de morfología y sintaxis del español"

| Section | Terms | CL | MS |
|---------|-------|----|----|
| 1 | 10 | 2 | 3 |
| 2 | 27 | 5 | 10 |
| 3 | 18 | 0 | 4 |
| 4 | 22 | 0 | 4 |
| 5 | 17 | 2 | 2 |
| 6 | 20 | 1 | 3 |
| All | 102 | 10 | 21 |

# 5 Experiments

## 5.1 Experiments with the Course "Data Bases"

**Experiment 1, Application of SAM.** Experiment 1 includes 10 mini-experiments: 5 for the textbook DB and 5 for the textbook TP. Each of them uses (a) 1 network constructed for the textbook, and, (b) 1 lexicon from 5 course/course section lexicons. Let us consider the DB network and the 1-st section lexicon. The network contains 55 terms, the lexicon includes 40 terms, but only 17 of them are shared by the network and lexicon. The values are shown in Tables 2, 4 and 6. Next, SAM activates the network and we obtain the resulting normalized activation of 1.77, see column 2 in Table 8. The other 9 mini experiments are done in the same way.

We present some examples of the activated networks. Figure 1 shows the activated network for the textbook "Procesamiento automático ...". This network results from the activation of terms from the course Sect. 1. Figure 2 shows a fragment of the activated network for the same textbook.

**Experiment 2, Application of CBM.** Experiment 2 also consists of 10 mini-experiments: 5 for the textbook DB and 5 for the textbook TP. Each of them uses (a) a lexicon related to the textbook, and (b) 1 lexicon from 5 course/course section lexicons. The necessary data are shown in Table 5. The value indicating the CBM performance is the number of shared terms (columns 3 & 4) divided by the course/course section lexicon (column 2). The results are presented in the mentioned Table 7, see column 3.

Expert Opinion. Expert Opinion reflects the opinion of the lecturer and uses the scale [−2, −1, 0, 1, 2], where: −2 means that the textbook has no any relation to the course, −1 means that the textbook includes some useful elements for the course, 0 means that the textbook reflects satisfactorily the contents of course, 1 means that the coverage of the course is good, and finally 2 means that the coverage of the course is very good. Speaking 'course' we mean both the course itself and its section. The evaluation takes into account the following 4 positions:

- mathematical (formal) models,
- representative examples,
- completeness of descriptions,
- text readability.

The result is presented in the column 4 of Table 8. The general conclusion based on EO is the following: (1) both SAM and CBM correctly show the better textbook for the whole course and CBM does it more contrastively; (2) both SAM and CBM correctly reflect the coverage of course sections in total but SAM gives slightly better result taking into account the assessments for Sects. 2 and 3.

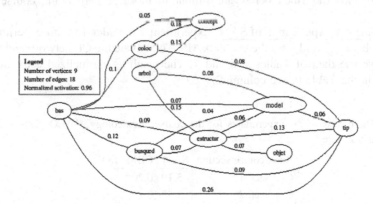

**Fig. 1.** The activated network for the textbook "Procesamiento automático…" with the lexicon of the course Sect. 1 (normalized activation = 0.96)

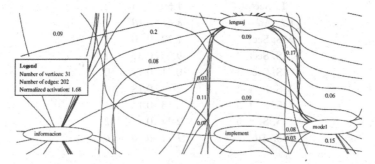

**Fig. 2.** Central part of the activated network for the textbook "Procesamiento automático …" with the lexicon of the course Sect. 3 (normalized activation = 1.68)

**Table 8.** The results of the experiments for the course "Data Mining". EO denotes the expert opinion

| Book/course-section | SAM | CBM | EO |
|---|---|---|---|
| DB, Sect. 1 | 1.77 | 0.43 | 2 |
| DB, Sect. 2 | 1.33 | 0.27 | 1 |
| DB, Sect. 3 | 1.17 | 0.34 | −1 |
| DB, Sect. 4 | 1.58 | 0.41 | 1 |
| *DB, All* | *3.51* | *0.34* | *1* |
| TP, Sect. 1 | 0.96 | 0.05 | −2 |
| TP, Sect. 2 | 0.80 | 0.09 | −2 |
| TP, Sect. 3 | 1.68 | 0.14 | 2 |
| TP, Sect. 4 | 0.97 | 0.06 | −1 |
| *TP, All* | *2.62* | *0.09* | *−1* |

## 5.2  Experiments with the Course "Lexicology…."

The experiments described below are similar to those related to the course "Data Bases".

Experiment 1, Application of SAM. Experiment 1 includes 14 mini-experiments: 7 for the textbook CL and 7 for the textbook MS. To activate the CL network and the MS network we use data of Tables 3, 5 and 7. The resulting normalized activations are presented in the Table 9, see column 2.

**Table 9.** The results of the experiments for the course "Lexicology…". EO denotes the gold standard performance

| Book/course-section | SAM | CBM | EO |
|---|---|---|---|
| CL, Sect. 1 | 3.19 | 0.20 | 1 |
| CL, Sect. 2 | 1.43 | 0.19 | −1 |
| CL, Sect. 3 | 0.00 | 0.00 | −1 |
| CL, Sect. 4 | 0.00 | 0.00 | −1 |
| CL, Sect. 5 | 0.12 | 0.12 | −1 |
| CL, Sect. 6 | 1.60 | 0.05 | −2 |
| *CL, All* | *8.61* | *0.10* | *−1* |
| MS, Sect. 1 | 7.12 | 0.30 | −1 |
| MS, Sect. 2 | 9.58 | 0.37 | 1 |
| MS, Sect. 3 | 0.41 | 0.17 | 0 |
| MS, Sect. 4 | 2.71 | 0.18 | 0 |
| MS, Sect. 5 | 0.13 | 0.12 | −1 |
| MS, Sect. 6 | 2.44 | 0.15 | −2 |
| *MS, All* | *21.12* | *0.20* | *0* |

Experiment 2, Application of CBM. Experiment 2 also consists of 14 mini-experiments: 7 for the textbook CL and 7 for the textbook MS. The results are presented in the mentioned Table 9, see column 3.

Expert Opinion. The lecturer uses here the same scales that were described above. The result is presented in the column 4 of Table 9. The general conclusion based on EO is the following: (1) both SAM and CBM correctly show the better textbook for the whole course but the difference of assessments is too high; (2) both SAM and CBM correctly reflect the coverage of course sections in total but some assessments should be more contrastive; (3) SAM gives slightly better result taking into account the coverage of Sects. 1 and 2.

## 6  Conclusion

Results. In this paper, we consider the problem of textbook selection for a given course or course section as a problem within Information Retrieval. Here, the database is comprised of a series of textbooks and a query by lexicon that describes the mentioned course or course section. To solve the problem, we compare two methods: (1) a spreading activation method (SAM) that measures textbook relevance using the activation of networks related to textbook contents, and (2) a method for textbook relevance measuring by using the coverage of the course lexicon by the textbook lexicon. This second method is named as the coverage-based method (CBM). The proposed applications employ a keyword list constructed using the criterion of term specificity and a normalized measure of network activation. Both methods have been tested against expert (the course author) opinion. The results show the following:

- both methods correctly select the textbook that better reflects the whole course and the sections having the best coverage by each textbook,
- SAM ensures better agreement with the expert opinion than CBM, but this difference is not very significant,
- some assessments result being too different and the others - too similar.

As the future work, we plan to develop this research in the following directions:

- further modifying SAM to obtain more understandable results,
- conducting experiments on other educational courses and textbooks.

**Acknowledgement.** Authors thank the reviewers from the MICAI-2017 Program Committee for their attention to this research and their valuable recommendations.

# References

1. Alexandrov, M., Danilova, V., Blanco, X.: A modified tripartite model for document representation in internet sociology. In: Chen, Q., Hameurlain, A., Toumani, F., Wagner, R., Decker, H. (eds.) DEXA 2015. LNCS, vol. 9262, pp. 323–330. Springer, Cham (2015). https://doi.org/10.1007/978-3-319-22852-5_27
2. Baeza-Yates, R., Ribero-Neto, B.: Modern Information Retrieval. Addison Wesley, Boston (1999)
3. Bourek, A., Alexandrov, M, Lopez, R.: Folksonomy - supplementing Riche expert based taxonomy by terms from online documents. In: Business and Engineering Applications of Intelligence and Information Systems, vol. 23, pp. 115–123. ITHEA Publication, Sofia-Rzeszov (2011)
4. Chantaca, C.: Apuntes de morfología y sintaxis del español. UNAM, Mexico (2008)
5. Crestani, F.: Application of spreading activation techniques in information retrieval. Artif. Intell. Rev. **11**(6), 453–482 (1995)
6. Gelbukh, A., Sidorov, G.: Procesamiento Automático del Español con Enfoque en Recursos Léxicos Grandes. Instituto Politécnico Nacional, Mexico (2006)
7. Lara, L.F.: Curso de lexicología, Colegio de Mexico (2006)
8. Lopez, R., Alexandrov, M., Barreda, D., Tejada J.: Lexisterm - the program for term selection by the criterion of specificity. In: Artificial Intelligence Applications to Business and Engineering Domain, vol. 24, pp. 8–15. ITHEA Publication, Sofia-Rzeszov (2011)
9. Manning, C., Raghavan, P., Schutze, H.: Introduction to Information Retrieval. Cambridge University Press, Cambridge (2008)
10. Olinger, D.: Selecting Textbooks and Other Curriculum Support Materials for Christian Schools, 7 p. Bju Press, Greenville (2005). http://www.bjupress.com/pdfs/ed-issues-whitepapers/selecting-textbooks.pdf
11. Silberschatz, A.: Fundamentos de Bases de Datos, 5th edn. Interamericana de España, McGrow Hill (2006)
12. Stefanovskiy, D., Alexandrov, M., Bourek, A., Hala, T.: Concept identification in document with network activation method. In: Transaction on Business and Engineering Intelligent Applications, vol. 29, pp. 93–97. ITHEA Publication, Sofia-Rzeszov (2014)
13. Troussov, A., Sogrin, A., Judge, J., Botvich, D.: Mining socio-semantic networks using spreading activation technique. In: Proceedings of I-KNOW-2008 and I-MEDIA, Graz, Austria, pp. 405–412 (2008)

# Image Processing and Pattern Recognition

# Behavior of the CIE L*a*b* Color Space in the Detection of Saturation Variations During Color Image Segmentation

Rodolfo Alvarado-Cervantes[1,2,3], Edgardo M. Felipe-Riveron[1(✉)],
Vladislav Khartchenko[2], Oleksiy Pogrebnyak[1],
and Rodolfo Alvarado-Martínez[3]

[1] Centro de Investigación En Computación, Instituto Politécnico Nacional,
Juan de Dios Batiz s/n, Col. Nueva Industrial Vallejo,
P.O. 07738, Mexico City, Mexico
rodolfo.alvarado.cervantes@gmail.com,
{edgardo,olek}@cic.ipn.mx
[2] Centro de Investigaciones Teóricas, Facultad de Estudios Superiores
Cuautitlán, Universidad Nacional Autónoma de México, Primero de Mayo S/N
Campo 1, Cuautitlán Izcalli, Mexico
vlad@unam.mx
[3] Departamento de Investigación En Electrónica de Control E Inteligencia
Artificial, Industrias Electrónicas Ateramex, S.a. de C.V, Papagayo #5 Col. Lago
de Guadalupe, 54760 Cuautitlán Izcalli, Mexico
ateramex@gmail.com

**Abstract.** In this paper, a study of the behavior of the CIE L*a*b* color space to detect subtle changes of saturation during image segmentation is presented. It was performed a comparative study of some basic segmentation techniques implemented in the L*a*b*, RGB color space and in a modified HSI color space using a recently published adaptive color similarity function. In the CIE L*a*b* color space we have studied the behavior of: (1) the Euclidean metric of a* and b* color components rejecting L* and (2) a probabilistic approach on a* and b*. From the results it was obtained that the CIE L*a*b* color space is not adequate to distinguish subtle changes of color saturation under illumination variations. In some high saturated color regions the CIE L*a*b* is not useful to distinguish saturation variations at all. It can be observed that the CIE L*a*b* has better performance than the RGB color space in low saturated regions but it has worse performance in most high saturated color regions; all high saturation regions are very sensitive to changes in illumination and a minimum change causes failures during segmentation. The improvement in quality of the recently published color segmentation technique to distinguish subtle saturation variations is substantially significant.

**Keywords:** CIELAB L*a*b* color space · Color metrics
Color categorization · Color image segmentation
Color segmentation evaluation · Synthetic color image generation

© Springer Nature Switzerland AG 2018
F. Castro et al. (Eds.): MICAI 2017, LNAI 10633, pp. 235–247, 2018.
https://doi.org/10.1007/978-3-030-02840-4_19

# 1  Introduction

Image segmentation consists of partitioning an entire image into different regions, which are similar in some predefined manner [1–3, 24]. Segmentation is an important feature of human visual perception which manifests itself, spontaneously and naturally. It is an important and difficult task in image analysis and processing. All subsequent steps, such as object recognition depend on the quality of segmentation [1–4, 24].

Color is an effective and robust visual feature to differentiate objects in an image. It is an important source of information in the segmentation process and may in many cases be used as a unique feature to segment objects of interest [1–3, 24].

Images with subtle changes of saturation are common in nature: The fading edges of clouds in the blue sky, changes of water vapor or mist on colored backgrounds; on aerial or satellite photographs of the seas, oceans, forests, deserts, etc. The colors of objects change its saturation due to the presence of some form of water steam in the middle.

Proper selection of the color space for color image processing is a very important aspect to be taken into account [2, 6, 8–10]. Several recent works [8, 16–18, 20, 21] use CIE L*a*b* or L*u*v* color spaces, which have some supposed advantages, such as the separation of lightness information (L*), as well as handling the chromatic color similarity as the Euclidean distance between the independent channels a*b* (or u*v*). These representations have the disadvantage that when managing the information of saturation and hue jointly in a*b* (or u*v*) channels, it is difficult to predict whether the similarity is due to some/one of these variables.

A comparative study [16] of several perceptually uniform color spaces (specifically: L*a*b*, L*u *v* and RLab) is presented in order to establish which color space is better for the segmentation of natural images. Only color information was used for comparative testing and excluded others. They conclude that with the color space L*u*v* the best results was obtained in both average discrimination capabilities and speed of processing.

In this paper we present a study of the behavior of the CIE L*a*b* color space to detect saturation variations during color image segmentation. For comparison purposes, we present the results using the Euclidean metric of the RGB channels and a recently published method [1, 5] using an improved color HSI space that keeps concordance with human color perception whilst eliminating known discontinuities of the classic HSI color space, and an adaptive color similarity function defined in that color space.

To carry out our study, synthetic color images with their associated ground truth were generated. The synthetic images were designed to evaluate the efficiency of achieved color information from given segmentation algorithms [11–15]. By the use and analysis of *receiver operating characteristic* (ROC) graphs [23] we obtained some proper characteristics of the segmentation methods under study.

The rest of the paper is organized as follows: In Sect. 2, we present the design methodology to generate synthetic images and benchmark. In Sect. 3, the results obtained with low and high saturated color images and their discussion are presented. Finally, in Sect. 4 the conclusions are given.

## 2  Design and Generation of Synthetic Images for Benchmark Testing

In this work we used the concepts and design considerations presented in Zhang and Gerbrands [14] and in [11–13, 15]. We created synthetic images with figure and background in color and selected a flower shaped image as the basic object to create our base test image (Fig. 1). For the CIE L*a*b* comparative tests were performed in a set of low and high saturated images with two different classification methods implemented in the L*a*b* color space [7, 20, 22]: (1) Using the minimum Euclidean distance of the *a and *b channels rejecting L* (as implemented by Matlab [7]), and (2) Using a probabilistic approach on the a* and b* channels [19, 20]. The L* value is excluded from the calculations with the intention of making them immune to changes in lighting. If L* would be used in the calculations of the distances, then additional errors would appear due to the shadows since shadows represent changes in luminance not in color.

The manner in which the tests were implemented is as follows: in the case of the minimum Euclidean distance of the a* and b* channels in the L*a*b* color space, the RGB image and the pixel samples (of figure and background) were previously transformed to the L*a* b* color space, discarding in all cases the lightness L* in order to calculate the Euclidean distance on the a* b* channels (color information) independently of the illumination.

Then, the centroids (average of the values a* and b* of the pixel samples) representing the colors of the figure and the background in the color space L*a*b* were calculated for each sample. The Euclidean distance from the centroid of each class to every pixel of the image is calculated to classify the pixels as figure or background according to the minimum distance. Details about this procedure can be consulted in [7]. Using the probabilistic approach, we also transformed the image and pixels samples (of figure and background) to the L*a*b* color space discarding in all cases the lightness L*. Then, the mean and standard deviation of the values a* and b* from the pixel samples are calculated. From this information, we approximated normal probability density function (PDF) of every pixel belongs to the object or background classes using Gaussians for every channel a* and b*. From this probability we calculated the likelihood [19]:

$$P^i_{1/2}(x) = \frac{p^i_1(F_i)}{p^i_1(F_i) + p^i_2(F_i)} \tag{1}$$

where $P^i_{1/2}(x)$ is the likelihood [19] function of the pixel $x$ belongs to the region 1 (figure region) with respect to the probabilities of $p^i_1$ (figure) and $p^i_2$ (background) for a given channel $F_i$, which can be a* or b* in this case. Similarly we calculate $P^i_{2/1}(x)$. To integrate the likelihood information of the two channels a* and b*, we multiplied the likelihood function of each channel:

$$P_{1/2}(x) = P^1_{1/2}(x) * P^2_{1/2}(x) \tag{2}$$

Similarly we calculated $P_{2/1}(x)$. Classification comes after obtaining the maximum between them and assign accordingly.

Segmentation tests were performed using the minimum Euclidean distance in RGB color space as reference. For comparison purposes, the segmentation results are shown in Figs. 6 and 10 as every third row of each color and in graphs shown in Figs. 8 (left) and 10 (left).

In the recently published method [1, 5] the following steps were performed:

1. Samples of both background and figure were taken, from which centroid and standard color dispersion was calculated.
2. The 24-bit RGB image (true color) was transformed to the modified HSI color space [1, 5].
3. For each pixel, the adaptive color similarity function [1, 5] to the centroids of figure and background was calculated creating two color similarity images (CSI).
4. Each pixel of the RGB image was classified by calculating the maximum value for each pixel position between the CSI images of the figure and that of the background.

This segmentation method can also be used directly in grayscale images without making any changes, achieving good results [1, 5]. On the contrary, the other tested methods that use the L*a*b* color space need to include the lightness L* to perform the segmentation of this type of images, since a* and b* values remain unchanged in the center of a*b* plane and would be blind to such images. To decide when the lightness L* must be considered in calculating the color distance is an additional task of the methods implemented in that space, contrary, the method presented in [1, 5] does it automatically when calculating the color similarity function using intensity distance as input.

The base shape of the synthetic test image was created with the following features:

• Concave and convex sections to make better the representation of real images, such as natural flowers.
• Extreme omnidirectional curvature in the entire image to hinder obtaining the edges applying mask edge detectors.
• The object was centered in the image.

The resulting flower-shaped object in the image is considered as the object of interest and the ground truth (GT) in all subsequent tests (Fig. 1).

**Fig. 1.** Flower-shaped ground truth

In addition to this object of interest, some features were imposed in order to hinder its color-based segmentation:

- Low saturation contrast. The contrast between the object and the background in all images was only due to saturation and very low for an observer, including some in which at a glance one cannot see the difference (e.g. Flower_5 in Fig. 3). The saturation contrast in low saturated test images was 0.05 and in the high saturated test images was 0.1.

The difference between the color characteristics of the object of interest and the background is called Delta by us and occurs in this study in saturation for each color of study. The tests were performed in color quadrants 0, 60, 120, 180, 240 and 300° and in low and high saturated images in two groups corresponding to the images flower_A, flower_B ... flower_F (Fig. 2) for low saturated images (with saturation = 0.1 and intensity = 1) and flower_Ah, flower_Bh ... flower_Fh (Fig. 3) for high saturated images (with saturation = 0.9 and intensity = 0.9).

- Blurred edges with an average filter. A sliding mean filter of size 3 × 3 pixels was applied to the whole image to blur the corners and to make detection of the object more difficult; such blurring was done to each of the RGB channels before the introduction of Gaussian noise.
- Introduction of Gaussian noise with SNR value = 5. The noise was applied to each of the RGB channels individually, and later we assembled the channels to create the noisy RGB color image.

Samples of pixels corresponding to the figure object were obtained by two squares of 2 × 2 starting at the pixel (84, 84) and (150, 150). Samples for background pixels were obtained by two squares of 2 × 2 starting at pixel (15, 15) and (150, 180).

The images were generated in the sectors 0, 60, 120, 180, 240 and 300° in low and high saturation regions, to which we later applied a faded shadow.

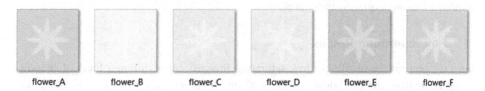

flower_A          flower_B          flower_C          flower_D          flower_E          flower_F

**Fig. 2.** Testing images with low saturation with delta in saturation

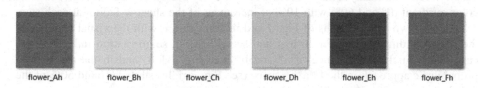

flower_Ah          flower_Bh          flower_Ch          flower_Dh          flower_Eh          flower_Fh

**Fig. 3.** Testing images with high saturation with delta in saturation

A shadow fading was applied to all noisy blurred images with the light center in the fixed coordinates (150, 150) in images of 256 × 256 pixels. It was applied gradually with 10% increments at each step. Figure 4 shows in detail for Flower 0 in low saturation. Figure 5 shows for Flower_0h in high saturation.

**Fig. 4.** Example in color quadrants with a faded shadow applied at 0° with low saturation

**Fig. 5.** Example in color quadrants with a faded shadow applied at 0° with high saturation

## 3   Results and Discussion

In this section we show graphically the results, both in the low saturated regions (see Fig. 6) and in the high saturated regions (see Fig. 10) for two color quadrant (0° and 60°) incrementing the level of shadow fading, in 10% at each step. The first position means no shadow and position 11 means 100% shadow fading.

We also show a variation of *receiver operating characteristic* (ROC) graphs [23] to visualize the values of hit rates (True Positives or TP rate) versus error rates (False Positives or FP rate) at the increasing of the shadow fading (Figs. 7, 8, 9 and 11, 12, 13). We show the numerical results for all color quadrants (0°, 60°, 120°, 180°, 240° and 300°). For this purpose all the images had the same post-processing: elimination of areas smaller than 30 pixels and a morphological closing with a circular structuring element of radius equal to two pixels.

### 3.1   Low Saturation Results

Here, we present the results for low saturation images with a different level of shadow fading comparing the Euclidean metric of a* and b* (every first row of each color), the probabilistic approach in a* and b* (every second row of each color), the Euclidean metric of the RGB channels (third row of every color) and the method using the adaptive color similarity function (fourth row of every color) included in Fig. 6 for two color quadrant (0° and 60°) with 10% of increment of the shadow fading at each step.

As is shown in the graphs of Fig. 7 and in coincidence with the visual analysis of the corresponding flower (Fig. 6 first and second rows), segmentation failures in the case of the Euclidean distance of a* and b* (see Fig. 7 left) and in the case of the probabilistic approach in the L*a*b* space (see Fig. 7 right) started around 50% of the faded shadow and continued increasing to levels of 80%–90% of false positives (errors rate) in all color quadrants (0°, 60°, 120°, 180°, 240° and 300°).

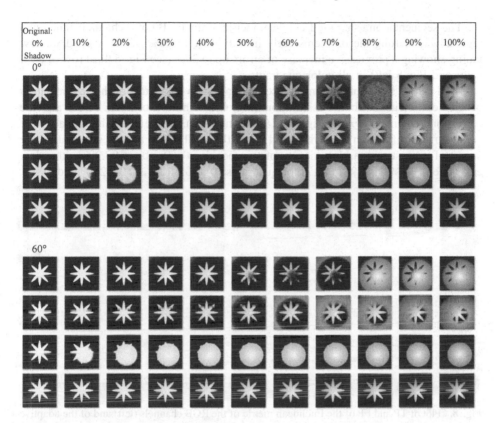

**Fig. 6.** Results of the color segmentation of low saturation images by the Euclidean metric of a* and b* parameters in the L*a*b* color space (first rows of each color), the probabilistic approach in a* and b* color channels (second rows of each color), the Euclidean metric of the RGB channels (third row of each color) and the method using the adaptive color similarity function (fourth row of each color), for two color quadrant (0° and 60°) with 10% increments of shadow fading at each step.

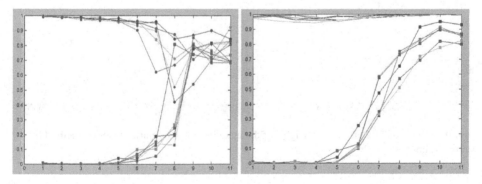

**Fig. 7.** Plot of true positives (TP) and false positives (FP) of the Euclidean distance of a* and b* (left) and the probabilistic approach on a* and b* (right) tested for low saturated images

The segmentation using the Euclidean metric of the RGB color channels failed in a regular way starting the problems early in only 10% to 20% of the applied shadow fading showing a progressive increase of errors up to 30% (see Fig. 6 third row of each color and Fig. 8 left) in all color quadrants.

As it can be seen from the images corresponding to the results of the segmentation of the test images with low saturation (Fig. 6 fourth row of each color) and the corresponding graphs (Figs. 8 right and 9 left and right), the method using the adaptive color similarity function [1, 5] behaved correctly in all cases, always segmenting the object of interest with a high hit rate of true positives (TP) above 99.2% with a low error rate of less than 1% in all color quadrants (0°, 60°, 120°, 180°, 240° and 300°).

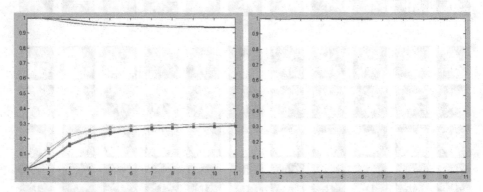

**Fig. 8.** Plot of TP and FP of the Euclidean metric of the RGB channels (left) and of the adaptive color similarity function method (right) tested for low saturated images

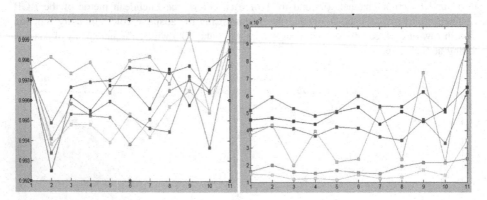

**Fig. 9.** Details of TP (left) and FP (right) of the adaptive color similarity function method in low saturated images

## 3.2  High Saturation Results

Here, we present the results for high saturated images with a different level of shadow fading comparing the Euclidean metric of a* and b* (every first row of each color), the probabilistic approach in a* and b* (every second row of each color), the Euclidean metric of the RGB channels (third row of every color) and the similarity function method (fourth row of every color). The results are shown in Fig. 10 for two color quadrant (0° and 60°) with 10% of increment of the shadow fading at each step.

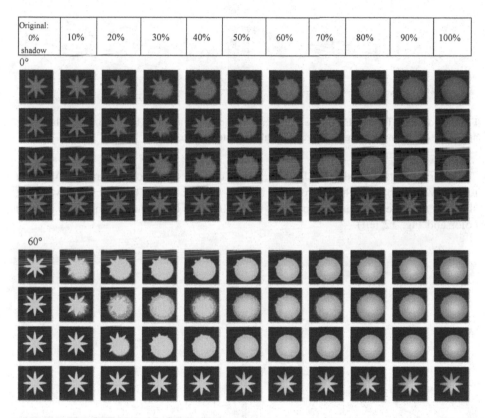

**Fig. 10.** Results of the color segmentation achieved between the Euclidean metric of the a* and b* parameters in the L*a*b* color space (first rows of each color), the probabilistic approach (second rows of each color), the Euclidean metric of the RGB channels (third row of each color) and the similarity function method (fourth row of each color), for two color quadrant (0° and 60°) of highly saturated images with 10% increments of shadow fading at each step

As is shown in the graphs of Fig. 11 and in coincidence with the visual analysis of the corresponding flower (Fig. 10 first and second rows of each color), segmentation failures in the case of the Euclidean distance of a* and b* (see Fig. 11 left) and in the case of the probabilistic approach in the L*a*b* space (see Fig. 11 right) started around

50% of the faded shadow and continued increasing to levels of 80%–90% of false positives (errors rate) in all color quadrants (0°, 60°, 120°, 180°, 240° and 300°).

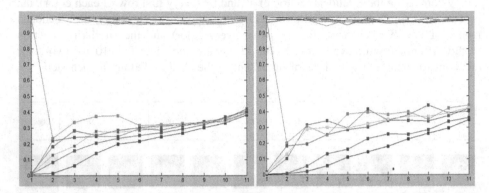

**Fig. 11.** Plot of TP and FP of the Euclidean metric of a* and b* (left) and the probabilistic approach on a* and b* (right) tested for high saturated images

The segmentation using the Euclidean metric of the RGB color channels failed in a regular way starting to have problems in 20% to 30% of the applied shadow fading showing a progressive increase of errors up to 30% (see Fig. 10 every third row of each color and Fig. 12 left).

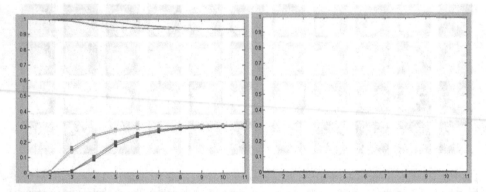

**Fig. 12.** Plot of TP and FP of the Euclidean metric of the RGB channels (left) and of the adaptive color similarity function method (right) tested for high saturated images

As it can be seen from the images corresponding to the results of the segmentation of the test images with high saturation (Fig. 10 fourth row of each color) and the corresponding graphs (Fig. 12 right and Fig. 13 left and right), the method using the adaptive color similarity function [1, 5] behaved correctly in all color quadrants (0°, 60°, 120°, 180°, 240° and 300°), always segmenting the object of interest with a high hit rate (TP) above 99.5%, only one result had 99.3% of hit rate. In all color quadrants had a low error rate below 0.5%. Details can be seen in Fig. 13 left and right.

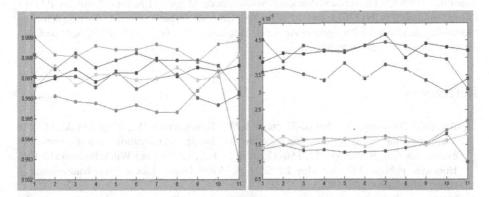

**Fig. 13.** Details of TP (left) and FP (right) of the adaptive color similarity function method in high saturated images

# 4 Conclusions

The results achieved show that the CIE L*a*b* color space is not adequate to distinguish subtle changes of color saturation under illumination variations. In some high saturation regions the CIE L*a*b* color space is not useful to distinguish saturation variations at all. It can be observed that the CIE L*a*b* has better performance than the RGB color space in low saturated regions but has a worse performance in most high saturated color regions. The segmentation algorithms using the CIE L*a*b* color space suffered errors in all cases at different levels of applied shadow.

The segmentation using the Euclidean metric of the RGB color channels failed in a regular way starting to have problems early at low levels of the applied shadow, showing a progressive increase of errors.

The method using the adaptive color similarity function performed well in low and high saturation color regions being practically immune to the increase of the shadow fading, with hit rates above 99% and errors rates below 1% in all cases of study. We have observed that the improvement in quality of this segmentation technique and its quick result is substantially significant.

It can be noticed that the non-consideration of the lightness parameter L* in calculating Euclidean distance and in the probabilistic approach in the CIE L*a*b color space did not made the methods immune to changes in lighting; so simple shadow can alter the quality of their results. This work is aimed to observe the performance of the CIE L*a*b* to detect subtle changes of saturation during color segmentation, and shows that it yields poor results and not equal for every color and level of saturation. Therefore all applications using that color space will have impoverished and unexpected results depending on the input images and illumination.

**Acknowledgements.** The authors of this paper wish to thank to the Centro de Investigación en Computación (CIC), Instituto Politécnico Nacional (IPN); México; Secretaría de Investigación y Posgrado (SIP), México; Centro de Investigaciones Teóricas, Facultad de Estudios Superiores Cuautitlán (FES-C), Universidad Nacional Autónoma de México (UNAM), Proyectos PAPIIT IN113316; PAPIIT IN112913 and PIAPIVC06, UNAM; Departamento de Investigación en Electrónica de Control e Inteligencia Artificial, Industrias Electrónicas Ateramex, S.A. de C.V., for their economic support to this work.

# References

1. Alvarado-Cervantes, .R., Felipe-Riveron, E.M., Khartchenko, V., Pogrebnyak, O.: An adaptive color similarity function suitable for image segmentation and its numerical evaluation. Col. Res. Appl. **42**, 156–172 (2017). E.C. Carter (ed.) Wiley Periodicals, Inc., Hoboken, published Online May 20, 2016 in Wiley Online Library (wileyonlinelibrary.com), https://doi.org/10.1002/col.22059
2. Plataniotis, K.N., Venetsanopoulos, A.N.: Color Image Processing and Applications, 1st edn. Springer, Berlin Heidelberg (2000). https://doi.org/10.1007/978-3-662-04186-4. 354 P.
3. Alvarado-Cervantes, R.: Segmentación de patrones lineales topológicamente diferentes, mediante agrupamientos en el espacio de color HSI, M.Sc. thesis, Center for Computing Research, National Polytechnic Institute, Mexico (2006)
4. Cheng, H., Jiang, X., Sun, Y., Wang, J.: Color image segmentation: advances and prospects. Pattern Recogn. **34**(12), 2259–2281 (2001)
5. Alvarado-Cervantes, R., Felipe-Riveron, E.M., Sanchez-Fernandez, L.P.: Color image segmentation by means of a similarity function. In: Bloch, I., Cesar, R.M. (eds.) CIARP 2010. LNCS, vol. 6419, pp. 319–328. Springer, Heidelberg (2010). https://doi.org/10.1007/978-3-642-16687-7_44
6. Angulo, J., Serra, J.: Modelling and segmentation of colour images in polar representations. Image Vis. Comput. **25**, 475–495 (2007). Centre de Morphologie Mathématique – Ecole des Mines de Paris, France
7. http://www.mathworks.com/help/images/examples/color-based-segmentation-using-the-l-a-b-color-space.html
8. Huang, R., Sang, N., Luo, D., Tang, Q.: Image segmentation via coherent clustering in L*a*b* color space. Pattern Recogn. Lett. **32**, 891–902 (2011)
9. Hanbury, A., Serra, J.: A 3D-polar coordinate colour representation suitable for image analysis, Technical report PRIP-TR-77, Pattern Recognition and Image Processing Group, Institute of Computer Aided Automation, Vienna University of Technology, Vienna Austria (2003)
10. Poynton, C.: (2002). http://www.poynton.com/PDFs/GammaFAQ.pdf
11. Zhang H., Fritts J., Goldman, S.: Image segmentation evaluation: a survey of unsupervised methods. Comput. Vis. Image Underst., 260–280 (2008) https://doi.org/10.1016/j.cviu.2007.08.003
12. Zhang, Y.J.: A survey on evaluation methods for image segmentation. Pattern Recognit. **29**(8), 1335–1346 (1996)
13. Zhang, Y.J.: A review of recent evaluation methods for image segmentation. In: Proceedings of the 6th International Symposium on Signal Processing and Its Applications, pp. 148–151 (2001)
14. Zhang, Y.J., Gerbrands, J.J.: On the design of test images for segmentation evaluation. In: Proceedings EUSIPCO, vol. 1, pp. 551–554 (1992)

15. Zhang, Y.J.: A summary of recent progresses for segmentation evaluation. In: Zhang, Y. J. (ed.) Advances in Image and Video Segmentation. IGI Global Research Collection, Idea Group Inc. (IGI), pp. 423–439 (2006). ISBN 1591407559, 9781591407553

16. Correa-Tome, F.E., Sanchez-Yanez, R.E., Ayala-Ramirez, V.: Comparison of perceptual color spaces for natural image segmentation tasks. Opt. Eng. **50**(11), 117203 (2011)

17. Gupta, S., Bhuchar, K., Sandhu, P.S.: Implementing color image segmentation using biogeography based optimization. In: International Conference on Software and Computer Applications, IPCSIT, vol. 9, pp 79–86. IACSIT Press, Singapore (2011)

18. Sengur, A., Guo, Y.: Color texture image segmentation based on neutrosophic set and wavelet transformation. Comput. Vis. Image Underst. **115**(8), 1134–1144 (2011). https://doi.org/10.1016/j.cviu.2011.04.001

19. Protiere, A., Sapiro, G.: Interactive image segmentation via adaptive weighted distances. IEEE Trans. Image Process. **16**(4), 1046–1057 (2007)

20. Bai, X., Sapiro, G.: A geodesic framework for fast interactive image and video segmentation and matting. In: IEEE 11th International Conference on Computer Vision, pp. 1–8 (2007)

21. Celik, T., Tjahjadi, T.: Unsupervised colour image segmentation using dual-tree complex wavelet transform. Comput. Vis. Image Underst. **114**, 813–826 (2010)

22. Matlab v 7.10.0.499: Image Processing Toolbox, Color-Based Segmentation Using K-Means Clustering (R2010a)

23. Fawcett, T.: An introduction to ROC analysis. Pattern Recogn. Lett. **27**, 861–874 (2006)

24. Gonzalez, R.C., Woods, R.E.: Digital Image Processing, 3rd edn, p. 954. Prentice Hall, Upper Saddle River (2008)

# Supervised Approach to Sky and Ground Classification Using Whiteness-Based Features

Flávia de Mattos[1], Arlete Teresinha Beuren[2],
Bruno Miguel Nogueira de Souza[3], Alceu De Souza Britto Jr.[1],
and Jacques Facon[4(✉)]

[1] Pontifícia Universidade Católica do Paraná, Curitiba, Brazil
flavia_100flavia@hotmail.com, alceubritto@gmail.com
[2] UTFPR Universidade Tecnológica Federal do Paraná, Santa Helena, Brazil
arletebeuren@utfpr.edu.br
[3] Universidade Estadual do Norte do Paraná, Bandeirantes, Brazil
brunomiguel@uenp.edu.br
[4] Universidade Federal do Espírito Santo, São Mateus, ES, Brazil
jacques.facon@ufes.br

**Abstract.** Sky/ground detection plays an important role in many applications such as unmanned control vehicle, dehazing process, cloud detection, for instance. This paper proposes a supervised sky-ground classification technique to color images. The novelty of the proposal is to evaluate the efficiency of whiteness indexes on the classification task. The strategy of the proposal consists in evaluating the power of whiteness indices in classification task. Eleven whiteness indices are used as features to feed a $SVM$ classifier. Experimental results onto 1200 images and numerical evaluations have highlighted that the combination of five whiteness indices is a interesting strategy to classify the sky and the ground.

**Keywords:** Sky · Ground · Segmentation · $SVM$ classifier
Whiteness index

## 1 Introduction

The detection of the sky region in an image provides many valuable information to define the horizon line and the size of the sky region, improve the quality of depth map estimation, measure the percentage of pollution, extract climate information, for instance. However, detecting the sky region still poses a challenge. The great variabilities of light, brightness and regions depending on the time of day and the weather make difficult the segmentation. Figure 1 depicts a cloudy image with sky, hill and obstacles.

We have observed that most of the proposed approaches to separat sky and ground are based on two categories: unsupervised or supervised approaches that use color information directly extracted from various color spaces. The amount of

F. Castro et al. (Eds.): MICAI 2017, LNAI 10633, pp. 248–258, 2018.
https://doi.org/10.1007/978-3-030-02840-4_20

Fig. 1. Image with sky, cloud, hill and obstacles.

color spaces proposed in the literature is very large, however, we believe that still few studies have been conducted to assess their influence. The second category are approaches based on horizon line estimation by means of edge detectors and Hough transform which suffer of low precision when obstacles such as road signs, cars, buildings in the images appear in the horizon.

We are proposing in this study to use the machine learning process from whiteness indices to sky/ground region segmentation in color images. And we want to answer to the following question: can whiteness indices have a contribution to the separation of the sky and ground, even if the sky is blue, rainy, clear or hazy?

The rest of the work is organized as follows. First, a summarized state of the art is described in Sect. 2. In Sect. 3, the whiteness indexes are described. In Sect. 4 the sky/ground segmentation strategy is described. Section 5 describes the experiments and the discussion of the results.

## 2   State of Art

De Croon et al. [1] present a technique based on segmentation of sky and not sky regions to avoid obstacles. The authors extracted visual features from the images as $RGB$, $HSV$ and $YCbCr$ pixel values, relative luminance around the pixel, presence of corners and borders using gradient, absolute and relative gradient in the blue channel, presence of corners characteristic of grayness, among others. Due to its ability to be fast and allow the real time execution, the feature values to classify regions as sky or not sky are mapped by means of decision trees. During the experiments, images of *LabelMe* database [2] depicting different environments as cities, forests, mountains, green pastures, snow areas, green pastures are used. After resizing the images to $120 \times 120$ pixels, 10% of the images formed the test set, while the remaining 90% are used as the training one. The results of image segmentation experiments were presented in a table (the ratio of the image classified as sky versus number of images), but no information about the accuracy and error rates is provided.

Lipschutz et al. [3] propose a Hough-based method to detect sky and earth in maritime images. After filtering the images by morphological erosion to remove weak edge detection, the images are smoothed by a Gaussian filter. Then the authors apply the Canny edge detector before applying the Hough transform. And the longest line found in the previous step is chosen as the sky and earth separation. The experiments were performed with 10 marine infrared images and 10 uncompressed colored visible light marine pictures, previously converted to grayscale images. The authors of the article evaluated the algorithm in terms of precision measured by the angle detected (in degrees) relative to a horizontal line and the line height above the center of the image (in pixels). They conclude that the angular deviation is very small, being $0.06°$ on average for infrared images and $0.21°$ to visible light images.

Williams and Howard [4] present a study to segment sky and ground for images of two different glaciers in Alaska. The Canny edge detector is applied to extract robust line segments from the image. Then the authors apply the Ramer-Douglas-Peucker polygonal approximation technique to preserve the strongest and less noisy segment candidates. Then, from a set of heuristics as color candidate region below and above the segment, weighted percentage of white pixels between the segment and the bottom of the image and also segment length, each remaining candidate segment is tested in order to verify that the candidate is actually part of the true horizon. The authors selected portions of continuous video recorded from field trials to evaluate the effectiveness of the proposed algorithm. Each video frame is processed to extract the horizon line. The assessment of the results is performed by means of 100 pictures manually labeled, indicating the foreground and background areas. From the viewpoint of classification, the average error rate was less than 2.5% of the amount of image pixels.

## 3   Whiteness Indices

A whiteness is an index that measures the relative degree of White. Whiteness indices are applied in some very specific areas such as dentistry [7,8], industrial applications as whitening of materials such as plastic [5]. There are few image applications using Whiteness indexes to segment images in the literature. Tables 1 and 2 describe the whiteness indices found in the literature. Equations with $R$, $G$, $B$ in their composition use $RGB$ color space channels. Similarly, equations with $H$, $S$, $I$ and $H$, $S$, $L$ use the $HSI$ or $HSL$ color spaces respectively. Since the whiteness indices were calculated for each pixel, to make easier the equation comprehension, the pixel rows and columns are omitted.

Table 1. Whiteness indices part 1.

| Whiteness index | Formulation |
|---|---|
| $ASTM$ $E313$ [5,6] | $W_{ASTME313} = 3.3388Z - 3Y$<br>Where the $RGB$ to $XYZ$ conversion is (Eq. 1):<br>$$\left\{ \begin{array}{c} X \\ Y \\ Z \end{array} \right\} = \left\{ \begin{array}{ccc} 0.4124564 & 0.3575761 & 0.1804375 \\ 0.2126729 & 0.7151522 & 0.0721750 \\ 0.0193339 & 0.1191920 & 0.9503041 \end{array} \right\} \left\{ \begin{array}{c} R \\ G \\ B \end{array} \right\} \quad (1)$$ |
| Berger [5,7] | $W_{Berger} = Y - aZ - bX$<br>Where $RGB$ to $XYZ$ conversion is described in Eq. 1<br>$a$ and $b$ are observer coefficients, tabulated as follows:<br>for $2^o$ observer $a = 3.440$ and $b = 3.895$<br>for $10^o$ observer $a = 3.448$ and $b = 3.904$ |
| $CIE$ [7,8] | $W_{CIE} = Y + 800(x_0 - x) + 1700(y_0 - y)$<br>Where $RGB$ to $XYZ$ conversion is described in Eq. 1<br>x, y the normalized chromaticity coordinates defined as:<br>$x = \frac{X}{X+Y+Z}$ and $y = \frac{Y}{X+Y+Z}$<br>$x_0$ and $y_0$ are the chromaticity coordinates<br>for the luminance of the origin observer<br>tabulated as $x_0 = y_0 = 0.3101$ |
| Ganz [5] | $W_{Ganz} = Y + Px + Qy + C$<br>Where $RGB$ to $XYZ$ conversion is described in Eq. 1<br>x, y the normalized chromaticity coordinates defined as:<br>$x = \frac{X}{X+Y+Z}$ and $y = \frac{Y}{X+Y+Z}$<br>$P, Q, C$ the nominal coefficients given<br>for luminance $D65/10^o$<br>tabulated as follows:<br>$P = -1868.322, Q = -3695.690, C = -1809.441$ |
| Harrison | $W_{Harrison} = 100 - R + B$<br>Where $R$ and $B$ are the red and blue intensities, respectively |
| Hunter [6] | $W_{Hunter} = 100 - \left( \left[ 220 \frac{(G-B)}{(G+0.242B)^2} \right] + (100 + \frac{G}{2})^2 \right)^2$<br>Where $R$ and $B$ are the red and blue intensities, respectively |
| Hunter lab [5,8] | $W_{HunterLab} = L - 3b$<br>Where $RGB$ to $XYZ$ conversion is described in Eq. 1<br>$XYZ$ to $Lab$ conversion is defined as follows:<br>$L = 100\sqrt{\frac{Y}{Y_n}}$<br>$b = 70\sqrt{\frac{0.00847X_n}{\frac{Y}{Y_n}}} \left( \frac{X}{X_n} - \frac{Z}{Z_n} \right)$<br>For luminance $D65/10^o$, $X_n, Y_n, Z_n$ values are tabulated as:<br>$X_n = 0.95047, Y_n = 1, Z_n = 1.08883$ |

# 4    Sky/Ground Classification

The proposed study aims to numerically evaluate the efficiency of different white-ness indices for the task of sky - ground classification. The classification protocole is designed to use the Support Vector Machine ($SVM$) classifier. The features are computed from whiteness indices for each pixel in a $N = 3 \times 3$ window:

– whiteness Index value of pixel $x(i,j)$. According to Eq. 5.

$$x(i,j) = \text{whiteness Index value} \quad (5)$$

**Table 2.** Whiteness indices part 2.

| Whiteness index | Formulation |
|---|---|
| Lanier [8] | $W_{Lanier} = 100 - \sqrt{(100 - L^*)^2 + a^{*2} + b^{*2}}$ <br> Where $L^*$ $a^*$ and $b^*$ are defined in Eqs. 2, 3 and 4: <br> $L^* = 116\Im\left(\frac{Y}{Y_n}\right) - 16$       (2) <br> $a^* = 500\left(\Im\left(\frac{X}{X_n}\right) - \Im\left(\frac{Y}{Y_n}\right)\right)$      (3) <br> $b^* = 200\left(\Im\left(\frac{Y}{Y_n}\right) - \Im\left(\frac{Z}{Z_n}\right)\right)$      (4) <br> Where $\Im(t) = \{\sqrt[3]{t}$ if $t > \delta^3\}$ <br> or $\Im(t) = \{\frac{t}{\delta^2} + \frac{4}{29}\}$ otherwise and $\delta = \frac{6}{29}$ <br> Here, $X_n$, $Y_n$ and $Z_n$ under luminance $D65$ with <br> $Y = 100$ are: <br> $X_n = 95.047$, $Y_n = 100.00$, $Z_n = 108.883$ |
| Stensby [6] | $W_{Stensby} = L^* + 3a^* - b^*$ <br> Where $L^*$ $a^*$ and $b^*$ are defined in Eqs. 2, 3 and 4 |
| Stephansen [5] | $W_{Stephansen} = 2B - R$ <br> Where $R$ and $B$ are the red and blue intensities |
| Taube [5] | $W_{Taube} = 4B - 3G$ <br> Where $R$ and $G$ are the red and green intensities |

– Mean $\mu$ for each whiteness index pixel that features the local behavior and reduces the influence of noise. Mean $\mu$ is defined as:

$$\mu(i,j) = \frac{1}{N} \sum_{i=1,j=1}^{N} x(i,j) \tag{6}$$

The $SVM$ classifier was designed to use the Radial Basis Function ($RBF$) kernel with values of $c = 1$ and gamma $= 0.0001$ in the $Weka$ environment (Waikato Environment for Knowledge Analysis) [9]. The choice of the $RBF$ kernel for the experiments is motivated by the fact that $SVM$ classifier hit rate with such kernel function is greater than 80% [10]. To evaluate the generalization capacity of our proposal, the cross-validation technique is used with 5-Folds: First the data set is divided into $k$ equal size subsets, then each subset is used for testing and the others for training. The choice of this evaluation method avoids overlapping test sets.

## 5    Experiments

To assess the efficiency of each whiteness index in our proposal, experiments were carried out using a database composed on images under uncontrolled illumination conditions. Our base was generated from a large base generated by Mihail et al. [11]. The generation of this large base was motivated by the difficulties of existing methods in dealing with appearance variations of sky regions. The large

**Fig. 2.** Some examples used in the experiments.

base contains external images captured in a wide range of weather and lighting conditions. And the authors kept five frames randomly selected for each day of the year. For each image, a binary mask (groundtruth) segmenting the sky and ground was generated. Our database totalizing 1200 images, with blue, rainy, clear, sunny or cloudy sky is divided into four categories of 300 images: city, sea, natural landscape and highway images. For each image, the ground-truth of sky /ground separation was obtained from the original dataset of Radu P. Mihail et al. [11]. While Fig. 2 depicts some examples used in the experiments with their respective groundtruth, Figs. 3 and 4 depict the images generated from the whiteness indices described in Table 1.

Table 3 shows the segmentation F-measure rates from each whiteness classified by means of $SVM$. $W_{Stephansen}$, $W_{Berger}$, $W_{ASTME313}$, $W_{HunterLab}$, and $W_{Taube}$ whiteness are the most performing indices with average F-measure rates higher than 89% for the four categories, city, sea, natural landscape and highway. The other whiteness indices are less efficient in our approach with F-measure rates lower than 71%.

With $W_{Stephansen}$, $W_{Berger}$, $W_{ASTME313}$, $W_{HunterLab}$, and $W_{TaubeW}$ indices, we may observe in Table 4 interesting results of average segmentation F-measure rates for each category .

From the results described in Table 4, we need point out that categorizing the images brought an interesting teaching about the classification power of whiteness indices. While the best average rate is obtained for city images with 96.23%, the worst score is obtained for natural landscape images with 87.89%.

Therefore these results show that the content of the images in each category has more influence on the classification than we had imagined.

From the individual results obtained for each category, our idea was to combine the five best indices and to repeat the sky/ground segmentation protocole by means of $SVM$ classifier. Table 5 shows the segmentation F-measure rates with $W_{Stephansen}$, $W_{Berger}$, $W_{ASTME313}$, $W_{HunterLab}$, and $W_{TaubeW}$ indices.

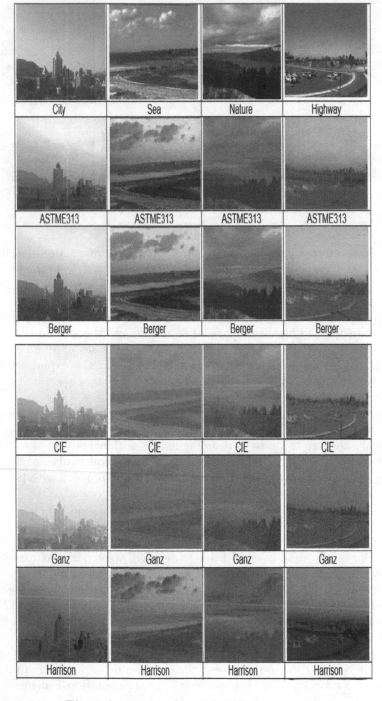

**Fig. 3.** Some examples used in the experiments.

**Fig. 4.** Some examples used in the experiments.

**Table 3.** F-measure rates from each whiteness and each category.

| Whiteness Index | F-measure (%) | | | | |
|---|---|---|---|---|---|
| | City | Sea | Natural landscape | Highway | Average |
| ASTM E313 | 95.41 | 89.41 | 84.31 | 88 | **89.28** |
| Berger | 96.81 | 91.66 | 88.41 | 90.61 | **91.87** |
| *CIE* | 66.71 | 67 | 61.1 | 67.01 | 65.46 |
| Ganz | 60.81 | 52 | 70 | 63 | 61.45 |
| Harrison | 60.92 | 69.01 | 63 | 65.87 | 64.70 |
| Hunter | 71.01 | 63.78 | 67.98 | 52.93 | 63.93 |
| Hunter lab | 96.31 | 94.31 | 90.81 | 90.81 | **93.06** |
| Lanier | 67.01 | 60 | 79.41 | 77 | 70.86 |
| Stensby | 68.001 | 66.01 | 68 | 63.31 | 66.33 |
| Stephansen | 97 | 92.91 | 90.31 | 91.81 | **93.01** |
| Taube | 95.91 | 90.31 | 85.41 | 88.53 | **90.04** |
| Average | 79.63 | 76.04 | 77.16 | 76.26 | 77.27 |

**Table 4.** F-measure rates from 5 five best whiteness indices and each category.

| Whiteness Index | F-measure (%) | | | | |
|---|---|---|---|---|---|
| | City | Sea | Natural landscape | Highway | Average |
| ASTM E313 | 95.41 | 89.41 | 84.31 | 88 | 89.28 |
| Berger | 96.81 | 91.66 | 88.41 | 90.61 | 91.87 |
| Hunter lab | 96.31 | 94.31 | 90.81 | 90.81 | 93.06 |
| Stephansen | 97 | 92.91 | 90.31 | 91.81 | 93.01 |
| Taube | 95.91 | 90.31 | 85.41 | 88.53 | 90.04 |
| Average | 96.23 | 91.66 | 87.89 | 89.99 | **91.44** |

We may observe that we have obtained higher classification rates for 3 categories, city, natural landscape and highway. In the case of category sea, we obtain a slight decrease in the classification rate with 0.05%.

To finish this analysis, the average F-measure rate for all the categories is also higher using the index combination with 91.94%

## 6    Conclusion and Future Studies

We have proposed a supervised sky/ground classification based on whiteness indexes. The features obtained from eleven whiteness indexes, still little known and almost exclusively used in the industry, were used to classify sky and ground by means of a *SVM* supervised classifier. The database used in the experiments, with blue, rainy, clear, sunny or cloudy sky, totalized 1200 images and

**Table 5.** F-measure rates combining the five best whiteness indices.

| Five best whiteness indices | F-measure (%) | | | | |
|---|---|---|---|---|---|
| | City | Sea | Natural landscape | Highway | Average |
| $W_{Stephansen} + W_{Berger} +$ $W_{ASTME313} + W_{HunterLab} +$ $W_{TaubeW}$ | 96.81 | 91.61 | 88.51 | 90.81 | **91.94** |

was divided in four categories of 300 images: city, sea, natural landscape and highway images. The sky and ground groundtruth was generated for each image.

From the numerical evaluation, we now may answer the question asked previously in the introduction (Sect. 1): can whiteness indexes contribute to the separation of sky and ground, even if the sky is blue, rainy, light or hazy?

From individual whiteness assessment, segmentation F-measure rates have shown that $W_{Stephansen} = 2B - R$, $W_{Berger} = Y - aZ - bX$, $W_{ASTME313} = 3.3388Z - 3Y$, $W_{HunterLab} = L - 3b$, and $W_{TaubeW} = 4B - 3G$ are the most promising indices. From a second numerical assessment combining the five best whiteness indexes $W_{Stephansen}$, $W_{Berger}$, $W_{ASTME313}$, and $W_{TaubeW}$, the results have highlighted that these five whiteness indices are very interesting features in the challenge of separating the sky from the ground.

We can also conclude that the combination of these five indices proves to be a better alternative in the classification process the four categories tested (city, sea, natural landscape and highway).

In future studies, we plan to incorporate other color index descriptors as blueness ones to increase the sky and ground classification rates. And we also plan to develop a classifying strategy to automatically categorize images into four or more classes.

# References

1. De Croon, G., De Wagter, C., Remes, B., Ruijsink, R.: Sky segmentation approach to obstacle avoidance. In: Proceedings of IEEE Aerospace Conference, pp. 1–16 (2011)
2. Russell, B.C., Torralba, A.T., Murphy, K.P., Freeman, W.T.: LabelMe: a database and web-based tool for image annotation. Int. J. Comput. Vis. **77**, 157–173 (2008)
3. Lipschutz, I., Gershikov, E., Milgrom, B.: New methods for horizon line detection in infrared and visible sea images. Int. J. Comput. Eng. Res. **3**, 226–233 (2013)
4. Williams, S., Howard, A.M.: Horizon line estimation in glacial environments using multiple visual cues. In: PIEEE International Conference on Robotics and Automation, ICRA, pp. 5887–5892 (2011)
5. Lin, J.: Factors affecting the perception and measurement of optically brightened white textiles. Ph.D. thesis, Graduate Faculty of North Carolina State University Raleigh, North Carolina (2013)
6. X-Rite: X-Rite: Color iQC and color iMatch color calculations guide, Version 8.0 (2012). http://www.xrite.com/service-support/product-support/formulation-and-qc-software/color-iqc

7. Puebla, C.P.: Whiteness assessment: a primer. Axiphos GmbH, Germany (2006)
8. Joiner, A., Hopkinson, I., Deng, Y., Westland, S.: A review of tooth colour and whiteness. J. Dent. **36**, s2–s7 (2008)
9. Smith, T.C., Frank, E.: Introducing machine learning concepts with WEKA. In: Mathé, E., Davis, S. (eds.) Statistical Genomics. MMB, vol. 1418, pp. 353–378. Springer, New York (2016). https://doi.org/10.1007/978-1-4939-3578-9_17
10. Van Geste, T., Suykens, J., Baesens, B.: Benchmarking least squares support vector machine classifiers. Mach. Learn. **54**, 5–32 (2004)
11. Mihail, R.P., Workman, S., Bessinger, Z., Jacobs, N.: Sky segmentation in the wild: an empirical study. Inference Corporation (2016). http://mypages.valdosta.edu/rpmihail/

# Vegetation Index Based on Genetic Programming for Bare Ground Detection in the Amazon

Julián Muñoz, Carlos Cobos[⊠], and Martha Mendoza

Information Technology Research Group (GTI),
University of Cauca, Popayán, Colombia
{julianfer, ccobos, mmendoza}@unicauca.edu.co

**Abstract.** Vegetation indices are algebraic combinations of spectral bands produced by satellite. The indices allow different vegetation covers to be identified by contrast evaluation. Vegetation indexes are used mainly in tasks of classification of satellite images, as well as chemical and physical land studies. An example is seen in the Normalized Difference Vegetation Index (NDVI) that shows up live green vegetation. This article describes the process of creating a new vegetation index that enables bare ground identification in the Amazon using genetic programming. It further shows how a threshold is automatically defined for the new index, a threshold that facilitates the task of photointerpretation and is not normally provided for other vegetation indexes. The new index, called BGIGP (Bare Ground Index obtained using Genetic Programming) showed significant values of contrast between the different covers analyzed, being seen to compete well with traditional vegetation indexes such as SR. The performance of BGIGP was also evaluated using the characteristics of 10448-pixel images from the "2017 Kaggle Planet: Understanding the Amazon from Space" competition, to classify bare ground against water, cloudy, primary, cultivation, road, and artisanal mine, obtaining a 93.71% of accuracy.

**Keywords:** Genetic programming · Remote sensing · Vegetation index
Definition of threshold

## 1 Introduction

Remote sensing has gained importance in recent years due to the emergence of advanced algorithms for image acquisition and processing [1]. These advances have enabled a greater understanding of data and spectral bands from both free access satellites such as Landsat, GOES, and MODIS, and private satellites such as Planet, RapidEye, QuickBird, and WorldView.

Applications in remote sensing have focused on studying the natural dynamics of the earth, analyzing the relationship between humans and deforestation, loss of biodiversity, and climate change [2]. The generation of vegetation indexes using spectral bands has been considered as one of the main applications of vegetation information extraction [3] for studying these human-environment relationships. Vegetation indices are combinations of expressions (spectral bands) through mathematical formulas [4]

© Springer Nature Switzerland AG 2018
F. Castro et al. (Eds.): MICAI 2017, LNAI 10633, pp. 259–271, 2018.
https://doi.org/10.1007/978-3-030-02840-4_21

whose objective is to enhance characteristics of interest in land cover. One approach for the construction of these mathematical formulas is based on the correct selection of spectral bands from satellite images (classic method) [5]. Another approach that has been quite successful in constructing vegetation indices relates to the use of genetic programming [6, 7]. Many vegetation indices are found in the state of the art [8, 9] that have been obtained through a classical approach or using genetic programming [10], but in none of them is a fixed threshold established to detect a specific cover. This is the primary motivation for this work, in which using a set of images in radiance values from a Planet satellite available via the "2017 Kaggle Planet: Understanding the Amazon from Space" competition, a new vegetation index and constant threshold were established that enable the classification of bare ground in the Amazon region. This is achieved by maximizing the fitness function related to the success rate in the detection of bare ground from a set of spectral values selected through the photointerpretation provided by the competition members. In addition to showing how the index was obtained, this work details the algorithm for obtaining the threshold, thus opening the way to expanding this approach based on genetic programming for other types of satellite information such as SAR satellites and Multi and Hyperspectral satellites.

The remainder of the paper is organized as follows. Section 2 presents related work. Section 3 presents the genetic program, the new vegetation index, and its corresponding threshold. Section 4 shows the experimental results on the dataset with the spectral values from Planet images. The results of measuring contrast between covers in the region are also shown and a visual inspection of the new vegetation index is carried out. Finally, some remarks and suggestions for future work are presented.

## 2  Related Work

Genetic programming (GP) has been widely used in the combination of satellite spectral bands for finding specific characteristics of a region and to generate vegetation indices that produce contrasts between the different covers of interest [1]. In 2007, Momm et al. in [11] used a hybrid approach between genetic programming and logistic regression, merging the treatment of dichotomous data (classes) with the quantitative results of expressions in genetic programming. The fitness function is defined by the model, the Kappa statistic, and the number of terms in the model. The result is an image that classifies water and not water, using a manually selected segmentation threshold.

An example of the use of GP to detect specific terrain characteristics can be observed in the method proposed in 2008 by Chion et al. in [3], in which, further supported by a regression model, was successful in quantifying the level of nitrogen in the vegetation. This research seeks to maximize the correlation between data measured in the field and the size of the formula obtained by the genetic program.

A vegetation index based on genetic programming called GPSVI was introduced in 2011 by Puente et al. in [7]. This index estimates the vegetation cover in soils to measure erosion. The fitness function depends on covariance and the cover management factor measured in the field.

In 2016, work related to finding a vegetation index using genetic programming and data from a hyper and multi-spectral satellite was carried out by Hernández et al. [1]. The fitness function was based on the Silhouette Score used primarily for clustering. The approach obtains a vegetation index for classifying two types of datasets with their respective ground-truth. Once the index is obtained, a classification process based on the minimum distance to the central tendency value of each sample is undergone to classify the datasets.

## 3  The Genetic Program and the New Vegetation Index

The genetic program used to find the new vegetation index is based on the proposal presented by Cobos et al. in [12] (it was originally used to obtain a new clustering index for web document clustering [13, 14]). The algorithm uses a representation of genes based on an expression tree, crossing one and two points of two parents, three classes of mutation algorithms, rank selection to generate a new generation and, to avoid premature convergence it uses a random re-initialization.

The representation of the gene is based on expressions (organized as trees) that are obtained from the combination of thirteen (13) basic attributes corresponding to the spectral bands of each pixel of an image, namely: (0) Red (R), (1) Green (G), (2) Blue (B), (3) Near-Infrared (NIR) and vegetation indices from the state of the art: (4) arvi, (5) cri, (6) evi, (7) ndvi, (8) ndwi, (9) savi, (10) sipi, (11) sr, and (12) tvi [2].

The fitness function of the genetic program seeks to maximize the number of successes in the classification of the bare ground-related pixels extracted from information from 12758 pixels of images taken from the "2017 Kaggle Planet: Understanding the Amazon from Space" competition. This dataset operates as the training dataset, D. To obtain this dataset the photo-interpretation technique [2] was used with support in labeling provided in the Kaggle competition for the different satellite images.

To evaluate and maximize the success rate, the genetic algorithm generates and evaluates (calculates fitness) different expressions. The fitness calculation is performed as a classification process based on each expression and a list of thresholds on the D dataset. To perform this task (fitness calculation) the following steps are performed:

(a)  generate an algebraic formula with the genetic program and then evaluate the formula in all registers $R_i \in D$ where $|D| = 12758$.
(b)  normalize the result of the operation in each record using min-max as indicated in Eq. (1)
(c)  Initialize $j = 1$ and $u_j = 0.05$.
(d)  classify all records by considering a dynamic threshold $u_j$ as indicated in Eq. (2), i.e. if the normalized value obtained is greater than the threshold $u_j$, the bare ground label (value 1) is assigned to the record $R_i$, otherwise the other cover label is assigned (value 0).
(e)  evaluate the success rate obtained for the threshold $u_j$ by comparing the true class in the training dataset as shown in Eq. (3).
(f)  increase threshold test iteration $j = j + 1$ and threshold $u_j = u_{j-1} + 0.05$.
(g)  repeat steps (d), (e) and (f) until $u_j < = 0.95$.

(h) return the higher success rate obtained and the threshold $u_j$ with which that success rate is achieved. At the best threshold, the inverse min-max operation is applied, as shown in Eq. (4), to return the threshold value in the true range of the expression (vegetation index).

$$X_i^* = \frac{X_i - X_{min}}{X_{max} - X_{min}}, \forall u_j \in U \tag{1}$$

where $X_i^*$ is the normalized value for the register $i$, $X_i$ is the value obtained from the evaluation of the algebraic formula of the new index, $X_{min}$ and $X_{max}$ are the maximum and minimum values of the evaluation of all the registers $R_i \in D$ for a threshold $u_j$ belonging to the threshold range $U$.

$$if\left(X_i^*\right) > u_j \rightarrow label = 1\ otherwise\ label = 0 \tag{2}$$

where **label** is the name of the label designated to distinguish bare ground (value 1). This evaluation is performed for all records with each of the thresholds.

$$TE_R^{u_j} = \frac{successes}{sucesses + failures} * 100\% \tag{3}$$

where $TE_R^{u_j}$ is the success rate for all registers $R_i$ with respect to the threshold $u_j$, where successes correspond to the times that the segmentation of the algebraic formula of the vegetation index coincided with the true class in the dataset $D$, failures is the mismatch between the true class and the index segmentation in Eq. (2).

$$U^R = U^* \times \left(U_{max} - U_{min}\right) + U_{min} \tag{4}$$

where the actual threshold $U^R$ of the vegetation index is calculated based on the specific normalized threshold of that solution $U^*$ (corresponds to one of the values $u_j$ ranging from 0.05 to 0.95 in steps of 0.05 and the maximum and minimum values of the index to which the fitness is being calculated.

Table 1 shows some solutions (vegetation indices) that the genetic program obtains. The indexes are in postfix notation (first the operands and then the operator recursively until reaching the root of the tree). For each solution **S**, the threshold value **U** that obtains the highest success rate for the expression is recorded, along with its corresponding success rate **TE** (Fitness). Indices in rows 2 and 3 correspond to the same expression, only the order has been changed.

The pseudo-code of the genetic program that maximizes the success rate for finding an index that classifies bare ground is shown in Fig. 1. Each step of the program is explained in more detail below.

**Initialize Algorithm Parameters:** To find an expression (index) and its corresponding threshold that maximizes the results of bare ground classification, the following parameters must be defined: Population Size (PS), Mutation Rate (MR), and Maximum Number of Generations (MNG) to stop the algorithm execution.

**Representation and Initialization:** Each individual or solution is represented as a tree where different expressions and a true field for the fitness value (objective function) are coded. The arguments for the expressions are: $0 for R, $1 for G, $2 for B, $3 for nir, and so on up to $12 for tvi. The operations managed in the genetic program were: +, −, *, /, and ln for natural logarithmic.

**Table 1.** Vegetation indices generated by genetic program for the detection of bare ground.

|   | S | Threshold | Fitness (success rate) |
|---|---|---|---|
| 1 | tvi arvi - B / | 6,44450491305019E-05 | 0,890186549615927 |
| 2 | B ln arvi + arvi + | 9,6603177529866 | 0,895046245493024 |
| 3 | arvi B ln + arvi + | 9,6603177529866 | 0,895046245493024 |
| 4 | evi sr - B sr * / cri + | -7,69062614858161E-05 | 0,901787113967707 |
| 5 | arvi R / G arvi * arvi R - / B ln - + | -9,31185082801432 | 0,906333281078539 |
| 6 | tvi tvi arvi * - B / | 7,2227355325264E-05 | 0,910330772848409 |
| 7 | B arvi - B / arvi - B / | 8,48612944793092E-05 | 0,912917385170089 |

```
01   Initialize algorithm parameters.
02   Randomly initialize population, which encode expressions as a Tree.
03   Calculate fitness value for each solution in population
04   For Generation = 1 to MNG (Maximum Number of Generations)
05       For I = 1 to PS (Population Size) step by 2
06           Select chromosome I as parent1 from current population.
07           Select chromosome I+1 as parent2 from current population.
08           Generate two intermediate offspring based on parent1 and
             parent2 using one or two-point crossover and include them
             in population.
09           Calculate fitness value for offspring.
10       Next For
11       Based on a MR (mutation rate), apply mutation using usual gene
         mutation, transposition of insertion sequence elements or root
         transposition, calculate fitness value for each new solution,
         and include new solutions in current population.
12       Select best PS solutions from current population to the new
         generation using Rank selection.
13       If Premature Convergence then Re-initialize population keeping
         best solution and calculate fitness value for each new chromo-
         some in population.
14   Next For
15   Select and return best chromosome.
```

**Fig. 1.** Pseudo-code for the genetic program.

**Crossover:** With the same probability, a one or two-point crossover is carried out. The crossover algorithm is explained in more detail in [12].

**Mutation:** The algorithm handles a low probability of mutation. When a solution is selected to mutate, one of the three options available is applied: usual gene mutation, transposition of insertion sequence elements, or root transposition. These have the same probability of being selected.

The genetic algorithm was executed generating multiple vegetation indices for the detection of bare ground. The vegetation index with the highest success rate (0.9129) was chosen in the training dataset (the last one in Table 1). The corresponding formula is: B arvi − B /arvi − B /. This formula expressed in order is presented in Eq. (5). This is the new vegetation index for the detection of bare ground in the Amazon that was obtained based on genetic programming (BGIGP).

$$BGIGP = \frac{\left[\left(\frac{B-arvi}{B}\right) - arvi\right]}{B} = \frac{1}{B}\left(1 - \frac{arvi}{B} - arvi\right) \tag{5}$$

where BGIGP is the new bare ground index based on genetic programming, B is the blue spectral band in radiance and arvi is the atmospherically resistant vegetation index.

The threshold value selected by the genetic algorithm for finding bare ground in the BGIGP index is: 8.486129E−05, i.e. any value greater than this threshold will be considered as bare ground in the new vegetation index. BGIGP and the threshold value can be multiplied by 10^5 to use "more natural" numbers.

# 4   Experimentation

The new vegetation index, BGIGP, was evaluated using two (2) tests: (a) Evaluation of the detection of bare ground on a test dataset and (b) Evaluation of the contrast percentage between bare ground and other vegetation cover present in the Amazon region.

## 4.1   Evaluation on Test Dataset

For the construction of the test dataset, pixels were also taken from images in the "2017 Kaggle Planet: Understanding the Amazon from Space" competition (available at https://www.kaggle.com/c/planet-understanding-the-amazon-from-space/data),    using the photo-interpretation technique [2] and the labels provided in the Kaggle competition. The dataset consists of 10448 records and has the same 13 attributes (R, G, B, NIR, arvi, cri, evi, ndvi, ndwi, savi, sipi, sr and tvi) as the training dataset. The dataset has two classes: bare ground (label 1) and another type of vegetation (label 0). The latter set includes water, habitation, primary, road, cultivation, agriculture, cloudy and artisanal mine. On applying BGIGP to the test dataset the confusion matrix was obtained together with the precision, recall and Kappa values shown in Table 2.

In general, the total precision of the BGIGP for the detection of bare ground is high, as corroborated by the Kappa statistic. The BGIGP has a high discrimination when detecting true bare ground of 96.85%. The number of samples classified incorrectly corresponded to 6.28%. It should be noted that BGIGP can be improved by enriching the training dataset, obtaining more varied samples of satellite images and vegetation cover.

**Table 2.** Confusion matrix for BGIGP evaluation.

| Classified as | True classes | | Total | Recall (%) |
|---|---|---|---|---|
| | Label 0 | Label 1 | | |
| Label 0 | **7302** | 81 | 7383 | 98.90 |
| Label 1 | 576 | **2489** | 3065 | 81.20 |
| Total | 7878 | 2570 | **10448** | |
| Precision (%) | 92.69 | 96.85 | 93.71 | |
| Kappa | 0.84081 | | | |

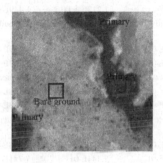

**Fig. 2.** Planet satellite image (true color) provided in the competition [16]. Extraction of four (4) regions of interest: bare ground and three samples of forest to conduct contrast measurements.

## 4.2  Evaluation of Contrast

The evaluation related to contrast analysis was made taking into account the contrast measure shown in Eq. (6) taken from [15]. To do this the contrast was measured between the bare ground and the different covers described above. The regions of interest were extracted from the satellite images provided in the Kaggle competition. Figure 2 shows an example.

$$C = |\bar{a} - \bar{b}| \tag{6}$$

where C is the contrast value, $\bar{a}$ is the average intensity of the bare ground and $\bar{b}$ the average intensity value of other vegetation cover.

The results of the contrast evaluation were applied on different satellite images belonging to the competition, so that the name is left as an identifier. In addition, the contrast values obtained from the SR vegetation index, also used for the detection of bare ground, were recorded. The results are shown in Table 3.

**Table 3.** Evaluation of contrast between bare ground and vegetation cover present in the Amazon. The contrast percentage is calculated by identifying the minimum and maximum spectral values of the BGIGP and SR vegetation indices.

| Image | Regions of interest | | | | Contrast | | |
|---|---|---|---|---|---|---|---|
| **train_124.tif** | 1-Bare ground | 2-Primary | 3-Primary | 4-Primary | C_1–2 | C_1–3 | C_1–4 |
| BGIGP | 8.883E-05 | 5.627E-05 | 6.182E-05 | 5.419E-05 | 31.6% | 26.2% | 33.6% |
| SR | 1.864E + 00 | 2.896E + 00 | 2.637E + 00 | 3.116E + 00 | 36.3% | 27.2% | 44.0% |
| **train_217.tif** | 1-Bare ground | 2-Primary | 3-Primary | 4-Primary | C_1–2 | C_1–3 | C_1–4 |
| BGIGP | 1.148E-04 | 5.327E-05 | 5.344E-05 | 4.626E-05 | 48.9% | 48.8% | 54.5% |
| SR | 1.498E + 00 | 2.446E + 00 | 2.260E + 00 | 2.412E + 00 | 54.7% | 44.0% | 52.8% |
| **train_19023. tif** | 1-Bare ground | 2-Cloudy | 3-Cloudy | 4-Cloudy | C_1–2 | C_1–3 | C_1–4 |
| BGIGP | 1.274E-04 | 6.088E-05 | 7.434E-05 | 7.936E-05 | 46.8% | 37.3% | 33.8% |
| SR | 1.376E + 00 | 9.323E-01 | 1.212E + 00 | 1.449E + 00 | 13.2% | 4.9% | 2.2% |
| **train_22614. tif** | 1-Bare ground | 2-Cloudy | 3-Cloudy | 4-Cloudy | C_1–2 | C_1–3 | C_1–4 |
| BGIGP | 1.246E-04 | 7.821E-05 | 6.001E-05 | 8.919E-05 | 25.1% | 35.0% | 19.2% |
| SR | 1.289E + 00 | 9.011E-01 | 8.419E-01 | 1.127E + 00 | 15.8% | 18.2% | 6.6% |
| **train_100.tif** | 1-Bare ground | 2-Water | 3-Water | 4-Water | C_1–2 | C_1–3 | C_1–4 |
| BGIGP | 1.296E-04 | 7.564E-05 | 7.764E-05 | 7.728E-05 | 39.2% | 37.8% | 38.0% |
| SR | 8.395E-01 | 7.611E-01 | 7.431E-01 | 7.373E-01 | 6.3% | 7.7% | 8.2% |
| **train_22614. tif** | 1-Bare ground | 2-Water with silt | 3-Water with silt | 4-Water with silt | C_1–2 | C_1–3 | C_1–4 |
| BGIGP | 1.241E-04 | 1.275E-04 | 1.259E-04 | 1.258E-04 | 1.9% | 1.0% | 0.9% |
| SR | 1.262E + 00 | 7.672E-01 | 7.444E-01 | 7.781E-01 | 20.1% | 21.0% | 19.7% |
| **train_32517. tif** | 1-Bare ground | 2-Water without silt | 3- Water without silt | 4- Water without silt | C_1–2 | C_1–3 | C_1–4 |
| BGIGP | 1.496E-04 | 3.178E-04 | 3.150E-04 | 3.095E-04 | 31.0% | 30.5% | 29.4% |
| SR | 9.998E-01 | 4.115E-01 | 4.369E-01 | 4.396E-01 | 19.4% | 18.6% | 18.5% |
| **train_33304. tif** | 1-Bare ground | 2- Water without silt | 3- Water without silt | 4- Water without silt | C_1–2 | C_1–3 | C_1–4 |
| BGIGP | 1.919E-05 | -5.109E-05 | -3.685E-05 | -4.486E-05 | 14.0% | 11.2% | 12.8% |
| SR | 8.510E-01 | 9.715E-01 | 1.070E + 00 | 9.371E-01 | 3.8% | 6.8% | 2.7% |
| **train_123.tif** | 1-Bare ground | 2- Cultivation | 3- Cultivation | 4- Cultivation | C_1–2 | C_1–3 | C_1–4 |
| BGIGP | 2.331E-04 | 4.236E-05 | 4.463E-05 | 4.602E-05 | 35.8% | 35.4% | 35.1% |
| SR | 1.110E + 00 | 3.373E + 00 | 3.112E + 00 | 3.346E + 00 | 60.4% | 53.4% | 59.7% |
| **train_1201.tif** | 1-Bare ground | 2- Cultivation | 3- Cultivation | 4- Cultivation | C_1–2 | C_1–3 | C_1–4 |
| BGIGP | 2.003E-04 | 2.268E-05 | 1.351E-05 | 1.324E-05 | 39.4% | 41.5% | 41.5% |
| SR | 9.685E-01 | 3.318E + 00 | 3.961E + 00 | 3.494E + 00 | 54.9% | 70.0% | 59.0% |
| **train_230.tif** | 1-Bare ground | 2- Habitation | 3- Habitation | 4- Habitation | C_1–2 | C_1–3 | C_1–4 |
| BGIGP | 1.126E-04 | 1.189E-04 | 1.130E-04 | 1.110E-04 | 6.1% | 0.3% | 1.6% |
| SR | 1.165E + 00 | 1.069E + 00 | 1.144E + 00 | 1.246E + 00 | 5.6% | 1.2% | 4.7% |
| **train_57.tif** | 1-Bare ground | 2- Artisanal Mine | 3- Artisanal Mine | 4- Artisanal Mine | C_1–2 | C_1–3 | C_1–4 |
| BGIGP | 1.472E-04 | 2.022E-04 | 1.956E-04 | 1.131E-04 | 17.4% | 15.3% | 10.8% |
| SR | 7.141E-01 | 3.564E-01 | 4.183E-01 | 1.101E + 00 | 10.2% | 8.4% | 11.0% |
| **train_207.tif** | 1-Bare ground | 2- Road | 3- Road | 4- Road | C_1–2 | C_1–3 | C_1–4 |
| BGIGP | 2.236E-04 | 2.893E-04 | 2.914E-04 | 2.721E-04 | 8.8% | 9.1% | 6.5% |
| SR | 1.309E + 00 | 9.333E-01 | 1.000E + 00 | 1.016E + 00 | 11.9% | 9.7% | 9.2% |
| **train_2605.tif** | 1-Bare ground | 2- Shadow | 3- Shadow | 4- Shadow | C_1–2 | C_1–3 | C_1–4 |
| BGIGP | 1.133E-04 | 9.868E-05 | 1.018E-04 | 9.830E-05 | 14.5% | 11.4% | 14.8% |
| SR | 1.265E + 00 | 1.070E + 00 | 1.025E + 00 | 9.904E-01 | 9.9% | 12.2% | 13.9% |

(*continued*)

**Table 3.**  (*continued*)

| Image | Regions of interest | | | | Contrast | | |
|---|---|---|---|---|---|---|---|
| train_19023.tif | 1-Bare ground | 2- Primary | 3- Cloudy | 4- Cultivation | C_1–2 | C_1–3 | C_1–4 |
| BGIGP | 1.275E-04 | 3.631E-05 | 6.178E-05 | 6.929E-05 | 64.1% | 46.2% | 40.9% |
| SR | 1.378E + 00 | 2.623E + 00 | 9.672E-01 | 2.092E + 00 | 37.1% | 12.2% | 21.3% |

| Image | Regions of interest | | | | | Contrast | | | |
|---|---|---|---|---|---|---|---|---|---|
| train 230.tif | 1-Bare ground | 2- Primary | 3- Habitation | 4- Cloudy | 5- Road | C_1–2 | C_1–3 | C 1–4 | C_1–5 |
| BGIGP | 1.180E-04 | 6.651E-05 | 1.162E-04 | 6.098E-05 | 1.371E-04 | 50.0% | 1.8% | 55.4% | 18.5% |
| SR | 1.096E + 00 | 1.926E + 00 | 1.025E + 00 | 7.999E-01 | 9.452E-01 | 48.4% | 4.2% | 17.3% | 8.8% |

In general, it can be observed that the BGIGP is competitive against the traditional SR index, surpassing it in the discrimination of such cover as water without silt, clouds, and cloud shadows. With respect to the other cover, BGIGP maintains a favorable contrast, except in Habitation, a cover indicating the presence of urbanized areas and for which a considerable amount of records was not obtained in the training dataset. A similar occurrence is found with the water with silt cover, where the vegetation index tends to detect bare ground mistakenly because the training set did not take these spectral values into account.

When performing contrast measurement on an image that has multiple cover, for example, in the training samples train_230.tif and train_19023.tif, the BGIGP index exceeds the SR index in most of the covers analyzed, except again in the covers of road and habitation for the same reasons as mentioned previously (the training dataset included hardly any samples of those covers). Figure 3 below shows the general performance of BGIP versus SR for different cover based on their average contrast percentage.

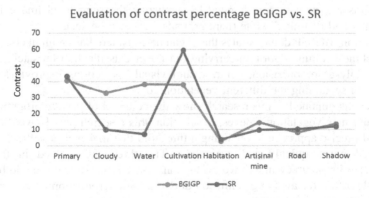

**Fig. 3.**  Contrast comparison between BGIGP and SR.

The BGIGP vegetation index can be competitive against the traditional SR index. It can be observed in Fig. 3 that the BGIGP surpasses in four (4) of the eight (8) covers selected, but, it is necessary to emphasize that in the covers in which the index did not win, it managed to be in a contrast range close to SR, except in Cultivation. With respect to this cover it is possible to improve the contrast by constructing a training dataset that stores more samples related to that cover and in general with the covers in which it loses.

Finally, a visual inspection of the BGIGP and the threshold provided in this research toward the classification (segmentation is the name more commonly used in this field) of bare ground on images in the "2017 Kaggle Planet: Understanding the Amazon from Space" competition was performed. The test consisted in constructing the images of the BGIGP vegetation index from the original Kaggle images, after which a segmentation was made based on the threshold obtained for bare ground. The resulting segmented images represent in white the detection of bare ground.

Each row of Fig. 4 shows the original Kaggle image (a) along with the vegetation index BGIBP (b) for the original image and then the classified (segmented) image with the threshold (c). Image 1.a (train_217.tif) features bare ground and forest, image 2.a (train_19023.tif) contains clouds, bare ground, and forests. Image 3.a (train_28273.tif) has water coverings, bare ground, forests, and agriculture. Image 4.a (train_32517.tif) has water with silt, agriculture, forests, and bare ground, and finally the covers present in image 5.a (train_230.tif) are habitation, bare ground, roads, forests, agriculture, and cloud cover.

Visual inspection revealed what was previously analyzed with the test dataset. BGIGP in image **4.a** confuses bare ground with water-silt, likewise with habitation in image **5.a**, but nevertheless, visually it can be seen in image **4.b** that there is a contrast between bare ground and water with silt. In Fig. **5.b** it can also be seen that the index has a considerable number of differentiable zones. From this it can be concluded that increasing the number of training samples, the selected threshold could be adjusted so that the new index presented in this investigation achieves the correct separability or a new index with a more precise threshold can be obtained.

The results related to images **1.a**, **2.a** and **3.a** have a high accuracy in detecting bare ground. This assertion is corroborated by analyzing the segmented image in which well-defined and delimited white (bare ground) areas can be seen.

In addition, BGIGP demonstrates that it can be considered as an input characteristic for a machine-learning algorithm carrying out cover classification on satellite images since in analyses of precision, contrast, and visual inspections it provides relevant details when separating the different vegetation cover.

The results obtained in this research show the potential of genetic programming in constructing new vegetation indexes. In addition, this research puts forward a simple, novel, and precise approach to obtaining a threshold that makes it possible to segment the desired cover quickly and accurately. The threshold selected in this work demonstrated its accuracy in the two evaluations carried out, so that it could become a suitable algorithm for avoiding confusion due to photointerpretation or in areas where there may be ambiguity in the classification process by experts.

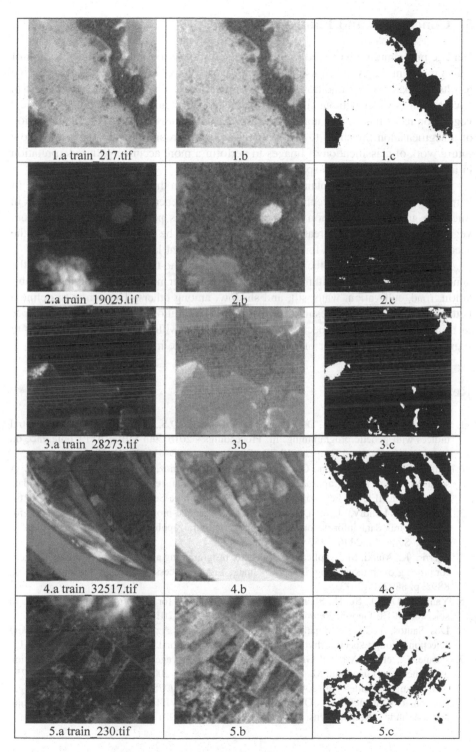

**Fig. 4.** True color satellite image, BGIGP vegetation index, classification by the new vegetation index.

## 5   Conclusions and Future Work

Genetic programming was used to produce a new vegetation index for the detection of bare ground in the Amazon using Planet images. The BGIGP presented competitive results compared to the traditional SR vegetation index, obtaining a greater contrast in covers such as water without silt, clouds, cloud shadows and artisanal mines. The new vegetation index has an advantage with respect to SR that is related to the identification of a segmentation threshold to find the areas of bare ground directly. This will allow future work of classification of images to perform a more accurate photointerpretation in areas where vegetation is sparse.

The approach used to obtain a suitable segmentation threshold for the detection of bare ground proved to be accurate, obtaining 93.71% general precision and 96.85% in true bare ground classification. With these results, it is possible to affirm that more vegetation indices can be created and a threshold can be specified in relation to the spectral ranges of the index for the detection of different land cover.

Regarding future work, the authors plan to enrich the training data set used in the genetic programming algorithm, incorporating a greater number of samples of habitation, road, cultivation, water-silt, and shadow, among others. The aim is to define a better index and a better threshold for that index. In addition, the research group hopes to bring this approach of spectral index construction with threshold identification to segmenting vegetation cover of interest in other satellite information sources.

## References

1. Hernandez Albarracin, J.F., Dos Santos, J.A., Torres, R.D.S.: Learning to combine spectral indices with genetic programming. In: Proceedings - 2016 29th SIBGRAPI Conference on Graphics, Patterns and Images, SIBGRAPI 2016, pp. 408–415. IEEE (2017)
2. Pencue-Fierro, E.L., Solano-Correa, Y.T., Corrales-Muñoz, J.C., Figueroa-Casas, A.: A semi-supervised hybrid approach for multitemporal multi-region multisensor landsat data classification. IEEE J. Sel. Top. Appl. Earth Obs. Remote Sens. 9(12), 5424–5435 (2016)
3. Chion, C., Landry, J.A., Da Costa, L.: A genetic-programming-based method for hyperspectral data information extraction: agricultural applications. IEEE Trans. Geosci. Remote Sens. 46, 2446–2457 (2008)
4. Djerriri, K., Malki, M.: Application of genetic programming and Landsat multi-date imagery for urban growth monitoring. In: SPIE - Image Signal Processing Remote Sensing XIX, vol. 8892, p. 889210 (2013)
5. Yang, H., Du, Q., Su, H., Sheng, Y.: An efficient method for supervised hyperspectral band selection. IEEE Geosci. Remote Sens. Lett. 8, 138–142 (2011)
6. Dos Santos, L.C.B., Guimaraes, S.J.F., Dos Santos, J.A.: Efficient unsupervised band selection through spectral rhythms. IEEE J. Sel. Top. Signal Process. 9, 1016–1025 (2015)
7. Puente, C., et al.: A novel GP approach to synthesize vegetation indices for soil erosion assessment. In: Giacobini, M., et al. (eds.) EvoWorkshops 2009. LNCS, vol. 5484, pp. 375–384. Springer, Heidelberg (2009). https://doi.org/10.1007/978-3-642-01129-0_42
8. Carlson, T.N., Ripley, D.A.: On the relation between NDVI, fractional vegetation cover, and leaf area index. Remote Sens. Environ. 62, 241–252 (1997)

9. Jiang, Z., Huete, A.R., Didan, K., Miura, T.: Development of a two-band enhanced vegetation index without a blue band. Remote Sens. Environ. **112**, 3833–3845 (2008)
10. Taghizadeh-Mehrjardi, R., et al.: Prediction of soil surface salinity in arid region of central Iran using auxiliary variables and genetic programming. Arid L. Res. Manag. **30**, 49–64 (2016)
11. Momm, H.G., Kuszmaul, J.S., Easson, G.: Integration of logistic regression and genetic programming to model coastal Louisiana land loss using remote sensing. In: American Society for Photogrammetry and Remote Sensing - ASPRS Annual Conference 2007, Tampa, Florida, pp. 1–8 (2007)
12. Cobos, C., Munoz, L., Mendoza, M., Leon Guzman, E., Herrera-Viedma, E.: Fitness function obtained from a genetic programming approach for web document clustering using evolutionary algorithms. In: Pavón, J., Duque-Méndez, N.D., Fuentes-Fernández, R. (eds.) IBERAMIA 2012. LNCS, vol. 7637, pp. 179–188. Springer, Heidelberg (2012). https://doi.org/10.1007/978-3-642-34654-5_19
13. Cobos, C., et al.: Clustering of web search results based on the cuckoo search algorithm and balanced Bayesian information criterion. Inf. Sci. (NY) **281**, 248–264 (2014)
14. Cobos, C., Duque, A., Bolaños, J., Mendoza, M., León, E.: Algorithm for clustering of web search results from a hyper-heuristic approach. In: Pichardo-Lagunas, O., Miranda-Jiménez, S. (eds.) MICAI 2016. LNCS, vol. 10062, pp. 285–316. Springer, Heidelberg (2017). https://doi.org/10.1007/978-3-319-62428-0_24
15. Li, S., Chen, X.: A new bare-soil index for rapid mapping developing areas using landsat 8 data. In: International Archives of the Photogrammetry, Remote Sensing and Spatial Information Sciences - ISPRS Archives, pp. 139–144. Copernicus GmbH (2014)
16. Kaggle Inc.: Planet: Understanding the Amazon from Space

# Driver's Drowsiness Detection Through Computer Vision: A Review

Muhammad Rizwan Ullah[1], Muhammad Aslam[2(✉)],
Muhammad Imran Ullah[3], and Martinez-Enriquez Ana Maria[4]

[1] Department of Computer Science, Superior University, Lahore, Pakistan
[2] Department of Computer Science, University of Engineering and Technology,
Lahore, Pakistan
maslam@uet.edu.pk
[3] Department of Electrical Engineering, COMSATS Institution of Information
Technology, Islamabad, Pakistan
[4] Department of Computer Science, CINVESTAV, Mexico City, Mexico

**Abstract.** Drowsiness and sleepiness of driver is an important cause of road accident on expressways, highways, and motorways. These accidents not only results in economic loss but may also in physical injuries, which could result permanent disability or even death. The aim of this research is to minimize this cause of road accidents. Safe driving requirement is unavoidable and to attain this, driver's drowsiness detection system is to be incorporate in vehicles. Drowsiness detection using vehicle-based, physiological, and behavioral change measurement system is possible with embedded pros and cons. Advancements in the field of image processing and development of faster and cheaper processors direct researches to focus on behavioral change measurement system for drowsiness detection. Computer vision based drowsiness detection is possible by closely monitoring the drowsiness symptoms like eye blinking intervals, yawning, eye closing duration, head position etc. The presented paper deals with merits and demerits of the drowsiness symptoms measurement mechanism and computer vision based drowsiness detection systems. The conclusion of the research is that by designing a hybrid computer vision based drowsy driver detection system dependability achieved. The proposed system is non-intrusive in nature and helpful in attaining safer roads by limiting potential accidental threat due to driver drowsiness.

**Keywords:** Drowsiness detection · Computer vision · Image processing
Eye blinking · Yawning · PERCLOS

## 1 Introduction

Transport systems are an essential part of human activities. Growth in roads infrastructures, advancements in vehicles and development of road safety laws are intend to reduce road accidents [1]. However according to a report published by WHO, death count of 1.25 million people per annum on road accidents has not reduced [2]. Changes in our lifestyle resulted in increased number of traffic accidents due to driver's drowsiness or sleepiness [3, 4]. National Highway Traffic Safety Administration

© Springer Nature Switzerland AG 2018
F. Castro et al. (Eds.): MICAI 2017, LNAI 10633, pp. 272–281, 2018.
https://doi.org/10.1007/978-3-030-02840-4_22

(NHTSA) estimates that approximately 25% of police reported accidents involves driver fatigue [5].

According to a study by the Sleep Research Center (UK), driver drowsiness causes up to 20% of accidents on monotonous roads [6]. While designing any vehicle, comfort zone and safety are the main factors and due to these comfort environment in the vehicle driver can go in sleeping mode [7]. In this situation of driver's drowsiness, the safety concerns are not properly address. To reduce this problem and to negate the deadly accidents, the driver continuous monitoring is required [8–10].

Different techniques have been reported for the detection of driver's drowsiness [11–13]. Subjective technique cannot be use in a real driving situation but is helpful in simulations for determining drowsiness [14]. Psychological signals like electrocardiogram (ECG), electroencephalogram (EEG), Electrooculography (EOG) can be utilize for drowsiness detection. A technique based on a psychological signal is more reliable [9, 15–17]. Vehicle movement based detection is another technique. Here information is obtain from sensors attached with steering wheel, acceleration pedal and/or body of the vehicle [11, 18, 19]. Signals collected from sensors are continuously monitor for the identification of noticeable variation in order to detect driver's drowsiness.

This paper is outlined as follows: Sect. 2 describes general drowsiness detection techniques. Computer vision based driver's drowsiness detection is presented in Sect. 3. Section 4 is for discussion on the prevailing drowsiness detection techniques and finally Sect. 5 concludes the paper.

## 2   General Techniques for Drowsiness Detection

A drowsy person behave differently and can be distinguished through visual monitoring. Computer vision based measurement of the driver's eye motion, eye blinking, head motion and/or head position utilized for the detection in Visual technique. A summary is presented in Table 1.

**Table 1.** Classification of drowsiness detection techniques.

| Category | Measurement | Characteristics |
|---|---|---|
| Subjective | Through questioners by professional | A well-defined reference developed by expert |
| Psychological | EEG, ECG, EoG etc. | Measurement through sensors attached with driver |
| Vehicular | Steering wheel movement, Acceleration, Lateral distance, etc. | Measurement with sensors attached to the vehicle |
| Visual | Eye blinking per minute, Yawning, Head pose, Head motion, etc. | Computer vision based measurement of the driver's behavior |

## 2.1  Subjective Measure Technique

Subjective measurement of level of drowsiness estimated on driver's personal judgment. Many scales devised but most commonly used drowsiness scale is the Karolinska Sleepiness Scale (KSS) [20]. This technique is essential for the measurement of drowsiness and helpful in defining the threshold level for any other drowsiness detection systems.

Rumagit et al. used real time driving simulator for drowsiness detection using eye gaze and correlate with KSS for evaluation [21]. A roadside test was designed to measure driver's fitness for continue driving [22]. At measurement site, volunteer drivers were stopped for the test, work-sleep data collection and KSS. Results obtained and information gathered were utilized to establish correlation and effectiveness of the test devised by Forsman et al. Jackson et al. utilized KSS for conformation of drowsiness association with slow eyelid closure with increased frequency and duration [23].

## 2.2  Psychological Measure Technique

For alertness and drowsiness stages, physiological signals are different. Taking advantage of this variation, psychological measures are taken with the help of dedicated sensors for the detection of drowsiness. A tabular survey on drowsiness detection with psychological technique is presented in Table 2.

**Table 2.**  Previous work on physiological drowsiness detection.

| Ref. | Sensors | Preprocessing | Feature extraction |
|------|---------|---------------|--------------------|
| [28] | EEG, ECG, EoG | Optimal wavelet packet, Fuzzy wavelet packet | The fuzzy MI-based Wavelet-packet algorithm |
| [29] | ECG | Band pass filter | Fast Fourier Transform (FFT) |
| [30] | EEG | Independent component analysis, Decomposition | Fast Fourier Transform (FFT) |
| [31] | EoG, EMG | Filtering & Thresholding | Neighborhood search |

Eye movement detection through EoG signal to identify drowsiness was utilized by many researchers. In this technique, the eye orientation monitored through electric field generation by the potential difference between cornea and retina of the eye [24]. Disposable electrodes at outer corner of each eye and one electrode at forehead are utilized to pick Rapid eye movements (REM) and Slow Eye Movements (SEM) signals [25]. REM and SEM occur when the driver is awake and drowsy respectively.

The Heart Rate (HR) significant variation between different drowsiness stages, make it a vital sign. HR easy determination through ECG is well understood technique [26]. Another important information from ECG, Heart Rate Variability (HRV) which is the ratio of Low Frequency (LF) and High Frequency (HF) is of great interest. HRV decreases as the drowsiness rating increases on KSS [27].

Row physiological signals are prone to noises and artifacts due vehicle movement. Therefore, an effective filtering technique is a must requirement before processing a physiological signal [32]. Statistical features are extracted, using various feature extraction techniques like Discrete Wavelet Transform (DWT) and Fast Fourier Transform (FFT), before further analysis [33]. Finally, Artificial Neural Networks (ANN) [34], Linear Discriminant Analysis (LDA), or other similar analysis were utilized for the drowsiness detection.

Physiological signals usage for drowsiness detection is accurate and reliable compared with other methods. However, physiological signals measurement is intrusive [28]. Some researchers have investigated wireless technology for minimizing the intrusiveness. Some other researchers, eliminate the intrusiveness by putting sensors on the steering, on the cost of bearable errors due to improper electrode contact, considering the importance of user friendliness [27].

### 2.3 Vehicle Movement Based Techniques

An indirect way to measure driver drowsiness is through vehicle-based measurements. In this technique, sensors are attached with some part of the vehicle like steering wheel and/or acceleration pedal. Signals collected from the sensors are analyzed for drowsiness detection. Steering wheel based drowsiness measurement is presented by Jung et al. [27]. Relatively larger variations in driving speed due to sleep deprivation was investigated [19].

Steering Wheel Movement (SWM) measurement using steering angle sensor is widely used for determining the level of driver drowsiness. Many researchers establish that normal drivers make more steering wheel reversals than sleep deprived drivers [35]. Lane change effect is cancelled out by considering only small movement (0.5° to 5°) of the steering wheel [36]. Hence, small SWMs make driver drowsiness detection possible. SWMs are greatly dependent on road geometry and it limit its usefulness.

Standard Deviation of Lane Position (SDLP) has gained the interest of researchers due to its simplicity and usefulness for drowsiness detection. SDLP is measured through software in the simulation environment and lane position is tracked through external camera in the field experiment [37]. Through experimental verification, Ingre et al. established a direct relationship between SDLP and KSS [38]. However, above experiment reveals poor correlation due to significant difference between selected subjects. Furthermore, SDLP is dependable on external factors like climate, lighting and road marking.

## 3 Computer Vision and Drowsiness Detection

Drowsiness never comes instantly but appear with visually noticeable symptoms. These symptoms generally appear even well before drowsiness in every driver. These includes Eye closing for longer time, High eye blinking rate, Heavy eyelids, Rubbing eyes, Yawing, Head nodding, Inability to focus and Hard to concentrate.

## 3.1  Template Matching Technique

In this technique, a template image presence in a larger image is checked through comparison. The template is an already stored image, especially selected for the comparison purpose. Both close and open eye templates are provided to the system. The system use pictures from the video to check the states of the eyes, calculate eyes closure time and compare with a predefined time for sleepiness and eye-blinking [39].

This technique of template matching is easy and simple, so most of researchers have used this technique. Bergasa et al. used this technique and confirms its effectiveness for drowsiness detection [40]. For faster eyes detection, adoption of Kalman filter algorithm was investigated by Tang et al. and ended up with promising results [41].

## 3.2  Eye Blinking Technique

This technique detects the level of drowsiness and sleepiness by calculating the eye blinking rate and eye closure duration. The reason is that when a driver felt drowsy, his/her eye blinking rate and gaze between eyelids are different from normal situations. Using eye blinking rate drowsiness detection methodology is presented in Fig. 1 where eye-blinking classification is carried out through computer vision.

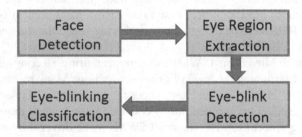

**Fig. 1.**  Computer vision based eye blinking classification

Ahmad and Borole monitor the position of irises and eye states in the technique [42]. They placed a camera at a suitable place in the vehicle and acquire video. Then by applying computer vision techniques to sequentially localize face, eyes and eyelids positions to measure ratio of closure.

## 3.3  PERCLOS Technique

PERCLOS means percentage of time eye closed in a given period. To sense the level of drowsiness PERCLOS is a well-known parameter. Yan et al. [43] consider that a human blinks once every 5 s on average that is 12 times blinks per minute. They tried gray-scale conversion and template matching for extracting data.

## 3.4  Yawning Technique

One of an important sign of fatigue is yawn. It is assume with a large vertical mouth opening compared. As compared to speaking, mouth is widely open in yawning process. Bhandari et al. detected yawn by face and then mouth tracking [44]. After yawn detection, the system alarms the driver.

# 4  Discussion and Recommendations

There are numerous techniques for drowsiness detection with embedded pros and cons. Each detection technique comes under a category depending upon the detection methodology and/or sensors used. The advantages and limitations of each category of drowsiness detection are presented in Table 3. The subjective technique, with real-time implementation limitation, is the simplest and provide basis for categorizing drowsiness. Psychological are promising with trustworthiness but embedded intrusiveness needed to be addressed without compromising reliability.

Table 3. Advantages and limitations of different techniques.

| Refs. | Category | Advantages | Limitations |
|---|---|---|---|
| [20–23] | Subjective | Simple, no sensors and no equipment | Not possible in real time |
| [28–31] | Psychological | Reliable, accurate, early detection | Intrusive, expensive |
| [19, 27, 35 38] | Vehicular | Non-intrusive, Ease of use, small sensors and moderate processing | Unreliable, late detection |
| [39–44] | Visual | Non-intrusive, Ease of use, proven hardware | Lighting conditions, background, tough threshold setting |

Vehicular based detection solved intrusiveness issue but not reliable due to late detection. Now comes the computer vision based technique which is non-intrusive, easy to implement due to major advancements in the field including immense processing power.

Only few researchers have tried combining computer vision based detection with other technique. Tran et al. [45] combine visual and vehicular technique. They focused on eye behavior for extraction of facial expression and extract SWM as vehicular technique. Lee and Chung [46] combined the visual and psychological techniques for drowsy driver detection. An android based smart phone is utilized to process data extracted from the wireless sensors. Video sensor and a bio-signal sensor captures the driver image and photoplethysmography (PPG) signal. Dynamic Bayesian network integrate the two features for more authentic driver's fatigue detection.

Nakamura et al. [47] faced the problem that some of the selected drivers did not show significant facial change of expression in their experiment. Their suggestion to overcome the shortfall is the use of EEG signal especially alpha channel. Authors proposed hybrid drowsiness detection is presented in Fig. 2. Here after detecting the eyes, two separate algorithms are used, one for PERCLOS and the other for eye-closing duration. Drowsiness detection in either case triggers the alarm for driver and co-passengers.

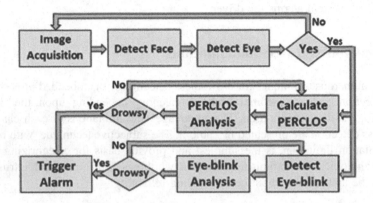

**Fig. 2.** Proposed hybrid drowsiness detection using image processing

In this paper, a comprehensive review of various methods to detect drowsiness while driving is presented. This article mainly focuses on computer vision based techniques. It is intended for the development of a new hybrid algorithm to eliminate the drawbacks of discussed methods.

## 5   Conclusion

Every year thousands of people died in road accidents. Mostly, the accident occurs due to the drowsiness of the driver. Such causes can be avoided by exploiting the advanced technology. The progress in the field of image processing and computer vision made it possible to detect the drowsiness of the driver by monitoring drowsiness visual symptoms. The paper is a comprehensive review on various methods to detect drowsiness with the focus on computer vision based detection. It is intended that computer vision based detection of the hybrid symptoms eliminate the drawbacks of discussed techniques. The proposed system is more reliable and dependable for driver drowsiness detection. It is non-intrusive in its nature. A reasonable number of road accidents are preventable with the use of computer vision based drowsiness detection.

## References

1. World Health Organization: Global status report on road safety 2015. World Health Organization (2015)
2. Peden, M., Toroyan, T., Krug, E., Iaych, K.: The status of global road safety: the agenda for sustainable development encourages urgent action. J. Australas. Coll. Road Saf. **27**, 37 (2016)

3. Arvind, P.D., Jivaji, M.J., Romi, K., Kamble, P.: Accident informer and prevention system. Int. J. Eng. Sci. **7**, 4772 (2017)
4. Murata, A., Urakami, Y., Moriwaka, M.: An attempt to prevent traffic accidents due to drowsy driving-prediction of drowsiness by Bayesian estimation. In: 2014 Proceedings of the SICE Annual Conference (SICE), pp. 1708–1715. IEEE (2014)
5. Ahmed, R., Emon, K.E.K., Hossain, M.F.: Robust driver fatigue recognition using image processing. In: 2014 International Conference on Informatics, Electronics & Vision (ICIEV), pp. 1–6. IEEE (2014)
6. Gonçalves, M., et al.: Sleepiness at the wheel across Europe: a survey of 19 countries. J. Sleep Res. **24**, 242–253 (2015)
7. Toda, T., Suzuki, K., Chen, G., Takami, I.: Robust control of active suspension—Improvement of ride comfort and driving stability using half car model. In: 2015 54th Annual Conference of the Society of Instrument and Control Engineers of Japan (SICE), pp. 548–553. IEEE (2015)
8. Borghini, G., Astolfi, L., Vecchiato, G., Mattia, D., Babiloni, F.: Measuring neurophysiological signals in aircraft pilots and car drivers for the assessment of mental workload, fatigue and drowsiness. Neurosci. Biobehav. Rev. **44**, 58–75 (2014)
9. Correa, A.G., Orosco, L., Laciar, E.: Automatic detection of drowsiness in EEG records based on multimodal analysis. Med. Eng. Phys. **36**, 244–249 (2014)
10. Jo, J., Lee, S.J., Park, K.R., Kim, I.J., Kim, J.: Detecting driver drowsiness using feature-level fusion and user-specific classification. Expert Syst. Appl. **41**, 1139–1152 (2014)
11. Saini, V., Saini, R.: Driver drowsiness detection system and techniques: a review. Int. J. Comput. Sci. Inf. Technol. **5**, 4245–4249 (2014)
12. Viljoen, E., Visser, J., Koen, N., Musekiwa, A.: A systematic review and meta-analysis of the effect and safety of ginger in the treatment of pregnancy-associated nausea and vomiting. Nutr. J. **13**, 20 (2014)
13. Veenendaal, A., Daly, E., Jones, E., Gang, Z., Vartak, S., Patwardhan, R.S.: Multi-view point drowsiness and fatigue detection. Comput. Sci. Emerg. Res. J. **2** (2014)
14. Murata, A., Naitoh, K., Karwowski, W.: A method for predicting the risk of virtual crashes in a simulated driving task using behavioural and subjective drowsiness measures. Ergonomics **60**, 714–730 (2017)
15. Dissanayaka, C., et al.: Comparison between human awake, meditation and drowsiness EEG activities based on directed transfer function and MVDR coherence methods. Med. Biol. Eng. Comput. **53**, 599–607 (2015)
16. Nguyen, T., Ahn, S., Jang, H., Jun, S.C., Kim, J.G.: Utilization of a combined EEG/NIRS system to predict driver drowsiness. Sci. Rep. **7**, 43933 (2017)
17. Wu, D., Lawhern, V.J., Gordon, S., Lance, B.J., Lin, C.-T.: Driver drowsiness estimation from EEG signals using online weighted adaptation regularization for regression (OwARR). IEEE Trans. Fuzzy Syst. **25**, 1522–1535 (2016)
18. Wang, X., Xu, C.: Driver drowsiness detection based on non-intrusive metrics considering individual specifics. Accid. Anal. Prev. **95**, 350–357 (2016)
19. Lawoyin, S., Fei, D.-Y., Bai, O.: Accelerometer-based steering-wheel movement monitoring for drowsy-driving detection. Proc. Inst. Mech. Eng. Part D: J. Automob. Eng. **229**, 163–173 (2015)
20. Åkerstedt, T., Hallvig, D., Kecklund, G.: Normative data on the diurnal pattern of the Karolinska sleepiness scale ratings and its relation to age, sex, work, stress, sleep quality and sickness absence/illness in a large sample of daytime workers. J. Sleep Res. **26**, 559–566 (2017)

21. Rumagit, A.M., Akbar, I.A., Igasaki, T.: Gazing time analysis for drowsiness assessment using eye gaze tracker. Telkomnika: J. Telecomun. Comput. Electron. Control 15(2), 919–925 (2017)

22. Forsman, P., Pyykkö, I., Toppila, E., Hæggström, E.: Feasibility of force platform based roadside drowsiness screening–a pilot study. Accid. Anal. Prev. 62, 186–190 (2014)

23. Jackson, M.L., et al.: The utility of automated measures of ocular metrics for detecting driver drowsiness during extended wakefulness. Accid. Anal. Prev. 87, 127–133 (2016)

24. Zhu, X., Zheng, W.-L., Lu, B.-L., Chen, X., Chen, S., Wang, C.: EOG-based drowsiness detection using convolutional neural networks. In: IJCNN, pp. 128–134 (2014)

25. Cona, F., Pizza, F., Provini, F., Magosso, E.: An improved algorithm for the automatic detection and characterization of slow eye movements. Med. Eng. Phys. 36, 954–961 (2014)

26. Chui, K.T., Tsang, K.F., Chi, H.R., Ling, B.W.K., Wu, C.K.: An accurate ECG-based transportation safety drowsiness detection scheme. IEEE Trans. Industr. Inf. 12, 1438–1452 (2016)

27. Jung, S.-J., Shin, H.-S., Chung, W.-Y.: Driver fatigue and drowsiness monitoring system with embedded electrocardiogram sensor on steering wheel. IET Intell. Transport Syst. 8, 43–50 (2014)

28. Khushaba, R.N., Kodagoda, S., Lal, S., Dissanayake, G.: Driver drowsiness classification using fuzzy wavelet-packet-based feature-extraction algorithm. IEEE Trans. Biomed. Eng. 58, 121–131 (2011)

29. Patel, M., Lal, S.K., Kavanagh, D., Rossiter, P.: Applying neural network analysis on heart rate variability data to assess driver fatigue. Expert Syst. Appl. 38, 7235–7242 (2011)

30. Lin, F.-C., Ko, L.-W., Chuang, C.-H., Su, T.-P., Lin, C.-T.: Generalized EEG-based drowsiness prediction system by using a self-organizing neural fuzzy system. IEEE Trans. Circ. Syst. I Regul. Pap. 59, 2044–2055 (2012)

31. Hu, S., Zheng, G.: Driver drowsiness detection with eyelid related parameters by support vector machine. Expert Syst. Appl. 36, 7651–7658 (2009)

32. Chen, L.-L., Zhao, Y., Zhang, J., Zou, J.Z.: Automatic detection of alertness/drowsiness from physiological signals using wavelet-based nonlinear features and machine learning. Expert Syst. Appl. 42(21), 7344–7355 (2015)

33. Silveira, T.D., Kozakevicius, A.D.J., Rodrigues, C.R.: Drowsiness detection for single channel EEG by DWT best m-term approximation. Res. Biomed. Eng. 31, 107–115 (2015)

34. Tabal, K.M.R., Caluyo, F.S., Ibarra, J.B.G.: Microcontroller-implemented artificial neural network for electrooculography-based wearable drowsiness detection system. In: Sulaiman, H.A., Othman, M.A., Othman, M.F.I., Rahim, Y.A., Pee, N.C. (eds.) Advanced Computer and Communication Engineering Technology. LNEE, vol. 362, pp. 461–472. Springer, Cham (2016). https://doi.org/10.1007/978-3-319-24584-3_39

35. Zhenhai, G., DinhDat, L., Hongyu, H., Ziwen, Y., Xinyu, W.: Driver drowsiness detection based on time series analysis of steering wheel angular velocity. In: 2017 9th International Conference on Measuring Technology and Mechatronics Automation (ICMTMA), pp. 99–101. IEEE (2017)

36. Otmani, S., Pebayle, T., Roge, J., Muzet, A.: Effect of driving duration and partial sleep deprivation on subsequent alertness and performance of car drivers. Physiol. Behav. 84, 715–724 (2005)

37. Liu, C.C., Hosking, S.G., Lenné, M.G.: Predicting driver drowsiness using vehicle measures: recent insights and future challenges. J. Saf. Res. 40, 239–245 (2009)

38. Ingre, M., Åkerstedt, T., Peters, B., Anund, A., Kecklund, G.: Subjective sleepiness, simulated driving performance and blink duration: examining individual differences. J. Sleep Res. 15, 47–53 (2006)

39. Królak, A., Strumiłło, P.: Eye-blink detection system for human–computer interaction. Univ. Access Inf. Soc. **11**, 409–419 (2012)
40. Bergasa, L.M., Nuevo, J., Sotelo, M.A., Barea, R., Lopez, M.E.: Real-time system for monitoring driver vigilance. IEEE Trans. Intell. Transp. Syst. **7**, 63–77 (2006)
41. Tang, X., Zhou, P., Wang, P.: Real-time image-based driver fatigue detection and monitoring system for monitoring driver vigilance. In: 2016 35th Chinese on Control Conference (CCC), pp. 4188–4193. IEEE (2016)
42. Ahmad, R., Borole, J.: Drowsy driver identification using eye blink detection. IJISET-Int. J. Comput. Sci. Inf. Technol. **6**, 270–274 (2015)
43. Yan, J.-J., Kuo, H.-H., Lin, Y.-F., Liao, T.-L.: Real-time driver drowsiness detection system based on PERCLOS and grayscale image processing. In: 2016 International Symposium on Computer, Consumer and Control (IS3C), pp. 243–246. IEEE (2016)
44. Bhandari, G., Durge, A., Bidwai, A., Aware, U.: Yawning analysis for driver drowsiness detection. Int. J. Eng. Res. Technol. **3**, 502–505 (2014)
45. Tran, D., Tadesse, E., Sheng, W., Sun, Y., Liu, M., Zhang, S.: A driver assistance framework based on driver drowsiness detection. In: 2016 IEEE International Conference on Cyber Technology in Automation, Control, and Intelligent Systems (CYBER), pp. 173–178. IEEE (2016)
46. Lee, B.-G., Chung, W.-Y.: Driver alertness monitoring using fusion of facial features and bio-signals. IEEE Sens. J. **12**, 2416–2422 (2012)
47. Nakamura, T., Maejima, A., Morishima, S.: Detection of driver's drowsy facial expression. In: 2013 2nd IAPR Asian Conference on Pattern Recognition (ACPR), pp. 749–753. IEEE (2013)

# Towards an Automatic Estimation of Skeletal Age Using $k - NN$ Regression with a Reduced Set of Tinny Aligned Regions of Interest

José Luis Tonatiúh Banda-Escobar[1], Salvador E. Ayala-Raggi[1(✉)],
Aldrin Barreto-Flores[1], Susana Sánchez-Urrieta[1],
José Francisco Portillo-Robledo[1], Alinne Michelle Sánchez-Tomay[1],
and Verónica Edith Bautista-López[2]

[1] Facultad de Ciencias de la Electrónica,
Benemérita Universidad Autónoma de Puebla, Av. San Claudio and 18 sur,
Col. Jardines de San Manuel, C.P. 72570 Puebla, Puebla, Mexico
tonatiuhbanda@gmail.com,
{saraggi,abarreto,surrieta,portillo}@ece.buap.mx,
michelle.stomay@correo.buap.mx
[2] Facultad de Ciencias de la Computación,
Benemérita Universidad Autónoma de Puebla, Av. San Claudio and 18 sur,
Col. Jardines de San Manuel, C.P. 72570 Puebla, Puebla, Mexico

**Abstract.** Human skeletal maturity has been typically estimated from radiographic images of the non-dominant hand through a subjective analysis performed by expert radiologists. In this paper we present a semi-automatic learning approach for estimating bone age. We consider five regions of interest, shortly *ROIs*, located between metacarpal and phalanges, which are obtained by placing strategic landmarks. *ROI* images are reshaped in the form of vectors which are merged in order to generate aligned feature vectors of each hand. The method consists of two stages, training and testing, for which radiographic images of female gender were used in a range of 1 to 18 years old. The training stage focuses on structuring the feature vectors of 300 bone-age-labeled images to generate a set of prototypes for a regression classifier. The second step is to approximate the bone age of a novel testing image, by computing its respective feature vector and comparing it with the set of prototypes. The age was determined using regression through a weighted $k - NN$ classifier. By using a set of 100 testing images, we demonstrate that it is possible to obtain an error comparable with state of the art algorithms by using only five small *ROIs* within the hand image.

**Keywords:** Skeletal maturity recognition · Bone age estimation
$k - NN$ regression · *ROI* alignment

© Springer Nature Switzerland AG 2018
F. Castro et al. (Eds.): MICAI 2017, LNAI 10633, pp. 282–293, 2018.
https://doi.org/10.1007/978-3-030-02840-4_23

# 1   Introduction

Bone age assessment, also known as skeletal maturity test, is a medical practice, commonly performed by radiologists, which provides important information for physicians from other areas who are looking for possible growth disorders. Typically, a radiographic image from the non-dominant hand (usually the left hand) is analyzed by the radiologist to accomplish the test. The useful range for bone age assessment is typically between 1 to 18 years because this is the most important period related to growth in children. Subsequently, after 18 years old the medical interest for estimating bone age decreases while changes in bone structure are small and less noticeable than at younger age.

The most common clinical methods for performing the bone age assessment are usually subjective because they are based on a visual comparison of the test radiographic image with a set of labeled standard images contained in a handbook [1]. In an attempt to reduce subjectivity, other methods like [2,3] are based on individually scoring different regions of different bones and then calculate a weighted sum in order to obtain the bone age. Although less subjective than the former method [1], the later [2] is time-consuming and impractical to perform on a day-to-day basis. Finally, the subjectivity inherent in the above traditional assessment methods causes the result to be different depending on the particular physician who performs it.

Inherent subjectivity present in traditional bone age assessment can be avoided by using computerized recognition approaches. Many of those approaches have been proposed [4-9]. Some of them work as expert systems and usually are based on extracting specific high level features from bones and comparing them with pre-established values defined by human experts [8]. Other approaches use again human defined high level features, but classification is carried out by machine learning methods that usually require a training stage based on a large set of examples [7,9,10].

In [9], Hsieh et al. calculate geometric features from *ROIs* defined over the Carpal bones for ages between 1 and 8 years, and propose an artificial neural network for estimating bone age. In [10], Giordano et al. automate the known clinical method from Tanner and Whitehouse [2] by applying image processing techniques to segment metaphysis, epiphysis, and diaphysis of bones and then calculate a feature vector composed by a reduced number of lengths and areas computed from those regions. Then, a classification algorithm based in hidden Markov models is used to estimate bone age.

In an attempt to develop pure machine-learning approaches, other authors like Spanpinato et al. [11] proposed not only to classify with known methods like neural networks, but to allow the machine to infer the classification features which better differentiate bone ages by using training examples. In a deep learning approach, they use a convolutional neural network to automatically learn features. Whole hand images are used and no special regions of interest are needed. Even though the accuracy of the above method is high (a MAE or Mean Absolute Error of 0.8 years), it must be mentioned that it requires a large amount of training images (1400 images taken from a data set described in [12]).

There is little work involving low-level features such as pixels. This happens because pixels in an image do not always represent the same place in the object to recognize. The same object in a second shot may have been displaced, rotated, scaled or even adopted another perspective. However, pixels can be used as classification features as long as images are properly aligned before carrying out the comparison. In [13] Ayala-Raggi et al. use the aligned appearance of the whole hand as a feature vector to be classified by a $k - NN$ regression classifier which computes bone age. An specially designed Active Appearance Model [14] for radiographic hand images, is computed to segment the test hand and align it to a *standard shape*. Then, it is compared with a data set of prototype aligned hands. Despite the method works (MAE of 1.8 years), we think the reduced data set they used is not enough to cope with the large number of features involved, the whole hand image is used to classify!.

In this paper, we show that by selecting a few, and very small, regions of interest, it is possible to reach a high accuracy in bone age estimation as long as those regions are properly aligned in scale and rotation.

According to [1, 2, 15] there are specific regions in a radiographic hand image that change markedly as the age changes. These regions are: 1. the carpal bones region, 2. the regions between metacarpal and proximal phalanges, and 3. the regions between proximal, middle and distal phalanges. Different methods for automatic bone age estimation use different regions. For instance, in [16] a total of 18 $ROIs$ are used, and 5 of these are the ones used by us. However, in [12], other 7 different $ROIs$ are utilized.

In this paper, we wanted to answer the question of whether it was possible to calculate bone age using only the five regions between metacarpal bones and proximal phalanges, which to our subjective opinion present a more noticeable appearance change, observed between 0 and 18 years, than the other regions.

In our work, pixels are used as low level features after a proper alignment of our small $ROI's$. We propose a simple but original method to compute the size (scale), of each $ROI$ based on the size of the hand in the image. Similarly, we also calculate a rotation angle in order to normalize $ROIs$ both in size and angle. Normalized $ROIs$ are merged to generate a feature vector.

## 2   System Overview

The proposed method for bone age estimation consists of two main stages: training and testing, as shown in Figs. 1 and 2. A pre-processing step is carried out in both training and testing stages as a first step before feature extraction. This step segments the hand in the picture, eliminates possible radiological markers and undesirable objects in the background, and finally adjusts the contrast of the images in order to homogenize them before entering the system.

A second step in both training and testing stages is a manually placement of the landmarks (points of interest) over strategic locations within radiographic image. The third step, also present in both stages, corresponds to segmentation and normalization in scale and angle of five $ROIs$ used to generate a feature vector.

Finally, the fourth step is different for training and testing. In training, we store the feature vector as an age-labeled prototype within a *prototypes* database. In testing, we use the feature vector as a test unlabeled prototype to be classified by a $k - NN$ regression classifier based on radial-basis functions. This regression classifier estimates bone age by regression from the age-labeled training prototypes stored during the training stage.

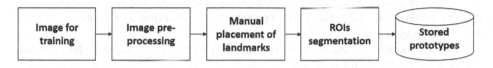

Fig. 1. Training stage.

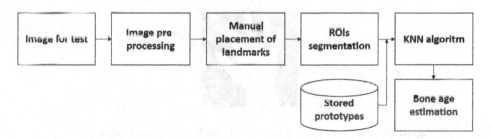

Fig. 2. Testing stage.

## 3   Image Pre-processing

Original radiographical images could be different each other, either by a different contrast or by intrusive objects or radiological markers present in the background surrounding the hand. In this section, we describe the two phases used for pre-processing radiological images.

### 3.1   Hand Segmentation

The contrast or intensity distribution in the $ROIs$ used in this paper must be adjusted in such a way that gray intensity of bone regions and gray intensity of background should be both the same two intensities in all images in our system so we can make comparisons between them. Since the $ROIs$ used in this paper are small regions located between metacarpal and phalangeal bones, then the amount of visible bone and background depend greatly on bone age. If the amount of visible bone is different in two images, we will obtain different gray intensities for bone and background when we apply the same contrast adjustment criterion to both images, for example an histogram equalization. In such a condition, it is not possible to compare the images satisfactorily.

In the whole hand image, even though the amount of bone is different for each bone age, this difference is much smaller and less noticeable than that present in our small selected *ROIs*. Therefore, instead of carrying out the contrast adjustment to each *ROI* separately, we decided to adjust the contrast to the whole hand images. However, the background surrounding the hand is not part of it, so we needed to segment the hand region in order to adjust the contrast only to this hand region.

Thus, a hand segmentation step is needed before carrying out the contrast adjustment of the hand region.

We use a variation of the *floodingfill* algorithm described in [17] to segment the hand's region. Once the hand is segmented, we use a binary mask such as that illustrated in Fig. 3 in order to make the contrast adjustment to that region.

**Fig. 3.** Example of a binary mask used for local contrast adjustment.

## 3.2   Contrast Adjustment

The binary image of the hand obtained in last section is used for adjusting the contrast only within the hand's region. We propose to perform this contrast adjustment by a using a simple linear mapping based on a *mean maximum* and a *mean minimum* values of the gray level intensities in the image. In order to calculate the *mean maximum* and a *mean minimum* values use compute first the mean $\mu$ and the standard deviation $\sigma$ of gray levels intensities. Then, the *mean maximum* can be calculated as $MeanMax = \mu + 1.5\sigma$ and the *mean minimum* as $MeanMin = \mu - 1.5\sigma$. From these two values it is possible to do a linear mapping of all the gray values to a new range between 0 and 255.

Figure 4 illustrates this process of contrast adjustment.

## 4   Manual Placement of Strategic Landmarks

In order to obtain five strategic *ROIs*, we propose a manual placement of 10 points of interest that we call *landmarks*, five of them located between proximal and intermediate phalanges, and the other five between metacarpal and proximal

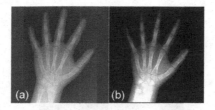

**Fig. 4.** Contrast adjustment of the hand's region. (a) Radiographical image with original contrast. (b) Radiographical image with corrected contrast

phalanges. The layout of the 10 landmarks is depicted in Fig. 5. In addition, we propose to locate the landmark exactly in the intermediate position between the bones where there is not some type of ossification, as is shown in Fig. 6.

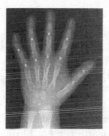

**Fig. 5.** Location of the 10 landmarks aimed to segment the proposed *ROIs*.

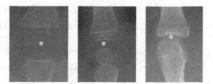

**Fig. 6.** Landmarks are located in the intermediate region where no ossification exists.

## 5   Segmenting *ROIs*

Once the process of placement of the landmarks is completed, the next step is segmenting the *ROIs*. In this paper we propose to use only five *ROIs* to determine bone age. The five landmarks located between proximal and intermediate phalanges are used just as a geometric reference aimed to be used for computing an inclination angle $\theta$ of the *ROI* with respect to the vertical, as shown in Fig. 7.

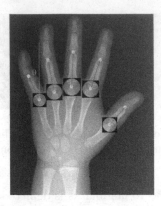

**Fig. 7.** Five *ROIs* used. Angle $\theta$ is computed by using the landmark location between proximal and intermediate phalanges in the same finger. The size or scale of the *ROI* is calculated using the distance between the two landmarks in the same finger multiplied by a constant factor.

The size of the *ROI* to segment is calculated based on the distance between the two landmarks in the same finger multiplied by a constant factor. We summarize the process for creating *ROIs* aligned in size and orientation in the following algorithm:

- Compute the distance between landmarks belonging to each finger.
- Multiply the distance by a parameter $D$. Thus, we obtain the size of the *ROI*.
- Segment the square *ROI* for each finger.
- Compute the angle $\theta$ between the vertical to the imaginary line between the two landmarks for each finger.
- Rotate each *ROI* so that the new angle $\theta$ is equal to zero.
- Resize each *ROI* to have a new size of $32 \times 32$
- Apply a circular binary mask to each *ROI* image ($diameter = 32$) in order to preserve only the same image pixels before the rotation.

Figure 8 shows the process already described. Once the five *ROIs* for a hand image are computed, the next step is to create a features vector or prototype which will be stored in a database or used as a test prototype for bone age estimation.

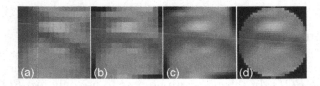

**Fig. 8.** The process of aligning and normalizing each *ROI*. (a) Inicial *ROI*. (b) Rotated *ROI*. (c) Resized *ROI*. (d) Masked *ROI*

# 6    Creating a Features Vector or Prototype

The prototype is created by reshaping or vectorizing each one of the five *ROIs* in such a way that its new size is $1 \times 1024$ (lines by columns) instead of $32 \times 32$. The five *line* vectors are then concatenated to form only one *line* vector with size of $1 \times 5120$. During the training stage, prototypes are stored, and each one is labeled with its corresponding actual bone age from the database. During testing, the created prototype will be analyzed by a $k - NN$ regression classifier to estimate its bone age.

# 7    $k - NN$ Regression Classifier

Bone age is finally estimated by a simple $k - NN$ regression classifier similar to the classifier used in [13], where ages of the nearest $k$ neighbors are weighted by a factor which depends on the Euclidean distance $d$ between the test prototype and each neighbor, and it is calculated as:

$$W_i = exp\frac{-d_i^2}{2\alpha^2}$$

where $\alpha$ is the smallest distance $(d_i)$ divided by 2. Finally, the estimated bone age is

$$age = \frac{\sum_{i=1}^{K} W_i BA_i}{\sum_{i=1}^{K} W_i}$$

where $(BA_i)$ are the respective bone ages of the $k$ prototypes.

# 8    Setup and Results

We used the public data set described in [12], which contains 1391 X-ray left-hand images of children of age up to 18 years old. These images have been evaluated for bone age by two different experts. Images in the data set are divided by gender (males and females) and by race (asian, afro-american, hispanic, and caucasic). Regarding race, in our approach, images were randomly mixed. In order to generate balanced training and testing sets, from each gender in the original dataset, we taken 300 images balanced in age and race for training, and other 100 different images balanced in age and race for testing. Therefore, a total of 800 images were used in our work.

## 8.1    Resizing the Original Images

Because the original images in the data set are different in size. Usually the vertical dimension (*lines*) is 256 and the horizontal dimension (*columns*) is less than 256 but not always the same. Then, we cropped the central part of images (where the hand is located) and merged two lateral bands which color was calculated from the pixels in each lateral edge of the cropped image. The final was a $256 \times 256$ image.

## 8.2    Estimating Bone Age

We tested our system for males and females separately using 100 test images with ages and races randomly mixed. Figure 9 shows two histograms of bone age for both test sets (males and females), showing a balance in age suitable for demonstrating the capability of our algorithm for estimating bone age independently of age and ethnicity.

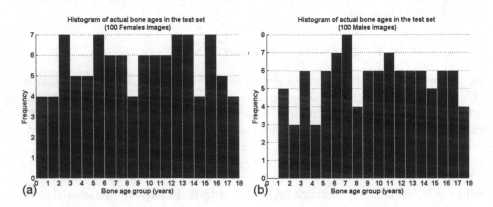

**Fig. 9.** Histograms of actual bone ages of the images used for testing (100 for each group). (a) Histogram for the female set. (b) Histogram for the male set.

300 images, different to those used for testing, of all ethnicities and ages were used for training. Each image was manually labeled with the 10 landmarks, and a prototype vector was created for each one. We test our system by computing the mean absolute error $MAE$ between the a vector formed with the 100 actual bone ages and a vector formed with 100 estimated bone ages returned by the system. Similarly, we computed the square root of the mean square error calculated between the above vectors.

The test was performed varying $k$ from $k = 2$ to $k = 26$, and we observed the best results in $k = 7$ for female images and $k = 10$ for male images as is shown in Fig. 10.

Finally, Fig. 11 illustrates graphically a comparison between actual bone ages and the estimated ones, sorted from lowest to highest. We observe in both plots a larger separation of actual and estimated age values just in the boundaries of the used age range, 0 and 18 years. The explanation could be the nature of $k - NN$ approach for *interpolating* but not for *extrapolating* ages.

Table 1 shows reported errors for different methods found in literature. In our case, by averaging MAE for females and MAE for males, we obtained a $MAE = 0.95$ years.

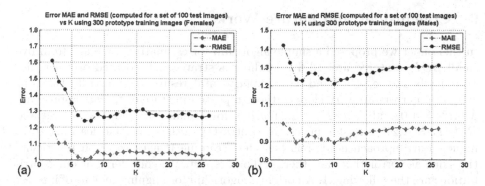

**Fig. 10.** Age error with 300 training images for each set of 100 test images, and varying $k$ parameter in $k - NN$ algorithm. (a) Age error (years) as a function of $k$ (females). (b) Age error (years) as a function of $k$ (males)

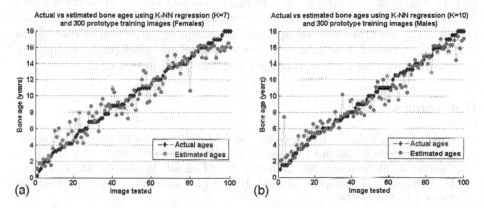

**Fig. 11.** Actual bone age vs estimated bone age, using 300 training prototypes and 100 test images where actual bone age was sorted from lowest to highest. $k$ is the optimum value for each group. (a) Actual bone age vs estimated bone age (females). (b) Actual bone age vs estimated bone age (males).

**Table 1.** Methods found in literature

| Method | Dataset | MAE (years) |
|---|---|---|
| Our proposed | Digital hand atlas database system [12] | * 0.95 |
| Ayala-Raggi et al. [13] | Imagen exakta laboratories (165 images) | 1.8 |
| Spampinato et al. [11] | Digital hand atlas database system [12] | 0.8 |
| Giordano et al. [10] | Private dataset (360 images) | 0.41 |

## 9   Conclusions and Future Work

In this paper we proposed a simple algorithm for estimating bone age from five small *ROIs* centered around five landmarks strategically located over a radiographically image of a hand. Our experimental results demonstrate that our estimation errors are very close to those reported in state of the art approaches $MAE = 1.0$ and $RMSE = 1.24$ *years* for females and $MAE = 0.89$ and $RMSE = 1.21$ years for males. In contrast to other machine learning techniques, our approach needs relatively few training images to reach practically the same age error that the other methods report. We consider that our contributions are the following: 1. An original algorithm for aligning regions of interest inside radiographical images. Our method calculates the size of the *ROIs* to be segmented based on the relative positions of the placed landmarks. Then, normalizes (in angle and scale) the *ROIs* in order to be used in the creation of feature vectors. 2. An original way to create aligned vectors of features useful for successful classification. 3. A way for obtaining consistent and discriminant classification features based on applying an adequate correction of contrast to the images involved. Finally, as a future work, we are developing a completely automatic algorithm for detecting the landmarks used in this work.

## References

1. Greulich, W., Pyle, S.: Radiographic Atlas of Skeletal Development of Hand and Wrist, 2nd edn. Standford University Press, Palo Alto (1971)
2. Tanner, J., Whitehouse, R., Cameron, N., Marshall, W., Healy, M., Goldstein, H.: Maturity and Prediction of Adult Height (TW2 Method), 2nd edn. Academic Press, London (1975)
3. Molinari, L., Gasser, T., Largo, R.: TW3 bone age: RUS/CB and gender differences of percentiles for score and score increments. Ann. Hum. Biol. **31**(4), 421–435 (2004)
4. Adeshina, S.A., Cootes, T.F., Adams, J.E.: Evaluating different structures for predicting skeletal maturity using statistical appearance models. In: Proceedings of the MIUA (2009)
5. Aja-Fernández, S., de Luis-Garcia, R., Martin-Fernandez, M.A., Alberola-López, C.: A computational TW3 classifier for skeletal maturity assessment. A computing with words approach. J. Biomed. Inf. **37**, 99–107 (2004)
6. Cunha, P., Moura, D.C., López, M.A.G., Guerra, C., Pinto, D., Ramos, I.: Impact of ensemble learning in the assessment of skeletal maturity. J. Med. Syst. **38**, 87 (2014)
7. Liu, H., et al.: Bone age pre-estimation using partial least squares regression analysis with a priori knowledge. In: 2014 IEEE International Symposium on Medical Measurements and Applications, MeMeA 2014, Lisboa, Portugal, 11–12 June 2014, pp. 164–167 (2014)
8. Niemeijer, M., van Ginneken, B., Maas, C., Beek, F., Viergever, M.: Assessing the skeletal age from a hand radiograph: automating the tanner-whitehouse method. In: Sonka, M., Fitzpatrick, J. (eds.) SPIE Medical Imaging, vol. 5032, pp. 1197–1205. SPIE, Bellingham (2003)

9. Hsieh, C.W., Jong, T.L., Chou, Y.H., Tiu, C.M.: Computerized geometric features of carpal bone for bone age estimation. Chin. Med. J. **120**(9), 767–770 (2007)
10. Giordano, D., Kavasidis, I., Spampinato, C.: Modeling skeletal bone development with hidden markov models. Comput. Methods Programs Biomed. **124**, 138–147 (2016)
11. Spampinato, C., Palazzo, S., Giordano, D., Aldinucci, M., Leonardi, R.: Deep learning for automated skeletal bone age assessment in x-ray images. Med. Image Anal. **36**, 41–51 (2017)
12. Gertych, A., Zhang, A., Sayre, J., Pospiech-Kurkowska, S., Huang, H.: Bone age assessment of children using a digital hand atlas. Comput. Med. Imaging Graph. **31**, 322–331 (2007). Computer-aided Diagnosis (CAD) and Image-guided Decision Support
13. Ayala-Raggi, S., Montoya, F., Barreto-Flores, A., Sánchez-Urrieta, S., Portillo-Robledo, J., Bautista-López, V.: A supervised incremental learning technique for automatic recognition of the skeletal maturity, or can a machine learn to assess bone age without radiological training from experts? Int. J. Pattern Recogn. Artif. Intell. (2017)
14. Cootes, T.F., Edwards, G.J., Taylor, C.J.: Active appearance models. IEEE Trans. Pattern Anal. Mach. Intell. **23**, 681–685 (2001)
15. Gilsanz, V., Ratib, O.: Hand Bone Age: A Digital Atlas Of Skeletal Maturity. Springer, Heidelberg (2005)
16. Kashif, M., Deserno, T.M., Haak, D., Jonas, S.: Feature description with SIFT, SURF, BRIEF, BRISK, or FREAK? A general question answered for bone age assessment. Comput. Biol. Med. **68**, 67–75 (2016)
17. Gonzalez, R.C., Woods, R.E.: Digital Image Processing, 3rd edn. Prentice-Hall Inc., Upper Saddle River (2006)

# Feature Selection from Image Descriptors Data for Breast Cancer Diagnosis Based on CAD

Laura A. Zanella-Calzada$^{(\boxtimes)}$, Carlos E. Galván-Tejada,
Jorge I. Galván-Tejada, and José M. Celaya-Padilla

Universidad Autónoma de Zacatecas, Unidad Académica de Ingeniería Eléctrica,
Jardín Juárez 147 Centro, Zacatecas, Mexico
lzanellac@uaz.edu.mx

**Abstract.** Breast cancer is an important public health problem worldwide among women. Its early detection generally increase the survival
rate of patients, however, is one of the biggest deficiencies to the present.
The purpose of this paper is to obtain a model capable of classifying
benign and malign breast tumors, using a public dataset composed by
features extracted from mammography images, obtained from the Breast
Cancer Digital Repository initiative. Multivariate and univariate models
were constructed using the machine learning algorithm based on CAD,
Random Forest, applied to the images features. Both of the models were
statistical compared looking for the better model according to their fitness. Results suggest the multivariate model has a better prediction capability than the univariate model, with an AUC between 0.991 and 0.910,
however, they were found five specific descriptive features that can classify tumors with a similar fitness as the multivariate model, with AUCs
between 0.897 and 0.958.

**Keywords:** Breast cancer diagnosis · Tumor classification · CAD
Machine learning · Random forest

## 1 Introduction

Breast cancer disease continues being a global health problem. Is the most common type of cancer among women and it's especially increasing on developing
countries [1]. According to the World Health Organization (WHO), approximately 521,000 women deaths worldwide were associated to breast cancer in
2012 [2] and according to the Instituto Nacional de Estadística y Geografía
(INEGI), in 2012, 15 out of 100,000 female deaths were associated to the disease
in Mexico, being the second cause of death in women [3].

One of the biggest issues of this disease is late detection, which is an important fact on reducing the survival rates; localized cancer leads to a 5-year survival
rate of 97.5%, whereas cancer that has spread to different body organs has a 5-
year survival rate of only 20.4%. Another important fact of breast cancer is

F. Castro et al. (Eds.): MICAI 2017, LNAI 10633, pp. 294–304, 2018.
https://doi.org/10.1007/978-3-030-02840-4_24

associated to its prevention, which results almost impossible because its causes still remain unknown [4].

At the present time, the best non-invasive tools for breast cancer early detection are diagnostic images, among which is mammography screening. This method has proven to be effective in asymptomatic and symptomatic women over 40 years [5], by reducing breast cancer mortality rates by 30–70%. The problem with mammograms is that they can be difficult to interpret because the sensitivity can be affected by the quality of the image and the level of experience of the radiologist [6, 7].

Recent studies have implemented algorithms to improve the detection of breast cancer by computer-aided design (CAD) aiming to obtain a better prognosis for the patient [8, 9]. These algorithms normally use different descriptive cancer features; however, it hasn't been found a standard set of features that gives an accurate tumors classification [10].

This research presents the search for a multivariate model for the classification of tumors. The search is carried out on: mammography assessments, ultrasound images features, clinical history, lesion segmentation, and selected pre-computed image-based descriptors.

A related work that suggest CAD to improve mammograms reading was the proposed by Pathel et al., with a new method for breast image segmentation in order of early diagnosis of breast cancer based on detecting micro-calcifications and a computer based on a decision system. The paper developed an adaptive K-means clustering algorithm [11]; however, the K-means method could make the model susceptible to overfitting, which would induce a poor model accuracy. In the work of Dheeba et al., was proposed a CAD system to detect breast cancer in mammograms through optimized swarm intelligence by neural networks that detect cancer. The primary focus is the neural network optimization to improve the detection accuracy, proving that this method has a better behavior than others recent works [12]; the drawback with this method is that it presents a high computational cost due to the possible solutions given by the number of samples; causing the problem to become exponentially more complex related to more samples. Moreover, Ramani presented a new approach to classify masses in mammography images. The extraction of mammogram features was performed using Symlet, SVD and weighted histogram Naive Bayes, and the algorithms used to classify extracted features were random forest and neural networks [13]. In the work of Karahaliou et al., it was proposed a wavelet - based contrast enhancement method to find the texture descriptors extracted from mammograms which can contribute to cancer diagnosis. To validate the ability of texture features to discriminate malignant lesions from benign, it was used the K-nearest neighbor classifier. Finally, to know the performance it was considered the area under the curve (AUC) and the receiver operating characteristic (ROC), which shown promising results on the diagnosis of breast cancer based on CAD that may contribute to the reduction of unnecessary biopsies [14].

The main purpose of this work is to develop a classification model capable of distinguishing between malign and benign tumors as a tool for the medical specialist in the breast cancer diagnosis. The classification model was constructed in base on the machine learning algorithm, random forest (RF), comparing a multivariate and univariate approach, looking for the highest fitness. The results suggest the multivariate model has a better prediction capability than the univariate classification model.

The original contributions of this work is to provide a model with a reduce number of descriptive features extracted from mammography images with an accuracy to classify breast tumors of at least 90% in order to provide a tool as a second opinion to the medical specialist, seeking to reduce the number of misdiagnoses and to contribute to the early diagnosis of breast cancer by reducing the work of extracting features from mammography images and by making the evaluation process faster.

This paper is organized as follows: an introduction to the diagnosis of breast cancer through CAD based on features extracted from images is in Sect. 1. Section 2 explains the methods followed to study the behavior of the multivariate and univariate models obtained with CAD with the different characteristics of mammography. Experimentation is presented in Sect. 3. Results are presented in Sect. 4; discussions and conclusions of these results are presented in Sect. 5. Finally in Sect. 6 future work of this approach is presented.

## 2 Materials and Methods

In this section is presented the process carried out on the development and analysis of the multivariate and the univariate models. Multivariate model is composed by the entire descriptive image features from the database which was subjected to the machine learning algorithm RF, while univariate models were developed using logistic regression as cost function. All models are composed by different type of descriptive features that were extracted from mammograms images. The univariate models contain the most significant features of the multivariate model.

The multivariate model was validated with a K-folds strategy, being previously trained with 70% of the original dataset and then it was subjected to a blind test with the 30% of the remaining data.

Both of the models, multivariate and univariate, were subjected to a statistical analysis in order to know their quantitative capability to classify tumors and being compared later between them.

Firstly, is presented a description of the dataset and a description of the data analysis performed, ending with the models validation carried out.

### 2.1 Dataset Description

In this paper we use the public available dataset Breast Cancer Digital Repository (BCDR). BCDR is a binary class data set due to the initial Breast Imaging Report and Database System (BI-RADS) classification of the result of the biopsy (Benign vs Malign). The BCDR dataset is composed by Digital Mammography data set number 1 (BCDR-D01), a film mammography-based repository composed by 64 women, rendering 143 segmentations; and Digital Mammography data set number 2 (BCDR-D02), a full field digital mammography-based repository composed by 164 women, rendering 455 segmentations. Subjects are in an age range of $58 \pm 11$ years old, with a maximum of 89 and a minimum of 23 [15].

Both of datasets are composed by 79 biopsy-proven lesions, including clinical data and image-based descriptors. All lesions are nodules or a combination of nodules with other abnormalities. From each of the 598 segmentations a total of 38 features were extracted: 11 features were extracted from the clinical and general data, 6 features were extracted from the intensity descriptors computed directly from the gray-levels of the pixels inside the lesion's contour identified by the radiologists, 13 texture descriptors features were computed from the gray-level co-occurrence matrix related to the bounding box of lesion's contour, and finally 8 features related to the shape and location descriptors of the lesion.

The clinical and general features are: age, breast density, mammography nodule, mammography calcification, mammography microcalcification, mammography axillary adenopathy, mammography architectural distortion, mammography stroma distortion, classification, image view and mammography type. The intensity descriptors features are: mean, standard deviation, skewness, kurtosis, minimum and maximum intensity values. The texture descriptors features are: energy, contrast, correlation, sum of squares, variance, homogeneity, sum average, sum entropy, sum variance, difference entropy, information measure of correlation 1 and 2. The shape and location descriptors features are: area, perimeter, center of mass, circularity, elongation, form, solidity and extent.

## 2.2   Data Analysis

All the data analysis was realized in the open source environment software R (version 3.3.1 2016-06-21 "Bug in Your Hair") [16]. In this work, as mentioned before, an univariate and multivariate searches were conducted. The multivariate search was conducted using the complete set of 27 descriptive features being subjected to the machine learning algorithm, RF. Clinical and general data features were removed to conserve only the image descriptors features.

RF is a robust machine learning technique that can handle classification problems based on bagging and random feature selection. This algorithm uses an out-of-bag (OOB) error, an unbiased estimate of the true prediction error, in which as the forest is built, each tree can be tested on the samples not used in building tree. RF uses the package randomForest (version 4.6-12 2015-10-07). Breiman et al., demonstrated that estimating the OOB error has the same result as estimating the error using a test set of the same size as the training set [17].

For this multivariate search, the dataset was initially separated in two sets. The first set contained 70% of the data, selected for the training process of the model, while the set that contained 30% of the data was selected for the testing process.

The train dataset was subjected to the RF algorithm to know the capacity of the model for the breast tumors classification. Then, the test dataset was subjected to the same process to compare the robustness of the model. This search was conducted ten times for each dataset with the purpose to prove that independently of its random function, the model keep stable. For this process was used a seed to keep reproducibility of the experiment.

Finally, for the univariate search was used the logistic regression cost function for each of the multivariate model features independently, due to the binary nature of the Benign/Malign outcome variable, looking for the features that present the biggest contribution for the tumors classification and thus discard the rest.

### 2.3 Model Validation

In order to validate the multivariate model, an over-fit test was done using the test dataset which contain 30% of the data as a blind test. Then, a statistical validation was done for each dataset, train and test, in order to evaluate the model with the Area Under Curve (AUC), the Receiver Operating Characteristic (ROC) and ODDS ratio parameters.

Finally, each of the univariate models were subjected to the same statistical validation as multivariate, to evaluate their ability to classify tumors and to demonstrate that the features of these univariate models are enough to classify benign and malign tumors in breast, in terms of sensitivity and specificity, making unnecessary the use of all the 27 features of the database.

## 3   Experiments

In this section is presented the process carried out on the experimentation of each of the models behavior. Firstly, is presented the data preprocessing which represents the extraction of features that are unable to contribute with the study purpose, followed by the development of the multivariate and univariate models. Finally, is described the model validation to evaluate the contributions of the results.

In Fig. 1 a flowchart of the overall methodology is presented. The image acquisition, lesion segmentation and feature extraction were carried out by an expert radiologist, depositing the data in the repositories used for this work (Fig. 1(A)). Then, the data analysis was realized in order to develop the multivariate and univariate proposed models for the tumors classification (Fig. 1(B)). Finally, each model was subjected to a validation process to evaluate its contribution to classify benign and malign breast tumors (Fig. 1(C)).

### 3.1   Dataset Preprocessing

Clinical and general data have to be obtained only by the radiologist, since it contains personal information of the patient and information of the interpretation of the mammography images by the specialist, therefore, these 11 features were removed from the dataset because they were unnecessary for this analysis.

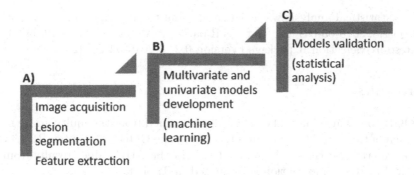

**Fig. 1.** Flowchart of the methodology followed. (A) Image acquisition realized by the radiologist (B) Models development (C) Models validation.

On the other hand, the dataset contained some missing values in the data, represented as Not a Number (NaN), which had to be imputed with the function $rfimput$ from the randomForest package. Additionally, a Z-Normalization was applied to avoid any outlier related problems. For this normalization, the whole data were subjected to the Eq. 1, where $x_i$ is the ith value of the feature $x$, $m(x)$ is the mean value of the feature values, $std(X)$ is the standard deviation value of the feature values and $z_i$ is the ith value of the Z-Norm feature z. As a result, all features mean is 0 and standard deviation is 1.

$$z_i = \frac{x_i - m(x)}{sdt(x)} \tag{1}$$

Later, were generated the train set and the test set, initially filtering the subjects with Benign outcome from the ones with Malign outcome (type of tumor) and each set was separated in two (70% and 30%) using an aleatory balanced selection. Then, both the sets containing 70% of the data were joined as were both sets containing 30% of the data.

The set containing 70% of the data (train set) was composed of 344 Benign outcomes and 75 Malign, while the set containing 30% of the data(test set) was composed of 147 Benign outcomes and 32 Malign.

### 3.2 Model Validation

The multivariate model was trained with the train set of the data and then was validated with a blind test using the test set or the 30% remaining data.

Later, a statistical analysis was performed on each of the models, obtaining the AUC, ROC and ODDS ratio, also the OOB error was obtained for the multivariate model. The AUC was calculated for each dataset (train and test) and model, for comparison. The OOB confidence interval error was obtained from the OOB value of ten RF realized with the purpose to prove that independently of its random function, the model keeps stable.

This statistical analysis was calculated using the packages: pROC R package (Version 1.8, 2015-05-04) [18], epitools R package (Version 0.5-7, 2012-09-30) [19] and ResourceSelection R package (Version 0.2-6, 2016-02-15) [20].

## 4    Results

The OOB confidence interval error results obtained from the multivariate model with each of the datasets (train and test) from the OOB value of ten RF (getting a variance error for the model under 1%) and the AUC values results from the statistical analysis information is presented in Table 1.

In Fig. 2(A), the ROC curve of the multivariate model with the train dataset is displayed, while in Fig. 2(B), the ROC curve with the test dataset is displayed.

**Table 1.** OOB error and AUC values results obtained from the multivariate model with the train and test datasets.

| Multivariate model | OOB error | AUC |
|---|---|---|
| Train dataset | 6.230% +/− 0.130% | 0.991 |
| Test dataset | 4.860% +/− 0.700% | 0.910 |

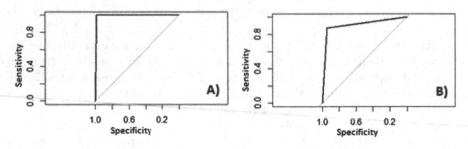

**Fig. 2.** ROC curves obtained from the multivariate model with each of the datasets. (A) Train dataset (B) Test dataset.

From the statistical analysis of the univariate model were obtained the AUC and ODD ratio values, and the ROC curves for each feature. From this results, the five most representative univariate models were extracted, according to their AUC values. The statistical information of these models is presented in Table 2. ROC curves for each of the univariate models are presented in Fig. 3; in Fig. 3(A) the ROC curve for the Correlation feature is shown, in Fig. 3(B) the ROC curve for the Area feature, in Fig. 3(C) the ROC curve for the Perimeter feature, in Fig. 3(D) the ROC curve for the Form feature and finally, in Fig. 3(E) the ROC curve for the Contrast feature.

**Table 2.** Results of statistical analysis obtained from the univariate models.

| Features | AUC |
|---|---|
| Correlation | 0.958 |
| Area | 0.948 |
| Perimeter | 0.937 |
| Form | 0.913 |
| Contrast | 0.897 |

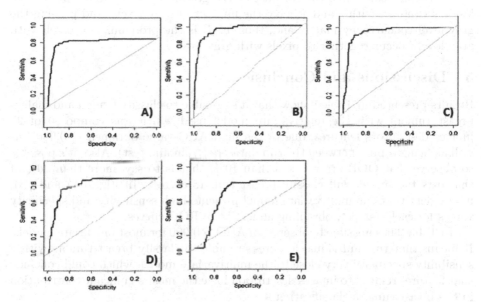

**Fig. 3.** ROC curves obtained from the univariate models with the best fitness. (A) Correlation feature (B) Area feature (C) Perimeter feature (D) Form feature (E) Contrast feature.

The features of each univariate model were obtained as follow:

$$Correlation = \frac{\sum_i \sum_j (ij)p(i,j) - \mu_x \mu_y}{\sigma_x \sigma_y} \qquad (2)$$

Equation 2 calculates the correlation of the segmented lesion, with $\mu_x$, $mu_y$, $\sigma_x$ and $\sigma_y$ being the means and standard deviations of $P_x$ and $P_y$, the partial probability density functions.

$$Area = |O| \qquad (3)$$

Equation 3 calculates the area of the segmented lesion, with $O$ being the set of pixels that belong to the segmented lesion.

$$Perimeter = length(E) \qquad (4)$$

Equation 4 calculates the perimeter of the segmented lesion, with $E$ being the edge pixels that belong to the segmented lesion.

$$Form = \frac{Perimeter * Elongation}{8 * Area} \tag{5}$$

Equation 5 calculates the form of the lesion's contour identified.

$$Contrast = \sum_i \sum_j (i - j)^2 p(i - j) \tag{6}$$

Equation 6 calculates the contrast of the gray-level of the bounding box of lesion's contour, with $i$ and $j$ being the number of gray levels, and p being the gray-level concurrency matrix and, thus, $p(ij)$ is the probability of pixels with gray-level $i$ occur together to pixels with gray-level $j$.

## 5   Discussions and Conclusions

Results presented in Table 1 show that it's possible to classify benign and malign breast tumors with the multivariate model used which was composed of 27 images descriptors features, due to the high AUC value obtained ($>0.900$), as well as being robust between the two datasets (train and test). Also, it's possible to observe that OOB error is less than 10%, that is to say, more than 90% of the tests the model will classify breast tumors correct. In Fig. 2(A) and (B), it's evident that the multivariate model presents high sensitivity and specificity values for each dataset, obtaining almost ideal ROC curves.

In Table 2 it's possible to observe an AUC $> 0.900$ for most univariate models. It means that this individual features are able to classify breast tumors with a sensibility-specificity very close to the multivariate model, which could conclude that features related to images description have the most significant contribution in the breast tumors classification.

Nevertheless, the disadvantaged is that most of the features of the univariate models presented in Table 2 are related to the tumor shape in the image, therefore they are dependent of the radiologist accuracy of delimiting the lesion segmentation. This presents a problem when using these characteristics to classify tumors, since obtaining the segmentations of different radiologists may induce errors.

On the other hand, the multivariate model through its analysis proved to be stable and to has a very small OOB variance error of 0.130% for the train dataset and 0.700% for the test dataset on its prediction to classify as shown in Table 1, which is acceptable in the maximum value under 1%. This demonstrate that there is not a dominant feature which can greatly affect the final result.

Finally, it can be proposed an emergent multivariate model, composed by the five features of the univariate models instead of the 27 features of the multivariate model, taking in consideration a cost-benefit analysis, since it's possible to have an error induced by the values obtained from the different radiologists but the features extraction work would be less, being necessary to extract only the five features of the model proposed, making the tumor classification easier and faster, obtaining a result with a considerable accuracy to be accepted as a second opinion after the medical specialist classification.

# 6   Future Work

From results presented in Sect. 4, it is possible to conclude that a deep feature selection could improve the final model accuracy and reducing the cost of extracting certain features of the mammography. Therefore, a feature analysis and selection must be carried on using several techniques of optimization, as genetics algorithms or a step wise feature selection. Also, contrasting between stochastic and deterministic feature selection approaches, searching for the technique that presents better prediction capabilities. Finally, increasing the number of samples with the purpose of decreasing the error classification, should improve the accuracy of the model.

**Acknowledgements.** This work was partially supported by the Laboratorio de Software Libre (Labsol) from Consejo Zacatecano de Ciencia Tecnología e Innovación (COZCyT). Also this work group thanks to Universidad Autónoma de Zacatecas (UAZ) for partially support the developed research.

# References

1. Chong, H.D., Cai, X., Chen, X., Hu, L., Lou, X.: Computer-aided detection and classification of microcalcifications in mammograms: a survey. Pattern Recognit. **36**(12), 2967–2991 (2003)
2. Adams, P.: The breast cancer conundrum (2013)
3. Brandan, M.E., Villaseñor, Y.: Detección del cáncer de mama: estado de la mamografía en México. Cancerología **1**(3), 147–162 (2006)
4. Dixon, A.M.: Diagnostic Breast Imaging: Mammography, Sonography, Magnetic Resonance Imaging, and Interventional Procedures (2014)
5. Wulaningsih, W., et al.: Serum calcium and the risk of breast cancer: findings from the swedish amoris study and a meta-analysis of prospective studies. Int. J. Mol. Sci. **17**(9), 1487 (2016)
6. Xia, C., Kahn, C., Wang, J., Liao, Y., Chen, W., Yu, X.Q.: Temporal trends in geographical variation in breast cancer mortality in china, 1973–2005: an analysis of nationwide surveys on cause of death. Int. J. Environ. Res. Pub. Health **13**(10), 963 (2016)
7. Houghton, L.C., et al.: Associations of breast cancer risk factors with premenopausal sex hormones in women with very low breast cancer risk. Int. J. Environ. Res. Pub. Health **13**(11), 1066 (2016)
8. Astley, S., Gilbert, F.: Computer-aided detection in mammography. Clin. Radiol. **59**(5), 390–399 (2004)
9. El Abbadi, N.K., Al Taee, E.J.: Breast cancer diagnosis by CAD. Int. J. Comput. Appl. **100**(5) (2014)
10. Eadie, L.H., Taylor, P., Gibson, A.P.: A systematic review of computer-assisted diagnosis in diagnostic cancer imaging. Eur. J. Radiol. **81**(1), e70–e76 (2012)
11. Moftah, H.M., Azar, A.T., Al-Shammari, E.T., Ghali, N.I., Hassanien, A.E., Shoman, M.: Adaptive k-means clustering algorithm for MR breast image segmentation. Neural Comput. Appl. **24**(7–8), 1917–1928 (2014)
12. Dheeba, J., Singh, N.A., Selvi, S.T.: Computer-aided detection of breast cancer on mammograms: a swarm intelligence optimized wavelet neural network approach. J. Biomed. Inform. **49**, 45–52 (2014)

13. Ramani, R., Vanitha, N.S.: Computer a ided detection of tumours in mammograms. Int. J. Image Graph. Signal Process. **6**(4), 54 (2014)
14. Karahaliou, A., et al.: Texture analysis of tissue surrounding microcalcifications on mammograms for breast cancer diagnosis. British J. Radiol. **80**(956), 648–656 (2007)
15. Moura, D.C., López, M.A.G.: An evaluation of image descriptors combined with clinical data for breast cancer diagnosis. Int. J. Comput. Assist. Radiol. Surg. **8**(4), 561–574 (2013)
16. Ripley, B.D.: The R project in statistical computing MSOR Connections. Newslett. LTSN Maths Stats OR Netw. **1**(1), 23–25 (2001)
17. Breiman, L.: Random forests. Mach. Learn. **45**(1), 5–32 (2001)
18. Robin, X., et al.: Package 'proc' (2017)
19. Aragon, T.: Epitools: epidemiology tools. R package version 0.5-7 (2012/2016)
20. Lele, S.R., Keim, J.L., Solymos, P., Solymos, M.P.: Package 'resourceselection' (2017)

# Fully Automated Segmentation of Abnormal Heart in New Born Babies

Attifa Bilal[1], Aslam Muhammad[2(✉)],
and Martinez-Enriquez Ana Maria[3]

[1] Department of CS and IT, Superior University, Lahore, Pakistan
attifa.bilal@superior.edu.pk
[2] Department of CS, UET, Lahore, Pakistan
maslam@uet.edu.pk
[3] Department of CS, CINVESTAV, D.F. Mexico, Mexico
ammartin@cinvestav.mx

**Abstract.** We show an intuitive method to segment the heart chambers and epicardial surfaces, including the colossal vessel dividers, in pediatric cardiovascular in Machine Resonance Imaging (MRI) of inherent coronary illness. Exact entire heart division is important to make tolerant specific 3D heart models for surgical arranging within the sight of complex heart abandons. Anatomical changeability because of inborn deformities blocks completely programmed chart book based division. Our intelligent division technique abuses master segmentations of a little arrangement of short-hub cut locales to consequently delineate the rest of the volume utilizing patch-based division. We too research the capability of dynamic figuring out how to naturally request client contribution to zones where division blunder is probably going to be high. Approval is performed on four subjects with twofold outlet right ventricle, a severe inherent heart imperfection. We demonstrate that procedures asking the client to physically fragment districts of enthusiasm inside short-hub cuts yield higher exactness with less client contribution than those questioning whole short-axis cuts. The proposed system validates the technique of automatic segmentation of heart using the combination of Dice matrices and active appearance model techniques which help the doctors to recognize heart disease.

**Keywords:** Congenital heart disease · Abnormal heart segmentation
Automatic detection of disease in MRI images

## 1 Introduction

As human life is not possible or even can't imagine without the normal working of heart. it works 24 h constantly. It never stops until a disease occurs or by natural death. The process of development of human heart completed in 43 days after confirmation of pregnancy with the resulting of four chambers walls (left ventricle, right ventricle, left atrium and right atrium) partially. Right atrium passes oxygenated blood to right ventricle and lungs then blood circulates in left atrium by using path of pulmonary veins. After the completion of above mentioned process atria, ventricles and tube veins start blooming in their size. There are four components which divide the heart into four

© Springer Nature Switzerland AG 2018
F. Castro et al. (Eds.): MICAI 2017, LNAI 10633, pp. 305–314, 2018.
https://doi.org/10.1007/978-3-030-02840-4_25

compartments which are septum, ventricular septum, septum secundum and atrioventricular. During the development of heart, there can be some weaknesses from female or genetic transformation which causes as a defect or abnormality of heart in new born children [2].

By using MRI imaging resource we proposed a technique which will automatically divides heart parts into slices to detect the defect in congenital heart. Diseases can be divides into major two types. (i) *Syndromic CHDs* (ii) Non-*Syndromic CHDs*. Magnetic resonance imaging (MRI) is an accurate technique and has a good control over precision to access the scanned view of heart parts and their functions [1]. Programmed calculation of VMS (ventricular muscle mass), VV (ventricular volumes) and functions is totally based on left ventricular, endocardial and epicardial boundaries. In this paper, technique used for automated segmentation of abnormal heart will increase the accuracy and ratio of detecting abnormality in congenital heart disease. In this paper, to get accurate visibility of MRI images as a binary images active shape model has been applied as 3D models.

Cardiovascular ailments cause 17.5 million passing consistently in the world [2]. The early analysis of the cardiovascular infections assumes an essential part in the recuperation. Cardiovascular MRI imaging utilizing cine MRI arrangements, considered as a critical instrument that utilized for assessing heart work.

Assessment of heart functions requires estimation of various cardiovascular parameters (i.e. launch portion (EF), Left Ventricle Mass (LVM), left ventricle volume, divider thickness, or divider thickening). These parameters depend on portioning the endocardial, and epicardial convoy ages through the left ventricle from the picture arrangements that are obtained from cardiovascular imaging strategy. The manual segmentation of these shapes from all dataset (i.e. untouched casings per all cuts) takes a great deal of time and exertion from the cardiologist.

Along these lines, the programmed division of parts of abnormal heart is vital, and can be considered as a challenging work. In the short-axis MRI picture, the blood pools like right and left ventricle are seem brilliant and all their surrounding structures seem dull (i.e. myocardium, lung, and liver) with various forces. Additionally the left ventricle resembles a roundabout in the short-hub picture [4].

There are a few methods utilized as a part of the left and right ventricle segmentation and left and right ventricular segmentation. Fully automated segmentation of heart has a great potential to improve surgical efficiency in children heart by applying specific 3D heart models. These models show accurate result to surgeons with better experience [3]. To develop such models to get structural view of child's MRI, which includes epicardial, entire blood pool and large vessels.

Manually to make segment of whole heart it consumes 3–5 h of surgeon interaction divide the 100–200 pieces which cover all parts of heart and great vessels [4, 5]. Whole heart segmentation is risky and challenging assignment even in normal objects. In previous research atlas based segmentation and deformable models have been used to make the divisions of an image [6]. Large set of database has been used to apply the parameters on objects.

The proposed technique segments the four chambers of heart automatically by combining Dice matric and active appearance model technique which showed result with high performance and precise accuracy. We are fully assured that the proposed technique is helpful to slicing the heart 3D model to detect the defect in new born child. It segments the pixels of desired portion of heart by inserting input image only which reduced the human interaction to make the segmentation manually.

Section 2 presents the review of previous work. Section 3 is about localization of the image in binary form after applying the thresholding techniques. Section 4 focuses on the division of the left ventricle which comprises of two principle steps. Section 5 explains the results with comparison with previous results. Evaluation of the results is also presented. Section 6 presents the conclusion and future work.

## 2  Related Work

As literature review, there is only few researchers' work on whole heart segmentation which needs less human interaction. There is no sufficient work has been acknowledged to make automatic segmentation of heart. This segment, the blueprint of the active appearance model technique is introduced. For points of interest, allude to [7]. It is richly incorporate learning shape and surface (appearance) inconstancy from cases all the while.

Imaging of the left ventricle utilizing cine short-hub MRI arrangements, considered as an imperative instrument that utilized for assessing cardiovascular capacity by ascertaining distinctive heart parameters. The manual division of the left ventricle in all picture successions takes a considerable measure of time, and hence the programmed division of the left ventricle is principle venture in heart work assessment. At that point, we changed picture pixels from Cartesian to polar directions for portioning the epicardial form. The after effects of the proposed strategy demonstrate the accessibility for quick and dependable division of the left ventricle.

The significant strides in the examination are as per the following: Preparing: (1) an arrangement of delegate pictures is picked and explained by specialists. (2) The preparation set is spatially adjusted utilizing a Procuresses Investigation. (3) A model shape is picked - i.e. a mean shape is assessed. (4) Appearance variety is gathered in a steady way, by building up a thin-plate or piece-wise relative twist between the model and every preparation case. (5) To determine a particular and minimal representation of the natural shape (historic points) and appearance (pixels) variety a primary segment examination (PCA) is performed on the adjusted preparing set (w.r.t. shapes and pixels). (6) The minimal parameterization from the PCA is then used to produce engineered pictures of the protest being referred to (e.g. left ventricle).

Division: (1) The model is naturally set in an underlying design over the (inconspicuous) picture. (2) Using a key segment multivariate straight relapse show, new pictures are produced to fit the concealed picture in the most ideal way. On the off chance that the procedure joins with an attractive outcome, a match (e.g. of the ventricle) is pronounced.

Step 1 of the division procedure is refined utilizing an initialization strategy depicted in [9, 10]. After a match has been pronounced, a further refinement [11] is proficient in light of the irregular tested advancement conspire, Simulated Annealing.

In the present review, 14 spatially relating short hub end diastolic X-rays were chosen from 14 people. The picked cut position spoke to low morphologic many-sided quality and high complexity. The pictures were obtained more than 15 heart cycles utilizing an ECG triggered breath-hold quick low point shot (FLASH) cinematographic beat succession. Cut thickness = 10 mm; field of view = 263 × 350 mm; lattice 256 × 256. The endocardial and epicardial forms of the left ventricle were clarified physically by setting 33 points of interest - i.e. relating focuses between and inside populaces along both the endocardial and epicardial shapes.

The comment was performed by two specialists. On the off chance that a heart disease is related with extra cardiac contortions as well as mental impediment, regularly a hereditary or ecological cause can be found, either by clinical acknowledgment of the phenotype, if conceivable took after by focused hereditary examination, or by screening for chromosomal numerical varieties [12]. More than 1200 disorders related with above mentioned diseases are recorded in the London Medical database [13], and a subset of the more successive disorders with particular heart imperfections is displayed in Table 1.

**Table 1.** Testing evaluation of the algorithm on dataset of 20 defected slices of heart

| Property | Sensitivity | Specificity | Dice metric |
|---|---|---|---|
| Endocardium area | 0.9661 ± 0.0625 | 0.9890 ± 0.0089 | 0.9037 ± 0.0747 |
| Epicardium area | 0.9432 ± 0.0766 | 0.9549 ± 0.0092 | 0.9261 ± 0.0473 |

Transformations in a portion of the qualities required in these disorders are likewise answered to bring about heart abandons without different elements related with the disorder. The frequencies of these changes in confined heart imperfections are as a rule extremely low [14]. The described types are founded in review of paper are genetic and non-genetic. In non-syndrome CHDs, in spite of the fact that it might be familial, a causative change can be recognized just in a little number of families, and a wide range of qualities can be involved [15].

There are some genetic defects or diseases which are found in heart patients like, atrioventricular septal defect mostly causes trisomy defect, atrial septal defect, bicuspid aortic valve, aortic valve stenosis, peripheral pulmonary artery stenosis, coarctation of the aorta, dilated cardiomyopathy, double outlet right ventricle, hypoplastic left heart syndrome, interruption of the aortic arch, pulmonary valve atresia, transposition of the great arteries, persistent ductus arteriosus, peripheral pulmonary artery stenosis, pulmonary valve stenosis, supravalvular aortic stenosis, total anomalous pulmonary venous return, tetralogy of Fallot and ventricular septal defect. These all mentioned defect are transferred as a genetics in new born children which causes heart disease [16].

Genetic guiding of such patients is consequently a test and the best symptomatic approach is not generally self-evident. A portion of the qualities included have a very particular phenotypic range of heart deformities, yet many are related with a heterogeneous range. In any case, the length of quality boards are not accessible for the hereditary screening of congenital heart defect, a decision for transformation screening must be founded on the sort of the found in the pro band or the family, who give a congenital heart defect.

## 3   Localization of Cardiac from MRI

Magnetic image resonance is a technique to get the clear view of an image of heart as a slice. So we used this facility for confining the general position of the heart in cardiovascular MRI pictures, we connected the calculation specified in [13]. This calculation relies on upon figuring the standard deviation between all pictures for various time periods in the center cut, to register the standard deviation delineate, used to decide the general position of the heart. The flowchart of that depict the means of this calculation appeared in Fig. 1.

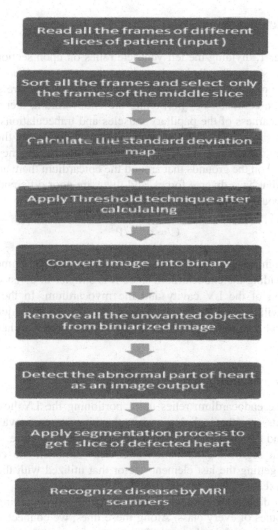

**Fig. 1.** Localization process of MRI image

As said, to get the outline, ought to decide the center cut that we will chip away at it. This is on the grounds that the heart has diverse perspectives along the long-hub (i.e. from zenith to base), as appeared in Fig. 1. In the center cut, we can see the left ventricle as a round shape, so there will be an awesome standard deviation between the myocardium, and the blood pool, as indicated by the development of the heart.

Subsequent to getting the standard deviation delineates, picture is converted to paired picture. The limit that utilized as a part of binarization, is computed in the wake of plotting the likelihood thickness capacity of the standard deviation values, and takes the edge esteem that gets 80% of the region under the likelihood thickness bend work.

# 4  Left Ventricle Segmentation

As appeared in Fig. 1, dividing the left ventricle relies on upon sectioning two unique shapes. The inside shape is called endocardium that encompasses the left ventricle blood pool, and the outside form that is called epicardium. There are a few challenges in fragmenting these contours. For portioning the endocardium, there are a few challenges as per the nearness of the papillary muscles and trabeculations inside the heart chamber that has a similar power of the myocardium. Additionally, there is some dark esteem in homogeneities inside the left ventricle hole itself. For the epicardium, the challenges produced on the grounds that around the epicardium there are diverse tissues (i.e. fat and lung) that have diverse forces, and there are poor difference between these tissues and the myocardium as calculated with Eq. (1).

$$C = 4\pi A/P^2 \tag{1}$$

A is Area of an image and P is presenting the parameters. To fragment these shapes, we will start in dividing the endocardium since it is simpler in division because of the great differentiation of the LV cavity and the myocardium. In the division of the endocardium, we will connect the calculation specified in [8]. Subsequent to portioning the endocardium, we will utilize the yield of division as a cover to help us in dividing the epicardium.

## 4.1  Endocardium Segmentation

The division of the endocardium relies upon portioning the LV hole, by separating diverse components (i.e. the inclination size, the biggest region value, the yield of middle channel, and the dim esteem) from every pixel in the picture. At that point, we apply the foremost segment examination (PCA) to diminish the component space measurement and getting the last element vector that utilized with the KNN classifier for dividing the pixels to blood or not.

This portion of division needs a preparation stage to help in taking in the classifier the principle attributes of every class. Along these lines, we connected our calculation on diverse patients. We took haphazardly 20 pictures from every patient for preparing. Amid setting up the preparation dataset, we should name the LV depression as class 1 and its encompassing territory as class 2. Along these lines, we did that by utilizing the manual division of the inward shape that connected with the dataset. We picked the components (utilized as a part of the division) because of the way of the LV hole that we need to fragment it. The LV pit seems splendid and the myocardium that encompasses it seems dim.

Thus, we have to enhance edges that encompass the LV cavity. For that we took the angle size and the biggest eigenvalue as elements. We get the slope greatness and the biggest eigenvalue at various scales (i.e. 1, 2, 4, 8, and 16) and take the most extreme over all scales (Fig. 2).

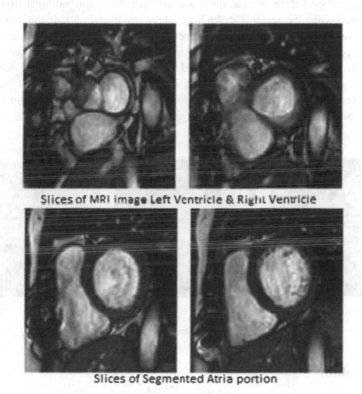

Slices of MRI image Left Ventricle & Right Ventricle

Slices of Segmented Atria portion

**Fig. 2.** Slices views of cardiac along the long-axis

## 4.2 Epicardium Segmentation

There are distinctive tissues (i.e. fat, lung, and liver) that encompass the myocardium, and these tissues have diverse force values. Additionally, the part of the epicardium before the correct ventricle is thin in thickness. These issues make the division of the epicardium is troublesome. For portioning the epicardium, we change over the sub image (removed from ROI picture) that focused in the focal point of the left ventricle cavity, and its sweep square with 30 pixels, from Cartesian to polar directions.

Subsequent to getting the polar picture of these pixels that cover this zone, we apply Canny [17] edge detection on this picture, to get polar edge delineate. Likewise, we change over the same sub image of the parallel picture of the left ventricle cavity (came about because of the past stage) to polar directions with a similar focus and for a similar range. At that point we utilized this picture as a parallel cover (subsequent to modifying it) to erase every undesirable edge (i.e. inside left ventricle hole, and endocardium as well) from the polar edge delineate to help us deciding the edge guide of the epicardium as it were.

As we specified before of that, there are low differentiation amongst myocardium and its encompassing tissues, this make little edges inside and outside the myocardium. Therefore, we erased the little associated segments in the edge guide to reach to the edges that speak to the epicardium shape at various parts. The main point at every section in the subsequent picture considered as edge point. In the wake of deciding all the edge focuses, we opposite the change of the edge guides facilitates from polar toward Cartesian, then get the arched body of these focuses, and get its limit outskirt that speak to the epicardial shape (Fig. 3).

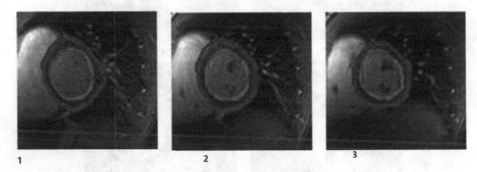

**Fig. 3.** Segmentation of epicardium slice in part 1, 2, and 3

## 5    Evaluation

To assess our work, we compute diverse parameters that used to gauge the execution of the division calculation. These parameters are affectability, specificity, and dice metric. Close to these parameters we computed the launch part (EF), and thought about its qualities from the programmed division calculation, and the manual division by connection investigation.

### 5.1    Sensitivity and Specificity

The affectability is the extent of genuine positives of the programmed division yield to the manual division yield (i.e. reference yield). The specificity is the extent of genuine negatives of the programmed division yield to the manual division yield.

These parameters were used for calculation as in Eq. (2 and 3).

$$S = TP/(TP + FN) \tag{2}$$

$$SP = TN/(FP + TN) \tag{3}$$

- Where S presents the sensitivity
- SP represents the specificity
- TP is original positive area (correctly classified as an object).
- FP shows the false positive area (classified as an object, but actually it is background).
- TN is presenting the true negative area which is correctly classified as a background.
- FN parameters are presenting the false negative area which has been classified as background, but in fact it is an object).

### 5.2 Dice Metric

The dice metric is a techniques which we used to make segment, DM, was calculated as in Eq. (2) It is a measure of contour overlap utilizing the contour areas automatically segmented (Aa), manually segmented (Am), and their intersection (As). DM is always between 0 and 1, with higher DM indicating better match between automatic and manual segmentations.

It is a measure of shape cover using the form ranges naturally divided (Aa), physically portioned (Am), and their crossing point 2. DM is dependably in the vicinity of 0 and 1, with higher DM demonstrating better match amongst programmed and manual divisions. After applying the both techniques parallel, it gives better result to make the automatic segmentation of abnormal heart.

## 6 Conclusion and Future Work

We displayed a precise intuitive strategy for entire heart division in inherent coronary illness which has been applied on 3D heart models. To the best of our insight, this is one of the best exhibits towards clinically useful picture division to empower routine utilization of 3D heart models for surgical arranging in CHD. We likewise demonstrate that dynamic learning approaches in which the client explains dubious ROIs have potential to additionally diminish division time.

Future work incorporates dynamic learning for self-assertively situated cuts or ROIs. More advanced dynamic learning methods that probabilistically display the normal blunder lessening given a hopeful return on initial capital investment could likewise yield enhanced division comes about with insignificant client exertion.

As it is limited only for new born babies heart detection so it can be further modified for the young blood as well as for further research as Ph.D. thesis.

# References

1. Gabriel Steg, P.: New developments in non-invasive cardiac imaging: critical assessment of the clinical role of cardiac magnetic resonance imaging. Eur. Heart J. **19**(9), 1282–1286 (1998)
2. World Health Organization of cardiovascular disease. www.who.int/cardiovascular_ diseases/en
3. Schmauss, D., Haeberle, S., Hagl, C., Sodian, R.: Three-dimensional printing in cardiac surgery and interventional cardiology: a single-centre experience. Eur. J. Cardio. -Thorac. **47**, 1044–1052 (2014)
4. Jacobs, S., Grunert, R., Mohr, F.W., Falk, V.: 3D-Imaging of cardiac structures using 3D heart models for planning in heart surgery: a preliminary study. Interact. Cardiovasc. Thorac. Surg. **7**(1), 6–9 (2008)
5. Valverde, I., et al.: Three-dimensional patient specific cardiac model for surgical planning in Nikaidoh procedure. Cardiol. Young **25**(4), 698–704 (2014)
6. Zhuang, X.: Challenges and methodologies of fully automatic whole heart segmentation: a review. J. Healthc. Eng. **4**(3), 371–408 (2013)
7. Arrington, C.B., et al.: Exome analysis of a family with pleiotropic congenital heart disease. Circ Cardiovasc Genet. **5**, 175–182 (2012)
8. Mitchell, S., Lelieveldt, B., Geest, R., Schaap, J., Reiber, J., Sonka, M.: Segmentation of cardiac MR image: an active appearance model approach. In: Medical Imaging 2000: Image Processing, San Diego, CA. SPIE, vol. 1. SPIE (2000)
9. Yifrah, S., Zadicario, E., Ju, T., Cohen-Or, D.: An algorithm for suggesting delineation planes for interactive segmentation. In: IEEE International Symposium on Biomedical Imaging, pp. 361–364. IEEE Press, New York (2014)
10. Veeraraghavan, H., Miller, J.: Active learning guided interactions for consistent image segmentation with reduced user interactions. In: IEEE International Symposium on Biomedical Imaging, pp. 1645–1648. IEEE Press, New York (2011)
11. Veeraraghavan, H., Miller, J.: Active learning guided interactions for consistent image segmentation with reduced user interactions. In: Biomed Imaging, pp. 1645–1648. IEEE (2011)
12. Settles, B.: Active Learning. Morgan & Claypool Publishers, San Rafael (2012)
13. Digilio, M.C., Marino, B., Giannotti, A., Dallapiccola, B., Opitz, J.M.: Specific congenital heart defects in RSH/Smith-lemli-opitz syndrome: postulated involvement of the sonic hedgehog pathway in syndromes with postaxial polydactyly or heterotaxia. Birth Defects Res. Part A: Clin. Mol. Teratol. **67**, 149–153 (2003)
14. Shi, W., et al.: Automatic segmentation of different pathologies from cardiac cine MRI using registration and multiple component EM estimation. In: Metaxas, D.N., Axel, L. (eds.) FIMH 2011. LNCS, vol. 6666, pp. 163–170. Springer, Heidelberg (2011). https://doi.org/10. 1007/978-3-642-21028-0_21
15. Wang, B., et al.: 4D active cut: an interactive tool for pathological anatomy modeling. In: IEEE International Symposium on Biomedical Imaging, pp. 529–532. IEEE Press, New York (2014)
16. Hirayama, Y.K., et al.: Phenotypes with GATA4/NKX2.5 mutations in familial atrial septal defect. Am. J. Med. Genet. A. **135**(4), 47–52 (2005)
17. Valverde, I., et al.: Three-dimensional patient-specific cardiac model for surgical planning in Nikaidoh procedure. Cardiol. Young **25**(4), 698–704 (2014)

# Time-Invariant EEG Classification Based on the Fractal Dimension

Rocio Salazar-Varas and Roberto Antonio Vazquez[✉]

Digital Signal Processing Group, Intelligent Systems Group,
Facultad de Ingeniería, Universidad La Salle México,
Benjamin Franklin 47, Col. Condesa, 06140 Mexico City, Mexico
rocio.salazar@ulsa.mx, ravem@lasallistas.org.mx

**Abstract.** Several computational techniques have been proposed in the last years to classify brain signals in order to increase the performance of Brain-Computer Interfaces. However, there are several issues that should be attended to be more friendly with the users during the calibration stage and to achieve more reliable BCI applications. One of these issues is related to the BCI's time-invariant robustness where the goal is to keep the performance using the information recorded in previous sessions to classify the data recorded in future sessions, avoiding recalibration. In order to do that, we have to carefully select the feature extraction techniques and classification algorithms. In this paper, we propose to compute the feature vector in terms of the fractal dimension. To evaluate the feasibility of the proposal, we compare the performance achieved with the fractal dimension against the coefficients of an autoregressive model using a linear discriminant classifier. To asses the time-invariant robustness of the fractal dimension, we train and evaluate the classifier using the data recorded during one day; after that, the trained classifier is evaluated using the data recorded in a different day. These experiments were done using the data set I from Brain-Computer Interface Competition III. The results show that the performance achieved with fractal dimension is better than the autoregressive model (which is one of the most common method used in BCI applications).

**Keywords:** Fractal dimension · Higuchi's method · Katz's method
EEG classification

## 1 Introduction

Brain-Computer Interfaces (BCI) provide an alternative communication path, different to motor channel, that allow a subject the control of a device only with brain activity, it means without muscular activity [1]. To relate the brain activity recorded with a specific mental event, different stages must be applied [2]. Firstly, the brain activity is recorded using different acquisition techniques such as electroencephalography (EEG), magnetoencephalography (MEG), electrocorticography (ECoG), among others. In BCI applications, the most used acquisition technique is the EEG. Then, the recorded signal is preprocessed (filtered

© Springer Nature Switzerland AG 2018
F. Castro et al. (Eds.): MICAI 2017, LNAI 10633, pp. 315–325, 2018.
https://doi.org/10.1007/978-3-030-02840-4_26

and amplified) in order to improve the signal quality, eliminating noise and artifacts such as the muscular. In the feature extraction stage, the most relevant information contained in the signal is extracted. Finally, this information is used to associate the recorded signal with a specific mental state.

Different feature extraction techniques have been proposed (in time and frequency domain) to extract relevant information from the signal related to a mental task [3,4]. However, to build reliable BCI applications, different issues must be attended in the feature extraction stage, such as [3]:

- Poor signal to noise ratio present in EEG signals.
- High dimensionality. Generally, the brain activity is recorded from several channels and the obtained feature vector presents high dimensionality.
- Time-variant behavior of the brain signals. Signals from brain activity vary rapidly over the time. This variation is more notorious in recordings from different sessions.
- Small training sets. It is desirable to perform small calibration sessions to avoid the calibration process results tedious for the users.

In this research, we are focused on the problem of the non-stationarity when the data used to train the BCI is recorded one day but the BCI is used on different days. Since the brain activity recorded is related not only with the mental task employed to control the BCI, but also with physiological activity, moods, environmental conditions, among others, it is desirable to develop a BCI system which provides a good accuracy, although the physiological or environmental conditions change. Therefore, it is important to select a robust feature which varies in the same way when a specific mental task is developed no matter other conditions as the mentioned above change, in other words, the feature must be time-invariant. In this sense, different solutions have been proposed, most of them apply adaptive methodologies focused on feature extraction or on classification stage [5,6]. However, it is still necessary to propose and adopt new methods to compute time-invariant features that extract underlying information contained in the recorded signal, related with the mental task developed, without the need to recalibrate the system each time it is used.

On the other hand, the fractal dimension (FD) is a metric related with the signal complexity, a fundamental characteristic of fractal objects is that their dimensions (e.g. length, area) are function of the scale of measurement [7]. Fractal geometry has the attraction of describe irregular shapes that Euclidean geometry is unable to describe. The FD has been used in image analysis mainly, e.g. in image segmentation [7–9]. Even more, in the biomedical signal processing field also has found application, for example in the electrocardiography signal analysis to detect different pathologies [10,11]. In the EEG signal analysis, the fractal dimension has been used to detect the onset of epileptic seizures [12,13] but also its behavior has been associated with the development of different mental tasks [14,15]. In that sense, due to its properties, the fractal dimension could be an interesting candidate to be evaluated as a time-invariant feature.

In this paper, we propose to use the FD as feature and evaluate its time-invariant robustness. The FD is computed through two methods commonly used:

Higuchi and Katz [16]. In the classification stage, a linear discriminant (LD) is employed. To evaluate the robustness of the FD, different conditions during the classification stage were established: using the data recorded in only one session to train and test the classifier and using the data from one session to train the classifier and the data from the other session to evaluate it. This robustness was evaluated in terms of the accuracy and the area under ROC (Receiver Operating Characteristic) curve. Furthermore, the classification results were optimized based on the information provided by the ROC curve. In order to assess the feasibility of the fractal dimension as feature, we compare the results obtained in classification stage against those obtained when the coefficients of an autoregressive (AR) model are used as features. The data used to validate the proposal was taken from the Data set I of the Brain-Computer Interface Competition III. After evaluating the experimental conditions, the results suggest that the performance achieved using the FD is better than the achieved through the AR coefficients.

This paper is organized as follow: In Sect. 2, a brief description of the theoretical concepts used in the proposal is given. In Sect. 3, the proposed methodology is described. In Sect. 4, the data set used to evaluate the proposal and the experimental results are exposed. Finally, in Sect. 5, the conclusions and future work from this paper are presented.

## 2  Background

In this section, we briefly review the theoretical concepts applied in the proposed methodology.

### 2.1  Fractal Dimension

Considering a time series $X = x(1), x(2), \ldots, x(N))$, where $N$ is the total number of samples in time, its fractal dimension (FD) could be obtained by different approximations [17]:

**Higuchi's Method.** This method computes the FD in the time domain. This method is based on a given finite time series $x_m^k$ constructed by following equation

$$
x_m^k = \left\{ x(m), x(m+k), x(m+2k), \ldots, x\left(m + \left\lfloor \frac{N-m}{k} \right\rfloor k\right) \right\} \tag{1}
$$

for $m = 1, 2, \ldots, k$, $m$ is an integer which indicates the initial time and $k$ is an integer indicating the discrete time interval between points and $\lfloor \cdot \rfloor$ means the integer part. The length $(L_m(k))$ of each $x_k$ is computed as

$$
L_m(k) = \frac{1}{k} \left\{ \left( \sum_{i=1}^{\left\lfloor \frac{N-m}{k} \right\rfloor} |x(m+ik) - x(m+(i-1)k)| \right) \frac{N-1}{\left\lfloor \frac{N-m}{k} \right\rfloor k} \right\} \tag{2}
$$

Finally, the FD of the signal section is solved from:

$$\langle L(k) \rangle \propto k^{-FD} \tag{3}$$

**Katz's Method.** Katz based his FD approximation on the measurement of planar curves. Katz did a correction to the estimation proposed by Mandelbrot ($FD = log(L)/log(d)$). According to Katz, the FD of a planar curve is given by [17]

$$FD = \frac{log(n)}{log(n) + log\left(\frac{d}{L}\right)} \tag{4}$$

where $n$ represents the total number of steps in the curve of number points $N$ (i.e. $n = N - 1$), $L$ is the total length of the curve (the sum of the distances between successive points), and $d$ is the distance between the first point of the sequence and the point of the sequence that provides the maximum distance, which can be expressed as:

$$d = max(distance(x(1), x(i))) \tag{5}$$

## 2.2 Auto Regressive Model

Considering a time series $X = x(1), x(2), \ldots, x(N))$, where $N$ is the total number of samples in time, employing an autoregressive model (AR) of order $p$, a new point could be expressed as a linear combination of its $p$ previous values

$$x(n) = \sum_{k=1}^{p} a_k x(n - k) + \epsilon(n) \tag{6}$$

where $\epsilon(n)$ expresses the innovation of the time series, uncorrelated with $x(l), (l < n)$, and $a_k$ are the coefficients of the AR model.

## 2.3 Linear Discriminant

The classification problem consists in assign to one class a new datum represented by its corresponding feature vector $\boldsymbol{y}$, using a classifier which was previously trained with a data set obtained to this goal. In BCI applications, one of the most used classifiers is the linear discriminant (LD).

LD establishes a surface decision in the features space which separates the points into two groups, each one related to one class [18]. The discrimination function can be written as

$$d = \boldsymbol{v}^T \boldsymbol{y} + v_0, \tag{7}$$

where $\boldsymbol{v}$ is a normal vector to the surface decision and $v_0$ is an offset value. The discrimination rule is

$$\text{if } d > th \quad \boldsymbol{y} \in \text{Class1},$$
$$\text{otherwise} \quad \boldsymbol{y} \in \text{Class 2}. \tag{8}$$

where $th$ is the threshold to determine to which class belongs a new sample. Commonly, this threshold is adjust to zero, but this value could be optimized.

# 3 Proposed Methodology

In this section, we explain the main steps of the proposed methodology. As a common BCI, the proposed methodology considers three main stages: preprocessing, feature extraction and classification.

Consider an EEG/ECoG recording in a matrix $A$ of dimensions $N \times M \times K$ where $N$ is the total number of samples in time, $M$ express the total number of channels (electrodes) used in the recording, and $K$ is the total numbers of trials.

In the first stage, the preprocessing is achieved using a common band pass filter. Once the signal has been processed, in the second stage, a feature vector is built computing the FD for each signal recorded from each one of the $M$ electrodes. Therefore, a feature vector $y$ of dimensions $1 \times M$ is obtained for each trial. Finally, in the third stage, a classifier is trained and tested with the feature vector obtained from the previous stage. A general scheme of the proposed methodology is shown in the Fig. 1.

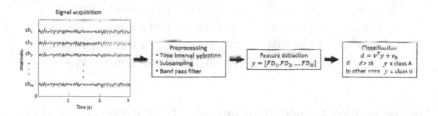

**Fig. 1.** Proposed methodology

# 4 Experimental Results

In this section, we describe a set of experiments which was carried out to evaluate the performance of the proposed methodology based on the fractal dimension as a feature extraction technique.

We use the Data set I from Brain-Computer Interface Competition III. It contains the electrocorticography recordings from one subject on two different days, the second session was recorded one week after the first session. The recordings were carried out using a $8 \times 8$ platinum electrode grid placed on the right motor cortex with a frequency sampling of 1000 Hz. In each trial, the subject was requested to imagine tongue or finger movement during three seconds. The data set from the first session contains 278 trials and from the second session contains 100 trials.

From the three seconds on which the subject is performing the mental task, we employed the two intermediate seconds (i.e. 0.5 s–2.5 s). The signals were subsampled to 250 Hz, and a Butterworth band pass filter of fourth order with cutoff frequencies 5 and 40 Hz was applied.

Under these conditions, the feature vector ($y$) was computed using the feature extraction techniques described in Sect. 2. For Higuchi's method the parameter $k$ was set to 8. For the case of the Katz's method, it was not necessary to define a value for $d$, it is set according to the characteristics of the signal in terms of Eq. 5. In addition, we compare the robustness of the FD techniques against the coefficients from an AR model of second order. Table 1, shows the mean value and the standard deviation of the fractal dimension and coefficients of the autoregressive model for both classes. These values were computed for the data recorded during first and second sessions. As it can be seen, the FD values computed by Katz's method provides greater differences between classes than Higuchi's method or AR coefficients.

Table 1. Mean values of FD and AR coefficients for both classes

| Method | 1st session | | 2nd session | |
|---|---|---|---|---|
| | Class 1 | Class 2 | Class 1 | Class 2 |
| FD Katz | $1.15 \pm 0.04$ | $1.34 \pm 0.11$ | $1.14 \pm 0.04$ | $1.34 \pm 0.12$ |
| FD Higuchi | $1.28 \pm 0.06$ | $1.30 \pm 0.07$ | $1.29 \pm 0.06$ | $1.31 \pm 0.06$ |
| AR coeff | $1.78 \pm 0.04$ | $1.77 \pm 0.04$ | $1.77 \pm 0.04$ | $1.76 \pm 0.04$ |
| | $-0.90 \pm 0.02$ | $-0.92 \pm 0.02$ | $-0.90 \pm 0.02$ | $-0.91 \pm 0.01$ |

The classification was performed through a linear discriminant and was carried out in four different conditions.

- For the first condition, the data recorded during the first session was used to train and evaluate the classifier. In this case 50% of the data was used to train the classifier and the remaining 50% was used to evaluate the performance. In order to avoid the data assigned to train or test set influence the classification process, a random cross validation of 30 iterations was performed.
- For the second condition, the data recorded during the second session was used to train and evaluate the classifier using the same procedure as in the first condition. This condition was also useful to evaluate the robustness of the features with a reduced number of training samples.
- For the third condition, the data recorded in the first session was used to train the classifier and the data recorded in the second session (one week after the first session) was used to evaluate it.
- The fourth condition was similar to the previous one, but in this case, the data recorded in the second session was used to train the classifier and the data recorded in the first session was used to it. As equal as in the second condition, this condition allows to evaluate the robustness of the features when the numbers of samples to train the classifier is reduced.

To evaluate the performance of the proposal, we compute the accuracy in terms of the percentage of samples correctly classified. The area under ROC curve was also computed.

The accuracy of the proposed methodology is shown in Table 2. As the reader can see, for the first and second condition, the FD provides a better accuracy than the AR coefficients (72.73%). It is also observed that the Katz's method reports higher accuracy (81.10%) compared with Higuchi's method (76.61%). Although the performance of the classifiers diminished when the number of samples for training was reduced, the accuracy achieved by the FD remains acceptable in contrast to the AR which drastically decreased (58.26%). These results confirm the fact that the FD can be used to discriminate between two different mental tasks.

The time-invariant robustness is analyzed from the third and fourth conditions when the data used to train and test the classifier is recorded in different days. The third condition shows that the FD also provides a better accuracy compared with the AR coefficients (70%). In the same way, Higuchi's method achieves a higher accuracy (81%) compared with Katz's method (73%). These results suggest that the FD is time-invariant robust since it provides an acceptable accuracy when the classifier is trained with data recorded from one day and tested with data from other day. However, when the number of samples for training the classifier is reduced (fourth condition), it seems that the robustness of the FD is affected, and the best performance is obtained with the AR coefficients (65.47%). Nonetheless, if we analyze the area under ROC curve, it is observed that the performance can be improved.

**Table 2.** Accuracy achieved with the proposed methodology under four conditions.

| Data | FD-Katz | FD Higuchi | AR |
|---|---|---|---|
| 1st session (Training and testing) | 81.10 ± 2.62 | 76.61 ± 2.33 | 72.73 ± 3.72 |
| 2nd session (Training and testing) | 76.13 ± 5.40 | 72.60 ± 4.61 | 58.26 ± 7.40 |
| 1st session (Training), 2nd session (Testing) | 73 | 81 | 70 |
| 2nd session (Training), 1st session (Testing) | 50 | 59 | 65.47 |

Table 3 shows the area under ROC curve for all tested conditions using the FD and the AR coefficients. As it can be seen, for first and second conditions, the area achieved by the FD is higher than the area obtained with the AR coefficients, these results are consistent with the accuracy reported above. On the other hand, for the third and fourth conditions, the area under ROC curve reflects a better performance than the reported with the accuracy, particularly the Katz's method. These results show that the LD classifier combined with the Katz's method ranks the samples more efficiently (in this case, in terms of the distance to the decision surface), suggesting that the FD extracts the underlying information of the signal related to the mental task which allows the LD classifier to rank the feature vectors correctly. Furthermore, based on this fact, the classifier could be optimized to improve its accuracy. So, the threshold used by the LD (Eq. 8) to determine to which class belong the samples must be adjusted. In order to do that, relevant information to adjust the threshold could be obtained from the plots shown in Figs. 2 and 3.

**Table 3.** Area under ROC curve achieved with the proposed methodology under four conditions.

| Data | FD-Katz | FD Higuchi | AR |
|---|---|---|---|
| 1st session (Training and testing) | $0.83 \pm 0.02$ | $0.88 \pm 0.03$ | $0.79 \pm 0.03$ |
| 2nd session (Training and testing) | $0.84 \pm 0.04$ | $0.81 \pm 0.05$ | $0.64 \pm 0.07$ |
| 1st session (Training), 2nd session (Testing) | 0.92 | 0.85 | 0.83 |
| 2nd session (Training), 1st session (Testing) | 0.79 | 0.71 | 0.71 |

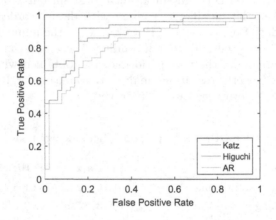

**Fig. 2.** ROC curve using the data from 1st session to train and the data from 2nd session to test.

One way to determine the best value for the threshold is to compute the distance to the point (0, 1) in the ROC plane. The index of the point nearest to (0, 1) indicates the position in the score vector that could be used as a threshold value. Following this approach, Table 4 shows the results achieved with the optimized classifier and the threshold value used to optimized the classifier. As it can be observed, in the case of first and second conditions, the accuracy does not show a notorious increment, in contrast with the third and fourth conditions. Furthermore, the Katz's method reach an accuracy of 87% under the third condition, which represent an improvement of 14 points. Although the AR method improves in 6 points, reaching an accuracy of 76%, the Higuchi's method obtains the second best accuracy (83%). These results suggest that the FD is a robust feature. For the fourth condition, the improvement using both FD methods is more remarkable. This fact reinforces the suggestion of the third condition in the sense that the FD is a robust time-invariant feature.

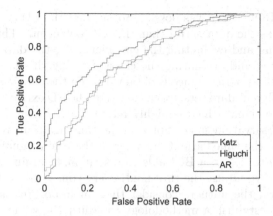

**Fig. 3.** ROC curve using the data from 2nd session to train and the data from 1st session to test.

**Table 4.** Optimized accuracy for the four conditions using the threshold value from ROC curve

| Data | FD-Katz | th | FD-Higuchi | th | AR | th |
|---|---|---|---|---|---|---|
| 1st session (Training and testing) | 81.62 ± 2.27 | −1.48 | 77.83 ± 2.07 | −0.59 | 74.50 ± 3.59 | −1.46 |
| 2nd session (Training and testing) | 78.20 ± 5.66 | −5.81 | 75.06 ± 4.80 | −4.44 | 65.20 ± 8.20 | −155.49 |
| 1st session (Training), 2nd session (Testing) | 87.00 | −2.78 | 83.00 | 0.55 | 76.00 | 2.70 |
| 2nd session (Training), 1st session (Testing) | 72.30 | 6.37 | 67.98 | 2.08 | 65.82 | −1.25 |

# 5 Conclusions and Future Work

In this paper, we proposed to use the fractal dimension to face the issue of time-variant behavior of the EEG/ECoG signals. The classification was carried out in different conditions: using the data recorded on one session to train and evaluate the classifier, and using the data recorded in one session to train and the data recorded in other session (one week after) to evaluate. The performance of the proposed methodology was evaluated in terms of the accuracy and the area under ROC curve.

In the case of training and evaluating the classifier with the data recorded in the same session, it was demonstrated that the accuracy achieved when FD is used as feature is better than the achieved when AR coefficients are employed, this fact confirms that FD is useful to discriminate brain signals from different mental tasks. Although for both FD and AR coefficients, the accuracy decreases when the data used to train and evaluate the classifier came from different sessions, it was demonstrated that optimizing the classifier, the accuracy achieved using FD is notoriously better than the achieved using AR coefficients.

Based on the ROC curve was possible to say that the LD classifier using the FD as feature ranks the data better than the AR coefficients. This fact occurs in both cases, training and evaluating the classifier using the data from the same session and training and evaluating the classifier using the data from different sessions. Since a good performance is obtained when the classifier is trained and evaluated with different data sets, we can say that the FD extracts the underlying information of the signal which is highly related to the mental task. This is a very important observation since expresses the time-invariant robustness of the FD, useful to face the time-variant behavior of the brain signals. In this sense, it will be possible to design a BCI able to discriminate brain signals making a brief recalibration (to adjust the threshold) every time it is used.

As future work, the authors consider that an important issue to improve the proposal is to establish a methodology to adjust the value of the threshold to optimize the classifier. Also, different classification techniques could be used to improve the accuracy of the proposed methodology such as artificial neural networks [19, 20] or spiking neural networks [21, 22].

**Acknowledgment.** The authors would like to thank Universidad La Salle México for the economic support under grant number NEC-03/15 and IMC-08/16.

# References

1. Yuan, H., He, B.: Brain-computer interfaces using sensorimotor rhythms: current state and future perspectives. IEEE Trans. Biomed. Eng. **61**, 1425–1435 (2014)
2. Nicolas-Alonso, L.F., Gomez-Gil, J.: Brain computer interfaces, a review. Sensors **12**, 1211–1279 (2012)
3. Lotte, F., Congedo, M., Lécuyer, A., Lamarche, F., Arnaldi, B.: A review of classification algorithms for EEG-based brain-computer interfaces. J. Neural Eng. **4**, R1 (2007)
4. Al-Fahoum, A.S., Al-Fraihat, A.A.: Methods of EEG signal features extraction using linear analysis in frequency and time-frequency domains. ISRN Neurosci. **2014** (2014)
5. Sun, S., Zhang, C.: Adaptive feature extraction for EEG signal classification. Med. Biol. Eng. Comput. **44**, 931–935 (2006)
6. Vaid, S., Singh, P., Kaur, C.: EEG signal analysis for BCI interface: a review. In: 2015 Fifth International Conference on Advanced Computing & Communication Technologies, ACCT, pp. 143–147. IEEE (2015)
7. Lopes, R., Betrouni, N.: Fractal and multifractal analysis: a review. Med. Image Anal. **13**, 634–649 (2009)
8. Menze, B.H., et al.: The multimodal brain tumor image segmentation benchmark (BRATS). IEEE Transactions Med. Imag. **34**, 1993–2024 (2015)
9. Islam, A., Reza, S.M., Iftekharuddin, K.M.: Multifractal texture estimation for detection and segmentation of brain tumors. IEEE Trans. Biomed. Eng. **60**, 3204–3215 (2013)
10. Acharya, R., Bhat, P.S., Kannathal, N., Rao, A., Lim, C.M.: Analysis of cardiac health using fractal dimension and wavelet transformation. ITBM-RBM **26**, 133–139 (2005)

11. Mishra, A.K., Raghav, S.: Local fractal dimension based ECG arrhythmia classification. Biomed. Signal Process. Control **5**, 114–123 (2010)
12. Cabukovski, V., Rudolf, N.d.M., Mahmood, N.: Measuring the fractal dimension of EEG signals: selection and adaptation of method for real-time analysis. WIT Trans. Biomed. Health **1** (1970)
13. Esteller, R., et al.: Fractal dimension characterizes seizure onset in epileptic patients. In: Proceedings of the 1999 IEEE International Conference on Acoustics, Speech, and Signal Processing, vol. 4, pp. 2343–2346. IEEE (1999)
14. Accardo, A., Affinito, M., Carrozzi, M., Bouquet, F.: Use of the fractal dimension for the analysis of electroencephalographic time series. Biol. Cybern. **77**, 339–350 (1997)
15. Boostani, R., Moradi, M.H.: A new approach in the BCI research based on fractal dimension as feature and adaboost as classifier. J. Neural Eng. **1**, 212 (2004)
16. Güçlü, U., Güçlütürk, Y., Loo, C.K.: Evaluation of fractal dimension estimation methods for feature extraction in motor imagery based brain computer interface. Proc. Comput. Sci. **3**, 589–594 (2011)
17. Polychronaki, G., et al.: Comparison of fractal dimension estimation algorithms for epileptic seizure onset detection. J. Neural Eng. **7**, 046007 (2010)
18. Fukunaga, K.: Introduction to Statistical Pattern Recognition. Academic Press, Cambridge (2013)
19. Garro, B.A., Vázquez, R.A.: Designing artificial neural networks using particle swarm optimization algorithms. Computational Intelligence and Neuroscience **2015** (2015). https://doi.org/10.1155/2015/369298
20. Garro, B.A., Sossa, H., Vázquez, R.A.: Design of artificial neural networks using differential evolution algorithm. In: Wong, K.W., Mendis, B.S.U., Bouzerdoum, A. (eds.) ICONIP 2010. LNCS, vol. 6444, pp. 201–208. Springer, Heidelberg (2010). https://doi.org/10.1007/978-3-642-17534-3_25
21. Vazquez, R.A., Garro, B.A.: Training spiking neural models using artificial bee colony. Comput. Intell. Neurosci. **2015**, Article ID 947098 (2015)
22. Cachón, A., Vazquez, R.A.: Tuning the parameters of an integrate and fire neuron via a genetic algorithm for solving pattern recognition problems. Neurocomputing **148**, 187–197 (2015)

# Jitter Approximation and Confidence Masks in Simulated SCNA Using AEP Distribution

Jorge Ulises Muñoz–Minjares[1]([⊠]), Yuriy S. Shmaliy[1]([⊠]),
Luis Javier Morales–Mendoza[2], and Osbaldo Vite–Chavez[3]

[1] Department of Electronics Engineering, Universidad de Guanajuato,
Guanajuato, Mexico
{ju.munozminjares,shmaliy}@ugto.mx
[2] Department of Electronics Engineering, Universidad Veracruzana,
Xalapa, Mexico
[3] Department of Electronics Engineering, Universidad Autonoma de Zacatecas,
Zacatecas, Mexico

**Abstract.** Jitter is inherent to the breakpoints of measured genome somatic copy number alterations (SCNAs). Therefore, an analysis of jitter is required to reduce errors in the SCNA estimation. The SCNA measurements are accompanied with intensive noise that may cause errors and ambiguities in the breakpoint detection with low signal-to-noise ratios (SNRs). We show that the asymmetric exponential power distribution (AEPD) provides much better approximation to the jitter distribution than the earlier proposed discrete skew Laplace distribution. Furthermore, we confirm that (AEP) distribution its suitable for computing the confidence upper and lower boundary limits used to guarantee an existence of genomic changes with a required probability. We test some simulated SCNAs measurements by the upper and lower confidence bound masks with several probabilities.

## 1 Introduction

The chromosomal changes called the *copy number alterations* (CNAs) are gains or losses of large segments in the deoxyribonucleic acid (DNA) of the genome, which are essential for all known forms of life. The somatic CNAs (SCNAs), which occur during the lifetime of an individual are recognized as mayor contributors to cancer development [1,2]. Despite a great progress in the chromosomal probing using most modern technologies to measure the genome chromosomal structure [3], the measurement noise still remains at a high level in the SCNAs data. Figure 1a gives an example of the SCNAs probes with a single breakpoint and two segments. Here, the $l$th segment $a_l$ and $(l+1)$th segment $a_{l+1}$ are perturbed by noise, which is recognized as white Gaussian with zero mean and the standard deviations $\sigma_l$ and $\sigma_{l+1}$ [5,6]. The segmental difference $\Delta_l = a_{l+1} - a_l$ corresponds to the breakpoint at $n = 200$. In the $l$th segment and $(l+1)$th segment, the segmental signal-to-noise ratios (SNRs) are specified as in [4,7],

© Springer Nature Switzerland AG 2018
F. Castro et al. (Eds.): MICAI 2017, LNAI 10633, pp. 326–337, 2018.
https://doi.org/10.1007/978-3-030-02840-4_27

$$\gamma_l^- = \frac{\Delta_l^2}{\sigma_l^2}, \quad \gamma_l^+ = \frac{\Delta_l^2}{\sigma_{l+1}^2} \tag{1}$$

for supposedly constant segmental values.

The uncertainty in the breakpoint location caused by the intensive noise is called "jitter". This phenomenon denotes a deviation to the left or to the right from the true breakpoint location [8]. The SCNA levels are estimated by simple averaging between the breakpoints, which reduces the variance of the segmental noise by the segmental length. However, in spite of several methods developed to refine the breakpoints [9–11], an accurate detection of the breakpoint locations often becomes unavailable due to low segmental SNRs. By virtue of the above, many approaches have been developed to provide denoising while preserving edges in such signals [12–15].

The jitter distribution in the SCNA breakpoints can be approximated with the discrete skew Laplace distribution depicted in Fig. 1b as SkL [16,17]. Even so, accuracy in the Laplace-based approximation becomes insufficient when the SNR exceeds unity [17]. There are several conditions under which the Laplace distribution becomes too rough and a more correct probabilistic model of jitter in the breakpoints is required; for example, when the SNR values are both low, $\gamma_l^-, \gamma_l^+ < 1$, and when they are extremely low, $\gamma_l^-, \gamma_l^+ \ll 1$.

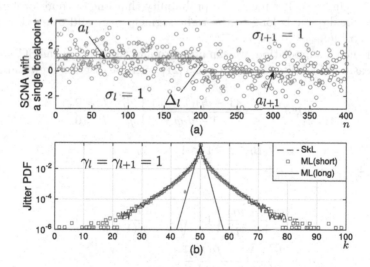

**Fig. 1.** Simulated SCNAs with a breakpoint at $n = 200$ and standard deviations $\sigma_l$ and $\sigma_{l+1}$ corresponding to SNRs $\gamma_l^- = \gamma_l^+ = 1$: (a) measurement and (b) jitter distribution. Here, ML (squared and solid) is the jitter pdf obtained experimentally using the ML estimator via a histogram over $10^5$ runs and SkL (dashed) is the Laplace distribution.

The CNVs estimation problem is thus to predict the breakpoints locations and the segmental levels with a maximum possible accuracy and precision acceptable for medical applications. Because of intensive noise [18], the estimates have to be accompanied with the confidence upper bound (UB) and lower bound (LB) masks considered in [19,20].

In this paper, we propose approximating the jitter distribution in the SCNAs breakpoints using the asymmetric exponential power function (AEPF) $\mathcal{EP}_\alpha$ when the SNR values becomes low and extra low. The $\mathcal{EP}_\alpha$ function can be used to approximate the experimentally measured jitter probability density function (pdf) with highest accuracy by finding the best fit for the measured data via the parameters $\alpha$, $\kappa$ and $\sigma$ of the Kolmogorov-Smirnov distance. Next, We test the derived distribution using simulated data and evaluate the approximation mean square error (MSE) for several SNRs levels related to the experimentally measured distributions. Finally, we establish adaptations to the equations for computing the confidence upper and lower boundary limits based us on the AEP distribution. Complementing the above with an example of simulated SCNAs measurements by the upper and lower confidence bound masks.

## 2   Jitter Distribution in the Breakpoints

The jitter distribution in the SCNA breakpoints can be derived if we suppose that all of the probes to the left of the breakpoint belong to the segment $a_l$ and all of the probes to the right from the breakpoint belong to the segment $a_{l+1}$, see Fig. 1a [21]. On the other hand, the probability that one or more probes to the left of the breakpoint belong to the right segment $a_{l+1}$ and otherwise produce the *jitter probability*.

Under such a supposition, we can approximate the jitter in the SCNA breakpoints measured in white Gaussian noise [21] with the discrete skew Laplace pdf [22],

$$p(k|d_l, q_l) = \frac{(1 - d_l)(1 - q_l)}{1 - d_l q_l} \begin{cases} d_l^k, & k \geqslant 0, \\ q_l^{|k|}, & k \leqslant 0, \end{cases} \tag{2}$$

where $0 < d_l = e^{-\frac{\kappa_l}{\nu_l}} = P(B_l)^{-1} - 1 < 1$, $0 < q_l = e^{-\frac{1}{\kappa_l \nu_l}} = P(A_l)^{-1} - 1 < 1$, $\kappa_l = \sqrt{\frac{\ln x_l}{\ln(x_l/\mu_l)}}$, $\nu_l = -\frac{\kappa_l}{\ln x_l}$,

$$x_l = \frac{\phi_l(1 + \mu_l)}{2(1 + \phi_l)} \left(1 - \sqrt{1 + \frac{4\mu_l(1 - \phi_l^2)}{\phi_l^2(1 + \mu_l)^2}}\right), \tag{3}$$

$$\mu_l = \frac{P(A_l)[1 - P(B_l)]}{P(B_l)[1 - P(A_l)]}, \tag{4}$$

$$\phi_l = \frac{P(A_l) + P(B_l) - 1}{[1 - 2P(A_l)][1 - 2P(B_l)]}, \tag{5}$$

$P(A_l)$ is the probability that all of the probes to the left from the breakpoint belong to $a_l$ and $P(B_l)$ is the probability that all probes to the right from the breakpoint belong to $a_{l+1}$.

The ordinary least squares (OSL) can be employed to detect the breakpoints in the maximum likelihood (ML) sense. By setting the segmental levels, $a_l$ and $a_{l+1}$, and the breakpoint location as variables, the MSE in the ML estimate can be minimized for the stepwise CNAs signal. So, the breakpoint location is said to be detected when the MSE in the ML estimate reaches a minimum.

In our simulation, the breakpoint location was detected $10^5$ times for each generated noise sequence with a constant SNR. The resolution of each iteration to generate the noise step was increased from 4 to 9 decimal values (in the short and long formats, respectively) to diminish the accumulated error. The histogram was plotted as a number of the events in the $k$ scale for each SNR. In order to avoid ripples, such a procedure has been repeated 5 times and the estimates were averaged. Normalized for a unit area, the histogram was accepted as the experimentally defined *jitter pdf*. Figure 1b shows the difference between the generated histograms using different formats in simulation. In turn, Fig. 2 illustrates a set of the jitter pdfs for different SNRs.

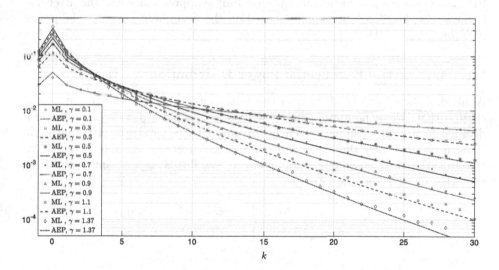

**Fig. 2.** Experimentally obtained one-sided jitter probability densities (markers) of the breakpoint location for equal segmental SNRs in the range of $M = 800$ points with a true breakpoint at $n = 400$. The experimental density functions were found using the ML estimator. The histogram was plotted over $10^5$ runs repeated 5 times and averaged.

## 2.1 Errors in the Discrete Skew Laplace-Based Approximation

Extensive investigations of the Laplace pdf (2) in applications to the SCNAs-like signals measured in Gaussian noise have revealed the following specifics [21]:

- Density (2) is reasonably accurate if the SNRs exceed unity, $\gamma_l^-, \gamma_l^+ > 1$, and highly accurate for $\gamma_l^-, \gamma_l^+ \gg 1$.

- The Laplace distribution (2) is also reasonably accurate if at least one of the segmental SNRs exceeds unity, $\gamma_l^- > 1$ or $\gamma_l^+ > 1$, and highly accurate if $\gamma_l^- \gg 1$ or $\gamma_l^- \gg 1$.
- The approximation error becomes large when $\gamma_l^-, \gamma_l^+ < 1$ and can be unacceptable if $\gamma_l^-, \gamma_l^+ \ll 1$.

A general conclusion is that the jitter distribution in the perceptible breakpoints can be fitted with the Laplace distribution (2) if the SNRs are relatively high [4,17]. Otherwise, the Laplace distribution can be inaccurate for taking any decision about the SCNAs structures via the estimates when the chromosomal changes are not brightly pronounces [19,20]. Thus, a more accurate approximation thus required.

# 3   Approximation of Jitter Distribution

In this section, we provide an efficient and simple approximation of the jitter distribution in the SCNA breakpoints based on the asymmetric exponential power distribution (AEPD).

## 3.1   Asymmetric Exponential Power Distribution

Analyzing the jitter distribution in the breakpoints, we have arrived at a conclusion that it can be approximated with a sub-Laplace distribution. We also decided to use an asymmetric generalization of the Gaussian and Laplace [23] laws in view of their simplicity and flexibility. A random variable $Y$ is said to have an AFPD, if there exist parameters $\alpha > 0$, $\theta \in \mathbb{R}$, $\sigma > 0$, and $\kappa > 0$ such that the pdf of $Y$ has the form of

$$f(x) = \frac{\alpha}{\sigma \Gamma\left(\frac{1}{\alpha}\right)} \frac{\kappa}{1+\kappa^2} \begin{cases} e^{-\frac{\kappa^\alpha}{\sigma^\alpha}|x-\theta|^\alpha}, & x \geqslant 0, \\ e^{-\frac{1}{\kappa^\alpha \sigma^\alpha}|x-\theta|^\alpha}, & x < 0, \end{cases} \tag{6}$$

where

$$\Gamma(a,x) = \int_x^\infty t^{a-1} e^{-t} dt, \, a > 0, \, x > 0, \tag{7}$$

is the incomplete gamma function. We will denote the distribution of $Y$ as $\mathcal{EP}_\alpha(\theta, \sigma, \kappa)$. The parameters $\theta$ and $\sigma$ represent the location and scale, respectively, while $\kappa$ corresponds to the controls skewness and $\alpha$ is the shape parameter. If $\kappa = 1$, the AFPD becomes symmetric about $\theta$. Otherwise, when $\kappa \neq 1$, letting $\alpha = 1$ transforms (6) to the discrete skew Laplace distribution [23]

$$f(x) = \frac{1}{\sigma} \frac{\kappa}{1+\kappa^2} \begin{cases} e^{-\frac{\kappa}{\sigma}|x-\theta|}, & x \geqslant 0, \\ e^{-\frac{1}{\sigma\kappa}|x-\theta|}, & x < 0. \end{cases} \tag{8}$$

An example of applications of $\mathcal{EP}_\alpha$ as an approximation is given in [24], where the MLEs parameters $\hat{\alpha}$, $\hat{\kappa}$ and $\hat{\sigma}$ were estimated for the growth distribution.

**Table 1.** MSEs Produced by the AEPD (6) for given $\hat{\alpha}$, $\hat{a}$, $\hat{\kappa}$ and $\hat{\sigma}$ in the reasonable SNR range.

| $\gamma^-, \gamma^+$ | $\hat{\alpha}$ | $\hat{\kappa}$ | $\hat{\sigma}$ | Error $Laplace$ | Error $\mathcal{EP}_\alpha$ |
|---|---|---|---|---|---|
| 0.1–0.1 | 0.46 | 1 | 4.75 | $7.28e^{-5}$ | $1.11e^{-7}$ |
| 0.2–0.2 | 0.52 | 1 | 3.33 | $7.62e^{-5}$ | $7.09e^{-8}$ |
| 0.3–0.3 | 0.54 | 1 | 2.49 | $7.53e^{-5}$ | $1.16e^{-7}$ |
| 0.4–0.4 | 0.56 | 1 | 2.08 | $7.16e^{-5}$ | $1.03\ e^{-7}$ |
| 0.5–0.5 | 0.57 | 1 | 1.77 | $6.81e^{-5}$ | $1.24\ e^{-7}$ |
| 0.6–0.6 | 0.58 | 1 | 1.56 | $6.45e^{-5}$ | $1.04e^{-7}$ |
| 0.7–0.7 | 0.59 | 1 | 1.43 | $5.9\ e^{-5}$ | $8.33e^{-8}$ |
| 0.8–0.8 | 0.6 | 1 | 1.3 | $5.68\ e^{-5}$ | $9.99e^{-8}$ |
| 0.9–0.9 | 0.602 | 1 | 1.18 | $5.24\ e^{-5}$ | $1.13e^{-7}$ |
| 1.0–1.0 | 0.61 | 1 | 1.11 | $5.03\ e^{-5}$ | $1.21e^{-7}$ |
| 1.1–1.1 | 0.614 | 1 | 1.04 | $4.71\ e^{-5}$ | $1.13e^{-7}$ |
| 1.2–1.2 | 0.622 | 1 | 0.99 | $4.41e^{-5}$ | $7.07e^{-8}$ |
| 1.37 1.37 | 0.628 | 1 | 0.9 | $3.90e^{-5}$ | $6.80e^{-8}$ |
| 1.50–1.50 | 0.635 | 1 | 0.85 | $3.58e^{-5}$ | $6.32e^{-8}$ |
| 2.0–2.0 | 0.647 | 1 | 0.7 | $2.62\ e^{-5}$ | $7.45e^{-8}$ |

## 3.2 Estimation of $\alpha$, $\kappa$ and $\sigma$

In order to use (6) as an approximation for the jitter distribution, one needs finding $\alpha$, $\kappa$ and $\sigma$ as functions of $\gamma_l^-$ and $\gamma_l^+$. We have found these constants by fitting the histograms with a highest accuracy and calculating the minimal Kolmogorov–Smirnov distance [25] defined as

$$d_{KS} = \max|F_0(x) - S_N(x)| \tag{9}$$

where $F_0(x)$ is the population cumulative distribution of equation (6), and $S_N(x)$ is the observed cumulative step function. The Kolmogorov-Smirnov distance is a common statistical measure called the "test of goodness of fit".

We calculate the distance $d_{KS}$ by (9) and select the minimum one to set the most appropriate vales of $\alpha$, $\kappa$ and $\sigma$ for various symmetric SNRs $\gamma^- = \gamma^+$. The results can be found in Table 1. We also approximate $\alpha$ and $\sigma$ in the mean square error (MSE) sense as

$$\alpha(\gamma) = 1 - \frac{a_1}{\gamma^{b_1}}, \tag{10}$$

$$\sigma(\gamma) = a_2 \gamma^{b_2}, \tag{11}$$

where $a_1 = 0.389$, $b_1 = 0.1394$, $a_2 = 1.142$ and $b_2 = -0.6289$. When the levels of SNR are different $\gamma^- \neq \gamma^+$ the values are calculated as $\alpha(\gamma^\pm) = \frac{\alpha(\gamma^+) + \alpha(\gamma^-)}{2}$

and $\sigma(\gamma^{\pm}) = \frac{\sigma(\gamma^+)+\sigma(\gamma^-)}{2}$. In order to calculate the value of $\kappa$, we modified the equation proposed in [23]

$$\hat{\kappa} = \left[\frac{\bar{X}_\alpha^-}{\bar{X}_\alpha^+}\right]^{\frac{1}{2(\alpha+1)}}, \tag{12}$$

where for the asymmetric case $\bar{X}^- = \gamma^+$ and $\bar{X}_\alpha^+ = \gamma^-$ and $\hat{\kappa} = 1$ otherwise.

## 4    Probabilistic Masks

Based on an analysis of Fig. 1a, It can be deduced that estimates of the SCNAs may have low confidence in presence of large noise, especially with small SNR $\gamma \leqslant 1$. Thus, each estimate requires confidence boundaries within which it may exist with a given probability. It is well illustrated in Fig. 2 in [19] to show that the breakpoint can be detected in a wide range and far from an actual location if to repeat probing. Otherwise, some segmental levels and breakpoints can be detected by an estimator close to actual ones, whereas some others not. In [19,20] is concluded that there is no other way but to find the confidence boundaries and probabilistic masks for these estimates.

Given an estimate $\hat{a}_l$ of the $l$th segmental level in white Gaussian noise, the probabilistic upper boundary (UB) and lower boundary (LB) can be specified for this estimate for the given confidence probability $P(\vartheta)$ in the $\vartheta$-sigma sense as [20]

$$\hat{a}_l^{\mathrm{UB}} \cong \hat{a}_l + \epsilon = \hat{a}_l + \vartheta\sqrt{\frac{\sigma_j^2}{N_l}} = \hat{a}_l + \vartheta\hat{\sigma}_l, \tag{13}$$

$$\hat{a}_l^{\mathrm{LB}} \cong \hat{a}_l - \epsilon = \hat{a}_l - \vartheta\sqrt{\frac{\sigma_j^2}{N_l}} = \hat{a}_l - \vartheta\hat{\sigma}_l. \tag{14}$$

where $\vartheta$ indicates the boundary wideness in terms of the segmental noise variance $\hat{\sigma}_l$ on an interval of $N_l$ points, from $\hat{n}_{l-1}$ to $\hat{n}_l - 1$.

Likewise, detected the $l$th breakpoint location $\hat{n}_l$, the jitter probabilistic left boundary $J_l^L$ and right boundary $J_l^R$ can be defined following [20] as

$$J_l^{\mathrm{L}} \cong \hat{n}_l - k_l^{\mathrm{R}}, \tag{15}$$
$$J_l^{\mathrm{R}} \cong \hat{n}_l + k_l^{\mathrm{L}}, \tag{16}$$

where $k_l^{\mathrm{R}}(\vartheta)$ and $k_l^{\mathrm{L}}(\vartheta)$ are specified by the jitter distribution in the $\vartheta$-sigma sense.

By combining (12) and (13) with (14) and (15), the probabilistic masks can be formed as shown in [20] to bound the CNV estimates in the $\vartheta$-sigma sense for the given confidence probability $P(\vartheta)$. An important property of these masks is that they can be used not only to bound the estimates and show their possible locations on a probabilistic field [19,20], but also to remove supposedly wrong breakpoints. Such situations occur each time when the masks reveal double UB and LB uniformities in a gap of three neighbouring detected breakpoints. If so, then the unlikely existing intermediate breakpoint ought to be removed.

Noticing that the segmental boundaries (12) and (13) remain the same irrespective of the jitter in the breakpoints, below we specify the masks for the jitter represented with the Laplace distribution (2) and AEP-based approximation (6).

## 4.1  Masks for AEPD Approximation

The confidence masks based on AEPD approximation are easily calculated using the equations described in [20] to Laplace distribution. For the Laplace distribution (2), the jitter left boundary $J_l^L$ (14) and right boundary $J_l^R$ (15) can be defined in the $\vartheta$-sigma sense if to specify $k_l^R(\vartheta)$ and $k_l^L(\vartheta)$ as shown in [21],

$$k_l^R = \left\lfloor \frac{\nu_l}{\kappa_l} \ln \frac{(1-d_l)(1-q_l)}{\xi(1-d_l q_l)} \right\rfloor, \tag{17}$$

$$k_l^L = \left\lfloor \nu_l \kappa_l \ln \frac{(1-d_l)(1-q_l)}{\xi(1 \quad d_l q_l)} \right\rfloor, \tag{18}$$

where $\lfloor x \rfloor$ means a maximum integer lower than or equal to $x$. Note that functions (16) and (17) were obtained in [21] by equating (2) to $\zeta(N_l) - \mathrm{ortc}(\vartheta/\sqrt{2})$ and solving for $k_l$.

The UB mask $\mathcal{EP}_l^{UB}$ and LB mask $\mathcal{EP}_l^{LB}$ for AEPD approximation can be formed by replacing in (17) and (18) the new values of $p_l$ and $q_l$ calculated from this distribution. Now, the equations to $p_l^{\mathcal{EP}}$ and $q_l^{\mathcal{EP}}$ can be defined as

$$p_l^{\mathcal{EP}} = e^{-\frac{\kappa^\alpha}{\sigma^\alpha}}, \tag{19}$$

$$q_l^{\mathcal{EP}} = e^{-\frac{1}{\kappa^\alpha \sigma^\alpha}}. \tag{20}$$

That allows us to specify the right-hand jitter $k_l^{\mathcal{EP}R}$ and left-hand jitter $k_l^{\mathcal{EP}L}$ by, respectively,

$$k_l^{\mathcal{EP}R} = \left\lfloor \frac{\sigma_l^{\mathcal{EP}}}{\kappa_l^{\mathcal{EP}}} \ln \frac{(1-d_l^{\mathcal{EP}})(1-q_l^{\mathcal{EP}})}{\xi(1-d_l^{\mathcal{EP}} q_l^{\mathcal{EP}})} \right\rfloor, \tag{21}$$

$$k_l^{\mathcal{EP}L} = \left\lfloor \nu_l^B \kappa_l^B \ln \frac{(1-d_l^{\mathcal{EP}})(1-q\mathcal{EP}_l)}{\xi(1-d_l^{\mathcal{EP}} q_l^{\mathcal{EP}})} \right\rfloor. \tag{22}$$

We finally define the jitter left boundary $J_l^{\mathcal{EP}L}$ and right boundary $J_l^{\mathcal{EP}R}$ as, respectively,

$$J_l^{\mathcal{EP}L} \cong \hat{n}_l - k_l^{\mathcal{EP}R}, \tag{23}$$

$$J_l^{\mathcal{EP}R} \cong \hat{n}_l + k_l^{\mathcal{EP}L}, \tag{24}$$

and use in the algorithm [20] previously designed for the confidence masks based on the Laplace distribution.

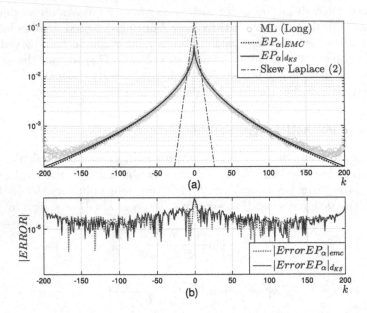

**Fig. 3.** Approximations of the experimentally measured jitter pdf (circles) for $\gamma_l^{\pm} = 0.1$ using the discrete skew Laplace distribution and the AEPD for $\alpha = 0.44$. Measurement points are provided by running the ML estimator $10^5$ times: (a) approximations and (b) absolute differences between the data and the approximations.

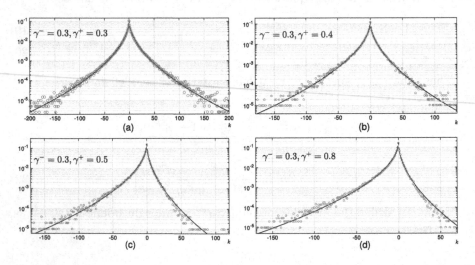

**Fig. 4.** Approximations of the experimentally measured jitter pdf (doted) for different SNR values using the AEPD (solid): (a)$\gamma_l^{\mp} = 0.3$, (b) $\gamma_l^{\mp} = 0.3, 0.4$, (c) $\gamma_l^{\mp} = 0.3, 0.5$ and (d) $\gamma_l^{\mp} = 0.3, 0.8$. Raw data are provided by running the ML estimator $10^4$ times.

# 5    Applications

The MSEs produced by the skew Laplace distribution (2) and the $\mathcal{EP}_\alpha$ approximation using (10), (11) and (12) are listed in Table 1. As can be seen, the approximation (6) with $\hat{\alpha}$, $\hat{\kappa}$ and $\hat{\sigma}$ produces smaller errors than the skew Laplace distribution (2). It can also be observed that the approximation $\mathcal{EP}_\alpha$ is much more accurate than (2) for any reasonably small $\gamma$. In Fig. 3a one can see how well the proposed approximation fits the measurement data obtained for $\gamma^\pm = 0.1$. It turned out that the difference between the experimental jitter distribution (ML) and the approximation obtained with (6) is very small, as shown in Fig. 3a. Figure 4a, b, c, and d sketch the proposed approximation for combined values of the SNR: $\gamma^- = 0.3$ and $\gamma^+ = 0.3, 0.4, 0.5, 0.8$. In this case, the value of $\hat{\alpha}$ is set constant with respect to $\gamma = 0.3$ at $\alpha = 0.54$. The confidence masks calculated based on the $\mathcal{EP}_\alpha$ approximation with simulated SCNAs are sketched in Fig. 5a. An analysis around the breakpoint $i_2$ is showed in Fig. 5b and c, computing the probability density function and the $\mathcal{EP}_\alpha$ approximation, respectively.

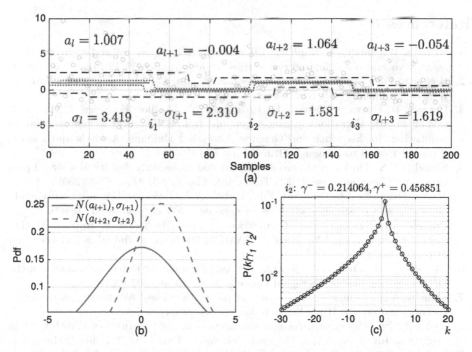

**Fig. 5.** (a) Simulated measurements of SCNAs with low segmental SNRs (circled) and $\mathcal{B}_l^{UB}$ and $\mathcal{B}_l^{LB}$ masks [20] (dashed) with a probability of 99.73% and an probability of 50% (doted), (b) segmental Gaussian densities for $\sigma_{l+1}$ and $\sigma_{l+2}$, and (c) Asymmetric Exponential Power approximation for jitter in the breakpoint $i_2$.

# 6   Conclusions

The AEPD employing the ML estimator parameters has appeared to be more accurate than the discrete skew Laplace distribution in the approximation of jitter in the breakpoints of the SCNAs. This is particularly true for low and extra low SNR values often observed in probes of small SCNAs. The parameters $\alpha$, $\kappa$ and $\sigma$ required to use the AEPD can be found experimentally for any reasonable SNR values. The AEPD-based approximation employs the Kolmogorov-Smirnov distance, which can be computed by minimizing the MSE. It is important to know that the coefficients $\alpha$, $\kappa$ and $\sigma$ are affected by the segmental SNRs in both the symmetric and asymmetric cases. We have also successfully calculated the upper and lower bounds for the confidence masks, which allow for decreasing errors generated by the skew Laplace distribution to avoid uncertainties and false decisions. Referring to the advantages of the proposed approximations, we now work on applications to massive probe data obtained using the micro-array of HR-CGH. We also seek simple relationships between the AEPD parameters and the segmental SNRs to use them in the confidence probabilistic masks.

# References

1. Hsin-Ta, W., Iman, H., Raphael, J.R.: Detecting independent and recurrent copy number aberrations using interval graphs. Bioinformatics **30**(12), i195–i203 (2014)
2. Hastings, P.J., Lupski, J.R., Rosenberg, S.M., Ira, G.: Mechanisms of change in gene copy number. Nat. Rev. Genet. **10**(8), 551–564 (2009)
3. Popova, T., Boeva, V., Manie, E., Rozenholc, Y., Barillot, E., Stern, M.H.: Analysis of somatic alterations in cancer genome: from SNP arrays to next generation sequencing. In: Sequence and Genome Analysis I Humans, Animals and Plants. iConcept Press Ltd., August 2013. Ed. by Ltd iP
4. Shmaliy, Y.S.: On the multivariate conditional probability density of a signal perturbed by Gaussian noise. IEEE Trans. Inf. Theory **53**, 4792–4797 (2007)
5. Munoz-Minjares, J.U., Shmaliy Y.S., Cabal, A.J.: Noise studies in measurements and estimates of stepwise changes in genome DNA chromosomal structures. In: Proceedings of International Conference on Pure Mathematics, Applied Mathematics, Computational Methods (PMAMCM 2014), Santorini Island, Greece, pp. 212–221 (2014)
6. Pique-Regi, R., Ortega, A., Tewfik, A., Asgharzadeh, S.: Detection changes in the DNA copy number. IEEE Signal Process. Mag. **29**, 98–107 (2012)
7. Shmaliy, Y.S.: Limiting phase errors of passive wireless SAW sensing with differential measurement. IEEE Sens. J. **4**, 819–827 (2004)
8. Joshi, A.: Speech emotion recognition using combined features of HMM & SVM algorithm. Int. J. Adv. Res. Comput. Sci. Softw. Eng. **3**(8), 387–393 (2013)
9. Hupe, P., Stransky, N., Thiery, J.P., Radvanyi, F., Barillot, E.: Analysis of array CGH data: from signal ratio to gain and loss of DNA regions. Bioinformatics **20**(18), 3413–3422 (2004)
10. Lemaitre, C., Tannier, E., Gautier, C., Sagot, M.F.: Precise detection of rearrangement breakpoints in mammalian chromosomes. BMC Bioinform. **9**(1), 286 (2008)
11. Wong, K., Keane, T.M., Stalker, J., Adams, D.J.: Enhanced structural variant and breakpoint detection using SVMerge by integration of multiple detection methods and local assembly. Genome Biol. **11**(12), 128 (2010)

12. Donoho, D.L.: De-noising by soft thresholding. IEEE Trans. Inf. Theory **41**, 613–627 (1995)
13. Tukey, J.W.: Exploratory Data Analysis. Addison-Wesley, Menlo Park (1971)
14. Lepski, O.V., Mammen, E., Spokoiny, V.G.: Optimal spatial adaptation to inhomogenous smoothness: an approach based on kernel estimates with variable bandwidth selectors. Ann. Stat. **25**, 929–947 (1997)
15. Rao B.D., Hari, K.V.S.: Effect of spatial smoothing on the performance of MUSIC and the minimum-norm method. In: Proceedings of IEEE, vol. 137(F), no. 6, pp. 449–458, December 1990
16. Picard, F., Robin, S., Lavielle, M., Vaisse, C., Daudin, J.J.: A statistical approach for array CGH data analysis. BMC Bioinform. **6**(1), 27–37 (2012)
17. Munoz-Minjares, J.U., Shmaliy, Y.S.: Approximate jitter probability in the breakpoints of genome copy number variations. In: Proceedings of 10th International Conference on Electrical Engineering, Computing Science and Automatic Control (CCE), Mexico City, Mexico, pp. 128–131 (2013)
18. Muñoz, J.U., Cabal, J., Shmaliy, Y.S.: Effect of noise on estimate bounds for genome DNA structural changes. WSEAS Trans. Biol. Biomed. **11**, 52–61 (2014)
19. Munoz-Minjares, J.U., Shmaliy, Y.S., Cabal-Aragon, J.: Confidence limits for genome DNA copy number variations in HR-CGH array measurements. Biomed. Signal Process. Control **10**, 166–173 (2014)
20. Muñoz-Minjares, J., CabalAragon, J., Shmaliy, Y.S.: Confidence masks for genome DNA copy number variations in applications to HR-CGH array measurements. Biomed. Signal Process. Control. **13**, 337–344 (2014)
21. Muñoz-Minjares, J., CabalAragon, J., Shmaliy, Y.S.: Effect of noise on estimate bounds for genome DNA structural changes. WSEAS Trans. Biol. Biomed. **11**, 52–61 (2014)
22. Kozubowski, T.J., Inusah, S.: A skew Laplace distribution on integers. Ann. Inst. Stat. Math. **58**, 555–571 (2006)
23. Ayebo, A., Kozubowski, T.J.: An asymmetric generalization of Gaussian and Laplace laws. J. Probab. Stat. Sci. **1**(2), 187–210 (2003)
24. Buldyrev, S.V., Growiec, J., Riccaboni, M., Stanley, H.E.: The growth of business firms: facts and theory. J. Eur. Econ. Assoc. **5**(2–3), 574–584 (2007)
25. Massey, F.J.: The Kolmogorov-Smirnov test for goodness of fit. J. Am. Stat. Assoc. **46**(253), 68–78 (1951)

# A Framework Based on Eye-Movement Detection from EEG Signals for Flight Control of a Drone

Eduardo Zecua Corichi$^{(\boxtimes)}$, José Martínez Carranza$^{(\boxtimes)}$,
Carlos Alberto Reyes García$^{(\boxtimes)}$, and Luis Villaseñor Pineda$^{(\boxtimes)}$

Department of computer Sciences, Instituto Nacional de Astrofísica,
Óptica y Electrónica (INAOE), Luis Enrique Erro # 1, 72840 Tonantzintla,
Puebla, Mexico
{corichiedu,carranza,kargaxxi,villasen}@inaoep.mx

**Abstract.** There is a considerable number of people with some disability they may go from partial limb disability to total incapacity. For these people, technology is an opportunity to bring them back some capabilities. In this work, we present a framework where we envisage a system that can be used by a disabled person who can not move but still possesses eye movements. Therefore, by using electroencephalographic (EEG) signals, we recognize and classify eye movements, which are then translated to control commands. Based on the latter, we developed an application to illustrate how such commands could be used to control a drone that could be used to deliver messages or carry out any other activity that involves the drone having to fly from a start point to a final destination. The results obtained in this study indicate that ocular movements are recognized with an accuracy of 86%, which suggests the feasibility of our approach.

**Keywords:** EEG · Decision tree · Classification · Drones control · PID

## 1 Introduction

The World Health Organization (WHO) states that between 250 000 and 500 000 people suffer each year worldwide spinal cord injuries [1], there are no reliable estimates of its global prevalence, but it is estimated that its annual global incidence is between 40 and 80 cases per million inhabitants, the core lessons are the most typical of paralysis cause. However, there are other diseases that affect motor neurons that should be considered (such as muscular dystrophy, myopathy distal lateral sclerosis amyotrophy or Guillain-Barre syndrome and Eaton-Lambert), these conditions can become completely paralyzed patient, clearing the individual mobility to move from a place and a need to communicate to someone else, leaving only the eye movement, blinking and electroencephalography signals for communication.

© Springer Nature Switzerland AG 2018
F. Castro et al. (Eds.): MICAI 2017, LNAI 10633, pp. 338–353, 2018.
https://doi.org/10.1007/978-3-030-02840-4_28

Recent research has focused on developing technology technologies exist to move a wheelchair [2] focused paralyzed or disabled people, but home environment that are difficult [3] or impossible to access due to the same architecture or the placement of furniture, making it entirely dependent on another person for many daily activities at home and drink a glass of water or send an emergency message to an individual in another room, in this case, a unmanned vehicles aerial (UAVs) or emph drones have more space of mobility and are currently are being used for various purposes among which are included surveillance, military efforts to provide security, tactical reconnaissance, mail, among others [4], used to access areas inaccessible or dangerous, being able apply these techniques in an environment indoor.

A communication approach with disabled people is to use the electrooculography (EOG) which consists of five electrodes placed on the face, around the eyes [5] capable of detecting the direction of eye movement in two dimensions (horizontal and vertical) and flicker, [12], on the other hand EEG signals collected from the human skull are fluctuations of electrical potentials that reflect activity in the underlying brain structures, particularly in the cerebral cortex below the surface of the scalp [6]. The oscillations produced by the EEG are classified according to with their relationship stimulation and may be spontaneous [7], usually the EEG signals are filtered signals eye movement by hiding brain signals of nearby channels in the eye, in some cases the EOG is used to remove the peaks of the EEG [8], using processing to remove the ECG signals, in this article these signals as commands are used Instead of treating them as noise.

This article intends to use EEG equipment acquisition to acquire and process EOG signals in order to reduce the amount of monitoring equipment in people disable to send command to UAVs to communicate whit other person or bring an object, this equipment is used for comfort and aesthetics that gives subtle compared to the EOG and it can hide in a bonnet. It is expected in future work using both signals (EEG and ECG) with the same system in order to obtain a variety of more extensive and complex commands, the objective of this research is to deal with the technology to send commands and interact with the environment through a drone by blinking and eye movement, which often are not affected by paralysis. The ability to communicate and interact with devices with the eye movement of the person makes these particularly relevant interfaces as an assistant for people with severe disabilities.

In this way and in order to describe in detail the proposed system, this paper is organized as follows: related work is presented in Sect. 2, the system and its main components are described in Sect. 3; the results are presented and discussed in Sect. 4; and finally the conclusions are broken down in Sect. 5 and acknowledgments.

## 2   Related Work

Scientists at the University of Texas at San Antonio (UTSA) are trying to turn science fiction into reality by developing technology that will allow soldiers to control a drone only with their minds remotely. Six professors from different university departments are working on various projects that have to do with the study of brain-machine interaction but was not the first university that can control drones with brain activity. In 2013, Professor Bin He of the University of Minnesota was the first person to show the flight of a small quadrocopter drone through a ring of balloons, entirely controlled with a cap with 64 electrode sensors placed on the head of a person [9]. For remotely flying the drone, the pilot imagined a fist, if it was imagined with his left hand, the drone veered to the left. The signals were sent wirelessly from the computer to the drone, but first, the signals sent by the brain cap had to be decoded and retransmitted as commands that the drone must run.

EEG has been used to examine the brain processes involved in tasks such as visual detection of a target [10] and visuomotor tracking [11]. By 2010, a consensus had been reached on the best approach to examine EEG data [12], but, particularly, two frequency bandwidths have received more attention. It has been found that the activity in the alpha range often decreases with increased task difficulty, whereas the opposite was observed in the activity in the theta range, particularly in the electrode positions in the mid-front line [13]; Electro-physiological experiments have shown that human's neurons in the visual cortex synchronize their firing at flashing light frequency, causing EEG responses which show the same frequency as the flashing stimulus [14].

Several authors have analyzed the relationship between EEG frequency and performance of different tasks, an EEG low frequency has been linked to a longer reaction time or to a greater number of errors [15]. The most common hypothesis was that the EEG performance ratio was modulated by the alert level [16]. It is beyond doubt that the alert level causes changes in both the EEG and performance. However, previous work reports with children have shown a positive correlation between the EEG delta power at rest and the response time (RT), and error ratio in visual attention and memory tasks carried out in different sessions.

In [17] shows a work that handles EEG equipment and eye tracking with a hybrid system for the combination of signals using these two systems are complemented to improve the results in order to control the direction of a pointer to position it in targets in a monitor using low-cost equipment, in this work is intended to reduce the amount of equipment mounted on the person and use the same EEG equipment to recognize eye movements.

## 3    System Description

All the experiments were performed on a computer with an Intel i7 quad-core processor with 8 GB of RAM and Ubuntu 14.4 OS running the Robot Operating System (ROS). A second computer with an AMD A10 processor with 12 GB of RAM with Windows 10 OS running Matlab 2015b and Weka 3.6. The whole system is divided into two parts: the first one is related to the acquisition of EEG data including its classification; the second stage involves the drone control using a PID controller to move to the specified position given the signals classification with feedback a system of tracking (Vicon).

## 3.1  Vicon Motion Capture System

The Vicon tracking system is a motion tracking system based on the use of monocular cameras that, through infra-red light, send a light beam to specific markers with a spherical shape and with a reflective coating, which bounces the light in all directions into the cameras [18]. Depending on the amount of reflected light and the location of each of the markers, each camera makes a triangulation returning the site of each marker in the space respecting to a reference proposed during equipment calibration and with pinpoint accuracy. These markers were placed in the drone's body so as not to stir on the flight and could be tracked at all times by the system at a frequency of 300 Hz.

## 3.2  BEBOP Drone

A Bebop drone from the company PARROT was used for the development of this work. This drone has a monocular fish-eye-type camera and four propellers. It can be controlled through computers or cell phones via WiFi communication, and it has a bottom ultrasonic sensor for measuring the distance between the ground and the drone, enabling it to remain stable during flight. This model has protections to operate indoors and outdoors.

## 3.3  PID Control

A PID controller (Proportional Integral Derivative) is a generic control mechanism over a closed-loop feedback, widely used in industry, the PID is a system that receives an error calculated from the desired output minus the obtained output, its output is used as input in the system that we want to control [19], the controller tries to minimize the error by adjusting the system information. A PID controller has three different parameters: the proportional, integral, and derivative, proportional value depends on the current error, integrally depends on past mistakes and derivative is a prediction of future errors. The sum of these three actions is used to adjust the process via a control element, like the position of a control valve or the power supplied to a heater.

By adjusting these three variables in the PID controller it can provide a control action designed for specific process requirements, the controller response can be described regarding the error control response, the degree to which the controller exceeds the setpoint and the level of system oscillation. Note that the use of PID control does not guarantee optimal system control or drone stability and gains adjustment of these systems is not trivial and needs to be modified depending upon conditions of each system and conditions of their environment, e.g., the drone is disturbed by their propellers rotation while flying depending on field.

To obtain the values of the agencies a controlled area was used and with tracking in the drone to analyze and adjust the gains, it is required that the team performs the activities as fast as possible without losing control or accuracy in the flight, for that purpose a proportion system giving a (40%) weight to the

Integral, (40%) weight of the derivative and (20%) proportional to give more smoothness to the speed when it reaches its destination.

For drone control system, a PID that calculates the error between the measured value and the desired value is used, this was applied in the context of a drone that has to reach a particular point in space, namely a reference point or waypoint. To this end, we use the Vicon system to know drone pose. Thus it is possible to calculate the error in between the current and the desired position. The PID sets the values to get closer to the waypoint, and the vehicle's velocity gets reduced as the vehicles get closer to the waypoint. Thus, our PID controller was implemented to control frontal displacement and to control rotation in yaw.

### 3.4   EEG Data Acquisition

EEG frequencies traditionally have been classified into different bands, Delta activity (1.5–3.5 Hz) is the main sleeping characteristic, but may be present in internal processes like mental calculations and memorization [20], Theta activity (4–7 Hz) may reflect a gatekeeper function of information flow through the hippocampus and the circuitry of target structures. Alpha activity (8–13 Hz) is more than a spontaneous frequency and is a prototype of dynamic processes that govern a large set of integrative brain functions. The Alfa patterns can be spontaneous, induced or evoked by stimuli, movements or related to memory. The fourth is the Gamma activity (25–100 Hz) which has been theorized that could be involved in the conscious perception process [21].

Emotiv EPOC diadem model was used for the acquisition of the signals, and it displays 14 channels (AF3, F7, F3, FC5, T7, P7, O1, O2, P8, T8, FC6, F4, F8, AF4) and 2 references (CMS, DRL) distributed in the cranial cortex as shown in Fig. 1(a). The system has a 256 Hz sampling frequency and is connected to a computer wirelessly through a USB connection.

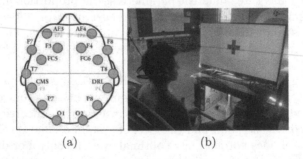

(a)                              (b)

**Fig. 1.** Our system is based on the processing of EEG signals: (a) Scheme that illustrates the electrodes location on the subject's head; (b) Display with red cross in the center to enable the subject to focus on a requested task to be recognized through the EEG signals. (Color figure online)

This work was carried out with a subject with an age of 25 years, with the aim of specializing the characteristics of electrical conduction [22] in the learning phase. Samples were collected while sitting and watching a screen with a red cross in the center with a white background, as shown in Fig. 1(b). This configuration was intended to reduce the involuntary movement of the eyes, which could be stimulated by visual distractions, also contributed to the reduction of noise in the signal recording. During the recordings, the subject to perform a movement of the eye (look up, look down, look left, look right, blinking) each time the change was carried out was requested, the user marked the start with a particular label at the beginning of performing the movement, Fig. 2 illustrates the recording process, during which the user performs an eye movement whilst wearing the diadem, signals are generated from the electrodes in the diadem, which are transmitted to the computer, these are the signals to be processed by our system, a total of 14 signals are available to be recorded in this process.

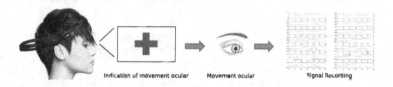

Fig. 2. Signal acquisition diagram.

## 3.5   Signal Processing Training

Given the fact that we are interested in recognizing eye movements, we selected to work with those channels closer to the eye, as recommended in [8] where the shows are more representative, these are the four channels classified as AF3, AF4, F7 and F8, see Fig. 3.

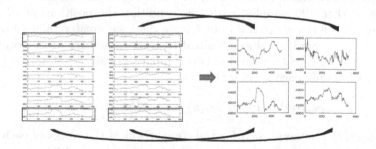

**Fig. 3.** From the 14 channels recorded with the Emotiv diadem, the channels AF3, AF4, F7 and F8 are then ones processed by our approach as these are argued to exhibit signal patterns that reflect the eye activity.

These four signals are given a single moving average filter to smooth the signal and highlight the shape of the eye movement using a $n = 55$, i is the location that is taken, D is the corresponding value in the signal, as it is shown in Eq. (1).

$$MA_n = \frac{\sum_{i=1}^{n} D_i}{n} \tag{1}$$

The human eye takes about 400 ms to complete a blink and the sampling time is 256 Hz, this leaves an interval in which the blink is recorded in 100 samples. The peaks and valleys are calculated in the signals (see Fig. 4).

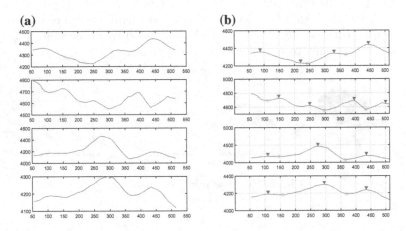

**Fig. 4.** (A) Signal passed by filter MA (B) Representative peaks movement.

To find the peaks that match the positions of the eye movements we compare the positive peaks of channels 1–4 and 3–4, compared with similar values, the peaks can have variations and do not occur at the same instant of time, taking into account these small variations we can know that the values are not in a range higher than 100 samples, with this condition the positions of the peaks and valleys of the signals that do not have a distance greater than 50 samples can be compared. Similar values obtained the total difference of the location of the peak with the Eq. (2), returning two comparison values 1–4 and 3–4 of the channels with a difference smaller than 50.

$$pick(ij) = PickPos_i(n) - PickPos_j(n) < 50 \tag{2}$$

This operation is performed for the comparison of the peaks of each of the channels, for the positive and negative values separately, resulting in one vector for each comparison with the different values of the peaks less than 50. Subsequently, this result is compared with the values of the other comparison vectors, obtaining the difference and dividing by the number of elements to scale the results in the same interval, doing this operation for the position values of the positive and negative peaks.

$$Dif_{ij} = \sum_{i=1}^{n} abs\left(\frac{(pick^+(ij)_i - pick^+(ij)_j)}{length(pick^+(ij))}\right) + \left(\frac{((pick^-(ij)_i - (pick^-(ij)_j)}{length((pickc^-(ij))}\right) \quad (3)$$

Seeking values which represent the minimum difference is compared, this indicates that the signals are more similar to the peaks since measures of signal comparison have been obtained. By selecting the most similar channels, the values of the peak positions are taken. The positions of the positive peaks of the selected channels are sockets, the difference values that position with the average of adjacent values within a range of ±50 samples starting from the sample to compare Eq. (4 it is calculated).

$$Dif_i = Valpic(pos_i) - \frac{(Valpic(pos_i - 50) + Valpic(pos_i + 50))}{2} \quad (4)$$

This operation is repeated for each of the values of each of the selected channels, are stored the in a table, these values are summed with the respective position and the maximum representing where the peak is located with more variation seeks to indicate where the change is generated in the signal and to find the negative peak of this signal the difference of the average positive peak location and the average location of the negative peaks is calculated, as shown in Eq. (5).

$$Dif = \frac{vulpick_i^- + valpick_j^-}{2} - \frac{valpick_i^+ + valpick_j^+}{2} \quad (5)$$

The resulting values are compared looking where the sign change occurs, the first negative values adjacent positions are selected, these values are added together and the minimum value is sought, this value represents the negative peak, the average of both negative positions are calculated as positive values calculated and missing values of more channels are obtained with these positions, generating a vector of nine values in row 8 calculated values and a value to indicate that movement it has been made. These operations are done for all samples collected, unitedly keeping the output values of the system, obtained as a result the values of the peaks where the coincidence with the channels is maximum and the intervals are in the range of the contemplative variations in the acquisition of the values of the signals of the eye (see Fig. 5).

Working with a fewer channels is also useful since it enables a faster processing, which ultimately is beneficial to our goal of achieving real-time communication with the drone.

Examples five channel signals corresponding to AF3 recorded at different times, in which the same subject performs the eye movement labeled shown flashing Fig. 6. it is noted that the pattern repeats the same motion [23] eye see Fig. 7, the aim is to recognize these movements eliminating all noise signals, contemplating the changes movement in the signal.

## 3.6  Computational Learning

To make the real-time system requires that the system will automatically assign each eye movements, to do this the system has to learn the characteristics of

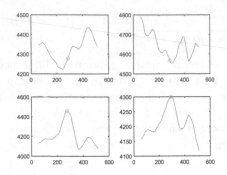

**Fig. 5.** Representative signal peaks.

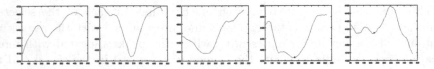

**Fig. 6.** Five samples of signals recorded from channel AF3 for the same subject performing the eye moment labelled as *blinking*, note that a patter can be drawn in these signals.

the signals, with the output values that were obtained above, for obtain a better classifier it comparing three conventional methods for classification:

- Decision trees
- Cluster
- Neural networks

Weka 3.8 was used to make the cluster and the decision tree and Matlab 2015 to the neural network, were selected to process the data differently, this in order to find you which is best suited to the characteristics of the information.

- The kmeans cluster showed an 83.3% of predicted values correctly.
- The neural network with hidden layers 8, after several genres, runs a 29% of correct values.
- J45 decision tree generated a 91% of predicted values correctly.

It can be observed that the kmean and the decision tree have good results since they can find representative parameters in the values to classify them, the neural network has poor results even after training several times, this can be due to the way of processing the information, since it does not have a pre-established start-up basis for the gains of neurons this makes it "random" fashion and established these values try to adjust the gains to obtain better results, the problem is when these values are not optimal and even if you want you can not perform well. In this case, it was selected with the classifier with the highest

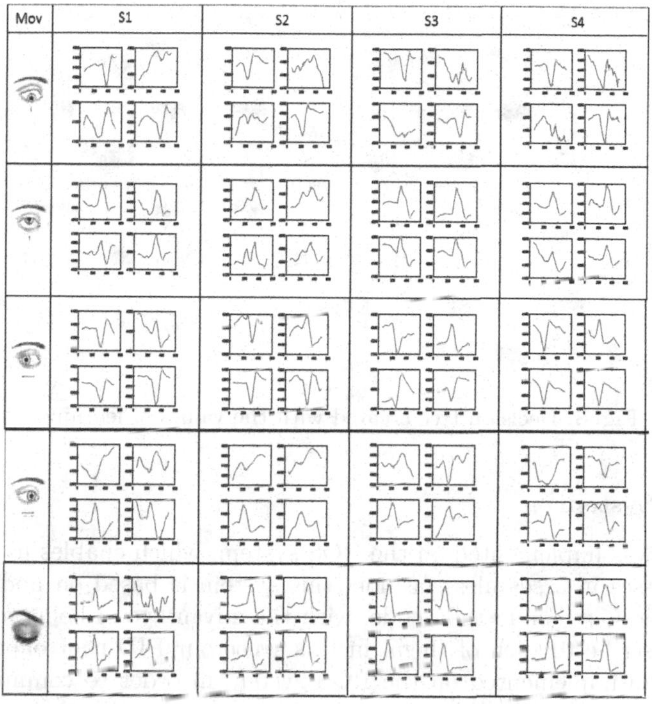

**Fig. 7.** Examples of signals recorded from a subject performing the eye movements to be recognized in this work, from to down: look up, look down, look left, look right, blinking.

percentage of correctly predicted values, the result decision tree shown in the image Fig. 8.

The internal number of each circle represents the order as the channels were chosen, the values next to the circles represent the condition to continue on this path. Finally, each square indicates the class to which it belongs, the whole decision tree is compiled in Matlab using conditions if-then.

## 3.7 Real-Time Signal Processing

We developed an interface program written in Matlab in order to communicate with the EpocSignalServer software is also licensed to Plymouth University and it is used to send the raw sensor data to external applications, such that for each one of the four channels, their raw data values from the Emotiv headset are continuously read and stored in matrix form in a time interval that does not exceed 3 s.

This information matrix is worked using the same method as described for learning, once calculated the feature vector that is applied to process the decision tree, the time it takes to process the information the program is 0.3 s, enough to detect even the fastest eye change caused by time.

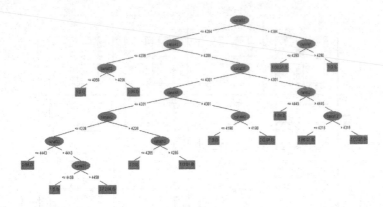

**Fig. 8.** Decision tree created with the values of learning.

## 3.8   ROS System

Our system was implemented on the ROS system, which enables us to communicate processes in a seamless fashion, this system is based on nodes that are launched from C++ or Python code, with the advantage of being able to publish and subscribe to each of them, in this sense our PID controller to control the drone was implemented on the ROS system in order to communicate our classification module, which generates drone commands, with the controller and ultimately with the drone via Wireless communication, the PID controller ran as a node in ROS and it subscribed to the classification node, the program responsible for generating the eye movements, which are used as flight commands to the drone. Depending on the classification, the drone performs an action: taking off, landing or flying to a certain area. The drone' pose was obtained from the Vicon system, which was read within the ROS node corresponding to the PID controller.

## 4   Experiments

In this section we present results from three sets of experiments: (1) assessment of our classification algorithm applied to a subset randomly selected from the database of eye movements; (2) assessment of our classification algorithm running in real time; (3) assessment of our classification algorithm integrated within our system in order to send command a drone upon subject's eye moment recognition. Each of eye movements to represent an instruction program for UAVs (see Table 3).

### 4.1   Classification Accuracy on the Database

The relation in between the number of total samples recorded and classified by our system in our database is shown Table 1, the number of samples is used for training and evaluate.

**Table 1.** Confusion matrix for random samples taken from the database.

| Mov | Blink-1 | Up-2 | Down-3 | Left-4 | Right-5 | Accuracy |
|---|---|---|---|---|---|---|
| Blink-1 | 90 | 5 | 0 | 0 | 5 | .90 |
| Up-2 | 5 | 73 | 3 | 0 | 3 | .86 |
| Down-3 | 1 | 2 | 84 | 2 | 0 | .94 |
| Left-4 | 0 | 0 | 0 | 95 | 0 | 1 |
| Right-5 | 3 | 4 | 1 | 2 | 65 | .86 |
| Accuracy | .90 | .86 | .95 | .95 | 89 | .91 |

The values in each row of the last column represent the percentages of each of the classes, and the value of the last row and last column represents the overall percentage of the system, we should highlight that the classification depends on the system calibration and noise entering to the channels so, in order to classify the eye movements, the channels must be represented with good intensity when generating movement and at normal speed [23]. Despite this, the classification accuracy is of 91% in average.

## 4.2   Real-Time Evaluation

The goal of this evaluation was that of assessing that our system was capable of classifying a subject's eye movement on-line, this is, as he performs the eye movement. For this, the user was asked to wear the diadem, look at the screen steering at the red cross, and then perform any of the five eye movements at his will. As soon as the signal is read from the diadem this goes into our system, after processing the resulting vector is compared to the decision tree and delivering the class to which belongs the movement, the same user was asked to perform this several times until 30 samples for each eye movement were carried out, the classification results for these samples are shown in Table 2, an average of 86% in classification accuracy was obtained, somewhat lower than when testing with the database off-line.

**Table 2.** Confusion matrix for real-time experiments.

| Mov | Blink-1 | Up-2 | Down-3 | Left-4 | Right-5 | Accuracy |
|---|---|---|---|---|---|---|
| Blink-1 | 26 | 2 | 0 | 2 | 0 | .86 |
| Up-2 | 0 | 24 | 0 | 3 | 3 | .80 |
| Down-3 | 0 | 0 | 22 | 8 | 0 | .73 |
| Left-4 | 0 | 0 | 0 | 28 | 2 | .93 |
| Right-5 | 0 | 0 | 0 | 0 | 30 | 1 |
| Accuracy | 1 | .92 | 1 | .68 | .85 | .86 |

## 4.3   Drone Control Assessment

A general overview of our system show Fig. 9 where eye movements are used to control a drone, Table 3 indicates what eye movement corresponds to what drone command. For the drone control commands, instructions were sent by an array of three numbers in the following way: the first digit has to be a take-off command, which was obtained via recognising the *look up* eye movement; the second digit indicates a target waypoint to which the drone has to fly, the three-way points options are set beforehand and labelled as 1, 2 and 3, associated to *look left*, *look right* and *blinking*, respectively; the last digit indicates the command for landing, which is obtained from recognising *look down*.

**Table 3.** Actions carried out according to eye movement classification.

| Class | Eye movement | Action |
|---|---|---|
| Class 1 | Look up | Taking off |
| Class 2 | Look down | Landing |
| Class 3 | Look left | Reaching point 1 |
| Class 4 | Look right | Reaching point 2 |
| Class 5 | Blinking | Reaching point 3 |

These were chosen in this way by the unusual behavior in a normal state, because it is more likely blinking, this action was taken as an intermediate value for reaching a point in space, after acknowledging the instruction takeoff, for the system to start operating, the user has to perform the *look-up* eye movement, otherwise either because the user did not choose the *look up* or because of miss-classification, the system will be halted until the expected eye command is recognized. If the latter is successful, then the user has to perform the next eye movement to choose a waypoint, and then he has to perform the *look down* eye movement, which corresponds to landing. After these values have been classified, these are saved in a text file, which is continuously being read by a node in ROS. This node validates the three numbers, and if these have the right syntax, this is takeoff, target waypoint, and landing, and if this is the case, then the commands are sent to the drone for this to perform the routine. Figure 9 shows the process of the whole system together, from data acquisition to drone's control system.

From the above, the subject was asked to perform the eye movements such in a way that the routine describe above could be executed by the drone. The subject was asked to repeat this ten times, where for each trial the target waypoint was randomly chosen by the subject, Table 4 summarizes the ten runs. Each column in the table is a trial containing two numbers in the format *subject's eye movement:recognized eye movement*. Note that per row; our system achieves an average accuracy of 86%. However, in terms of the routines, 8 out of the 10 trials were valid and safe to be sent to the drone, since take off and landing was correctly classified, which was important for the drone to execute a safe flight.

**Table 4.** Drone commands via subject's eye movements classified in real time.

| Drone Command/class | Trial | | | | | | | | | | |
|---|---|---|---|---|---|---|---|---|---|---|---|
| | subject's eye movement:classified eye movement | | | | | | | | | | |
| | 1 | 2 | 3 | 4 | 5 | 6 | 7 | 8 | 9 | 10 | Accuracy |
| Taking off/1 | 1:1 | 1:1 | 1:1 | 1:1 | 1:1 | **1:4** | 1:1 | 1:1 | **1:4** | 1:1 | 0.8 |
| Target way point/{3, 4, 5} | 4:4 | 3:3 | 4:4 | **5:1** | 5:5 | 5:5 | 4:4 | 5:5 | 4:4 | 4:4 | 0.9 |
| Landing/2 | 2:2 | 2:2 | 2:2 | 2:2 | 2:2 | 2:2 | 2:2 | 2:2 | **2:1** | 2:2 | 0.9 |
| **Average accuracy** | | | | | | | | | | | **0.86** |

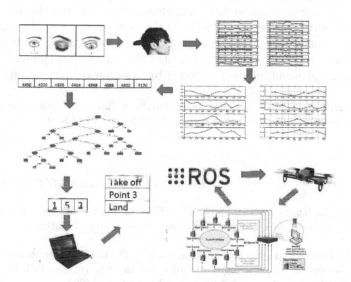

**Fig. 9.** Diagram of the full system proposed in this work.

For the review of this paper, we prepared a representative video of our system, the reviewers can find it at: https://www.dropbox.com/s/u5tblsaktvy65m0/Towards20Real-Time20Control20of20Drones.wmv?dl=0.

Table 4 is divided into columns which separate each of the experiments, each of the rows (from top to bottom) represent the ordered values taken at each of the instants, each of these contains two numbers, the first indicates the value that was captured in the classifier and the second is the value of the actual classification.

## 5   Conclusions

In this paper we have presented results based on the use of EEG for recognition of eye movement triggered by a visual stimulus and that when recognized, is used to send control commands to a drone system focused as an assistant for disabled persons who can not move. Our proposal includes an example that illustrates the translation of eye movements into control commands to operate a UAV. The eye movements are captured via EEG from an emotive diadem, the eye movement signals are then segmented and recognised automatically using a classification scheme. The recognised segments are translated into the flight commands.

The oscillations produced by the EEG can be classified according to their relationship with stimulation, in this case the stimuli corresponded to eye movement test subjects and these oscillations were classified into five categories, whose recognition triggers control command. We obtained a classification accuracy of 86%, which was sufficient for the purposes of this paper.

However, for future work we have considered improving the classification and complement it with a detector of false positives as sending a wrong command the drone can be catastrophic, also considered working with the recognition of some other kind of expressions such as grimacing, winks and even thoughts. Finally, we aim at experimenting in less controlled tests scenarios such as outdoors.

**Acknowledgments.** This work has been partially funded by the Royal Society through the Newton Advanced Fellowship with reference NA140454.

# References

1. McDonald, J.W., Sadowsky, C.: Spinal-cord injury. Lancet **359**(9304), 417–425 (2002)
2. Gautham, G., Kumar, K., Manjunath, S., Khaleel, M.M.P.: Wheel chair movement control using eye blink sensors and smart phone. Imp. J. Interdiscip. Res. **2**(7) (2016)
3. Henry, P., Krainin, M., Herbst, E., Ren, X., Fox, D.: RGB-D mapping: using depth cameras for dense 3D modeling of indoor environments. In: The 12th International Symposium on Experimental Robotics. ISER, Citeseer (2010)
4. Parasuraman, R., Cosenzo, K.A., De Visser, E.: Adaptive automation for human supervision of multiple uninhabited vehicles: effects on change detection, situation awareness, and mental workload. Mil. Psychol. **21**(2), 270 (2009)
5. Mala, S., Latha, K.: Demystification of electrooculogram signals: an introductory approach to activity recognition
6. Donoghue, J.P.: Connecting cortex to machines: recent advances in brain interfaces. Nat. Neurosci. **5**, 1085–1088 (2002)
7. Başar-Eroglu, C., Strüber, D., Schürmann, M., Stadler, M., Başar, E.: Gamma-band responses in the brain: a short review of psychophysiological correlates and functional significance. Int. J. Psychophysiol. **24**(1), 101–112 (1996)
8. Croft, R., Barry, R.: Removal of ocular artifact from the EEG: a review. Neurophysiol. Clin./Clin. Neurophysiol. **30**(1), 5–19 (2000)
9. LaFleur, K., Cassady, K., Doud, A., Shades, K., Rogin, E., He, B.: Quadcopter control in three-dimensional space using a noninvasive motor imagery-based brain-computer interface. J. Neural Eng. **10**(4), 046003 (2013)
10. Makeig, S., et al.: Electroencephalographic brain dynamics following manually responded visual targets. PLoS Biol. **2**(6), e176 (2004)
11. Huang, R.-S., Jung, T.-P., Delorme, A., Makeig, S.: Tonic and phasic electroencephalographic dynamics during continuous compensatory tracking. NeuroImage **39**(4), 1896–1909 (2008)

12. Klimesch, W., Freunberger, R., Sauseng, P., Gruber, W.: A short review of slow phase synchronization and memory: evidence for control processes in different memory systems? Brain Res. **1235**, 31–44 (2008)
13. Gevins, A., Smith, M.E., McEvoy, L., Yu, D.: High-resolution EEG mapping of cortical activation related to working memory: effects of task difficulty, type of processing, and practice. Cereb. Cortex **7**(4), 374–385 (1997)
14. Picton, T.: Human brain electrophysiology. Evoked potentials and evoked magnetic fields in science and medicine. J. Clin. Neurophysiol. **7**(3), 450–451 (1990)
15. Valentino, D.A., Arruda, J., Gold, S.: Comparison of QEEG and response accuracy in good vs poorer performers during a vigilance task. Int. J. Psychophysiol. **15**(2), 123–133 (1993)
16. Makeig, S., Jung, T.-P.: Tonic, phasic, and transient EEG correlates of auditory awareness in drowsiness. Cogn. Brain Res. **4**(1), 15–25 (1996)
17. Kim, M., Kim, B.H., Jo, S.: Quantitative evaluation of a low-cost noninvasive hybrid interface based on EEG and eye movement. IEEE Trans. Neural Syst. Rehabil. Eng. **23**(2), 159–168 (2015)
18. Ribo, M., Pinz, A., Fuhrmann, A.L.: A new optical tracking system for virtual and augmented reality applications. In: Proceedings of the 18th IEEE Instrumentation and Measurement Technology Conference, IMTC 2001, vol. 3, pp. 1932–1936. IEEE (2001)
19. Åström, K.J., Hägglund, T.: Advanced PID control. Systems and Automation Society, ISA-The Instrumentation (2006)
20. Harmony, T., et al.: EEG delta activity: an indicator of attention to internal processing during performance of mental tasks. Int. J. Psychophysiol. **24**(1), 161–171 (1996)
21. Duzsaki, G.: Rhythms of the Brain. Oxford University Press, Oxford (2006)
22. Baumann, S.B., Wozny, D.R., Kelly, S.K., Meno, F.M.: The electrical conductivity of human cerebrospinal fluid at body temperature. IEEE Trans. Biomed. Eng. **44**(3), 220–223 (1997)
23. Herrmann, C.S.: Human eeg responses to 1–100 hz flicker: resonance phenomena in visual cortex and their potential correlation to cognitive phenomena. Exp. Brain Res. **137**(3–4), 346–353 (2001)

# Design of Blind Robust Estimator
# for Smart Sensors

Miguel Vazquez-Olguin[1], Yuriy S. Shmaliy[1(✉)], Oscar Ibarra-Manzano[1],
and Luis Javier Morales-Mendoza[2]

[1] Universidad de Guanajuato, 36885 Salamanca, Mexico
Shmaliy@ugto.mx
[2] Universidad Veracruzana, 93390 Poza Rica, Mexico

**Abstract.** Efficient implementation of low cost transducers for industrial applications requires smart sensor with embedded accurate and
blind filtering algorithms. In this paper an iterative, blind, and unbiased finite impulse response (UFIR) filter having prediction capabilities
is proposed as an alternative to the Kalman filter (KF) for smart sensors design. The robustness of the UFIR filter is proved analytically. The
predictive properties of UFIR filter allow getting a high accuracy and
precision when measurements are provided with missing data, which is
demonstrated based on a short-time and long-time temperature probing.

## 1 Introduction

Advances in micro-electromechanical systems (MEMS) and semiconductor
devices have led to the development of low cost transducers. Depending on the
application, these devices could be massively implemented in order to improve
sampling over a certain measurement area. However, the estimation capabilities
of these low cost transducers may underperform in particular applications. To
increase the reliability of such devices, a "smart sensor" [1] with filtering properties should be developed. A smart sensor is a device responsible for sensing,
signal conditioning, signal processing and signal communication [2,3]. The estimation performed by a smart sensor must be capable of real-time operation,
unbiasedness, robustness, blind operation and predictive features [4–7].

In the past decades, several algorithms have been implemented with this aim
using the Kalman filter (KF). In [8,9], an orientation tracking system was developed using the KF as a fusion sensor. The KF was implemented in a smart sensor
in order to cancel the torque ripples in harmonic drive systems in [10]. In [11],
the KF and the extended KF (EKF) were used to improve WiFi fingerprinting
by using a smart micro-electromechanical system. The KF is a popular choice as
an estimator, because of its fast computation and optimal estimates. Nonetheless, the lack of robustness against the imprecisely defined noise statistics, model
errors and its nature as a Bayesian estimator [12] makes it unsuitable for smart
sensors in many cases.

Experience has proven that better performance is attributable to the finite
impulse response (FIR) filters [13–15] operating with most recent data. Several

© Springer Nature Switzerland AG 2018
F. Castro et al. (Eds.): MICAI 2017, LNAI 10633, pp. 354–365, 2018.
https://doi.org/10.1007/978-3-030-02840-4_29

fast FIR algorithms have been developed to be suitable for the implementation in smart sensors. In [16] a receding horizon (RH) Kalman FIR filter was designed that operates similarly to KF. A fast recursion-based algorithm was developed in [17] for deterministic time-invariant control systems. In [18], an iterative $p$-shift unbiased FIR (UFIR) algorithm was designed to completely ignore the noise statistics and initial values, while reducing the output noise variance as a reciprocal of $N$. This algorithm provides filtering with $p = 0$, RH filtering with $p = 1$, $|p|$-lag smoothing with $p < 0$, and $p$-step prediction with $p > 0$. It is important that the prediction capability of the algorithm can be employed to process data with missing measurements [19]. Fast Kalman-like algorithms were designed for optimal UFIR filtering in [20] and for bias-constrained optimal FIR filtering in [21].

Unlike the KF-based estimators, UFIR filtering does not need any information about the noise statistics. Suboptimal estimates are guaranteed by this filter on the optimal horizons of $N_{opt}$ points. By virtue of this, the UFIR algorithm generally demonstrates better robustness against temporary model errors, imprecisely defined noise statistics and temporary measurement errors [22] than the KF. Furthermore, its performance can be improved by adapting the generalized noise power gain (GNPG) to operation conditions [23]. These particular features of the iterative UFIR filtering algorithm point out to new opportunities in smart sensor design. In this paper, we design a blind predictive UFIR filtering algorithm suitable for the implementation in smart sensors under missing data.

## 2   Measured Quantity and Process Model

Let us consider an environmental quantity $Q(t)$ represented through a $K$-state vector $x_k \in \mathbb{R}^K$ whose dynamics is described by the following sate-space equations:

$$x_k = A_k x_{k-1} + u_k + B_k w_k, \tag{1}$$

$$\tilde{y}_k = H_k(A_k x_{k-1} + u_k), \tag{2}$$

$$y_k = \alpha_k(H_k x_k + v_k) + (1 - \alpha_k)\tilde{y}_k + e_k, \tag{3}$$

$$z_k = y_k - e_k, \tag{4}$$

where measurements of $Q(t)$ are provided by a linear sensing device, $u_k \in \mathbb{R}^K$ and $e_k$ are the control and calibration signals, respectively. Here, $A_k \in \mathbb{R}^{K \times K}$ is the process matrix, $B_k \in \mathbb{R}^{K \times M}$ is the process noise matrix, $H_k \in \mathbb{R}^{1 \times K}$ is the sensor matrix. The mutually independent and uncorrelated noise vectors $w_k \in \mathbb{R}^M$ and $v_k$ have zero mean, $E\{w_k\} = 0$ and $E\{v_k\} = 0$. Covariances $Q_k = E\{w_k w_k^T\}$ and $R_k = E\{v_k v_k^T\}$, are unknown along with their distribution.

Missing data are highly possible to occur under real operation conditions, especially in industrial applications. By taking advantage of the digital nature of the smart sensors, it is possible to implement an indicator of signal quality, where good ($\alpha_k = 1$) or bad ($\alpha_k = 0$) data are represented via a binary output. If data are lost, the algorithm is capable of replacing the missing measurement with $\tilde{y}_k$ (2) in which the previous state $x_{k-1}$ can be substituted with the estimate.

Let $\hat{x}_{k|r}$ be the estimate of $x_k$ at time index $k$ through measurements from past up to and including at time-index $r$. We will also consider the following variables: $\hat{x}_k^- \triangleq \hat{x}_{k|k-1}$ is the *a priori* state estimate, $P_k^- \triangleq P_{k|k-1} = E\{(x_k - \hat{x}_k^-)(x_k - \hat{x}_k^-)^T\}$ is the *a priori* estimate covariance, $\hat{x}_k \triangleq \hat{x}_{k|k}$ is the *a posteriori* state estimate, and $P_k \triangleq P_{k|k} = E\{(x_k - \hat{x}_k)(x_k - \hat{x}_k)^T\}$ is the *a posteriori* error covariance matrix.

Under these assumptions, we now proceed to design a robust blind predictive Kalman-like UFIR filter. It is important to notice that, under real operation conditions, the statistics of the noise process can not be easily obtained, therefore the KF could generate bad estimates. Thus, we resort to the UFIR filter, since it does not require any information about noise.

## 3   UFIR Filtering Algorithm

As stated before, due to the ability of the UFIR filter to ignore the noise statistics, higher robustness can be achieved [22]. At a test stage, the only tunning parameter, the optimal horizon length of $N_{\mathrm{opt}}$ points, can be found by minimizing the mean squared error (MSE) [24,25].

The UFIR filter operates with data measured on a horizon $[m, k]$, from $m = k - N + 1$ to $k$, to satisfy the unbiasedness condition

$$E\{\hat{x}_k\} = E\{x_k\}. \tag{5}$$

The convolution-based UFIR estimate found on $[m, k]$ for $\alpha_k = 1$ is stated in [26,27] as

$$\hat{x}_k = \mathcal{H}_{m,k}(Z_{m,k} - L_{m,k}U_{m,k}) + S_{m,k}U_{m,k}, \tag{6}$$

where $U_{m,k} = [\, u_m^T \; u_{m+1}^T \; \cdots \; u_k^T \,]^T$ and the homogeneous UFIR filter gain is

$$\mathcal{H}_{m,k} = (C_{m,k}^T C_{m,k})^{-1} C_{m,k}^T, \tag{7a}$$

$$= G_k C_{m,k}^T, \tag{7b}$$

where $G_k = (C_{m,k}^T C_{m,k})^{-1}$ is called the generalized noise power gain (GNPG) [27]. The extended observation vector $Z_{m,k}$ and the mapping matrix $C_{m,k}$ can be written as

$$Z_{m,k} = [\, y_m - e_k \; y_{m+1} - e_{m+1} \; \cdots \; y_k - e_k \,]^T, \tag{8}$$

$$C_{m,k} = \begin{bmatrix} H_m (\mathcal{F}_k^{m+1})^{-1} \\ H_{m+1} (\mathcal{F}_k^{m+2})^{-1} \\ \vdots \\ H_{k-1} A_k^{-1} \\ H_k \end{bmatrix}, \tag{9}$$

where the product of system matrices is defined by

$$\mathcal{F}_k^r = \begin{cases} A_k A_{k-1}...A_r, & r < k+1 \\ I & r = k+1 \\ 0 & r > k+1 \end{cases}, \tag{10}$$

and auxiliary matrices are given by

$$S_{m,k} = \Big[ \underbrace{\mathcal{F}_k^{m+1} \ \mathcal{F}_k^{m+2} \ ... \ A_k \ I}_{N} \Big], \tag{11}$$

$$L_{m,k} = \bar{C}_{m,k} S_{m,k}, \tag{12}$$

$$\bar{C}_{m,k} = \mathrm{diag}\Big( \underbrace{H_m \ H_{m+1} \ ... \ H_k}_{N} \Big). \tag{13}$$

Although the batch form (7a) is short, it might not be suitable for smart sensors, because of the computational complexity. Therefore, we next present a fast predictive iterative form of the UFIR filter.

## 3.1  Predictive Iterative UFIR Filtering Algorithm

As stated in [28], the iterative form of the UFIR filter is obtained by running iterations from $l = m + K$ to $l = k$. The initial estimate is found using (7b) in a short batch form on a usually small horizon $[m, m + K - 1]$.

Once $\hat{x}_{m+K-1}$ and $G_{m+K-1}$ are obtained, the estimate $\hat{x}_k$ is found at the last iteration step using the following equations:

$$G_l = [H_l^T H_l + (A_l G_{l-1} A_l^T)^{-1}]^{-1}, \tag{14}$$

$$K_l = G_l H_l^T, \tag{15}$$

$$\hat{x}_l^- = A_l \hat{x}_{l-1} + u_k, \tag{16}$$

$$y_l = \begin{cases} y_l, & \alpha_l = 1 \\ H_l \hat{x}_l^-, & \alpha_l = 0 \end{cases}, \tag{17}$$

$$\hat{x}_l = \hat{x}_l^- + K_l(y_l - e_k - H_l \hat{x}_l^-). \tag{18}$$

A pseudo code of this algorithm is given as Algorithm 1.

If $u_k = 0$ and $e_k = 0$, the homogeneous case of the algorithm is obtained. As can be seen, Algorithm 1 does not require any information about noise and the initial values. Note that, unlike KF, the finite impulse response of this filter makes it more robust against uncertainties under real operating conditions [7], as errors of the previous estimates are not considered in the actual estimate.

The horizon $N_{\mathrm{opt}}$ can be found at a test stage by minimizing the trace of the error covariance matrix $P_k$ as

$$N_{\mathrm{opt}} = \arg\min_N \{\mathrm{tr}\, P_k(N)\}. \tag{19}$$

---

**Algorithm 1.** Predictive Iterative UFIR Algorithm

---

    **Data:** $y_k$, $e_k$, $u_k$, $\alpha_k$
    **Result:** $\hat{x}_k$

1  **begin**
2     **for** $k = N - 1 : \infty$ **do**
3        $m = k - N + 1$,   $s = m + K - 1$;
4        $G_s = (C_{m,s}^T C_{m,s})^{-1}$;
5        **if** $\alpha_k = 0$ **then**
6           | $y_k = H_k(A_k \hat{x}_{k-1} + u_k)$;
7        **end if**
8        $\tilde{x}_s = G_s C_{m,s}^T Z_{m,s}$;
9        **for** $l = s + 1 : k$ **do**
10          $G_l = [H_l^T H_l + (A_l G_{l-1} A_l^T)^{-1}]^{-1}$;
11          $\tilde{x}_l^- = A_l \tilde{x}_{l-1} + u_l$;
12          $\tilde{x}_l = \tilde{x}_l^- + G_l H_l^T (y_l - e_l - H_l \tilde{x}_l^-)$;
13        **end for**
14        $\hat{x}_k = \tilde{x}_k$;
15     **end for**
16  **end**
17  † First data $y_0$, $y_1$,..., $y_{N-1}$ must be available.

---

When the reference signal is unavailable, $N_{\text{opt}}$ can be estimated by minimizing the trace of the derivative of the mean square value of the residual $V_k = E\{(y_k - H_k \hat{x}_k)(y_k - H_k \hat{x}_k)^T\}$ [25] as

$$N_{\text{opt}} \cong \arg \min_N \left\{ \frac{\partial}{\partial N} \operatorname{tr} V_k(N) \right\}. \tag{20}$$

The latter option may be unique if the test stage is not assumed.

## 4    Robustness of UFIR Filter and KF

In this section we analyze the robustness between KF (Algorithm 2) and UFIR filter. It is known that a KF estimator will produce more random errors if the bias correction gain exceeds an optimal value and more bias errors otherwise [29]. The bias correction gain is affected mostly by the three factors: imprecisely defined noise statistics, temporary model errors, and temporary measurement errors.

### 4.1    Imprecisely Defined Noise Statistics

Imprecise noise covariances can be modeled by substituting $Q_k \leftarrow \alpha^2 Q_k$ and $R_k \leftarrow \beta^2 R_k$, where $\alpha = 1$ and $\beta = 1$ stand for completely known noise. To ascertain the effects of $\alpha$ and $\beta$ on the robustness of KF, a stationary mode is

**Algorithm 2.** Recursive KF Algorithm

**Data:** $\hat{x}_0$, $P_0$, $Q_k$, $R_k$

**Result:** $\hat{x}_k$, $P_k$

1 **begin**

2    **for** $k = 1, 2, \cdots$ **do**

3      $\hat{x}_k^- = A_k \hat{x}_{k-1} + u_k$ ;

4      $P_k^- = A_k P_{k-1} A_k^T + B_k Q_k B_k^T$ ;

5      $K_k = P_k^- H_k^T (H_k P_k^- H_k^T + R_k)^{-1}$ ;

6      $\hat{x}_k = \hat{x}_k^- + K_k(y_k - e_k - H_k\hat{x}_k^-)$ ;

7      $P_k = (I - K_k H_k)P_k^-$ ;

8    **end for**

9 **end**

considered where $P_{k-1} \cong P_k^-$ in line 4 of Algorithm 2 produces the discrete-time algebraic Lyapunov equation [30]

$$P_k^- - A_k P_k^- A_k^T = \alpha^2 B_k Q_k B_k^T , \tag{21}$$

which solution is known to be an infinite sum [31],

$$P_k^- = \alpha^2 \sum_{i=0}^{\infty} A_k^i B_k Q_k B_k^T (A_k^i)^T = \alpha^2 \Sigma_k . \tag{22}$$

We next substitute (22) into line 5 of Algorithm 2 and write the Kalman gain as

$$\bar{K}_k \cong \alpha^2 \Sigma_k H_k^T (H_k \alpha^2 \Sigma_k H_k^T + \beta^2 R_k)^{-1}$$

$$= \Sigma_k H_k^T \left( H_k \Sigma_k H_k^T + \frac{\beta^2}{\alpha^2} R_k \right)^{-1} . \tag{23}$$

Equation (23) suggest that the optimal value of $\bar{K}_k = K_k$ is achieved when $\alpha = \beta = 1$. If $\bar{K}_k > K_k$, the random errors dominate and, if $\bar{K}_k < K_k$, the bias errors grow, meaning that:

1. Random errors will grow if $\alpha > 1$ and/or $\beta < 1$.
2. Bias errors will dominate when $\alpha < 1$ and/or $\beta > 1$.
3. Errors may compensate if $\alpha = \beta$ or $(\alpha, \beta) < 1$ or $(\alpha, \beta) > 1$.

KF is indeed more accurate when $\alpha$ and $\beta$ are both range close to unity. Otherwise, the UFIR filter that is not affected by changes in $\alpha$ and $\beta$ may be more accurate.

### 4.2 Temporary Model Errors

The effect of temporary model errors can be observed by allowing $A_k \leftarrow \eta A_k$ with $\eta \neq 1$ during a short time under the imprecisely defined noise statistics:

$Q_k \leftarrow \alpha^2 Q_k$ and $R_k \leftarrow \beta^2 R_k$. Here $\eta$ affects both filters, therefore we rewrite $K_k$ and $G_l$ as

$$\bar{K}_k \cong \Sigma_k H_k^T \left( H_k \Sigma_k H_k^T + \frac{\beta^2}{\alpha^2 \eta^2} R_k \right)^{-1}, \tag{24}$$

$$\bar{G}_l = \left[ H_l^T H_l + \frac{1}{\eta^2} (A_l G_{l-1} A_l^T)^{-1} \right]^{-1}. \tag{25}$$

It follows, by $\alpha = \beta = 1$, that robustness of both filters to changes in $\eta$ is near equal. Otherwise, $\alpha$ and $\beta$ may dramatically increase errors caused by $\eta$ in the KF. Such an effect is not seen in the UFIR filter.

### 4.3   Temporary Measurement Errors

To model measurement errors, we substitute $H_k$ with $\mu H_k$, where $\mu = 1$ denotes accurate measurements, and retain $Q_k \leftarrow \alpha^2 Q_k$ and $R_k \leftarrow \beta^2 R_k$. We then transform $K_k$ and $G_l$ to

$$\bar{K}_k \cong \frac{1}{\mu} \Sigma_k H_k^T \left( H_k \Sigma_k H_k^T + \frac{\beta^2}{\alpha^2 \mu^2} R_k \right)^{-1}, \tag{26}$$

$$\bar{G}_l = \frac{1}{\mu^2} \left[ H_l^T H_l + \frac{1}{\mu^2} (A_l G_{l-1} A_l^T)^{-1} \right]^{-1} \tag{27}$$

and infer the following. When the second components dominate in the parentheses of (26) and brackets of (27), the UFIR filter has higher robustness, because the gain $1/\mu^2$ is better compensated by the reciprocal of $1/\mu^2$ in (27) than $1/\mu$ in (26). Moreover, $\alpha$ and $\beta$ may dramatically deteriorate the KF performance that also speaks in favor of the UFIR filter.

The UFIR filter does not need previous information about noise statistics, making it a more robust estimator than the KF in real-world applications where noise statistics and model errors are not clearly defined [12–14,16,20,21,32–34]. Such conditions can be met, for example, in industrial environments where impulsive noise is present due to random machinery activation or when estimating CO concentration in urban areas, where many environmental variables make it impossible to determine the model errors.

## 5   Experimental Verification

In order to demonstrate the predicting capabilities of Algorithm 1, we consider the temperature measurements database available from [35]. The samples were taken using a multisensor device developed by Pirelli Labs and a commercial temperature sensor. Figure 1 shows the data of 30 weeks, where each point corresponds to one hour averaging. It can be observed some readings of 0°C, which corresponds to missing data. The time span from week 24 to week 26 presents

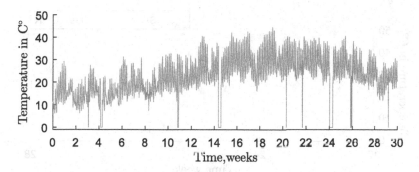

**Fig. 1.** 30 weeks measurements of temperature with missing data [35,36].

several missing points. This period of time was selected to demonstrate the superior performance of the predictive UFIR filter on an off-line manner.

To find the UFIR estimates, we suppose that the temperature changes linearly on an averaging horizon of $N = 24 \times 7 = 168$ points that corresponds to one week. The state-space model is defined with $u_k = 0$, $e_k = 0$, $H_k = [\,1\ 0\,]$, and

$$A_k = \begin{bmatrix} 1 & \tau \\ 0 & 1 \end{bmatrix},$$

where $\tau = t_k - t_{k-1}$ is the sampling time. The noise processes are considered to be zero mean with unknown distributions.

Figure 2 shows the estimation capabilities of Algorithm 1 over an interval with no missing data. As can be seen, the UFIR filter produces estimates, which track the mean of the noisy measurements. If some data are lost, the basic UFIR filter (deleting lines 5–7 of Algorithm 1) tends to use the zero values to produce the average. That increases the estimation error as shown in Fig. 3 and produces undesirable excursions.

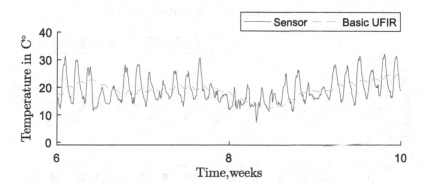

**Fig. 2.** Temperature estimation without missing data.

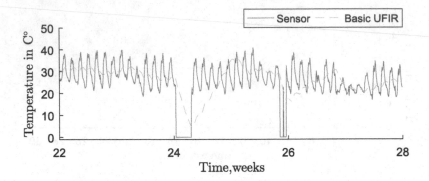

**Fig. 3.** Temperature estimation with missing data.

By implementing the predictive capabilities in Algorithm 1, the UFIR filter is able to bridge a gap between the measurements by eliminating the excursions and generating much better results as sketched in Fig. 4.

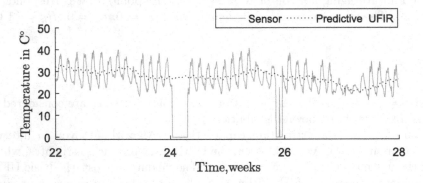

**Fig. 4.** Temperature estimation by the predictive UFIR.

Finally, in Fig. 5 we show the estimates of the temperature rate where, again, the basic UFIR causes larger excursions where data are lost.

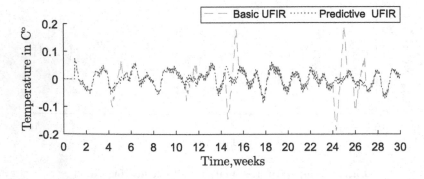

**Fig. 5.** Estimated second state of the model corresponding to temperature rate.

# 6    Conclusions

Like the KF, the UFIR filter is a universal estimator. However, several advantages against KF are attributable to the UFIR filter, which make it a better option for smart sensors design. The UFIR filter offers better robustness that was demonstrated analytically. The UFIR filter does not require any information about noise and the initial values, which are commonly not well-known if many real scenarios. The predictive property of the UFIR filter allow for accurate prediction of the missing data and bridging the gaps over uncertainties. Although the results shown in this work were obtained by using previously saved data, the iterative form of the UFIR algorithm is suitable for the implementation in near real-time on small devices such as smart sensors, which have limited computational resources. This filter is suitable for estimating a wide range of physical variables such as pressure, humidity, acceleration, flow, etc. As long as the space-state model is available and the noise present in the measurements is of zero mean nature.

# References

1. Giachino, J.M.: Smart sensors. Sens. Actuators 10(3–4), 239–248 (1986)
2. Frank, R.: Understanding Smart Sensors. Artech House, Northwood (2000)
3. Song, E.Y., Lee, K.: Understanding IEEE 1451-networked smart transducer interface standard - what is a smart transducer? IEEE Instrum. Meas. Mag. 11(2), 11–17 (2008)
4. Swanson, D.C.: Signal Processing for Pntelligent Sensor Systems with MATLAB, 2nd edn. CRC Press, Boca Raton (2011)
5. Kirianaki, N.V., Yurish, S.Y., Shpak, N.O., Deynega, V.P.: Data Acquisition and Signal Processing for Smart Sensors. Wiley, Chichester (2002)
6. Zhao, F., Guibas, L.J.: Wireless Sensor Networks: An Information Processing Approach. Elsevier, Amsterdam (2004)
7. Vazquez-Olguin, M.A., Shmaliy, Y.S., Ibarra-Manzano, O.: Blind robust estimation with missing data for smart sensors using UFIR filtering. IEEE Sens. J. 17(6), 1819–1827 (2017)
8. Won, S.H.P., Golnaraghi, F., Melek, W.W.: A fastening tool tracking system using an IMU and a position sensor with Kalman filters and a fuzzy expert system. IEEE Trans. Ind. Electron. 56(5), 1782–1792 (2009)
9. Sabatelli, S., Galgani, M., Fanucci, L., Rocchi, A.: A double-stage Kalman filter for orientation tracking with an integrated processor in 9-D IMU. IEEE Trans. Instrum. Meas. 62(3), 590–598 (2013)
10. Taghirad, H.D., Belanger, P.R.: Torque ripple and misalignment torque compensation for the built-in torque sensor of harmonic drive systems. IEEE Trans. Instrum. Meas. 47(1), 309–315 (1998)
11. Zhuang, Y., Li, Y., Qi, L., Lan, H., Yang, J., El-Sheimy, N.: A two-filter integration of MEMS sensors and WiFi fingerprinting for indoor positioning. IEEE Sens.S J. 16(13), 5125–5126 (2016)
12. Simon, D.: Optimal Estimation: Kalman, $H_\infty$, and nOnlinear Approaches. Wiley, Hoboken (2006)

13. Jazwinski, A.H.: Stochastic Processes and Filtering Theory. Academic, New York (1970)
14. Kwon, W.H., Han, S.: Receding Horizon Control: Model pRedictive Control for State Models. Springer, London (2005). https://doi.org/10.1007/b136204
15. Shmaliy, Y.S., Ibarra-Manzano, O.: Time-variant linear optimal finite impulse response estimator for discrete state-space models. Int. J. Adapt. Control. Signal Process. **26**(2), 95–104 (2012)
16. Kwon, W.H., Kim, P.S., Park, P.: A receding horizon Kalman FIR filter for linear continuous-time systems. IEEE Trans. Autom. Control. **44**(11), 2115–2120 (1999)
17. Han, S.H., Kwon, W.H., Kim, P.S.: Quasi-deadbeat minimax filters for deterministic state space models. IEEE Trans. Autom. Control. **47**(11), 1904–1908 (2002)
18. Shmaliy, Y.S.: Linear optimal FIR estimation of discrete time-invariant state-space models. IEEE Trans. Signal Process. **58**(6), 3086–3096 (2010)
19. Shmaliy, Y.S., Arceo-Miquel, L.: Efficient predictive estimator for holdover in GPS-based clock synchronization. IEEE Trans. Ultrason. Ferroelectr. Freq. Control. **55**(10), 2131–2139 (2008)
20. Zhao, S., Shmaliy, Y.S., Liu, F.: Fast computation of discrete optimal FIR estimates in white gaussian noise. IEEE Signal Process. Lett. **22**(6), 718–722 (2015)
21. Zhao, S., Shmaliy, Y.S., Liu, F.: Fast Kalman-like optimal unbiased FIR filtering with applications. IEEE Trans. Signal Process. **64**(9), 2284–2297 (2016)
22. Vazquez-Olguin, M., Shmaliy, Y.S., Ibarra-Manzano, O.: Distributed unbiased FIR filtering with average consensus on measurements for WSNs. IEEE Trans. Ind. Inform. **13**(3), 1440–1447 (2017)
23. Fu, J.B., Sun, J., Fei, G., Lu, S.: Maneuvering target tracking with improved unbiased FIR filter. In: 2014 International Radar Conference, pp. 1–5, October 2014
24. Pak, J.M., Ahn, C.K., Shmaliy, Y.S., Shi, P., Lim, M.T.: Switching extensible FIR filter bank for adaptive horizon state estimation with application. IEEE Trans. Control. Syst. Technol. **24**(3), 1052–1058 (2016)
25. Ramirez-Echeverria, F., Sarr, A., Shmaliy, Y.S.: Optimal memory for discrete-time FIR filters in state space. IEEE Trans. Signal Process. **62**(3), 557–561 (2014)
26. Shmaliy, Y.S., Khan, S.H., Zhao, S., Ibarra-Manzano, O.: General unbiased FIR filter with applications to GPS-based steering of oscillator frequency. IEEE Trans. Control. Syst. Technol. **25**(3), 1141–1148 (2017)
27. Shmaliy, Y.S., Ibarra-Manzano, O.: Noise power gain for discrete-time FIR estimators. IEEE Trans. Signal Process. **18**(4), 207–210 (2011)
28. Shmaliy, Y.S.: An iterative Kalman-like algorithm ignoring noise and initial conditions. IEEE Trans. Signal Process. **59**(6), 2465–2473 (2011)
29. Shmaliy, Y.S., Khan, S., Zhao, S.: Ultimate iterative UFIR filtering algorithm. Measurement **92**, 236–242 (2016)
30. Sima, V.: Algorithms for Linear-Quadratic Optimization. Marcel Dekker, New York (1996)
31. Kailath, T., Sayed, A.H., Hassibi, B.: Linear Estimation. Prentice-Hall, Upper Saddle River (2000)
32. Ahn, C.K., Han, S., Kwon, W.H.: $H_\infty$ FIR filters for linear continuous-time state-space systems. IEEE Signal Process. Lett. **13**(9), 557–560 (2006)
33. Ahn, C.K.: Strictly passive FIR filtering for state-space models with external disturbance. AEU-Int. J. Electron. Commun. **66**(11), 944–948 (2012)
34. Pak, J.M., Ahn, C.K., Lim, M.T., Song, M.K.: Horizon group shift FIR filter: alternative nonlinear filter using finite recent measurements. Measurement **57**, 33–45 (2014)

35. UCI Machine Learning Repository: Air Quality Data Set. University of California, Irvine, CA, USA, June 2017. https://archive.ics.uci.edu/ml/datasets/Air+Quality
36. De Vito, S., Massera, E., Piga, M., Martinotto, L., Di Francia, G.: On field calibration of an electronic nose for benzene estimation in an urban pollution monitoring scenario. Sens. Actuators B **129**(2), 750–757 (2008)

# Author Index

Printed in the United States
By Bookmasters